TIME
SPECIAL EDITION

TAYLOR SWIFT
A MAGICAL ERA

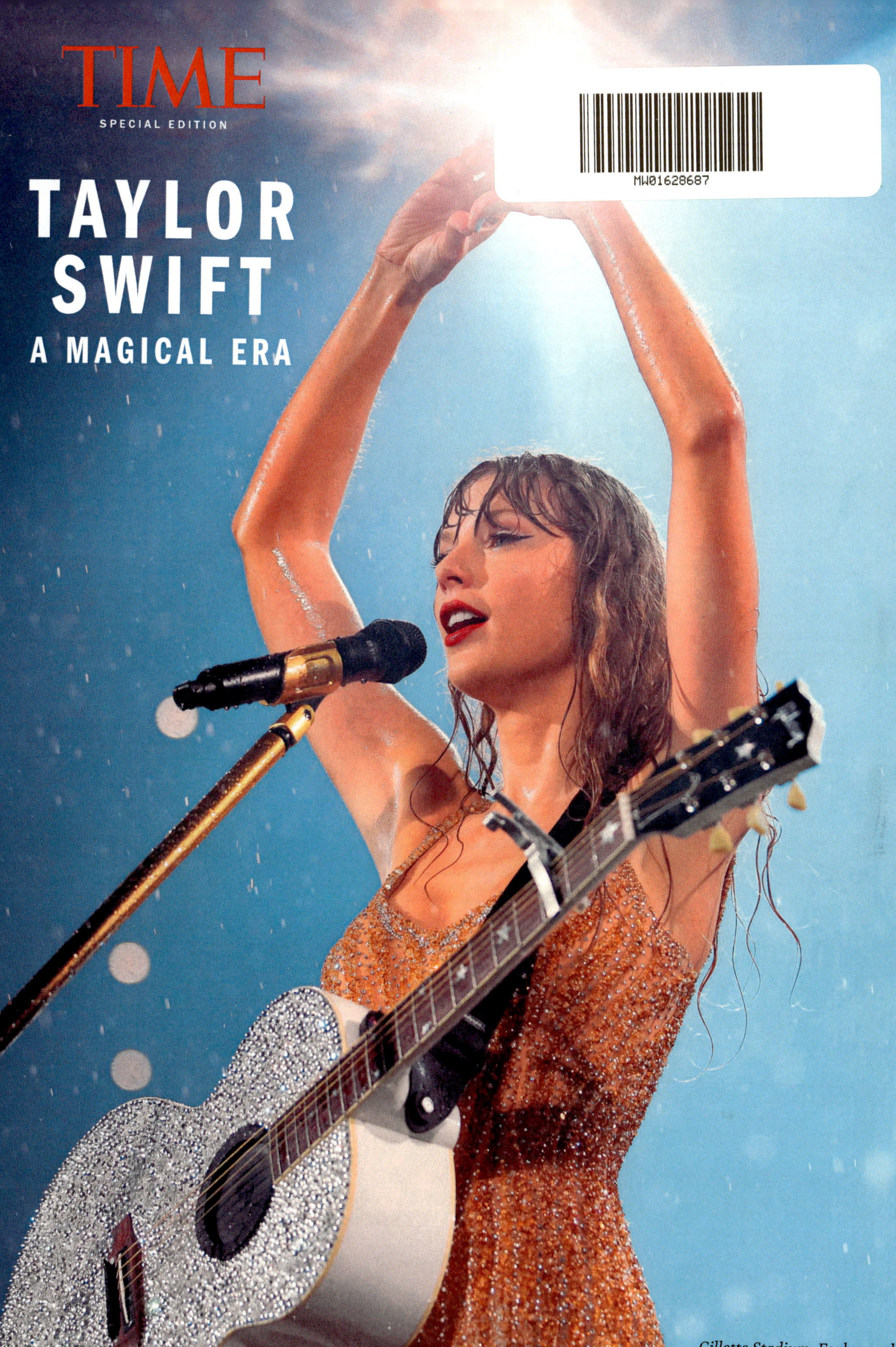

Gillette Stadium, Foxborough, Massachusetts, May 2023.

MetLife Stadium, East Rutherford, New Jersey, May 2023.

CONTENTS

During the Cincinnati stop on the Eras Tour, Swift sang a set from her 2017 album, Reputation.

A VERY GOOD YEAR

Through the blockbuster Eras Tour, the continued success of *Midnights*, and seismic-like activity in Seattle, Taylor Swift has outdone herself. Again.

BY SHANNON CARLIN

TAYLOR SWIFT'S 2023 ERAS TOUR HASN'T just been a pop culture phenomenon—it's been a geological one, too. At Swift's back-to-back sold-out shows in July 2023 at Lumen Field in Seattle, the crowd—an astonishing 72,000 fans each night—was so loud that it registered the equivalent of a 2.3-magnitude earthquake on the Richter scale.

The reaction was quickly dubbed a "Swift Quake" after the "Beast Quake" that rocked Lumen in 2011 when the Seattle Seahawks scored a last-minute game-clinching playoff touchdown. Yet the zealous football fans were no match for Swifties, seismologist Jackie Caplan-Auerbach told CNN after the second show. "The shaking was twice as strong as Beast Quake," she said. "It absolutely doubled it."

To use the language of seismology, there are foreshocks, there are mainshocks, and then there's Taylor Swift, whose tectonic year has seemingly defied the laws of physics—at least as they relate to the music industry. When she announced her career-spanning Eras Tour in November 2022, the demand for presale tickets was so staggering, it broke Ticketmaster's website. That meltdown spurred a congressional hearing into the ticketing industry and accomplished something even more rare: a showing of bipartisanship between Republicans and Democrats. Swift has not only sold out every venue she has played since then, she has sold more tickets in 2023 than the year's next two highest grossers combined. (They would be Bruce Springsteen and Harry Styles.) Fans who haven't been lucky enough to nab a ticket have taken to "Taylor-gating," setting up camp outside a venue in hopes of hearing the singer. During Swift's three-night stint in Nashville, there were reportedly 32.8 percent more visitors in Nissan Stadium's parking lot than inside the 69,000-seat arena.

It's not just stadiums that have benefited from Swiftmania—it's the global economy. Analysts estimated that by the time Eras completes its last concert date, it could generate $5 billion in economic activity. In July, the Federal Reserve Bank of Philadelphia announced that the singer's three-night stand in the City of Brotherly Love had led to the best month of hotel revenue since the pandemic began, while Las Vegas credited her with helping to bring tourism back to pre-COVID-19 levels. Hoping to get in on the action, Canadian prime minister Justin Trudeau tweeted an invite that echoed lyrics from several Swift songs: "It's me, hi. I know places in Canada would love to have you." (A month later, Swift announced a string of 2024 dates in Toronto.)

The tsunami of enthusiasm has put Swift on track to become the biggest touring artist in the world. "I do think this is unlike any tour we've ever seen—or may ever see," says Mara Klaunig, a senior analyst at economic consultancy Camoin Associates. "The closest thing I can think of is Beatlemania. She's just one of those once-in-a-generation stars that captivates all of us."

Pent-up demand is one reason for Eras' success—it had been five years since Swift's last tour, an extended break due mostly to the pandemic. But after 17 years, 10 studio albums (plus four rerecorded ones), and thousands of headlines, Eras is also the culmination of a boundary-pushing career. In that time span, Swift has vaulted from Nashville darling to one of the biggest pop stars in the world. When she speaks, people listen, and she has used her voice to take on Spotify, Apple, and rapper Kanye West. She has shown support for the LGBTQ+ community and criticized sexist double standards. After she testified against a radio DJ she said had groped her, Swift was named a 2017 TIME Person of the Year, alongside other silence breakers including the creator of the #MeToo movement, activist Tarana Burke.

Swift's honesty and vulnerability have helped her build a deep rapport with her fans, but she is also a savvy marketer who knows how to entice an audience. She has invited Swifties into her home for secret listening parties, even going so far as to bake cookies for her guests. She leaves Easter eggs in her albums' liner notes and social media posts that turn her fans into super sleuths. "I've trained them to be that way," Swift told *Entertainment Weekly* in 2019. "I love that they like the cryptic hint-dropping. Because as long as they like it, I'll keep doing it."

SOME CRITICS HAVE CALLED SWIFT DISINGENUous or calculating for positioning herself as the underdog when she is one of the highest-paid entertainers in the world. But Emily Simonian, a licensed marriage and family therapist in the Washington, D.C. area, says she's seen firsthand how Swift's music has helped her patients, often women in their 20s and early to mid-30s. "She wears her heart on her sleeve and has publicly experienced heartbreak and pain, which has endeared her to fans," Simonian says. "Particularly those of the same generation, who maybe feel she is a peer. I think that her relatability and accessibility is her secret sauce."

In Swift, fans see someone who isn't afraid to fight for what she believes in. A prime example: her battle to gain back control of her music. In 2019, music executive Scooter Braun bought the rights to her first six albums when he purchased her former label, Big Machine Records. After posting on her Tumblr page that the deal left her "sad and grossed out" and accusing Braun of bullying her, Swift two months later announced she would rerecord her earliest albums, dubbing them "Taylor's Versions."

In doing so, Swift joined an impressive roster of music talent that has fought to regain financial and artistic control of their back catalog. Frank Sinatra, Chuck Berry, and Little Richard all recut their classic hits. More recently, so have R.E.M., the B-52s, and Wheatus. But what started out as a financial and artistic decision for Swift seems to have morphed into an emotional endeavor. When she announced *Fearless (Taylor's Version)*, she said that rerecording the 2008 album made her "fully appreciate it in its whimsical, effervescent, chaotic entirety" and all the more determined to continue with the project. *Fearless (Taylor's Version)* became the first rerecorded album in history to reach

Phoebe Bridgers was one of Swift's special guests when the Eras Tour hit Nashville in May.

No. 1. Both *Red (Taylor's Version),* which came out in late 2021, and *Speak Now (Taylor's Version),* from July 2023, topped the Billboard charts, edging Swift past Barbra Streisand to become the female artist with the most No. 1 albums.

Swift's Eras Tour, her sixth, caps off an especially prolific period for her. In 2019, she released *Lover*, a back-to-basics pop album that celebrated romance and debuted at No. 1 on the Billboard 200. In 2020, she released *Folklore* and *Evermore*, which veered into indie territory and earned her some of the best reviews of her career. When Swift picked up her album of the year Grammy in 2021 for *Folklore*, she joined Sinatra, Stevie Wonder, and Paul Simon as the only artists to win the award three times. Last year's *Midnights*, a raw collection of electro-pop songs, has produced her longest-running No. 1 single to date, "Anti-Hero." "It's me, hi, I'm the problem, it's me," she sings in what could be described as a self-aware anthem for the therapy generation.

Then there was opening night in Glendale, Arizona, when Swift, as she would for each Eras performance, played 44 songs across three hours, a feat that even drew praise from New England Patriots coach Bill Belichick. In the early weeks of the tour, there seemed to be a viral moment every night: the surprise songs, the special guests, the celebrities who showed up knowing who the real star was.

In the meantime, *Midnights,* basking in the glow of the blockbuster tour, is on track to become the best-selling album of the year, moving almost twice as many copies as every other title already released in 2023. And that's on top of the millions of copies the album sold in 2022. The only person who could possibly beat Taylor Swift now might be, well, Taylor Swift. On September 1, AMC released its first presale tickets to *Taylor Swift: The Eras Tour,* the fall 2023 concert film. Within three hours, the chain had sold a record-breaking $26 million in tickets. Seismic activity, indeed—or maybe just Swiftian, as the singer continues to do things the only way she knows how: her way. ☐

IT'S TAYLOR SWIFT'S ERA

Wherever the superstar goes—and in 2023, that included 24 venues in 24 cities on 66 nights—her fans will follow.

BY JEANNIE KOPSTEIN AND MARIAH ESPADA

At Atlanta's Mercedes-Benz Stadium in April, Swift became the first artist to sell out three nights at the venue, for a total of about 180,000 fans. As she had throughout the tour, she played two surprise acoustic songs for the audience each night. On April 28, shown here, the numbers were "The Other Side of the Door" and "Coney Island."

YOU DON'T HAVE TO BE A SWIFTIE TO have been touched in some way by Taylor Swift's Eras Tour, a stadium arena experience that kicked off in March 2023. The show, which pays homage to every era of the artist's 17-year career, was set to become the biggest tour of all time just a third of the way through its run.

If you live in one of the locales where Swift, 33, performed, your city likely saw a boost in revenue from the hundreds of thousands of concert attendees who traveled from near and far. If you don't—or simply couldn't snag tickets due to the cost or the now infamous Ticketmaster snafu—chances are you've seen clips of the three-and-a-half-hour show from celebrities' and fans' Instagram stories.

While there's much to say about the music, costumes, and production, the impact of the Eras Tour has been starkly reflected in the numbers: an estimated $1.4 billion in tickets by the series' end, according to projections from Pollstar, and hundreds of millions of streams, reaching a nearly 80 percent spike in those listening to Swift's music catalog in the weeks after the tour kicked off.

The Eras Tour stands in a league of its own, even among classic groups such as the Rolling Stones, who have been hitting the road for decades; peer artists Harry Styles and Beyoncé, who also had major tours this year; and Adele, who has a sold-out Las Vegas residency under her belt. The U.S. leg was supposed to come to an end on August 9 after 53 shows, but Swift extended her run, adding dates in cities including New Orleans, Indianapolis, and Toronto. The blockbuster concert series went international in August, starting with four shows in Mexico City, and as of press time was to continue its five-continent run through November 2024.

The reasons for Eras' success are manifold. For one, Swift's timing has been exceedingly good: Post-pandemic, the tour is a welcome outing for concertgoers itching for an immersive live music experience. The sheer depth and breadth of Swift's music catalog has also been a factor, says Nora Princiotti, a staff writer at the *Ringer* and cohost of the podcast of *Every Single Album: Taylor Swift*. "She can go three-and-a-half hours and it's just hit after hit after hit," Princiotti says. Then there's the Swiftie phenomena itself. The singer's fans appreciate how connected she is to her body of work—she writes or cowrites all of her songs, has been protective of her music in the streaming boom, and

Swift played six sold-out shows at SoFi Stadium outside Los Angeles, resulting in a $320 million bump to L.A. County's GDP.

SoFi Stadium

DADS ARE
SWIFTIES
TOO

ERAS
FEARLESS
Speak Now
RED
1989
reputation
Lover
folklore

TS

Swifties have dropped an estimated $1,300 to $1,500 each in ancillary spending during the Eras Tour.

is now releasing rerecordings of her discography to reclaim their master rights.

The Economic and Cultural Impact of the Eras Tour

If ticket sales do hit the $1.4 billion mark as expected, the Eras Tour will become the biggest concert series in history, blowing past Elton John's multiyear farewell tour, which wrapped in July 2023 with $939 million in receipts.

But the money goes far deeper than just ticket revenue. If the current rate of spending continues, the Eras Tour is projected to generate close to $5 billion in economic impact. "If Taylor Swift were an economy, she'd be bigger than 50 countries," Dan Fleetwood, president of research and insights at QuestionPro, an online survey firm, told GlobeNewswire.

On the opening night in Glendale, Arizona, the concert brought in more revenue for local businesses than Super Bowl LVII, which was held in February 2023 in the same stadium. To use the Arizona event as a yardstick for the Eras Tour, Swift performed the equivalent of two to three Super Bowls every weekend, including all six of the sold-out shows she did in Los Angeles in August.

Typically, tickets to a live performance generate hundreds of dollars in ancillary local spending. But for the Eras Tour, Swifties on average dropped more than $1,300 each on things such as outfits and costumes, merchandise, dining, and travel. Some 91 percent of those fans seemed unfazed by the sum, telling QuestionPro that they would do it again, given the chance. The governor of Illinois credited the singer with reviving the state's tourism industry after her three nights in Chicago. She was even mentioned in a report by the Federal Reserve Bank of Philadelphia, which said she had

CONTINUED ON PAGE 16

The Eras Tour opened on March 17 in Glendale, Arizona, ceremoniously renamed "Swift City" by the mayor in celebration. The concert brought in more revenue for local businesses than the 2023 Super Bowl, which was held in the same stadium. During her 1989 set, Swift rocked a pink crystal Roberto Cavalli skirt set, one of many sparkly numbers by the designer that have appeared on the tour.

CONTINUED FROM PAGE 13

boosted that city's hotel revenue.

The enthusiasm has been so great that some cities along the way have experienced supply shortages. For example, in the song "You're on Your Own, Kid" off the *Midnights* album, Swift mentions "friendship bracelets." On cue, thousands of fans lined up at craft shops and elsewhere for beads, sequins, and thread so they could fashion armlets spelling out the names of Swift songs, colloquialisms, and Easter eggs. Not all shops were able to keep up with the demand.

What makes the Swiftian spending spree even more notable is that it comes amid broader economic challenges, such as inflation, which remained stubbornly high in some places, and climbing interest rates. "There's a cost of living crisis, and people are still forking out thousands of dollars to see Taylor Swift," says Alice Enders, a music industry analyst and a former senior economist at the World Trade Organization.

What's more, the Eras Tour has become a cultural phenomenon, making headlines globally, nationally, and, of course, locally. Minneapolis renamed itself "Swiftie-apolis"; Santa Clara, California, took on the moniker "Swiftie Clara" and made the singer its honorary mayor; New Jersey governor Phil Murphy adjusted the name of the state's sandwich to Taylor Swift Ham, Egg, and Cheese for her. World leaders including the president of Chile, the mayor of Budapest, and Canadian prime minister Justin Trudeau all asked the singer to bring Eras to their countries. In July, the FBI tweeted out a Taylor Swift pun.

Princiotti says that as a fan, it's been gratifying but something of a disconnect to see the globe embrace Swift so enthusiastically. "I think a lot of fans feel like they've spent their entire lives defending their love of her," she says. "And there's something very strange in seeing the U.S. government, or all of these various municipalities, just desperate to get a little sliver of the clout that comes from just being somewhat associated with Taylor Swift."

Beyond the Concert Tickets

In terms of ancillary spending, one of the standouts has been tour merchandise. Decked out in beaded bracelets and with drawings of the number 13 (Swift's favorite) on their hands, Swifties by the thousands have lined up, waiting for hours, to snag their $75 hoodies, $55 long-sleeve shirts, and $45 T-shirts. They have also been clamoring to get their hands on physical copies of Swift's music—and the star has responded to their demands, so far issuing more than 20 versions of *Midnights*, on CD, LP, and cassette in various colors, with different artwork. One suite of covers for the vinyl editions that debuted in late 2022 fit together to form a clock face; there was also an edition of *Midnights*, released late last year, that came with bonus tracks.

"Streaming has taken over the purchase of the physical album product, but Taylor Swift is among the artists who still make money from vinyl and CDs because they've become collector's items for

This dollhouse-style backdrop—shown here at the May 2023 show in Nashville—appeared behind Swift one room at a time. Fans recognized the set from Swift's "Lover" music video.

her fans," Enders explains.

Notably, sales of *Midnights* in 2023 have come on top of an already phenomenal 2022 for the album, when it sold 945,000 copies in vinyl. The number made *Midnights* not only the top-selling vinyl record of that year, but its first-week vinyl sales were the highest since at least 1991. One out of every 25 vinyl records sold in 2022 was a Taylor Swift album, and in 2023, she became the first artist in history to simultaneously occupy at least seven of the top 10 spots on Billboard's Vinyl Albums Chart. "This moment for her is like an excellent HBO miniseries that's not just a primary narrative, but also a B plot and a C plot where the main narrative is the tour, but underneath that we have the album rerecordings," says Charlie Harding, a music journalist and cohost of the podcast *Switched on Pop*.

The Success of Swift's Rerecording Project

Take Swift's "Taylor's Version" rerecording project, which the pop star announced in 2019 after music mogul Scooter Braun bought her prior music company, Big Machine Label Group, including the masters to her first six albums.

CONTINUED ON PAGE 20

Throughout the tour, when Swift performed her surprise acoustic songs, she often changed her costume on stage, delighting fans. For the first night of her Kansas City stop (seen here), she pulled on a pleated yellow dress over her jeweled 1989 outfit and then played "Never Grow Up" and "When Emma Falls in Love."

CONTINUED FROM PAGE 17

To wrest artistic and financial control from Braun, Swift began to rerecord and release those early albums. So far, there have been three installments: *Fearless (Taylor's Version)*, *Red (Taylor's Version)*, and *Speak Now (Taylor's Version)*, with the rerecorded editions all including additional "vault songs" that didn't make it onto the original albums. The fourth installment is the rerecording of her synth-pop crossover hit, *1989*. Swift revealed that news in closing out her six-show Los Angeles stint. And she made the official announcement in her signature Swiftian way on August 9. For numerolgists, that's 8/9, and October 27, 2023, is nine years to the day after *1989's* initial release in 2014. Swift primed the pump for *1989 (Taylor's Version)* by releasing several vinyl and special-edition deluxe CDs for preorder on her website.

"It's kind of like the Marvel Cinematic Universe," says Harding. "We're in the Taylor Swift cinematic universe at any given moment. There's endless amounts of discussion to be had at every level of this world that she's created, and each one I think serves a different audience."

Making Music History

Fans, meanwhile, have embraced Swift's attempt to claim her music back, opting to stream the rerecordings more than the original versions, thus dethroning the catalog once owned by Braun. (He sold the rights to Shamrock Capital in November 2020.) And they have helped propel their star to the forefront of several music records. *Speak Now (Taylor's Version)* made history when it went straight to the top of the *Billboard* 200 chart as her 12th No. 1. Even more remarkably, within days of the release of *Speak Now (Taylor's Version)*, Swift held 23 of the top 50 spots of Spotify's U.S. Top 50.

With more tour stops on the horizon—plus the debut of *Taylor Swift: The Eras Tour* in movie theaters this fall (it broke presale records on the first day tickets became available)—Eras seems to be exceeding even Swift's expectations. On the last night of the first U.S. leg of the series, she told the crowd, "I figured it would be fun, but I did not know it would be like this." In Harding's view, Swift has figured out both the recipe for financial success and spectacular longevity. "Taylor Swift has the capacity to be around for a whole lifetime," he says. "The big question I have is: Where do you go from here?" ☐

In Santa Clara, California, sister band HAIM, longtime friends of Swift, joined her on stage to perform "No Body, No Crime." Those outfits? A nod to the evil stepsister dresses HAIM donned in Swift's music video for the song "Bejeweled."

Born on December 13, 1989, Swift has long claimed 13 as her lucky number and has used it in various ways throughout her career. During her Fearless *set in Los Angeles, she played a jewel-encrusted guitar decorated with the digits.*

1

BECOMING TAYLOR

At 15, she landed a record deal. By 16, she was a fixture on the country scene. And at 24, with the release of *1989,* Taylor Swift hit next-level fame as America's powerful crossover princess.

In April 2002, 12-year-old Swift performed the National Anthem before a Detroit Pistons–Philadelphia 76ers game.

FROM TIME'S NOVEMBER 24, 2014, COVER STORY

AN ALL-AMERICAN VOICE

With the release of the 2014 album *1989*, Swift crossed over from country fame to pop superstardom.

BY JACK DICKEY

AT 8 O'CLOCK ON THE MOST EXCITING night of her life, America's most important musician was leading several dozen fans in a performance of "Happy Birthday" directed toward a young woman named Caylee, who had just turned 21. She presented Caylee with a bottle of champagne and a card. "Do you know what kind of drinker you are yet?" the 24-year-old superstar asked the 21-year-old as she put her arm around her. "Are you a happy drunk?"

Earlier that day, in the same Manhattan event space, Taylor Swift had charmed music-biz executives while waiters circulated with frenched lamb and lobster canapés. Her fifth album had come out that morning. She greeted bosses from iHeartMedia–formerly Clear Channel, recently rechristened–and took pictures with them and their awe-struck daughters.

By evening, the waiters had switched to pizza, the crowd had turned civilian, and Swift had replaced her sleek all-black ensemble with a navy dress with white polka dots and a gold necklace that read *t.s. 1989*. When she entered the room, the brigade of fans, prevailingly female and in their late teens and early 20s, queued behind Caylee like supplicants in want of benediction.

Swift is happy to minister to them. "They're discovering the music that tells them how they are going to live their lives and how they should feel and how it's acceptable to feel," she says. "I think that's kind of exciting." She has recently started speaking to her fans about two connected matters of importance to her: the music business and feminism.

On November 3, 2014, almost all of Swift's music vanished from Spotify, the online streaming service that claims more than 50 million active users, more than 10 million of whom pay for an ad-free and mobile-ready version. Her departure came as a surprise to plenty of those users. She says it shouldn't have; she believes that Spotify's particular model devalues her work. "With Beats Music and Rhapsody," Swift says, naming two competing services,

"you have to pay for a premium package in order to access my albums. And that places a perception of value on what I've created. On Spotify, they don't have any settings or any kind of qualifications for who gets what music." Swift's decision made such an impact that Spotify's CEO, Daniel Ek, wrote a blog post defending his business. A Spotify spokesperson told TIME that total payout for Swift's streaming over the past 12 months globally was $2 million. Swift's label, which receives only a portion of the payments, says it collected $496,044 from domestic streams during that period.

The Spotify dustup made one thing especially clear: More than anyone else, Swift knows how to create albums people will pay for. According to Nielsen SoundScan, Swift was the nation's best-selling artist in 2008 and 2010 and No. 2 in 2012, the last three years she released albums. There's every reason to expect her to finish No. 1 in 2014. Her first-week figure of 1.287 million copies sold for her new album, *1989,* bests any album's sales week since 2002's *The Eminem Show.*

Swift and Eminem have something else in common: The two are the most successful writer-artists to break in and sustain such levels of popularity since the 1990s began. Among Swift's pop peers, Rihanna and Miley Cyrus lean far more heavily on outside songwriters, while Lady Gaga and Beyoncé haven't matched her sales. Swift is the only artist to have three albums sell a million copies in their first week since 1991, when SoundScan started keeping track. Before *1989,* she sold nearly 70 million digital tracks. *Billboard* named her its woman of the year for 2014, the second time she's received that distinction in the award's eight-year history. Her last tour grossed $150 million—the biggest tally country music had ever seen. She has 46 million Twitter followers, putting her in striking distance of Barack Obama, if still behind Katy Perry and Justin Bieber, her reported antagonists.

Yet as financially secure as Swift may be, she worries a great deal about her industry's future, and her own, periodically falling into, as she puts it, "rabbit holes of self-doubt and fear." She says, "It's a really important thing that I manage my anxiety when it comes to the future, because, you know, I have very few female role models. That scares me sometimes." She says she looks up to Mariska Hargitay, the *Law & Order: SVU* actress: "She's one of the highest-paid actresses—actors in general,

Swift in Nashville in 2006 at age 16, at the start of her career. Opposite: An undated photo from her childhood.

Swift appeared with Brad Paisley and Kellie Pickler at the 2007 Country Music Association Awards in Nashville.

women or men—on television, and she's been playing this very strong female character for so many years now." Swift once gave Hargitay and her husband a ride home from an Ingrid Michaelson concert. She later named her cat Olivia Benson, after Hargitay's *SVU* character.

She likes to think, she says, about what her grandchildren will say one day—it's easier than worrying about her millions of fans. She knows that one way or another, the grandkids will tease her. "But I'd really rather it be 'Look how awkward your dancing was in the "Shake It Off" video! You look so weird, Grandma!' than 'Grandma, is that your nipple?'"

Hiding in Plain Sight

"Shake It off," *1989*'s lead single, had been out for a little over a month when I visited Swift in September at her parents' home in suburban Nashville for the first of a series of interviews this fall. The song, sonically Swift's danciest to date and her second Billboard No. 1, covers the business—significant to her—of bad publicity and "haters" in the world at large.

SHE FLEW TO NASHVILLE AT AGE 11 AND HANDED HER DEMO CD OF COVERS TO RECORD LABELS ALL ALONG MUSIC ROW, BUT STRUCK OUT.

In person, Swift is taller and thinner than you might expect, and more sharp and sarcastic. She speaks in a low voice, engagingly and crisply, pronouncing every *t*. We sat at a table on a patio beside a babbling pool, and she tucked her legs underneath her while we talked.

Surely every parent with an ambitious child knows by now the origin story of Taylor Alison Swift. Born in, yes, 1989, in Reading, Pennsylvania, to Scott, a financial adviser at Merrill Lynch, and Andrea, then a marketing executive for a mutual fund, Swift lived on a Christmas-tree farm before moving to the nearby town of Wyomissing. As a child, she wrote (stories, poems, diary entries) and performed (musical theater, national anthems) whenever she could. She even won a nationwide poetry contest in fourth grade. But country songwriting—Swift has said Faith Hill, Shania Twain, and LeAnn Rimes inspired her—scratched the itch better than anything that preceded it. She flew to Nashville at age 11 and handed her demo CD of covers to record labels all along Music Row, but she struck out. She tried again at 13 with songs she had written and fared better, earning a development deal with RCA Records. But RCA wanted her to record other people's songs, and she didn't like that. Besides, the deal had little chance of becoming something real. She opted out and accepted a generous publishing contract with Sony/ATV. She was the youngest songwriter the company had ever signed.

In eighth grade, Swift talked her parents into relocating to Hendersonville, Tennessee, outside Nashville, with her younger brother, Austin, in tow. She would write at her publisher's office for a few hours each week after school, recounting her day and griping about the flaky boys for whom she had no patience. Her mom would pick her up afterward. While performing at an industry showcase, Swift caught the attention of longtime promotions executive Scott Borchetta. When Borchetta started his own record label soon afterward, in 2005, he snapped up not only Swift but also an investment in his business from her father. The next year, her first album, *Taylor Swift,* came out. Three months after its release, the Recording Industry Association of America (RIAA) would certify it as gold, en route to the five-times-platinum certification it would receive by 2011. Easy enough, right?

Nope. Everyone who works with Swift cites her uncommon determination and exacting nature. Arturo Buenahora Jr., the former Sony/ATV executive who first signed Swift, says that even at 14 the singer would decline the help of 40-year-old men with long track records of country-hitmaking success. Ryan Tedder, who has written and produced songs for artists from Beyoncé to U2 and wrote two songs with Swift for *1989,* noticed her focus too. "Ninety-five times out of 100, if I get a track to where we're happy with it, the artist will say, 'That's amazing.' It's very rare to hear, 'Nope, that's not right,'" he says. Liz Rose, Swift's most frequent cowriter, says scores of young women have requested her services in recent years, hoping to "write a Taylor Swift song." Rose has to tell each one, "Honey, no. Only Taylor Swift could write those songs."

It isn't just that Swift pulls nearly all her material from her own life. She writes, at her finest, with a poet's delicate touch and a dramatist's nose for conflict. From the first line of her first single, 2006's "Tim McGraw," she stood apart: "He said the way my blue eyes shined put those Georgia stars to shame that night/I said, 'That's a lie.'" In that song, and throughout that first album, Swift presented herself as an unlikely mix of coquettish and world-weary, eager and ready to fall in love and equally ready to lose it all. The debut had songs of infatuation and songs of vengeance, all of them mercifully less twangy and anesthetizing than what the rest of mainstream country had to offer.

And off she went, collecting admirers from an older generation with its own songwriting bona fides. Kris Kristofferson, Bruce Springsteen, Dolly Parton—all were wowed by Swift's craft and poise. At her best she can write stories like Joni Mitchell's and set them to melodies as memorable as Pharrell's. But she can also sell like ABBA, traverse genres—proving stronger than the format constraints that have strangled scores of high-profile artists—and attract an audience that seems more vast and more loyal than any other artist's. She has introduced to her fans an earnestness and craft, a form of romanticism, that seems to be in short supply elsewhere in society. And she has pulled it off in an era seemingly dead set against such triumphs—one in which audiences are far more likely to splinter than to coalesce—all while masquerading to many as a teen idol, hiding in plain sight.

Along for the Ride

One day in early 2014, Tedder, the producer, songwriter, and OneRepublic front man, was walking down Abbot Kinney Boulevard in Venice, California, when he got a call from Swift. She wanted his help on her new album, and the energetic Tedder knew it was a match from the start. "If anyone else's bloodstream has trace amounts of Red Bull, hers does," he says. She told him that she loved the '80s, and she wanted snapshots of every era of pop from her life. Most important, Tedder says, Swift said she wanted him to ditch every notion he had of her sound. "There is no country on this album. Pretend I'm this new artist who just needs to make this album that defines her career," she told him.

Even though *1989* is her fifth album, released eight years after her first, it may indeed come to

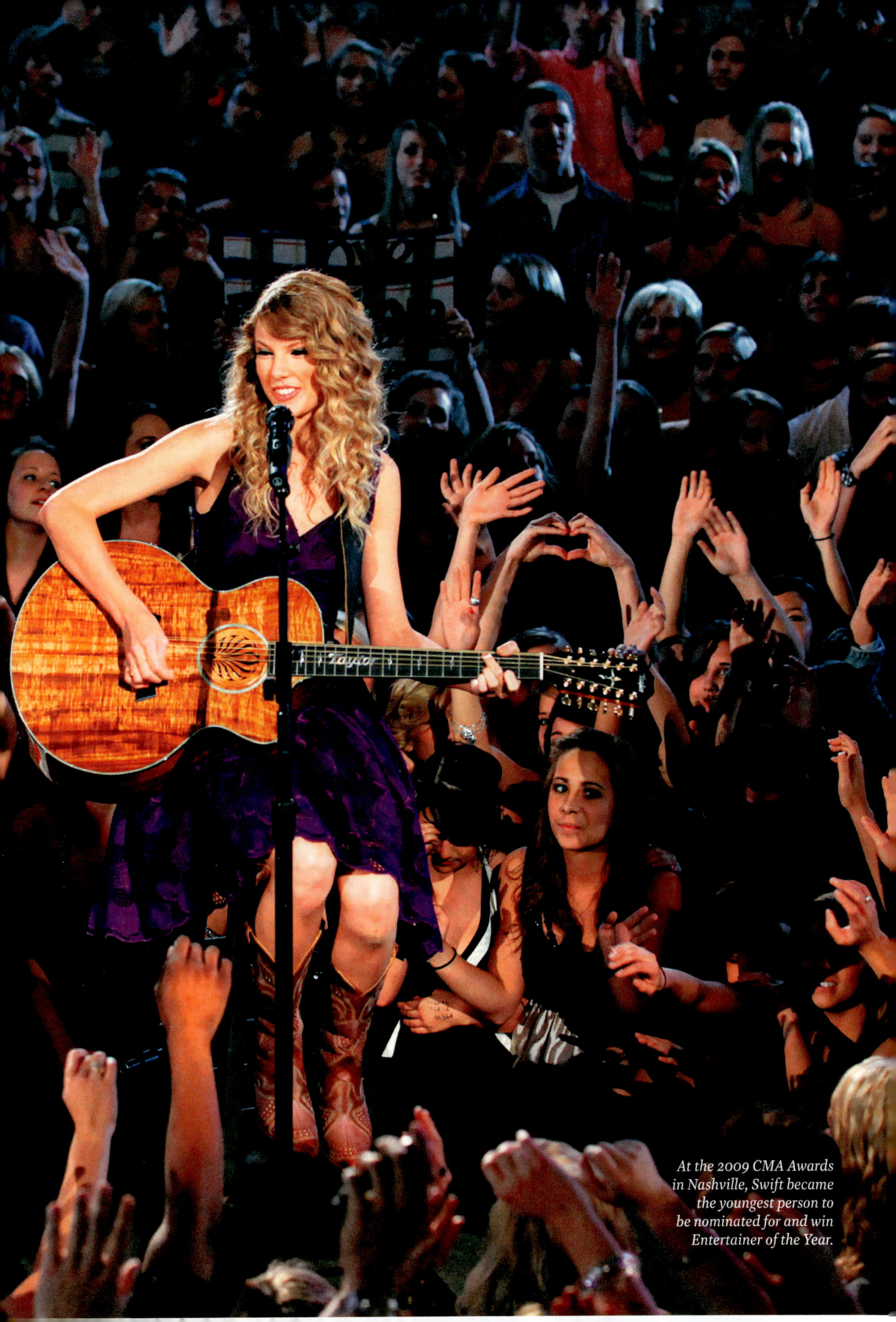

At the 2009 CMA Awards in Nashville, Swift became the youngest person to be nominated for and win Entertainer of the Year.

Swift in October 2010, around the time of the release of her third album, Speak Now.

define her career. It marks Swift's split from Nashville, both literal and figurative. The old marriage was always one of convenience. The Pennsylvania-reared Swift—no more authentically country than a coastal Cracker Barrel—found in Nashville a chance to make it on the strength of her songs. Had New York City or Los Angeles, the nation's other two music-making capitals, found Swift first, surely they would have sanded down her rough edges, straightened the curls from her hair. Since Swift had been in Nashville, earnestly, from the start of her career, she was welcome to stay as long as she liked.

Her country writing had always been sharp, even by the genre's tough standards. Her second album, *Fearless,* offered "Fifteen," which situates Swift's ninth-grade romantic troubles alongside those of her real-life best friend Abigail and builds and builds until: "Back then, I swore I was gonna marry him someday, but I realized some bigger dreams of mine/And Abigail gave everything she had to a boy who changed his mind, and we both cried." Some of Swift's detractors said she was crusading for chastity, but the lyrics capture too the wrenching myopia that all high schoolers suffer.

Her catalog is filled with songs like that, songs that on second and third listen transcend their narrative focus. Take "Enchanted," on 2010's *Speak Now*, the album Swift wrote without any assistance from cowriters. On first pass, the nearly six-minute-long track sounds like the work of an obsessive, unrelatable mind. But listen again and you hear a song about all of life's impossible relationships—like the crush that persists for just two stops on the subway—and the dueling senses of opportunity and futility that pervade all affairs of the heart.

While recording 2012's *Red*, Swift found herself in need of a new sound. Borchetta, the president of her record label, heard a version of her song "Red" produced by her usual collaborator Nathan Chapman. Borchetta says, "The song was brilliant—great melody. But I told them that the way it was recorded, guys, the production just doesn't match the song. It needs a pop sound." So Chapman and Swift asked if they could take another crack at it. They did—and it was worse, Borchetta says, than the first pass. "And Taylor basically said, 'All right, would you call Max?'"

"Max" is 43-year-old Max Martin, perhaps the most successful pop songwriter of the past 20 years, trailing only two guys named McCartney

Swift rehearsed before her 2013 Red Tour. Opposite: With her backup dancers.

and Lennon. Martin, who is based in his native Sweden and rarely gives interviews, made his name in the late 1990s writing and producing R&B-inflected bubblegum-pop hits for Britney Spears, the Backstreet Boys, and NSYNC. After that era gave way, he found a second life helping Pink and Katy Perry develop their electronic sound. Martin and his protégé, Johan "Shellback" Schuster, made for unusual collaborators for Swift, given how tight she had kept her pre-*Red* circle. But she was ready to experiment, and they were ready to help. "We Are Never Ever Getting Back Together," the bouncy single the three made, became Swift's first No. 1 on the Billboard Hot 100. "I Knew You Were Trouble," a rocking electronic track, would later hit No. 2.

Her goal with *1989*, she says, was a "sonically cohesive" album, one that didn't straddle genres as *Red* and *Speak Now* had. And she has achieved it with an album louder, snappier, and poppier than anything she's released before. Tedder says it was entirely Swift's doing. "People will look for a hole to punch in the Taylor Swift poster and say, 'Oh, you've got Max Martin, me, Jack [Antonoff] from Fun—established hitmakers.' But I think any one of us will tell you, it's really Taylor. We're acting as editors. She's driving. We're along for the ride."

On *1989*, Swift changes thematically, too, deadpanning about her man-eater reputation in "Blank Space" and describing for the first time a girl who cheats on her tomcat boyfriend in "Style." The old Swift rarely explored gray areas. Yet, she says, "when you're growing up and essentially publishing your diary for the world to read, you end up incorporating new themes as these themes become evident to you in your own life."

Her life is full of new themes. Around the time of her previous album release, in 2012, the public seemed to know Swift best as a serial dater—John

Mayer and Jake Gyllenhaal were among her famous boyfriends—and a new queen of the kiss-and-tell. Before that, Swift was best known to nonfans for the time Kanye West filched her mic at the 2009 MTV Video Music Awards to say that Beyoncé, not Swift, deserved the award for best female video.

But since 2012, Swift's public image has morphed in tandem with her private life. Her last public relationship ended in January 2013, and afterward she cut her hair, made a bunch of new friends, and moved from Nashville to New York City, where she bought a $19.9 million pair of Manhattan penthouses that had once belonged to the director Peter Jackson. Soon she became, judging by photographs, a fixture on the city's sidewalks, though she was trapped inside more than she'd like: "If I'm in the mood to be held accountable for every single article of clothing on my body—whether it matches, if it clashes, if it's on trend—then I go out. If I'm not interested in undergoing that kind of debate and conversation . . . I just don't go out." At least the city's paparazzi are polite, she says.

The Two Taylors

Swift likes to tell a story about how she came to be named Taylor. Well, she likes to tell two. The first is that she was named for James Taylor, the gentle "Fire and Rain" singer whom her parents adored. And the other: "My mom named me Taylor because she thought that I would probably end up in corporate business—my parents are both finance people—and she didn't want any kind of executive, boss, manager to see if I was a girl or a boy if they got my résumé."

The businesswoman wound up in Swift anyway. She has sponsorships with Diet Coke and Keds, and for the sake of album sales she has aligned herself not only against Spotify but with Target. More than a third of Swift's first-week sales came at the retailer, where among the store-exclusive bonus tracks on *1989* are Swift's intimate voice memos explaining her craft. Like so many millennials born into the upper middle class, Swift has benefited from the demise of the concept of selling out. By now, Americans are used to brands' ubiquity, and her product placement is hardly intrusive. What does it matter, really, that "Style" premiered in a Target commercial rather than in a small concert? Swift says her big sales figures matter "because I realize how important of a statement it makes to everyone to whom statements are very important."

1989 looks backward with its synthesizers, drum machines, and Polaroid-centric aesthetic, but Swift also brought back the past with the hoopla surrounding its release. In 1989, the U.S. music industry (top sellers: Madonna, Janet Jackson, Fine Young Cannibals) brought in more than $12 billion,

Swift writing lyrics from Red*'s "Holy Ground" on her arm. Opposite: A performance from the Red Tour, 2013.*

adjusted for present-day inflation, according to the RIAA. In 2013? Less than $7 billion. Swift says she wanted to make "an album that's really an album-album–highlighted, underlined, all-caps, exclamation points at the end of it." Not too many artists have free rein to do that. But Swift's fans, enamored and protective of her after years of confessional and moving songs, will support her—and her business prerogatives—whatever the industry headwinds.

Her fans' loyalty extended so far as to police online leaks of *1989* in the days before its release. Album sales mattered to her, and so too would they matter to her fans. Swift later told NPR that it was the first time an album of hers had leaked but not trended on Twitter, and she thanked the Swifties for it. From them, Swift says, she has enjoyed "extreme, unconditional, wonderful loyalty that I never thought I'd receive in my life, not from a best friend, not from a boyfriend, not from a husband, not from a dog."

The fans she assembled on the night of Caylee's 21st birthday were of that loyal breed. Swift herself had selected them from Twitter, Tumblr, and Instagram, with vetting help from her staff, to attend the final evening in a series of "*1989* Secret Sessions." All summer, she had invited groups of her most fervent followers to her homes (in Manhattan, Los Angeles, Nashville, and Watch Hill, Rhode Island) and to a hotel room in London to preview her forthcoming album. Once they signed nondisclosure agreements, she would bake for them and give them little bits of commentary about the tracks. Then they would pose with her for goofy Polaroid shots.

On this final night, though, with the album finally in stores en route to selling nearly 1.3 million copies in its first week, the session had turned a little less secret than the others. Swift played her songs live, two of them for the first time, on a downtown rooftop, simulcasting the performance on Yahoo and iHeart's stations to an audience worldwide. Behind her, the towers of the Financial District punctured early-evening amber skies. And the lights atop the Empire State Building—a versatile LED rig installed just two years ago—danced to the beat of Swift's just-released songs. Four years earlier, Swift first sang, "How the kingdom lights shined just for me and you." On the ground, no one understood what was going on. But on the roof, Swift's fans shimmied and shivered, warding off the evening's chill and gazing up at their queen while she looked out over her vast new kingdom. □

'This Is Risky'

Back in 2014, the singer discussed Spotify, timid managers, and female role models.

BY JACK DICKEY

Not everything could fit into the previous article, so here's more of what Swift told TIME.

Why did you leave Spotify? I'm in an office of people who are upset they can't stream your music.

Everybody's complaining about how music sales are shrinking, but nobody's changing the way they're doing things. They keep running toward streaming, which is, for the most part, what has been shrinking the numbers of paid album sales.

With Beats Music and Rhapsody you have to pay for a premium package in order to access my albums. And that places a perception of value on what I've created. On Spotify, they don't have any settings, or any kind of qualifications for who gets what music. I think that people should feel that there is a value to what musicians have created, and that's that. [Swift's music returned to Spotify in 2017.]

What was the goal of your new album, *1989*?

With *1989*, I was really putting my neck on the line, because I was the one saying I needed to change directions musically. And my label and management were the ones saying, "Are you sure, are you positive? This is risky." And I was the one who had to come back every time and say, "No, this is what we're doing." When I put forth an album cover that didn't have half my face on it and tried to convince my label that this was the best way to sell an album, you know, I got some kind of interesting side-glance looks. But I knew that this was the best cover to represent this record, because I wanted there to be an air of mystery.

What does writing a song do for you?

I see a lot of celebrities build up these emotional walls around themselves where they let no one in, and that's what makes them feel very lonely at the top. I just keep writing songs. And I kind of stay open to feeling humiliated and rejected, because before being a quote-unquote celebrity, I'm a songwriter. Being a celebrity means you lock your doors and close your windows and don't let people in. Being a songwriter means you're very attuned to your intuition and your feelings, even if they hurt.

Is there someone you look to as a model of where you'd like your career to go? Are there women you look up to?

We're taught to find examples for the way we want our lives to wind up. But I can't find anyone, really, who's had the same career trajectory as mine. So when I'm in an optimistic place, I hope that my life won't match anyone else's life trajectory, either, going forward. I do have female role models in the sense of actresses like Mariska Hargitay. I think she has a beautiful life and an incredible career, and I think she's built that for herself. And Ina Garten, the Barefoot Contessa. I really love her business and how she sticks to who she is, and how people relate to it. In other industries, I have female role models. I just struggle to find a woman in music who hasn't been completely picked apart by the media, or scrutinized and criticized for aging, or criticized for fighting aging—it just seems to be much more difficult to be a woman in music and to grow older. I just really hope that I will choose to do it as gracefully as possible.

It's the same thing as living your life based on what your grandkids will say one day. I'm sure there will be things that my grandkids make fun of me for, no matter what.

Swift is known for mining her own life for material and for writing or cowriting all of her songs.

Does it annoy you when people say you don't write your own songs, or that someone else is pulling the strings of your career?
I haven't heard any of the people I respect in the music industry or in journalism saying that they think I don't write my own songs. I think when I put out *Speak Now*, which was my third album, and I decided I was just going to write it entirely on my own, to me that was enough of a statement. I felt like I could move on from that. And we all know it's a feminist issue. My friend Ed [Sheeran], no one questions whether he writes everything.

As a female celebrity, having your body scrutinized in a way that doesn't happen for male celebrities—how do you deal?
I refuse to buy into these comparisons, because you don't see it happening to men. All you seem to see is "Which New Mother Is Sexier?" "Who's the Hotter Mama?" "Who's Got the Better Booty?" If we continue to show young girls that they are being compared to other girls, we're doing ourselves a huge disservice as a society. I surround myself with smart, beautiful, passionate, driven, ambitious women. Other women who are killing it should motivate you, thrill you, challenge you, and inspire you rather than threaten you. The only thing I compare myself to is me two years ago, or me one year ago. You just try to lead by example, and you hope that someday, if we talk about feminism enough, maybe we'll start to actually see it make a difference in the way young girls perceive themselves and each other. □

In Arlington, Texas, during the 2018 Reputation Stadium Tour.

LOOK WHAT YOU MADE ME DO

Unpacking a viral video, snake GIFs and all.

BY CADY LANG

MAKE NO MISTAKE ABOUT IT—TAYLOR Swift always has plenty of feelings about what you think of her and the headlines she's made in recent years, something she reiterated relentlessly in the first single, "Look What You Made Me Do," off her 2017 album *Reputation*.

If the track and album title (and all those creepy snake GIFs) weren't obvious enough clues, the video for the song drove home that fact that Swift feels keenly about being critiqued as a public figure. The video, which debuted at the 2017 MTV Video Music Awards—the setting for many a dramatic narrative in Swift's life—showed the pop princess's character viciously confronting her own past personas as well as the dramas that have surrounded her, from her highly scrutinized romantic relationships to her years-long feud with Kanye West that flared up explosively in 2016 when Kim Kardashian (then married to West) went after Swift on social media.

While the overall theme of the "Look What You Made Me Do" video was overt enough, there were plenty of hidden references to Swift's catalog that you might have missed.

She made clear she intended to bury her past personas, including Nils Sjoberg. To explain: Swift once helped pen a song called "This Is What You Came For" with ex-boyfriend Calvin Harris. However, once the pair broke up, it came out that Swift had cowritten the song and provided some vocals under the pseudonym Nils Sjoberg—a revelation that spurred a series of tweets from Harris accusing the singer of stirring up drama and referencing her longtime feud with fellow pop princess Katy Perry. As the "Look What You Made Me Do" video opened, an undead version of Taylor Swift (which some fans saw as a continuation of her persona from the "Out of the Woods" music video) dug a grave as the tombstone of Nils Sjoberg hovered in the background. On an equally pointed note, the main tombstone from which zombie Swift emerged read "Here Lies Taylor Swift's Reputation."

She even went so far as to reference where she felt that her reputation began getting attacked: Lying in the grave that a zombie-like Swift filled with dirt was Swift clad in the dress the star wore to the 2014 Met Gala—the start of her *1989* era, when Swift's personal and professional life often made headlines. (For example, a few months after the gala, the music video for Swift's single "Shake It Off" was released and drew criticism for what was seen as its stereotypes about Black women.)

Swift wanted viewers to remember her 2017 lawsuit win: The shot of her reclining in a bathtub full of jewels showed a lone dollar bill amid the sparkling baubles, a reference to the single-digit damages she sought from David Mueller, the former Colorado radio DJ who Swift alleged had groped her. Swift's lawyer, in his closing argument, had noted that the reason his client had asked for only $1 was because it was a "single symbolic dollar, the value of which is immeasurable to every women in this situation," meaning that it affects all women, in all financial situations, and that every woman should be able to say that it's wrong.

The throne scene took on trust issues: At the time, Swift had begun appropriating the snake imagery she was pelted with on social media following her controversy with Kimye. In the "Look What You Made Me Do" video, she sat on a golden throne while being served tea by slithering reptiles. If you looked closely enough, you could see that the arms of the throne read "Et Tu Brute," a reference to the betrayal that Julius Caesar suffered at the hands of his onetime ally Brutus, which some interpreted as Swift feeling vulnerable amid potential betrayal. The phrase was also inscribed in gold on the columns of her snake-filled palace.

Meanwhile, Swift sipped tea in the video like Kendall Jenner in a much-commented-on Instagram post from the era. It all unfolded in the wake of Kim Kardashian's infamous 2016 Snapchat, where the reality star shared

Top: The video references a Vogue *shoot and Beyoncé (above). Opposite, from top: Kendall Jenner and cats.*

the phone conversation between Swift and Kanye West about West's song "Famous." Included in the lyrics was a verse where West rapped about one day having sex with Swift—which reignited the two stars' long-running feud. A few days after the Snapchat release, Jenner, Kardashian's half sister, posted an image on Instagram where she posed with her legs crossed, drinking a bottle of water. She captioned it "tea time," possibly a reference to the pasttime of "spilling tea," or gossiping. The teatime segment of the "Look What You Made Me Do" video had more than a few similarities to Jenner's post, in both her stance (crossed legs) and style (sleek hair and slit gown). Swift's dress was also by Balmain, a brand that has long championed the Kardashian/Jenner family. And then, of course, Swift was literally sipping tea in the shot.

Then there was the car-crash scene—probably definitely a poke at Swift's longtime foe Katy Perry—in which Swift drove a gold luxury sports car down a dead-end street and barreled into a pole, sending glass spraying everywhere. When the car door opened to flashing paparazzi lights, Swift emerged sporting angular bangs and a flashy dress that evoked Perry's style at the time. Another hint that Swift had Perry on her mind: She wore a leopard-print coat and had a leopard in the front seat of the car. (Perry's fans are called "Katy Cats.") And finally, there was the mock Grammy that Swift clutched after the crash. That could have been interpreted as that Swift was still thinking about the 2014 Grammys, at which *Red* did not win album of the year, but it could also have been a dig at Perry. (The two famously made up a few years later, with Perry making a cameo in the "You Need to Calm Down" video.)

The singer also appeared to acknowledge her fraught past with streaming companies: Swift famously pulled her music from Spotify in 2014 because the streaming service was paying her such a small royalty fee, and she later called out Apple Music for offering music free during a trial period when the service first launched. While Swift has settled her differences with both Spotify and Apple, she has been credited with influencing the streaming business model, which she seemed to reference in the video by committing a "robbery" in a bank with an LED sign that glared "streaming company" in the background.

She also leaned into the stereotypes that she's been teased for: Her henchwomen's disguises were cat masks, a not-so-subtle-reference to Swift's obsession with her Scottish Fold felines, named Meredith Grey, after the lead character in the long-running television show *Grey's Anatomy,* and Olivia Benson, the hero of *Law & Order: Special Victims Unit.* Swift has joked about possibly becoming a "crazy cat lady" one day.

In a number of places in the video, Swift nodded to criticism in the media and on socials that her group of friends—her "squad"—consisted largely of supermodels or Victoria's Secret Angels. Detractors objected in particular to Swift's 2015 music video for the song "Bad Blood," about friendship and betrayal, which featured model and actor friends including Selena Gomez, Kendrick Lamar, Lena Dunham, Hailee Steinfeld, Cara Delevingne, and Zendaya, among many others.

In the "Look What You Made Me Do" video,

Swift seemed to acknowledge those who didn't like her squad. In one shot, she led a biker gang of photogenic and leggy girls on motorcycles, an obvious homage to a 1991 *Vogue* editorial shoot "Wild at Heart" by fashion photographer Peter Lindbergh, which featured supermodels Linda Evangelista, Naomi Campbell, and Cindy Crawford as a biker gang. Later in the video, Swift positioned herself as the dominatrix-esque leader of a factory of expendable robotic model types who were attending "Squad U."

Having built a career—empire—on writing songs about love and about being lovelorn, Swift also addressed her own love life. In a new scene, Swift stood in the center of a row of men who danced behind her while wearing black "I ♥ T.S." crop tops that mimicked a tank top with the same phrase that her ex the actor Tom Hiddleston sported at one of Swift's famous Fourth of July parties. The internet resourcefully pointed out that there were eight men in Swift's lineup, which if you wanted to go very deep could coincide with the eight high-profile ex-boyfriends Swift had by that point (Hiddleston, Calvin Harris, Harry Styles, Conor Kennedy, John Mayer, Jake Gyllenhaal, Taylor Lautner, and Joe Jonas).

In her music video, Swift used a jet to remind her fans that *Reputation* would be her sixth studio album by emblazoning it with the phrase "TS6." The plane is used as the backdrop to the final segment of the video, in which she seemed to actively try to shed her past personas: The message was loud

In an infamous moment at the 2009 VMAs (below), Kanye West interrupted Swift's acceptance speech. Opposite: In 2015, on stage with Hailee Steinfeld, Gigi Hadid, Lily Aldridge, and Lena Dunham.

and clear when Swift appeared atop a mountain of her former selves, including the geeky, bespectacled "You Belong With Me" Taylor, the top-hat-wearing "Red" Taylor, and the ringlet-adorned, glitter-dress-loving, guitar-strumming country music Taylor. They were all overshadowed by the *Reputation-era* Swift, who was clad all in black and out for revenge.

In the segment, she also returned to her reputation for famous friends: Her "You Belong with Me" persona looked nearly identical to the one that debuted in 2008 except that the "Junior Jewels" T-shirt she wore in "Look What You Made Me Do" was covered with the signatures of her various celebrity pals, including but not limited to Selena Gomez, Blake Lively and Ryan Reynolds, Lena Dunham, Gigi Hadid, Todrick Hall (who also appeared in the video), Martha Hunt, and Ed Sheeran.

Her various iterations might have pointed to the track list for *Reputation*: At the video's close, 15 different Taylor personas (ranging from her silver-dress-clad, 2009 VMAs "Taylor, I'mma let you finish" Taylor to her 2017 angry, wearing-all-black *Reputation* Taylor) stood in a lineup, which one Tumblr user pointed out corresponded to a theory that there are 15 songs on the new album (and for what it's worth, fans said Swift herself liked the theory on Tumblr).

However, Swift took her biggest shots with the conversation that her multiple selves have with one another. The star relied on the 15 different personas she created to voice the critiques that others have made of her, with some extremely pointed scenes.

"You Belong with Me" Taylor was criticized by "Into the Woods" zombie Taylor and the other Taylors for her "surprised" face, something Swift has been made fun of for on multiple occasions, especially at awards shows. *Reputation* Taylor then called "Into the Woods" zombie Taylor a "bitch," and zombie Taylor promptly rebuked her by saying, "Don't call me that!" It was a pointed reference to the very public disagreement that Swift and Kanye West had over his reference to her in "Famous."

"Teardrops on My Guitar" Taylor was then accused of being fake by "Red" Taylor, which prompted the younger personality to burst into tears, while another Taylor from the *Reputation* era weighed in, accusing Swift of "playing the victim... again."

However, the most biting reference might have been the comments the fur-clad *Reputation* Swift delivered to the glamorous 2014 Met Gala Swift. As she snapped a storm of selfies, Met Gala Swift informed her sister Swifts that she was "getting receipts" so that she could "edit them later"—a remark that was interpreted as a jab at Kim Kardashian, who's known for raising the selfie to an art form (and who has a coffee-table Rizzoli book to prove it). The theory was that by talking about editing the images, the Swift character was suggesting Kardashian had manipulated the phone call that she shared of Swift and Kanye talking about "Famous."

As a final self-aware note, the 2009 VMAs Swift echoed her infamous (and later deleted) Instagram post where she declared that she would "very much like to be excluded from this narrative."

Responded all the other Taylors, in unison: "Shut up!" ☐

At the 2019 TIME 100 Gala in New York City.

2

QUEEN OF THE EASTER EGGS

Among her many commercial and artistic talents, Taylor Swift has mastered how to bury messages about her IRL travails and dramas in her songs and videos.

Swift kicked off Pride Month 2019 by performing Lover's lead single "ME!" at iHeartRadio's Wango Tango show in Los Angeles.

DIGGING INTO *LOVER*

The 2019 album was meaty, gossipy, and packed with up-tempo electropop.

BY RAISA BRUNER

IT WAS AUGUST 23, 2019, AND AT LONG LAST, *Lover* had arrived. Taylor Swift's seventh studio album, clocking in at a meaty 18 tracks—her longest ever—was finally available to the star's legion of fans. And did *Lover* deliver. Described by Swift as "a celebration of love, in all its complexity, coziness, and chaos," *Lover* not only gave Swifties a boatload of up-tempo electropop songs, it served up a tantalizing labyrinth of Easter eggs, celebrity name-checks, and meta references only die-hard fans would understand.

Fans wasted no time diving in and then took to social media to speculate about the allusions (perceived or real) from Swift's history. TIME got in on the fun, too, digging into *Lover* track by delicious track. Here's where we landed.

1. "I Forgot That You Existed"

Swift kicked things off with a light mission statement of sorts, insisting that she'd moved on—whether it was from an ex or a feud was a mystery. She did, however, borrow a phrase from Drake when she sang that she was "In my feelings more than Drake, so yeah," calling back to the rapper's 2018 hit "In My Feelings." She also seemed to throw shade at her critics: "Got out some popcorn as soon as my rep started going down."

2. "Cruel Summer"

Swift's summers used to be all about her annual celebrity-studded Fourth of July party at her estate in Rhode Island. But in "Cruel Summer," the singer

suggested the season had taken on a different meaning because of a love interest ("I don't wanna keep secrets just to keep you"), possibly a reference to her then boyfriend, actor Joe Alwyn. In a bit of cross-referencing, it seemed that Swift pal Ellen DeGeneres had foreshadowed "Cruel Summer" when she appeared in the video for "You Need to Calm Down" sporting a "Cruel Summer" tattoo.

Other "Cruel Summer" chitchat revolved around the lyric "Devils roll the dice, angels roll their eyes." To sharp-eyed fans, the phrase was familiar because they'd seen it in the music video for "Lover" (which dropped before the album release) as the name of a board game. Swifties who kept tabs on the star during the promotional tour for *Lover* might have noticed that she often wore a small dice insignia.

3. "Lover"

Put out as a single a week before the album, the title track, "Lover," was an acoustic, folksy tune that was, yes, a love song. It also hid some important references to Swift's body of work and her evolving sense of self. On *Reputation*'s "New Year's Day," the singer had waxed poetic about an after-party scene. In

Above: The "Lover" video. Opposite: With Miley Cyrus. "Miss Americana & the Heartbreak Prince" referenced a song Swift sang in Hannah Montana: The Movie.

"Lover," she was all about the house party ("We can leave the Christmas lights up 'til January"; "This is our place, we make the rules"). In the bridge, which took the tone of singsong wedding vows, Swift seemed to wink at tabloid coverage of her romantic life ("Swear to be overdramatic and true to my lover"). More references to her private life could be read into the music video, which took place in a snow globe; there was a faux board game called "King of Hearts" (there's a "King of My Heart" song on *Reputation*) and a painting of her new kitten.

4. "The Man"

"The Man" was chock-full of observations about the sexist double standards around Swift's choices. Some alluded to her dating life ("They'd say I played the field before I found someone to commit to, and that would be okay for me to do"), while others took aim at haters ("How much of this I deserve, what I was wearing, if I was rude"). The singer even name-checked Leonardo DiCaprio, famous for his yacht parties on the Mediterranean Sea ("I'd be just like Leo in Saint Tropez"). This was familiar territory for Swift. "A man does something strategic. A woman does the same thing? Calculated. A man stands up for himself. A woman throws a tantrum," she told radio host Elvis Duran in a 2019 interview. "You can go on and on. A man is confident, a woman is smug... where we need to continue talking about gender equality as a whole subject is, it starts at perception."

5. "The Archer"

It's not a surprise that Swift, the subject of relentless media attention and troll activity and an antagonist or protagonist in many a public feud, would be drawn to archery imagery. "I've been the archer, and I've been the prey," she sang in "Archer," a track that referenced combat and that Swift released on an Instagram Live. During the stream, the singer pointed to a few additional bow-and-arrow allusions in videos for other *Lover* songs—among them the scene in "You Need to Calm Down" where pop artist Hayley Kiyoko shot an arrow into a bull's-eye emblazoned with the number 5, and the cupids playing in the band in the "ME!" video. What Swifties weren't sure about was what the archery image was referencing: her breakup with former bestie Karlie Kloss? Her breakup with former boyfriend Joe Alwyn?

6. "I Think He Knows"

"I Think He Knows," a love song that echoed the first flush of a big crush, contained a few important references. One was to a mysterious address, 16th Avenue, which forms Music Row in the city of Nashville, where Swift keeps a home. Another was the "indigo eyes" of a love interest. Some wasted no time before speculating there was an Alwyn connection; for the record, he has blue eyes.

7. "Miss Americana & the Heartbreak Prince"

Throughout her career, Swift has played on classic American high school tropes—marching bands, football teams and cheerleaders, prom queens. In 2008, Swift, who missed her own high school prom, even held a prom-themed party after her hit "Our Song" reached the top chart spot. She returned to the theme in "Miss Americana & the Heartbreak Prince," singing, "Now I'm feeling hopeless, ripped up my prom dress, running through rose thorns." Yet she seemed to be done with the so-called cool kids and ready to move on, identifying herself as the "most likely to run away with you." And she engaged in some Easter egg games with her past recordings. "You know I adore you, I'm crazier for you than I was at 16, lost in a film scene," the song began. That was a reference to the tune "Crazier" that Swift performed in 2009's *Hannah Montana: The Movie.*

8. "Paper Rings"

So apparently Swift really, really liked someone—enough to forgo "shiny things" for more mundane "paper rings." This song was a breathless, rock-tinged ride, but it snuck in some callbacks to specific Swift moments: "I want to drive away with you," she sang, recalling older tracks like "Getaway Car." "I want your dreary Mondays," she added, which sounded like a follow-up to the "I want your midnights" of *Reputation*'s "New Year's Day."

9. "Cornelia Street"

"Cornelia Street" sounded sweet and whimsical as a song title, but it actually referred to a real place: an iconic street in New York's West Village where Swift has history. (There's also a Cornelia Street in North London, although she hasn't been spotted there.) Swift has written New York–centric songs ("Welcome to New York" on *1989*) in the past, but "Cornelia Street" updated her connection to the city. "We were a fresh page…filling in the blanks as we go" seemed like an expansion of the lyrics of "Blank Space" on *1989* ("I've got a blank space, baby—and I'll write your name"). She was also vocal about being an avid journal writer and returned to the subject of drinking with her lover, as she did on 2017's "Delicate" on *Reputation.* And then there were the Cornelia roses Swift used to decorate promotional performances at the time *Lover* came out, which now are clear references to this song.

10. "Death by a Thousand Cuts"

One of the album's sadder songs, "Death by a Thousand Cuts" saw Swift in pain. ("You said it was a great love, one for the ages/But if the story's over, why am I still writing pages?") Pages and journals were a recurring motif across the album for Swift, who was also handing out blank journals to fans at listening sessions. "Paper cut stings from my paper-thin plans" could be taken many ways—in one interpretation, maybe those paper rings from a few songs ago weren't holding up so well. And a number of her other lines in "Death by a Thousand Cuts" called back to other songs and imagery from her oeuvre, from "Gave up on me like I was a bad drug"—see "Lord save me, my drug is my baby" in "Don't Blame Me," from *Reputation*—to the boarded-up windows of "Call It What You Want," also from *Reputation,* that were reiterated here.

11. "London Boy"

If you were confused by this song opening with the distinctive voice of actor Idris Elba, who was talking about driving someone around on his scooter, it helps to know that Elba was (and is) both a Londoner and a costar of Swift's in the film adaptation of the musical *Cats*. The voice clip was from an appearance he made on James Corden's talk show (Corden was another *Cats* actor). Online, Swifties linked the title, "London Boy," to Swift's ex Alwyn, who, like Elba, is also British. As for the song's content, "London Boy" was basically a litany of British references—from "uni" (the U.K.'s term for college) to "best mates" (best friends) to places like Camden Market, Highgate, the West End, Bond Street, Brixton, Hackney, the Heath, and Soho.

12. "Soon You'll Get Better," featuring the Chicks

The music video for "ME!" dropped in April 2019, months before Lover, and it hinted that country royalty the Chicks would make an appearance on the album. (The video included a photo of the Chicks on the wall while Swift sang, "There's a lot of cool chicks out there.") Swift was good as her word and featured the band in the song "Soon You'll Get Better," which was perhaps Lover's most tender track and had the singer sounding close to tears in some spots. Fans theorized that the subject was her mom, Andrea, who has battled cancer. In an essay for *Elle* published in March 2019, Swift opened up about her family's struggles with the disease. "Both of my parents have had cancer, and my mom is now fighting her battle with it again. It's taught me that there are real problems and then there's everything else. My mom's cancer is a real problem," she wrote. In "Soon You'll Get Better," she echoed that sentiment: "This won't go back to normal, if it ever was/It's been years of hoping...soon you'll get better." Swift is known to be close to her mom, making this song an especially poignant one.

13. "False God"

"False God" was Swift at her most downtempo as she compared a romantic relationship with a religion ("I know heaven's a thing/I go there when you touch me/ Honey, hell is when I fight with you/But we can patch it up good/Make confessions and we're begging for forgiveness/Got the wine for you"). She also flicked at a transatlantic entanglement ("We were stupid to jump in the ocean separating us/Remember how I'd fly to you?") and New York again ("You're the West Village/You still do it for me, babe"). And there's the line "I can't talk to you when you're like this," which Swift said in French ("*Je ne peux pas parler toi comme ça*") in the opening for the "ME!" music video.

14. "You Need to Calm Down"

In "You Need to Calm Down," Swift doubled down on her lyrical and visual references. The video for the song featured everything from a cat face on a watch (she loves cats, of course) to a phone case that spelled out "L-O-V-E-R" to a back tattoo that showed off a snake metamorphosing into a cloud of butterflies (a nod to her evolution out of the *Reputation* era and into the *Lover* one). There were star cameos from the likes of Laverne Cox, the men of *Queer Eye*, Ciara, Adam Rippon, Billy Porter, and

many more. There was a protest march that Swift later explained was a reference to the protesters who regularly bother her fans during shows. There was a drag queen pageant in which the ladies were dressed up as the many faces of pop today (Lady Gaga, Cardi B, and Beyoncé among them), alluding to the way the media often pits female stars against one another. There was Katy Perry herself as a hamburger (the outfit Perry donned for the 2019 Met Gala afterparty) hugging Swift, in a French fries costume—officially quashing the two singers' much-written about feud.

Above: Katy Perry and Swift in the "You Need to Calm Down" video. Opposite: Swift and her mom in 2015.

15. "Afterglow"

"Afterglow" was an apology song—"I don't wanna do this to you...it's all me, just don't go, meet me in the afterglow." It was also filled with Swift's favorite metaphors, particularly the color blue—which popped up regularly throughout the album—as well as the lyric "Fighting with a true love is boxing with no gloves," which conjured up memories of her battle-ready "Bad Blood" phase.

16. "ME!" featuring Brendon Urie

As a reintroduction for Swift following the maximalist electronic sound of the *Reputation* era, "ME!" came across as bright, brassy, and positive. She kicked things off in the music video with a repetition of sorts. Where "You Need to Calm Down" featured a tattoo of a snake transforming into a cloud of butterflies, "ME!" brought the image to life with a snake slithering along the ground, hissing, opening its mouth and then dispersing into a swarm of the winged creatures. Then came the subtle hints: more cats, a wall of paintings featuring literal chicks, lots of rainbows (nodding to Swift's more public status as an LBGTQ+ ally), cinematic flicks at works including the *Umbrellas of Cherbourg*, *Mary Poppins*, *Singin' in the Rain*, and *Moulin Rouge!*, her new kitten, and a heart-shaped kaleidoscope (a reference to lyrics from her older song "Welcome to New York"). Lyrically, "ME!" was a little more oblique. But fans recognized that Swift singing "I know that I went psycho on the phone" was a wink to a line from *Reputation*'s "Look What You Made Me Do" ("The old Taylor can't come to the phone right now. Why? Because she's dead!"), while the rest of "ME!" is primarily an affirmation of self and a show of newfound confidence.

17. "It's Nice to Have a Friend"

Light and plinking, "It's Nice to Have a Friend" echoed one of Swift's early songs—"Mary's Song (Oh My My My)" from her 2006 debut album, about childhood friends who grew up and got married. That was also the fate of the protagonists in this song, who go from "School bell rings, walk me home/Sidewalk chalk covered in snow" to "Church bells ring, carry me home/Rice on the ground looks like snow" in the space of a few verses. There was also a mention of the "pink sky, up on the roof"—pink being another of the colors that Swift had tied this album to visually.

18. "Daylight"

Swift finished things off on a bright note. "I once believed love would be burning red," she sings, "but it's golden, like daylight." That's a direct throwback to her album *Red*, of course. Other lyrics on "Daylight" were hinted at in her promotional materials, such as the "love letters" she shared on Spotify that included the lines "Luck of the draw only draws the unlucky... I wounded the good and I trusted the wicked/Clearing the air, I breathed in the smoke." In a live stream ahead of the album release, Swift said that the project as a whole "felt aesthetically to me very daytime, very sunlit fields," which became clear on "Daylight." □

FOLKLORE: A PANDEMIC EXPERIMENT

While the world was in lockdown, Swift hit the drawing board.

BY RAISA BRUNER

IF THERE'S ONE THING WE KNOW ABOUT Taylor Swift, it's that she works hard. In *Miss Americana*, a documentary about her, the intense pace of Swift's life—and the similarly intense pressures of the scrutiny she finds herself under—was laid bare for all to analyze.

But then the coronavirus pandemic swept in and, presumably, cleared her pop-star slate. Swift was left with her privacy as lockdowns shuttered us all into our homes. On social media, she was neither cryptically silent nor strategically active; she seemed, for the first time in a long time, like she was just living her life and drinking wine on her couch like many of the rest of us, big plans on hold.

But even in her downtime, curtains drawn on her celebrity, Swift was creating. The July 2020 release of *Folklore*, her 16-track (17 counting the bonus number) eighth album, came as a surprise even to devout followers: Only 11 months after *Lover*, it was the first time she'd put out a project on less than a two-year schedule. Swift didn't bother with the extensive release tease of her past albums; she announced her new work on a Thursday, rolled it out on a Friday, and then sat back to enjoy the weekend response.

A New Sound

In dropping *Folklore*, Swift was clear and direct about the intent of her work. She shared the names of all the major collaborators: pop producer and longtime musical partner Jack Antonoff, whom she called "musical family"; her "musical heroes," Aaron Dessner from the moody rock band the National and indie god Justin Vernon of Bon Iver; a mysterious collaborator named William Bowery.

That, and the gray-scale, woodsy images with which she teased the release, announced her new direction: alternative pop-folk. In her delicate, confessional singing and melodies there were hints of fellow artists such as Lana Del Rey, for whom she

During the 2021 Grammy Awards, Swift performed songs from sister albums Folklore *and* Evermore.

The music video for "Cardigan" showed Swift being transported to whimsical worlds through her piano.

expressed admiration, on "Cardigan," and Phoebe Bridgers on "Seven." There was the twinkling Postal Service–referencing intro on "The Last Great American Dynasty," the blissed-out orchestral wall of sound on "Epiphany," and the serving of elegiac Sufjan Stevens keys on "Invisible String."

Despite her start as a darling of the Nashville country scene, Swift has always been a musical chameleon. She evolved into rock-pop by *1989*, stretched herself into hip-hop on the spiky *Reputation*, and went full-throated pop on *Lover*. *Folklore* was what a lot of fans had been waiting for all along: a lengthy, emotionally wrought indie album. Its heart was folk storytelling; its production was every kind of thing fans have heard and loved on breakup albums in the last decade. Its vision was a gray-blue soundscape, an autumnal album dropped on us in the heat of summer, the first full project of this kind from Swift, inhabiting a truly melancholy space she's mainly hinted at in past ballads.

But those ballads have often been her most poignant work. *Folklore* met her at exactly the right point. While the rest of us were still adjusting to pandemic life, still engaged in important conversations about our country's racist history, the unhurried tempo of *Folklore* felt like a balm.

"And Some Things You Just Can't Speak About"

It would be fruitless to break down every Swift lyric; the songwriting can be poetically obtuse, and she's telling many stories, from many characters' points of view, with many aching regrets. Swift has historically been one of our most confessional pop stars, often mining her personal archives for material. *Folklore* was a little more, well, folkloric: "The lines between fantasy and reality blur, and the boundaries between truth and fiction become almost indiscernible," she said in an advance statement about the content. Still, she buried plenty of Easter eggs in her lyrics for fans to unpack.

The album's opening song, "The 1," was an ode to what could have been. The "who" of it all, of course, remained murky: "But we were something, don't you think so?/Roaring twenties, tossing pennies in the pool/And if my wishes came true/It would've been you."

As avid listeners well know, Swift loves riffs on the past. She also loves to weave in references to her old music, a trail of bread crumbs for fans to follow from era to era. "To kiss in cars and downtown bars was all we needed," she sang on "Cardigan," and it sounded a lot like an echo of her lyrics on *Lover*'s "Cornelia Street" ("We were in the backseat, drunk on something stronger than the drinks in the bar"). And when she sings "You drew stars around my scars" on the same song, close followers might flash back to the "guitar string scars" of "Lover."

Every song on *Folklore* had those kinds of winks, reinforcing the universe that Swift has crafted and expanded. "Mad Woman," for instance, was the story of a "misfit widow getting gleeful revenge," according to the singer's note on social media. But lines such as "And women like hunting witches too" hearkened back to the *Reputation* era ("They're burning all the witches even if you aren't one," she sang on "I Did Something Bad").

Some numbers were more mysterious than

others. "Exile," which featured Bon Iver, reeked with the exquisite pain of parting. "Hoax," a quiet piano ballad, detailed a relationship flawed but lasting. ("No other sadness in the world would do" is a devastatingly universal reminder of that bittersweet sensation.)

"The Last Great American Dynasty," in contrast, was specific and historical: the story of socialite Rebekah Harkness, the prior inhabitant of Swift's expansive Rhode Island estate. On "Epiphany," Swift dove into the experience of another historical character: her grandfather, Dean, when he landed on the beaches of Guadalcanal in 1942. "And some things," she sang after describing a harrowing moment of war, "you just can't speak about."

OK, What About "Betty"?

In her liner notes, the star wrote that the album contained a collection of three songs that she refered to as the Teenage Love Triangle. "These three songs explore a love triangle from all three people's perspectives at different times in their lives," she noted. Listeners, reading between plotlines of betrayal, heartache, and teen angst, concluded that the tracks were "Betty," "Cardigan," and "August."

"Betty," in which Swift returned most directly to her country roots, generated some of the earliest attention. That was at least in part because of one thread that could be read as vaguely autobiographical—which some fans were keen to do. The characters in the song, Betty, James, and Inez, happened to have the same names as Blake Lively and Ryan Reynolds' three children. Given that Lively and Reynolds (who've since had a fourth child) were part of Swift's friend circle, her fans found a connection to their hero's IRL world.

The Quarantine Album

During quarantine, with so few events to attend, live music mostly canceled, and many artists postponing their work, album releases found new resonance—whether they came from Taylor Swift or not.

But Swift, being Swift, was always destined to conjure up a powerful reaction. Throughout 2020, Swift's public dispute with music manager Scooter Braun over her music catalog made headlines and raised questions about the ownership artists have over the music they create. Prior to that, she often drew tabloid scrutiny for everything from her romantic life and fashion choices to her political activity (or lack of it) to her celebrity friendships, and her multiple and long-running feuds.

Her response often has been to write it all out: to address past relationships, excavate heartbreak and frustration, and insist on resilience. That *Folklore* was foggy, that it relied more on smart songwriting and less on speculation about her personal life and complicated visual cues, suggested it was bound for a long shelf life.

Quarantine had us all dragging up old memories and wondering what was still real. *Folklore* wasn't the album that would drive worries away and replace them with sparkle. It was the work of an artist who was extending her ambitions to look back and get a little lost in the memory haze, digging out an old favorite cardigan for comfort. ◻

FINDING MEANING IN *EVERMORE*

The sister album to *Folklore* was a cozy, poetic throwback to simpler times and high school crushes gone awry.

BY RAISA BRUNER

TAYLOR SWIFT DIDN'T HAVE TO RELEASE A whole extra album in December 2020. Just months earlier, she'd already surprise-dropped *Folklore*, an album that topped many critics' year-end lists (including TIME's). But after a lifetime in the spotlight, Swift seemed ready to upend all expectations, whether in the business of her music or the art itself. And if, as she explained in a preemptive Instagram post, she had more to say after finishing *Folklore*—well, no one was raising their hand to complain.

Evermore both expanded on the themes of *Folklore* and served as a companion album: It was cozy and retrospective, dreamy and poetic without being obtuse. It was still pop, but it was filtered through the light leaks of a cabin in the woods and wrapped up in the homespun imagery Swift put out alongside it. (Never underestimate the power of a carefully staged album promo shot. To wit: the pop superstar in a plaid flannel coat, her hair braided, crunching through a barren winter field.)

For *Evermore*, Swift brought back the same team she had on *Folklore*: the National's Aaron Dessner, longtime producer Jack Antonoff, and Justin Vernon of Bon Iver, as well as William Bowery, the pseudonym of her then boyfriend Joe Alwyn. She also fit in a song featuring the National and a track with HAIM, the sisters who the next year competed against (but lost to) Swift for the 63rd Grammys' album of the year prize. "To put it plainly, we just couldn't stop writing songs," Swift wrote on Instagram in advance of the release. "To try and put it more poetically, it feels like we were standing on the edge of the folklorian woods and had a choice: to turn and go back or to travel further into the forest of this music. We chose to wander deeper in."

What Was New on *Evermore*?

While *Folklore* was full of musical surprises for listeners unprepared for this new Swiftian era, *Evermore*

Swift released her second quarantine album, Evermore, *less than six months after* Folklore.

came across as more of an album of meditations. It featured Swift finessing clever turns of phrase, finding pleasure in playing around with the cadences of her lines, the plucks of her guitar, and the stories—both fictional and personal—that she can weave. "Champagne Problems," for instance, breathlessly recounted the story of an ill-fated proposal: "Sometimes you just don't know the answer 'til someone's on their knees and asks you/'She would've made such a lovely bride, what a shame she's f-cked in the head,' they said/But you'll find the real thing instead, she'll patch up your tapestry that I shred."

Taken as a whole, the free-flowing collection that was *Evermore* sounded like Swift made the album for herself and didn't stop to second-guess anything. To use her own back-to-nature metaphor, after so many years deep in the woods of superstar perfectionism, *Evermore* was a different kind of forest entirely—one to get lost in.

What Connected *Evermore* Back to *Folklore*?

At the time of *Evermore's* release, Swift described the recording as a "sister album," and that was very much the case. *Folklore* had come across as a muted, autumnal palette of sounds, moving Swift from the hyper-produced pop of *Reputation* and *Lover* to a low-key alternative genre with space to breathe. *Evermore* came off as *Folklore's* winter companion, full of songs rendered in pastel shades of lingering sadness and regret. At 15 tracks (plus two bonus numbers on the deluxe version), *Evermore* was about the same length as its predecessor, just right for another long solo walk in the woods.

But there were some notable differences. First, where *Folklore* carried forward the signature sound of producer Antonoff with subtle '80s touches and synth-pop highs on many songs, on *Evermore,* he was only credited as a producer on one song ("Ivy," which hearkened back to *Folklore's* "Invisible String" with its bluegrass guitar plucks). Second, Dessner's band the National made a full appearance on "Coney Island," including vocals from lead singer Matt Berninger. And finally, in an album highlight, Swift picked up the pace to have fun with HAIM on "No Body, No Crime," her version of a murder ballad à la the Chicks' "Goodbye Earl," replete with harmonica licks.

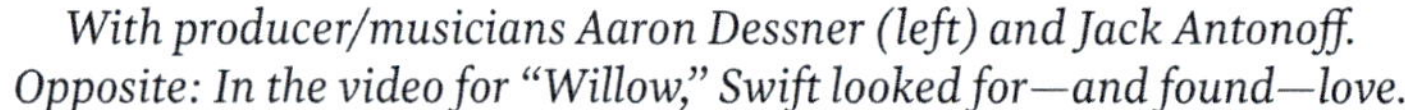

With producer/musicians Aaron Dessner (left) and Jack Antonoff.
Opposite: In the video for "Willow," Swift looked for—and found—love.

Who Are Marjorie and Dorothea?

Two of Swift's new songs were named after women. One was highly personal, and the other was a fictional projection. The emotional ballad "Marjorie" was named for her maternal grandmother, Marjorie Finlay, an opera singer who passed away in 2003. Tender and full of remembrances of tiny missed moments, "Marjorie" resonated with many who had lost a loved one recently.

"Dorothea," meanwhile, sounded more upbeat—albeit wistful about what could have been. In the song, Swift dreamed about a hometown girl who left for a shinier life in Hollywood, singing from the perspective of the person left longing for her from afar. "It's never too late to come back to my side," she sang. "If you're ever tired of being known for who you know, you know you'll always know me." At the time, she shared on social media that it was a story from her imagination, although I like to read it as Swift singing to herself.

Like the love triangle she sketched in "Betty," "Cardigan," and "August" on *Folklore*, "Dorothea" hinted at a whole universe of high school crushes gone awry. It was fertile territory for Swift, whose persona and lyricism have always been so closely tied to the imagery of young Americana. And it echoed further on its partner track, "'Tis the Damn Season," a song that hit home for millennials longing to disconnect from regular life and rekindle flames of the past.

What Other Lyrics or References Were Important?

As always, Swift gave listeners a thicket of references scattered throughout. Her universe was then and remains now an unfailingly rich and complex one to get lost in. Words, scenes, and themes fans had seen throughout her career popped up again: scars, the color gold, champagne, imagery of ships, the downside of beauty, the aftermath of parties, places in New York, the unresolved parts of relationships, insecurity, nostalgia.

And the album closed out on a contemplative note that seemed to come full circle back to *Folklore*, which had included "Exile," a collaboration with Bon Iver. In "Exile," Swift and Bon Iver had explored a soured relationship. In the song "Evermore," Swift seemed to return to the exes, who had moved on. "Been down since July," she sang. "Hey December, guess I'm feeling unmoored. Can't remember what I used to fight for. . . . This pain wouldn't be for evermore," she finished off, hinting at future hope. Winter, after all, couldn't last forever. ☐

MIDNIGHTS AND SLEEPLESS NIGHTS

Late at night, the singer says, she dwells on personal terrors and insecurities. So she poured her angst into 13 tracks, recruited her celeb pals for some videos, and produced her biggest release yet.

BY SHANNON CARLIN

WHEN TAYLOR SWIFT ANNOUNCED THE release of her tenth studio album, *Midnights,* in August 2022, she called it the story of "13 sleepless nights scattered throughout my life." The songs, written during those wee hours when Swift should have been asleep, resulted in a collection that the star has called her most self-reflective yet—an exploration of her insecurities, guilt, shame, and revenge fantasies. In other words, the kinds of things that would keep anyone up way past their bedtime. Unlike most of us, though, Swift turned those scary hours into something beautifully chaotic.

As always, the rollout of *Midnights* was highly choreographed. There were months of Easter eggs and a teaser that ran during the third quarter of *Thursday Night Football* on Prime Video. Shortly before *Midnights* dropped on October 21—at midnight, naturally—Swift revealed that the album would be a visual one. She said she had reteamed with cinematographer Rina Yang (who had worked on Swift's short-film adaptation of "All Too Well") to make a "music movie" for each track (many starring celebrity friends, including Laura Dern, the sisters of HAIM, comedian Mike Birbiglia, and burlesque dancer Dita Von Teese). Three hours later, Swift shared that there would be seven bonus tracks. At 8 a.m., the "Anti-Hero" video premiered; it was followed by a #TSAntiHeroChallenge on YouTube Shorts. And let's not forget Swift's turn on TikTok, where she played something called "Midnights Mayhem with Me." The object of the game: to reveal the titles of *Midnights'* 13 tracks by spinning a bingo cage. Each ball corresponded to a track from the album.

Need help sorting it all out? Here's our take on *Midnights.*

Taylor Swift at Her Most Vulnerable

While *Folklore* and *Evermore*, Swift's back-to-back pandemic albums, told the stories of other people—

Swift before the release of her 10th studio album, Midnights.

Betty, James, Inez, Rebekah Harkness—*Midnights* marked the star's return to first-person lyrics, and she was more candid than ever. Consider, for example, track 5, "You're On Your Own, Kid," in which she explored the pressures she feels under the spotlight. "From sprinkler splashes to fireplace ashes/I gave my blood, sweat, and tears for this/I hosted parties and starved my body/Like I'd be saved by a perfect kiss."

The *Midnights* Collaborators

The record was produced by Swift's longtime collaborator Jack Antonoff, who coauthored 11 out of the record's 13 songs, and whom, Swift wrote, she considered a "co-pilot on this adventure."

The most notable cameo on *Midnights* was alt-pop fave Lana Del Rey, who appeared on the love song "Snow on the Beach," which she cowrote with Swift and Antonoff. Actor and former Lolawolf singer Zoë Kravitz—who has been recording a solo album with Antonoff—popped up as a cowriter and background vocalist on the album's opener, "Lavender Haze." *Teen Wolf* actor Dylan O'Brien played drums on that track, and his clapping skills could be heard on another, "Question...?" which also featured Antonoff; Antonoff's sister, Rachel; and Swift's brother, Austin, according to *Entertainment Weekly*. Swift's ex Joe Alwyn, who penned songs for *Folklore* and *Evermore* under the pseudonym William Bowery, cowrote *Midnights'* piano ditty "Sweet Nothing."

A Chaotic 3 a.m. Surprise

As the clock struck 3 on the East Coast on October 21, 2022, Swift released seven bonus songs that didn't make the cut for *Midnights* but that she said were just too good to lock away in the vault. *Midnights (3am Edition)* included three tracks cowritten by her *Folklore* and *Evermore* collaborator Aaron Dessner— "The Great War," "High Infidelity," and "Would've, Could've, Should've"—plus outtakes of her recording sessions with Antonoff, including "Bigger Than the Whole Sky," the synth-heavy "Paris," the slinky "Glitch," and electropop closer "Dear Reader."

The Swiftiest of All

Some of Swift's most repeatable (and meme-able) lines surfaced in "Anti-Hero," about the star's insecurities and anxieties. "It's me, hi, I'm the problem, it's me," she sang in the chorus, later adding, "I'll stare directly at the sun, but never in the mirror." The song's best lyric might have been the (seemingly) Liz Lemon–inspired "Sometimes I feel like everybody is a sexy baby/ And I'm a monster on the hill." But let's not overlook "Vigilante Sh-t," where she sings, "I don't dress for women/I don't dress for men/Lately I've been dressing for revenge."

The Joe Alwyn Effect

While Swift and Alwyn broke up in the spring of 2023, they were a couple throughout the making of *Midnights*—six years altogether, according to media reports—and many consider him to be the muse behind the new album's unabashed and slightly

"Anti-Hero" referenced a number of Swift's personal fears (above). Opposite: At a Midnights *listening party.*

unhinged love songs. The *Mad Men*–inspired "Lavender Haze" was about being in the honeymoon phase and trying to protect the relationship—"the real stuff," as Swift wrote on Instagram—from tabloid rumors and other intrusions.

On "Sweet Nothing," Swift characterized Alwyn as one of the few people who did not want something from her. "Everyone's up to something/I found myself running home to your sweet nothings," she sang. "Outside they push and shovin'/ You're in the kitchen humming/All that you ever wanted from me was sweet nothing." In "Mastermind," she talked about setting her sights on Alwyn first. "I laid the groundwork and then, saw a wide smirk/On your face, you knew the entire time," she sings. "You knew that I'm a mastermind/And now you're mine/Yeah, all you did was smile."

Taylor Is Gonna Taylor

Swift is nothing if not self-referential, and never more so than on *Midnights*. A few not-so-veiled shout-outs to her previous albums included "You're on Your Own, Kid," where she talked about a high school crush who sounded a lot like the boy she pined for on the *Fearless* tracks "You Belong with Me" and "Hey Stephen." Revenge-themed "Karma" definitely had a *Reputation* vibe, and the wine-soaked "Maroon" felt like the coda to *Red*, right down to the color choice. Swift even sampled herself, specifically *1989's* "Out of the Woods" on "Question...?" Was it a clue that *1989 (Taylor's Version)* was coming soon?

Fans also pointed out that the visual component of *Midnights* was a walk down memory lane, with Swift wearing costumes that echoed looks she wore in earlier videos, including "Endgame," "Ready for It," and "Blank Space." In the video for "Anti-Hero," which Swift wrote and directed, *It's Always Sunny in Philadelphia* actress Mary Elizabeth Ellis made a cameo as Swift's greedy daughter-in-law, wearing a dress from the 2009–2010 Fearless Tour.

A fan on Twitter (now X) went so far as to characterize the rollout of *Midnights* as "the Taylor Swift Multiverse of Madness" for all the callbacks to her earlier work. Swift isn't the same person who made those albums, and *Midnights* proves how much she's grown as an artist.

Still, some old habits die hard. □

SINGING WITH THE STARS

Swift is not only one of the most powerful entertainers in the world—she has collaborated with a who's who of the music business.

Role Model

Madonna was promoting her album *Rebel Heart* when she invited Swift to join her at the 2015 iHeartRadio Music Awards. At the time, Swift had just crossed over from country to pop, and she seemed thrilled to be on stage with the Material Girl. Why wouldn't she be, said TIME, noting: "Madonna's ability to reinvent her sound and her image has provided precedent for any number of pop stars, including one who recently switched genres entirely."

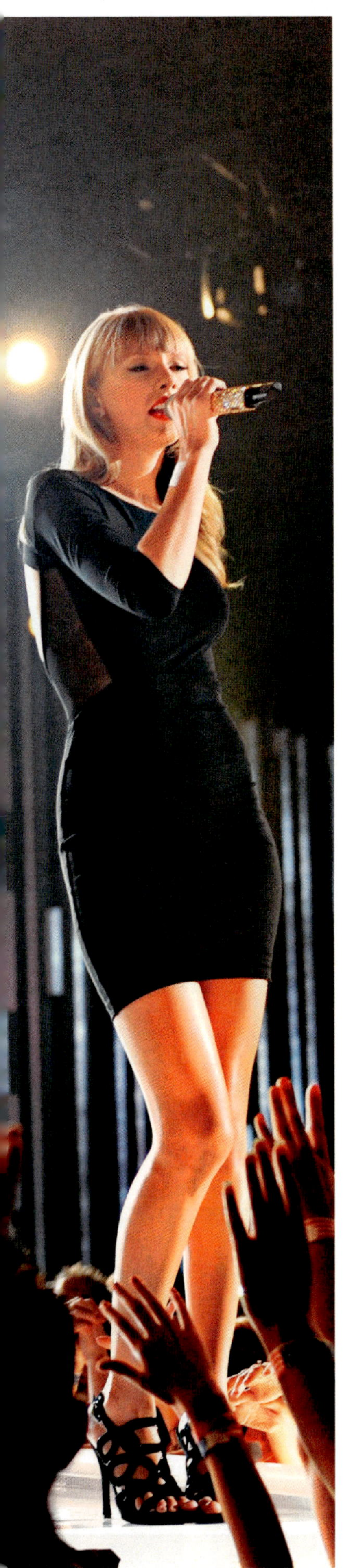

↑

I Write the Songs

During her 2011–2012 Speak Now World Tour, Swift started penning the lyrics from other artists' songs on her left arm before each show. When word reached Ed Sheeran that his track "Lego House" had made the limb, he got in touch with Swift through her manager. The two became fast friends, recording and performing together numerous times. In 2014, Sheeran joined Swift on stage to kick off the European leg of her Red Tour at London's 02 Arena.

←

Local Heroes

In 2006, Swift entered the music scene with her debut single, "Tim McGraw," a nod to the country music star, her idol. Seven years later, she recorded "Highway Don't Care" with McGraw himself. Swift, McGraw (in cowboy hat), and fellow country singer Keith Urban performed the number together on a 2013 CBS special, *Superstar Summer Night,* that McGraw hosted.

↑

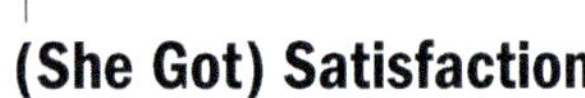

(She Got) Satisfaction

Rolling Stones front man Mick Jagger happened to be in Nashville in September 2015, right before Swift was set to perform at the Bridgestone Arena as part of the 1989 World Tour. Naturally, she had his number, and she texted to see if he'd join her on stage. Jagger's concern: What should he wear? A blue leather jacket, it turned out, which the rocker sported with his usual flair as he and Swift sang a version of "(I Can't Get No) Satisfaction."

→

Making Up

It went down like this. When the 2015 MTV Video Music Award nominations were announced in July of that year, Swift's "Bad Blood" got a nod for video of the year. Rapper Nicki Minaj's "Anaconda" did not. Minaj tweeted her disappointment, which Swift took as a jab. Minaj said that wasn't the case, but a feud was born. Yet just a month later, the two seemed to bury the hatchet when Swift joined Minaj for the VMAs' opening number, Minaj's "The Night Is Still Young."

↑
Old School
Mick Jagger was not the only rocker to join Swift in Nashville during her 2015 hometown concerts. One night, the pop star brought out Aerosmith's Steven Tyler, whom she met when she was making her debut in the pop world and Tyler was exploring the country music scene. The two sang Aerosmith's "I Don't Want to Miss a Thing."

←
My Brilliant Friend
Swift and Selena Gomez—who became besties back in 2008 when they were both dating Jonas brothers—treated fans in Los Angeles to a duet during Swift's stint at the Staples Center (now the Crypto.com Arena) in 2015. They belted out Gomez's "Good for You," which went on to be nominated for song of the summer at that year's VMAs.

Glitter Bomb

Swift opened the 2019 Billboard Music Awards with her single "ME!" featuring Brendon Urie of Panic! at the Disco. Urie wowed fans by descending from the sky with an umbrella, à la Mary Poppins, to join Swift on stage at the MGM Garden Arena in Las Vegas.

Good Rap

The surprise guest for Swift's sold-out MetLife Stadium concert in East Rutherford, New Jersey, in May 2023: Bronx rapper Ice Spice. The duo performed their song "Karma," from Swift's *Midnights (The Til Dawn Edition),* live for the first time, thrilling the crowd of more than 70,000.

3

A WOMAN IN FULL

In the male-dominated music industry, Swift doesn't hesitate to stand up for herself—and her music. That's made Swifties love her even more.

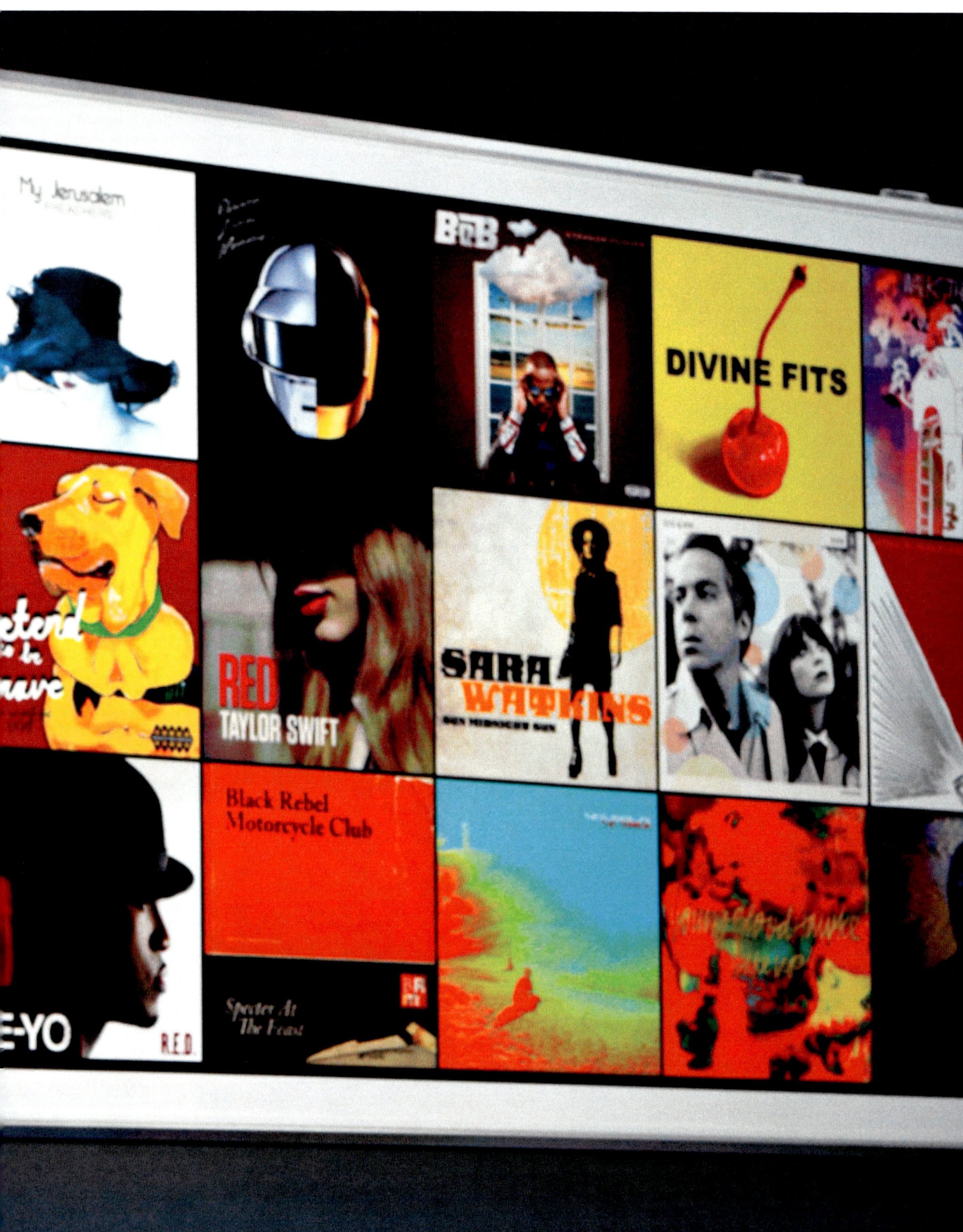
My Jerusalem
B.o.B
DIVINE FITS
RED
TAYLOR SWIFT
SARA
WATKINS
Black Rebel
Motorcycle Club
Specter At
The Feast
E-YO
R.E.D.

Apple senior executive Eddy Cue showed a new iTunes interface at a company conference in 2013.

WHEN TAYLOR TOOK ON APPLE

In a 2015 blog post read 'round the music world, the 25-year old star demanded action—and she got it.

BY JACK DICKEY

LOTS OF 25-YEAR-OLDS WRITE BLOG POSTS. One would have to imagine the incidence is even more pronounced among 25-year-old creative types who have not yet been ground into submission by the machinery that makes the American culture industry levitate and whirr. It's exceedingly rare that one of those blog posts accomplishes anything, except perhaps a phone call from a parent who wants the author to give law school another shot.

It's exceedingly surprising, when the proper nouns are stripped away, that a 25-year-old's blog post—on a *Sunday*—could compel Apple, the world's most valuable company (by market cap), to change course *later that day* on an already-announced major consumer product, one that had presumably occasioned dozens of previous meetings and strategy sessions.

But this is a story about Taylor Swift, who was, in 2015, even before the aforementioned Sunday missive, already the biggest thing going in popular music. With a series of strategic keystrokes, she became something even bigger: a commercial power with the resolve to fight the continued devaluation of recorded music and get things done.

The brouhaha began when Apple announced on June 8, 2015, that it would launch its own streaming music service, one with the presumable aim of eating into the 60 million users Spotify said it had at the time. Apple Music even announced its price as $9.99 per month, the same figure Spotify was charging for its premium subscription.

Spotify, too, had been the subject of intense criticism from artists and labels about its comparatively meager royalty payments. After Swift yanked her music off the platform in November 2014, her label told TIME that over the prior 12 months it had been paid less than $500,000 for domestic streaming of Swift's music, despite her status as one of the service's most popular artists. (Spotify claimed Swift's payout for global streaming, including the U.S., had been $2 million over that period.)

THE BROUHAHA BEGAN WHEN APPLE ANNOUNCED THAT IT WOULD LAUNCH ITS OWN STREAMING MUSIC SERVICE.

Back then, what Swift and others reasoned was that any music service offering a free ad-supported option, as Spotify was doing, could not offer artists a worthwhile fee. (Country singer Rosanne Cash said in June 2014 that her songs were streamed 600,000 times over an 18-month period—and that she had received $114.)

At its launch, Apple Music took a different tack. It enticed subscribers with three free trial months of service—months during which it would not compensate labels for music streamed. Hence Swift's ire and Tumblr post, "To Apple, Love Taylor." By nightfall, Eddy Cue, an Apple senior executive, had tweeted that the company would reverse course and pay artists out of its own pocket. Cue told *Billboard* at the time, "When I woke up this morning and saw what Taylor had written, it really solidified that we needed to make a change." He said he called Swift directly to tell her the news.

There's been a rich tradition in America of mass-media artists fighting the corporate interests in their workplaces, from the founding of Mary Pickford and Charlie Chaplin's United Artists in 1919 all the way to Matt Damon and Ben Affleck writing *Good Will Hunting* because they didn't think they would get cast in parts they wanted. But even in that context, Swift's evangelism stood out. One imagines that few artists could mobilize a fan base like hers—nursed as it has been on free, on-demand content—to pressure Apple. But there they were, having earned their tribute, in Swift's victory tweet early Monday: "I am elated and relieved. Thank you for your words of support today. They listened to us."

During her career, Swift has benefited from a cultural change; many millennials are more sympathetic to corporations than their predecessors might have been. Her listeners came of age, prevailingly, in the era of free or cheap music—not one in which a teen might have to shell out two to three weeks worth of allowance to buy a CD. In 2015, as today, some music fans look at labels as champions for beleaguered artists rather than conglomerates hell-bent on ripping fans off. And Swift's fans looked to Apple as an artist-supporting American triumph capable of doing better.

Funny (or not so funny) enough, Apple Music and several music labels were under investigation by two state attorneys general for anticompetitive practices—were they colluding to crush Spotify? (The investigations quietly petered out.) Apple had been in similar straits two years earlier when a judge ruled that it had colluded with book publishers against Amazon to fix ebook prices; the company agreed to a $450 million settlement. Apple was fine, and Taylor Swift was fine. The group imperiled, as it has been since the music industry began to shrink, was (as Swift put it) "the new artist or band ... the young songwriter ... the producer who works tirelessly," not to mention the rank-and-file at the record label.

Swift cast her lot with them, and she cajoled Apple into taking baby steps toward the same, which is a feat. Swift appeared to not only be the sole artist who could make a mass audience pay full freight for its listening choices; she was the only one who could make it feel altruistic while doing so. That's big. I, for one, can't wait until Swift the blogger finds out what's happened to the journalism business. □

An Unlikely Duo

Once Swift and Apple Music made up in 2015, they joined forces to collaborate on a documentary, a commercial, and more. BY AVA ERICKSON

Not only did publicity around the tiff between Apple Music and Swift help create consumer awareness for the platform, it also nudged other artists into signing on and got the ball rolling with subscribers. Six months into Apple Music's life, the service had about 10 million users. (Today, the number is an estimated 88 million.) Once Swift and Apple Music made up, they collaborated on a number of projects, including these.

The 1989 World Tour Live

Directed by Jonas Åkerlund, this two-hour-plus documentary features footage from Swift's November 2015 concert in Sydney, Australia, as well as behind-the-scenes clips and interviews from other shows on the tour. Apple Music has since released *Wiz Khalifa: Behind the Cam*, a 2019 documentary about the hip-hop star's personal life; *Harry Styles: Behind the Album*, a 2017 film about Styles' process creating his debut album; and *Kygo: Stole the Show,* chronicling the Norwegian DJ and record producer's rise to fame in 2016.

Apple Music + Taylor Swift Ad

In a 2016 television commercial, Swift ran on a treadmill while listening to a workout playlist featuring Drake and Future's song "Jumpman" on Apple Music. The clip went viral for its comedic moment when Swift lost focus—and her footing. According to iTunes, sales of "Jumpman" jumped fourfold in the week following the ad's debut, and the #Gymflow playlist went to No. 5 Apple Music playlist of the week.

Swift's Mood Playlists

In 2022, Swift released three exclusive playlists through Apple Music with a voice memo giving some background explaining her choices. Quill Pen Songs, featuring "Anti-Hero" and "Ivy," were marked by "period-piece detail," she said; Fountain Pen Songs, with "Champagne Problems" and "Cruel Summer," had narrative lyrics; and Glitter Gel Pen Songs, with "22" and "You Belong with Me," featured classic pop tunes. Other artists who have created special playlists for Apple Music include Ed Sheeran and Billie Eilish.

'I Was Angry'

In 2017, the pop star talked with TIME about her sexual assault testimony earlier that year.

BY ELIANA DOCKTERMAN

In August 2017, Taylor Swift testified in an open courtroom about being sexually assaulted. The appearance came two months before film mogul Harvey Weinstein would be accused of having sexually harassed women for decades, and also before #MeToo swept the nation. Swift's words inspired other women to speak out, and in December 2017, she was recognized by TIME as one of the Silence Breakers who helped spur a powerful movement.

The singer-songwriter's story dated to 2013, when she took a photo with a Colorado radio DJ after an interview. During that photo, Swift said, DJ David Mueller reached under her skirt and grabbed her rear end. Swift privately reported the incident to the station where Mueller worked, and he was fired. Mueller then sued Swift for defamation. She countersued for a symbolic $1—and won.

Swift refused to be bullied on the stand. Her straightforward testimony was lauded by many for its fierceness. When asked why the pictures taken during the assault didn't show the front of her skirt wrinkled as evidence of any wrongdoing, she said simply, "Because my ass is located at the back of my body." When asked if she felt guilty about Mueller losing his job, she said, "I'm not going to let you or your client make me feel in any way that this is my fault. Here we are years later, and I'm being blamed for the unfortunate events of his life that are the product of his decisions—not mine."

Swift's clear-eyed testimony marked one of several major milestones in the conversation around sexual harassment. She responded in writing to questions from TIME about her experience. Her answers were lightly edited.

Why was it important for you to come forward about what happened to you?
In 2013, I met a DJ from a prominent country radio station in one of my preshow meet and greets. When we were posing for the photo, he stuck his hand up my dress and grabbed onto my ass cheek. I squirmed and lurched sideways to get away from him, but he wouldn't let go. At the time, I was headlining a major arena tour, and there were a number of people in the room that saw this. I figured that if he was brazen enough to assault me under those risky circumstances, imagine what he might do to a vulnerable young artist if given the chance. It was important to report the incident to his radio station because I felt like they needed to know. The radio station conducted its own investigation and fired him. Two years later, he sued me.

How did you feel when you testified?
When I testified, I had already been in court all week and had to watch this man's attorney bully, badger, and harass my team, including my mother, over inane details and

A court sketch of Swift during the 2017 trial. Opposite: Denver store Craftsy showed support.

ridiculous minutiae, accusing them and me of lying. My mom was so upset after her cross-examination that she was physically too ill to come to court the day I was on the stand. I was angry. In that moment, I decided to just answer the questions the way it happened. This man hadn't considered any formalities when he assaulted me, and his lawyer didn't hold back on my mom—why should I be polite? I'm told it was the most amount of times the word "ass" has ever been said in Colorado Federal Court.

How have people responded to your story?

People have been largely very supportive since the trial began, but before that, I spent two years reading headlines referring to it as "the Taylor Swift Butt-Grab Case," with internet trolls making a joke [of it]. The details were all skewed. Most people thought I was suing him. There was an audible gasp in the courtroom when I was named as the defendant. Once it hit the news that I was in Denver dealing with this, there was an outpouring of support on social media, and I have never appreciated it more. I spoke to Kesha on the phone, and it really helped to talk to someone who had been through the demoralizing court process.

After this experience, what advice would you give to your fans?

I would tell people who find themselves in this situation that there is a great deal of blame placed on the victims. You could be blamed for the fact that it happened, for reporting it, and for how you reacted. You might be made to feel like you're overreacting. My advice is that you not blame yourself and do not accept the blame others will try to place on you. You should not be blamed for waiting 15 minutes or 15 days or 15 years to report sexual assault or harassment, or for the outcome of what happens to a person after he or she makes the choice to sexually harass or assault you.

Is this a watershed moment for the way we think about sexual assault and harassment in culture?

I think that this moment is important for awareness, for how parents are talking to their children and how victims are processing their trauma, whether it be new or old. The brave women and men who have come forward have all moved the needle in terms of letting people know that this abuse of power shouldn't be tolerated. Going to court to confront this type of behavior is a lonely and draining experience, even when you win, even when you have the financial ability to defend yourself. Even though awareness is higher than ever about workplace sexual harassment, there are still many who feel victimized, afraid, and silenced by their abusers and circumstances. When the jury found in my favor, the man who sexually assaulted me was court-ordered to give me a symbolic $1. To this day he has not paid me that dollar, and I think that act of defiance is symbolic in itself. ◻

The documentary captured Swift preparing for her performance at the 2019 VMAs.

TAYLOR'S REAL LIFE

The 2020 documentary *Miss Americana: Taylor Swift* was an intriguing but incomplete sketch of an icon in transition.

BY RAISA BRUNER

IN JANUARY 2020, WHEN THE DOCUMENTARY *Miss Americana: Taylor Swift* was released, the star hadn't been to a Grammys ceremony since 2016, when—at 26—she had taken home three trophies, including her second album of the year win for the multiplatinum *1989*. Still, the awards show loomed large in *Miss Americana*, which debuted on Netflix and traced Swift's life in the years that followed her big AOTY night. One of the documentary's most revealing vignettes took place when Swift learned that *1989*'s divisive follow-up, *Reputation*, had failed to earn a single nomination in any of the Grammys' major categories. "This is fine," she declared into her phone, studiously calm but also obviously, palpably hurt. "I just need to make a better record."

There was a lot going on in that reaction. Like most superstars, Swift doesn't need the Grammys nearly as much as they need her, so she could have shrugged off her snub. After all, it's not like the

Swift in 2018 at the moment she learned Reputation *had not been nominated for any major Grammy Award.*

Recording Academy is known for its consistent good taste. (The year before *Reputation* was passed over for album of the year consideration, Bruno Mars' bland *24K Magic* beat out far superior works by Kendrick Lamar, Childish Gambino, Jay-Z, and Lorde.) Or she could have gone to the opposite extreme, raging against her exclusion from an honor to which she, as one of the most successful pop musicians in the world, might feel entitled. Instead—ever beholden to the opinions of others—she accepted the outcome as valid criticism. At that point in her career, Swift was still striving for the approval she sought as a teenage country prodigy. "My entire moral code as a kid and now is a need to be thought of as good," she admitted early in the film. The cursory, unfocused, overly stage-managed but occasionally fascinating *Miss Americana* was, more than anything else, the story of how a pop star stopped worrying and learned to speak her mind.

Directed by Lana Wilson—a filmmaker best known for such serious fare as the 2013 documentary *After Tiller*, about third-trimester abortion providers—*Miss Americana* was a bit of a hodgepodge. Interviews that read as intimate but didn't always provide new insight into Swift's experience sat alongside performance footage and short clips of casual hangouts with friends and family. A scene in which Swift, her beloved mom, Andrea, and Andrea's giant dog endured turbulence at mealtime on an airplane was pure physical comedy. In the studio, we watched her bang out hits from 2019's album *Lover* with a pro's finesse and the glee of a musician who savors the songwriting process. The result was less a cohesive story than a patchwork of mismatched topics that Wilson attempted to stitch together with threads of an extremely public, ever-intensifying Taylor Swift narrative.

Those who don't do social media or follow celebrity news might not have realized that the singer had a rocky few years immediately after *1989*'s triumph—at least by the standards of an industry juggernaut who'd never stopped selling out stadiums or releasing hit records. April 2016 brought Kanye West's "Famous," on which the rapper mused, "I feel like me and Taylor might still have sex/Why? I made that bitch famous" (a reference to the episode, seven years earlier, when he humiliated both Swift and himself by interrupting her MTV VMAs acceptance speech to protest that "Beyoncé had one of the best videos of all time"). The lyric reignited West and Swift's long-running feud and was amplified by extra drama on social media. Meanwhile, during the all-important 2016 presidential election, Swift declined to endorse either Hillary Clinton or Donald Trump in a move that some perceived as self-serving.

Wilson rehashed the well-documented Kanye spat at a length that felt excessive in an 85-minute film, digging up snarky blog posts, nasty hashtags, and invasive if also somewhat inane red-carpet interviews. Swift framed the VMAs incident, which happened when she was 19, as a formative trauma. Clearly, Wilson's aim was to contrast the singer's nearly lifelong identity as America's sweetheart—a rise recounted in montages that followed her tween days as a Nashville newbie to teen country phenom to 20-something pop eminence—with a period in which she increasingly found herself in the cultural crosshairs, tarred as a liar, a selfish careerist, a privileged white woman eager to paint herself as a victim.

MISS AMERICANA CULMINATED IN A THRILLING SCENE WHERE SWIFT FACED DOWN A CABAL OF MIDDLE-AGED WHITE GUYS.

As Swift—who, to her credit, came across as genuine and self-critical offstage—pointed out, it was impossible for her to do anything without inviting the accusation that everything she does is calculated. *Reputation*, an attempt to hit back at the haters and regain control of the narrative by authoring her own self-deprecating villain edit, was a case in point. Especially with that history in mind, Wilson's effort to recount how her subject became the brave, outspoken Taylor was undermined by the fact that she was allowed to sidestep some obvious questions: What was going on with Swift and her then-boyfriend, Joe Alwyn? What factored into her decision to appear in the critically maligned *Cats* film? How did she parse the complicated racial and gender politics underlying her feud with Kanye? Why did it take her so long to denounce the white supremacists who notoriously made her their patron saint, dubbing Swift an "Aryan goddess"?

The film did address why Swift stayed mum on such mainstream political debates as the 2016 election, during which everyone from the lowliest reality TV stars to Beyoncé and Oprah entered the fray. Convinced that no one wanted to hear the opinion of a young entertainer and cowed by the example of the Chicks, who alienated conservative country listeners by vocally opposing the Iraq War, she followed her team's advice to keep her views to herself. As she told it, facing down a DJ who groped her in a high-profile sexual assault case (which she won) was what convinced her to speak out in defense of her beliefs. Wilson captured her ranting, in her own enviably eloquent way, in support of the Violence Against Women Act.

Miss Americana culminated in a thrilling scene where Swift faced down a cabal of middle-aged white guys, including her dad, who didn't want her to come out against right-wing Tennessee Senate candidate Marsha Blackburn in the 2018 midterms (Blackburn won a narrow victory, despite Swift's efforts). She did it anyway, those who disagreed be damned, because, Swift insisted, the election was a matter of "right and wrong." It seemed the old good-girl Taylor was finally dead.

That wasn't the only moment in the film that revealed more about Swift's personality and struggles than the reflections on Kanye. In another moving scene, she spoke for the first time about an eating disorder that for many years had her scrutinizing the way her body looked in every poorly composed paparazzi photo and starving to fit into a size 00. Were these "calculated" disclosures? The long list of glaring omissions—as well as Wilson's reticence to investigate how Swift's political awakening affected her daily life offstage and outside the boardroom—make it hard to argue otherwise. Yet they did come across as genuine. With a more elegant, purposeful structure or at least more time to explore her toughest choices, *Miss Americana* might have offered a satisfying portrait of the real Taylor. Instead, the film came off more like a sketch. After an album as bright and vivid as *Lover*, I can't imagine I was the only one hoping for more color. □

Fans waited for Swift at the Toronto International Film Festival in 2022.

MASTER OF HER MUSIC

In the wake of a fight with her old label, Swift is rereleasing her back catalog—and reaping the artistic and financial benefits.

BY RAISA BRUNER

IF YOU PAY CLOSE ATTENTION, YOU CAN hear it: There's a new lushness in the opening banjo twangs and an extra beat when she sings "Just say yes." But the difference between the 2008 version of Taylor Swift's "Love Story," which helped propel the singer to pop stardom, and the 2021 rerelease of that same song is subtle. Called "Taylor's Version" on streaming platforms, the updated mix was a part of *Fearless (Taylor's Version)*, which arrived in April 2021 as the first of the artist's rerecordings of her back catalog. Next came *Red (Taylor's Version)* in November of that year; then *Speak Now (Taylor's Version)* in July 2023; and in October 2023, *1989 (Taylor's Version)*, the project's fourth installment.

In the rerecordings so far, the lyrics and production haven't changed that much: It's Swift's business that's shifted. Now 33, she has recently cycled through a full indie-pop era—as shown by her Grammy-winning turn on *Folklore* and her subsequent album, *Evermore*—and embarked on the Eras Tour, which has been dominating the cultural conversation throughout 2023. Simultaneously, she has been amping up her battle with the music industry to manage the means, method of production, and distribution of her work.

Art makes us feel things, a craft at which Swift is a master. Art also makes money, and she is equally adept at that. Her goal now: to make sure her art stays within her control. It's a pipe dream for artists of any kind, but Swift has power that most don't, and her very personal fight to reshape the way wealth from creative work is distributed is a power-

ful potential model for wrestling compensation back from industry forces.

Swift signed to Big Machine Records in 2005 as a fresh-faced Nashville singer with a guitar and long blonde hair. The contract expired in 2018, but not before she rocketed to radio-play heights with hits like "I Knew You Were Trouble" and crossed into the pop stratosphere. Her agreement with Big Machine did not give Swift ownership of the masters—the original recordings—so when she switched labels to Universal Music Group's Republic Records, she made sure to secure ownership of her future masters. Changing labels, carving out more agency, updating contract terms—these steps are par for the course for a successful artist. People change, and so do the contracts that govern them.

Master Recording Profits

Swift's behind-the-scenes moves became front-page news when Big Machine Label Group was sold to private-equity group Ithaca Holdings, which at the time was owned by Scooter Braun, a music manager. Braun sold Swift's masters to Shamrock Holdings for a reported $300 million in 2020, and in 2021 sold Ithaca to a South Korean outfit. On a business level, Braun's move was smart: Swift's master

Manager Scooter Braun (left) and Big Machine founder Scott Borchetta.

recordings reap profits whenever the songs are streamed or bought. On the personal front, it was contentious. Swift claims Braun, who manages acts like Justin Bieber and rapper Quavo, has repeatedly bullied her, and she slammed the sale publicly and promised to rerecord those original six albums, this time with the masters under her own control. Anyone who hits play on an old version of Swift's early songs right now will still pay into the bank of Braun. Her hope, it seems, is to override those archival works with the new versions. "Artists should own their own work for so many reasons," she wrote in a February 2021 Instagram post, "but the most screamingly obvious one is that the artist is the only one who really knows that body of work." Her choice stirred up responses across the music world and forced the public to take a long look at the music industry's quiet corporate machinations.

Not the Usual Artist

Artists regularly chafe against their record label contracts; see Kanye West, who very publicly vented against his own contractual obligations in 2020 (before a series of escalating controversies moved the conversation further and further from his music). But rarely do they go through the hassle of rerecording and rereleasing old work. Swift, though, is not your usual artist. She had time—a whole year of it, while the pandemic put her touring schedule on pause. And she is meticulous about how her work is consumed and perceived, from the aesthetics of her album covers to the comments she makes on Tumblr fan blogs. Given her unique position, platforms like Spotify have everything to gain by supporting her new versions. Meanwhile, the fans who are the most active streamers of her old music have become well aware of her intentions and will abide by her wishes. Swift is in the rare position to want to upend the system and actually have the power to do so.

A Decade's Worth of Vocal Maturity

In addition to the subtle production updates that Swift has made to the rerecordings, listeners may also hear in her voice the maturity that an extra decade can provide. The star has also been sharing new tracks from her so-called vault, the first of which was "You All Over Me" with Maren Morris, a song that had been scrapped from the original *Fearless* but which Swift included on *Fearless (Taylor's Version)*. Similarly, *Speak Now (Taylor's Version)* added six vault songs and tweaked a lyric from 2010's "Better Than Revenge," which critics for years had complained could be read as slut-shaming.

What has been truly different about Swift's "new" work has been the intention behind it, and the developments that have brought her to the place to own it. Every musician is a business, a startup with limited equity to portion out to labels, publishers, and other stakeholders. As the business grows, the musician is left with a smaller and smaller piece of the pie. Greater equity was the central consideration of Swift's label change—along with greater certainty that all who contributed to making the art itself would benefit from their work.

"There was one condition that meant more to me than any other deal point," she wrote at the time: ensuring that profits from the future sale of Spotify shares would be returned to artists. That this financial nitty-gritty is what excited Swift most might seem at odds with her image as a singer-songwriter who performs on sets that look like a cottage in a fairy-tale forest. But that persona hides Swift's savvy. She's long understood that artists, even those with brands as powerful as hers, are vulnerable to exploitation. After building an empire writing deeply personal songs, should selling her story really come so cheap? □

Record-Breaking Rerecordings

How Swift's first three (Taylor's Version) albums compare to the originals. **BY AVA ERICKSON**

To say Taylor Swift's decision to rerecord her old albums was a good one is an understatement. As with ticket sales for the singer's concerts—her first tour, in 2009, grossed more than $60 million, and her latest, the Eras Tour, is on track to gross around $1.4 billion, according to Pollstar—the (Taylor's Version) albums are breaking all kinds of records. Here's a look at how the first three have performed.

Fearless (Taylor's Version), top left, debuted in April 2021, and in the first year it earned one million equivalent album units—a measurement that accounts for streaming, song downloads, and traditional album sales. The 2008 *Fearless* earned 242,000 equivalent album units over the same time period.

Red (Taylor's Version), bottom right, debuted at No. 1 on the Billboard 200 chart in November 2021. It earned almost 2 million equivalent album units in a year, compared with the 2012 *Red*, which earned 220,000. *Red (Taylor's Version)* also outperformed *Fearless (Taylor's Version)*, doubling its equivalent album units for the first year.

Speak Now (Taylor's Version), top right, debuted in July 2023, with 716,000 in equivalent album sales the first week, shy of the 2010 edition (which sold more one million copies) but eclipsing both the *Fearless* and *Red* rerecordings. *Speak Now (Taylor's Version)* also notched the second-biggest week for a vinyl album since 1991, and all 22 of the rereleased tracks debuted on the Billboard Hot 100 .

Swift announced the release of 1989 (Taylor's Version) on August 9, 2023, during her concert at SoFi Stadium outside Los Angeles.

TIME

Editor in Chief Sam Jacobs
Managing Editor Lily Rothman
Creative Director D.W. Pine

TAYLOR SWIFT

DOTDASH MEREDITH PREMIUM PUBLISHING
Editorial Director Kostya Kennedy
Creative Director Gary Stewart
Editorial Operations Director Jamie Roth Major
Manager, Editorial Operations Gina Scauzillo
Associate Manager, Editorial Operations Ariel Davis
Editor Eileen Daspin
Art Director Lan Yin Bachelis
Senior Photo Editor C. Tiffany Lee
Photo Editor Steph Durante
Writers Raisa Bruner, Shannon Carlin, Jack Dickey, Eliana Dockterman, Ava Erickson, Mariah Espada, Jeannie Kopstein, Cady Lang
Copy Chief Tracy Guth Spangler
Researcher Tresa McBee
Production Designer Sandra Jurevics
Premedia Trafficking Supervisor Sophia Mozena
Premedia Imaging Specialist Don Atkinson
Color Quality Analyst Sarah Schroeder
Production Director Patrick McGowan
Production Managers Kyle Dirks, Ashley Schaubroeck, April Gross

Vice President & General Manager Jeremy Biloon
Vice President, Group Editorial Director Stephen Orr
Executive Publishing Director Megan Pearlman
Senior Director, Brand Marketing Jean Kennedy
Associate Director, Brand Marketing Katherine Barnet
Associate Director, Business Development & Partnerships Nina Reed
Senior Manager, Brand Marketing Geoffrey Wohlgamuth
Brand Manager, Brand Marketing Mia Rinaldi

Special thanks Gabby Amello, Brad Beatson, Farah Ameen

DOTDASH MEREDITH
President, Lifestyle Alysia Borsa

Swifties have drawn 13s on their hands for years (the singer, born on December 13, considers the number lucky), but for the Eras Tour, they added a new tradition, loading their arms with friendship bracelets spelling out Swift references.

CREDITS

Front covers
(with guitar) Emma McIntyre/TAS23/Getty Images; (with microphone) Kevin Mazur/TAS Rights Management/Getty Images

Back cover
(from top) Emma McIntyre/TAS23/Getty Images; John Shearer/TAS Rights Management/Getty Images

1 TAS Rights Management/Getty Images **2-3** Sarah Yenesel/EPA-EFE/Shutterstock

A Very Good Year
4-5 Taylor Hill/TAS23/Getty Images **7** John Shearer/TAS23/Getty Images

It's Taylor Swift's Era
8-9 Terence Rushin/TAS23/Getty Images **10-11** Allen J. Schaben/Los Angeles Times/Getty Images **12** (from top, from left) Rachel Wisniewski/The Washington Post/Getty Images; Kevin Mazur/TAS23/Getty Images; Natasha Moustache/TAS23/Getty Images; Jutharat Pinyodoonyachet/The New York Times/Redux; Jefferee Woo/Tampa Bay Times/ZUMA/Alamy; Emma McIntyre/TAS23/Getty Images; Jutharat Pinyodoonyachet/The New York Times/Redux; Zack Wittman/The New York Times/Redux; Justin L. Stewart/ZUMA/Alamy; Jutharat Pinyodoonyachet/The New York Times/Redux; Grace Smith/MediaNews Group/The Denver Post/Getty Images; Terence Rushin/TAS23/Getty Images **13** Brittany Murray/MediaNews Group/Long Beach Press-Telegram/Getty Images **14-19** John Shearer/TAS23/Getty Images (3) **20-21** Jeff Kravitz/TAS23/Getty Images **22-23** Emma McIntyre/TAS23/Getty Images

Becoming Taylor
24-25 Hainsley Brown/eyevine/Redux **26-27** Jesse D. Garrabrant/NBAE/Getty Images **28** Splash by Shutterstock **29** Mark Humphrey/AP **30** Rick Diamond/WireImage/Getty Images **32-33** Terry Wyatt/UPI/Shutterstock **34-35** Art Streiber/AUGUST **36** Christie Goodwin/TAS/Getty Images **37** Christopher Polk/TAS/Getty Images **38** Kevin Mazur/TAS/Getty Images **39** Mark Metcalfe/TAS/Getty Images **40-41** Matt Irwin/Trunk Archive **42-43** Matt Winkelmeyer/TAS18/Getty Images **46** Christopher Polk/Getty Images **47** Larry Busacca/LP5/Getty Images

Queen of the Easter Eggs
48-49 Agency/NurPhoto/Shutterstock **50-51** John Salangsang/Shutterstock **53** AJ Pics/Alamy **54** Kern/WireImage/Getty Images **57** TAS Rights Management 2021/Getty Images **61** Peggy Sirota/Trunk Archive **62** Kevin Mazur/Getty Images for The Recording Academy **65** Kent Nishimura/Los Angeles Times/Contour RA/Getty Images **66** Chris Sweda/Chicago Tribune/Tribune News Service/Getty Images **68-69** Kevin Mazur/Getty Images **70-71** (from left) Kevin Winter/ACMA2013/Getty Images; Gareth Cattermole/TAS/Getty Images **72-73** (from left) John Shearer/LP5/Getty Images; Mario Anzuoni/Reuters/Redux **74-75** (from left) Christopher Polk/TAS/Getty Images; John Shearer/LP5/Getty Images **76-77** (from left) Kevin Winter/Getty Images; Kevin Mazur/TAS23/Getty Images

A Woman in Full
78-79 David Fisher/Shutterstock **80-81** Stephen Lam/Reuters/Redux **83** (left) Mark Metcalfe/Getty Images **84** Theo Stroomer/Getty Images **85** Splash by Shutterstock **86-88** © Netflix/Courtesy Everett Collection (2) **90-91** Wesley Lapointe/Los Angeles Times/Getty Images **92** Kevin Mazur/Getty Images **94** Kevin Winter/TAS23/Getty Images **95** Jutharat Pinyodoonyachet/The New York Times/Redux **96** Kevin Mazur/Getty Images

TROPHY COLLECTOR

Fans always hope to see Swift at the VMAs, but given that the star has been performing dozens of three-hour-plus arena shows on her Eras Tour, they would have understood if she'd sat out the 2023 event. What was never in doubt for Swifties: that she would win in multiple categories. They were excited to see her take home 9 of the 11 awards she was up for, including best pop video for "Anti-Hero," which was presented—along with some friendship bracelets—by a reunited NSYNC.

Made in the USA
Las Vegas, NV
07 March 2024

86821018R00059

NUEVO ESPAÑOL EN MARCHA

LIBRO DEL ALUMNO

Francisca Castro Viúdez
Ignacio Rodero Díez
Carmen Sardinero Francos
María Elena Arévalo Alvarado
Alma Edith Bautista Alférez
Elena Jiménez Martín

¿Cómo es *Nuevo Español en marcha 1*?

NUEVO ESPAÑOL EN MARCHA 1 es un curso de español para el nivel A1 del *Marco común europeo de referencia*. Al final de este nivel los estudiantes podrán comunicarse de forma elemental, pero correctamente, en pasado (pretérito), presente y futuro (*voy a* + infinitivo), y conocerán aproximadamente unas 1000 palabras fundamentales. Además, podrán dar información básica sobre sí mismos y sobre los otros, así como desenvolverse en una serie de situaciones prácticas.

1 Portada
Incluye los contenidos que se van a trabajar en la unidad.

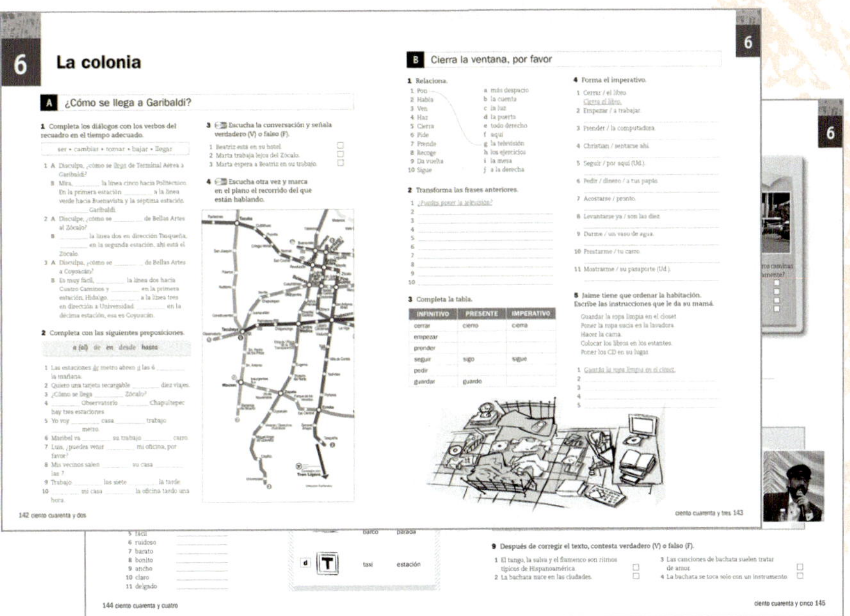
6 La colonia

A ¿Cómo se llega a Garibaldi?

B Cierra la ventana, por favor

6 Cuaderno de ejercicios y anexos

- Cuaderno de ejercicios y soluciones.
- Actividades en parejas.
- Verbos regulares e irregulares.
- Transcripciones.

5 Gramática y vocabulario
Resume los contenidos gramaticales y el vocabulario organizado por familias léxicas.

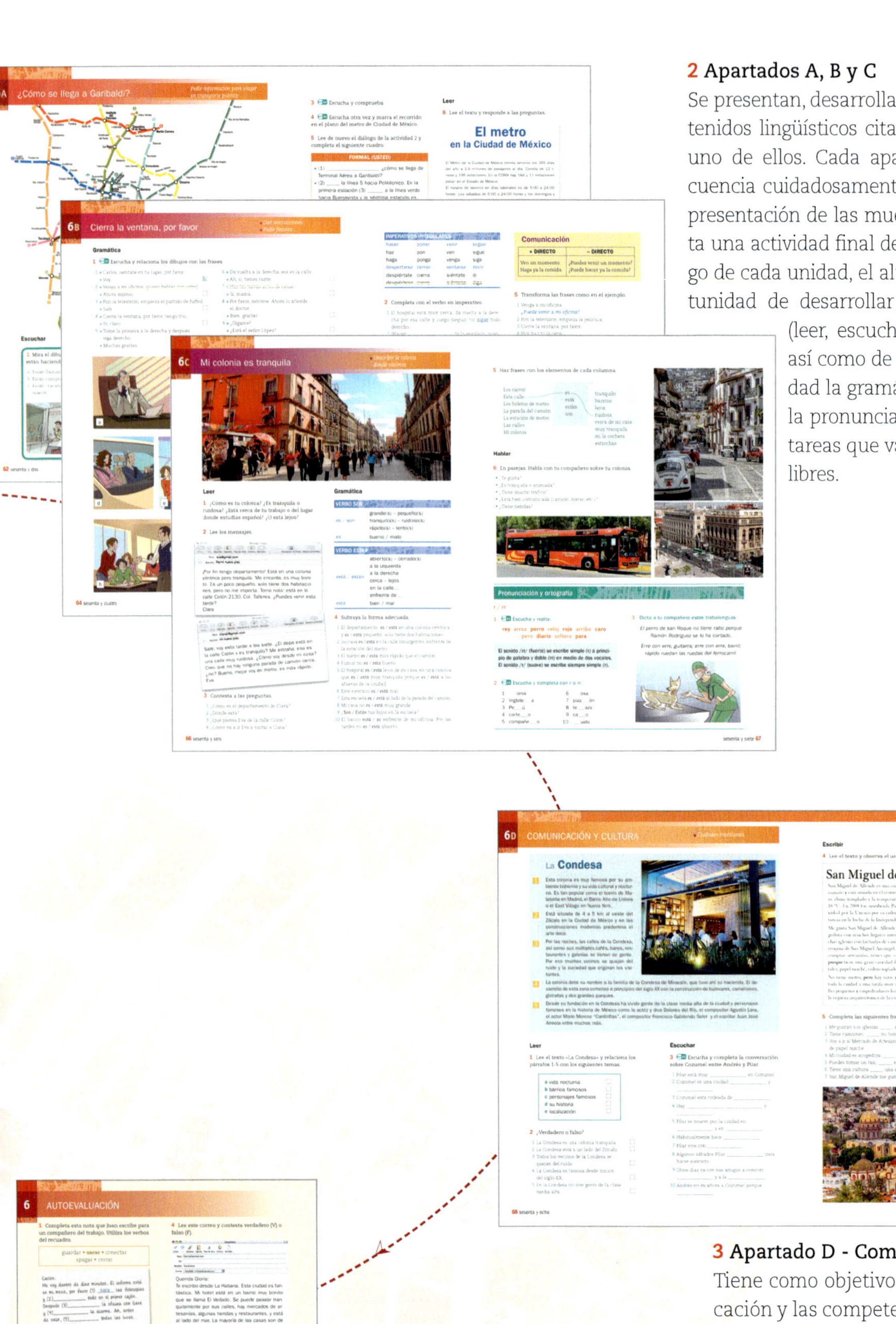

2 Apartados A, B y C

Se presentan, desarrollan y practican los contenidos lingüísticos citados al inicio de cada uno de ellos. Cada apartado sigue una secuencia cuidadosamente graduada, desde la presentación de las muestras de lengua hasta una actividad final de producción. A lo largo de cada unidad, el alumno tendrá la oportunidad de desarrollar todas las destrezas (leer, escuchar, escribir y hablar) así como de trabajar en profundidad la gramática, el vocabulario y la pronunciación, en una serie de tareas que van de muy dirigidas a libres.

3 Apartado D - Comunicación y cultura

Tiene como objetivo desarrollar la comunicación y las competencias tanto socioculturales como interculturales del estudiante. Las actividades están agrupadas según las cuatro destrezas lingüísticas: leer, escuchar, escribir y hablar.

4 Autoevaluación

Actividades destinadas a recapitular y consolidar los objetivos de la unidad. Se incluye un test con el que el alumno podrá evaluar su progreso según los descriptores del *Portfolio europeo de las lenguas*.

Contenidos

ANTES DE EMPEZAR

A ¡Hola! Me llamo Maribel

1 Lee y escucha.

Maestra: ¡Hola! Me llamo Maribel y soy la maestra de español. Vamos a presentarnos. A ver, empieza tú, ¿cómo te llamas?
Estudiante 1: Me llamo Marcelo.
Maestra: ¿De dónde eres, Marcelo?
Estudiante 1: Soy brasileño, de Porto Alegre.
Estudiante 2: Yo me llamo Isabelle y soy francesa.

2 Practica con tus compañeros.

- ■ ¡Hola!
- ● ¡Hola!
- ■ ¿Cómo te llamas?
- ● Me llamo ___________.
- ■ ¿De dónde eres?
- ● Soy (de) ___________.

3 Completa el cuadro.

PAÍS	NACIONALIDAD	
	masculino	femenino
1 Alemania	alemán	
2 España		española
3 Brasil	brasileño	
4 Francia		francesa
5 Italia	italiano	

Saludos

4 Escucha y repite.

VOCALES				
A	E	I	O	U
a	e	i	o	u

CONSONANTES				
mayúscula	**minúscula**	**nombre**	**sonido**	**ejemplos**
B	b	be	/b/	abuelo, bien
C	c	ce	c + a, o, u = /k/ c + e, i = /θ/	casa, cosa, cuatro cerrado, cine
D	d	de	/d/	día, dos
F	f	efe	/f/	fumar
G	g	ge	g + a, o, u = /g/ gu + e, i= /g/ g + e, i = /x/	gato, pago, agua guerrero, guitarra genio, giro
H	h	hache	–	hotel, hospital
J	j	jota	/x/	jefe, jirafa
K	k	ka	/k/	kilogramo
L	l	ele	/l/	león, limón
M	m	eme	/m/	México, mira
N	n	ene	/n/	nada, no
Ñ	ñ	eñe	/ɲ/	niña, año
P	p	pe	/p/	pan, pera
Q	q	cu	qu + e, i = /k/	quince, queso
R	r	erre	/r/ /rr/	pera, Corea, rosa, ramo, arroz
S	s	ese	/s/	casa, sol, paseo
T	t	te	/t/	tomate, tú
V	v	uve (ve)	/b/	vaca, ven, vino
W	w	uve doble (doble u)	/u/ o /gu/ /b/	William wolframio
X	x	equis	/ks/	examen, éxito
Y	y	i griega (ye)	/i/ /ʝ/	(Juan) y (Luis) yogur, yo
Z	z	zeta	z + a, o, u = /θ/	zapato, cazo, azul

Conjuntos de letras

CH	ch	(che)	/t͡ʃ/	chocolate
LL	ll	(doble ele)	/ʎ/	llave, camello, lluvia

5 Escucha.

ca	casa
que	queso
qui	quiero
co	color
cu	cuatro

ga	gato
gue	guerra
gui	guitarra
go	agosto
gu	agua

za	zapato
ce	cerrado
ci	cine
zo	zoológico
zu	azul

ja	jamón
je / ge	jefe / genio
ji / gi	jirafa / gitano
jo	jota
ju	julio

6 Lee en voz alta las siguientes palabras.

región	paz	quien
gente	chocolate	catorce
joven	ácido	pequeño
ejemplo	cereza	guitarra

¿Con B o con V?
(En Latinoamérica: *b = be larga; v = be corta*)
***V**eracruz, **B**ilbao, Isa**b**el, **V**icente.*

¿Con G o con J?
***G**enio, ro**j**o, **j**irafa, **g**itana.*

¿Con H o sin H?
***H**otel, agua, **h**uevo, **h**elado.*

7 Escucha y señala la palabra que deletrean.

1 ROMERO	☑	RODERO	☐
2 DÍEZ	☐	DÍAZ	☐
3 GONZÁLEZ	☐	GONZALVO	☐
4 RIBERA	☐	RIVERA	☐
5 JIMÉNEZ	☐	GIMÉNEZ	☐
6 PADÍN	☐	BADÍN	☐

8 Pregunta a cinco compañeros su nombre y apellido. Sigue el modelo.

- ■ ¿Cómo te llamas?
- ● Fabio.
- ■ ¿Con be o con uve?
- ● Con be.
- ■ ¿Y de apellido?
- ● Oliveira.
- ■ ¿Cómo se escribe?
- ● O-ele-i-uve-e-i-erre-a.
- ■ ¿Así está bien?
- ● Sí, muy bien.

SÍLABA TÓNICA

Si la palabra lleva tilde, esta indica la sílaba tónica.
*ca**fé** **mé**dico **ár**bol*

Si no hay tilde, se pronuncia más fuerte la última cuando la palabra acaba en consonante (excepto **n** y **s**).
*Ma**drid** espa**ñol** ha**blar***

Se pronuncia más fuerte la penúltima si la palabra termina en vocal, en **n** o **s**.
***je**fe ven**ta**na e**xa**men **cri**sis*

9 Subraya la sílaba tónica de las palabras del recuadro.

ale<u>mán</u> • alemana • japonés • maestro
estudiante • maestra • brasileño
hospital • estudiar • libro
lección • compañero • madre

10 Escucha, comprueba y repite.

Para la clase

¿Puede repetir, por favor?

¿Cómo se dice "orange"?

¿Cómo se escribe?

Perdone, no entiendo.

¿Qué significa "arroz"?

11 Seguro que conoces algunas palabras en español. Relaciónalas con las imágenes.

1 fiesta	☐	6 flamenco	☐	11 salsa	☐
2 hotel	☐	7 tango	☐	12 playa	☐
3 cine	☐	8 bar	☐	13 mariachi	☐
4 hospital	☐	9 chocolate	☐	14 guitarra	☐
5 restaurante	☐	10 café	☐	15 siesta	☐

12 6 Escucha y repite.

13 ¿Conoces otras palabras en español?

C Mapas de México y América Latina

El español

El español o castellano es la lengua oficial de España y de 19 países latinoamericanos. Es la segunda lengua más hablada después del chino; la hablan más de 450 millones de personas. El español viene del latín, igual que el francés, el italiano, el portugués y el rumano. En España, también son lenguas oficiales el catalán, el gallego y el euskera.

Saludos

- Saludar y presentar a otra persona
- Nacionalidades
- Profesiones: el género
- *Tú* y *usted*
- Preguntar y dar el número de teléfono y la dirección
- **Cultura:** Fórmulas de tratamiento (*tú* y *usted*)

1A Mucho gusto

- *Saludar y presentar a otra persona*
- *Nacionalidades*

Hablar

1 Mira las fotos y señala dónde están.

1 En una oficina.	☐	3 En clase.	☐
2 En un hotel.	☐	4 En una cafetería.	☐

Escuchar

2 (7) Escucha y lee.

EN CLASE

Isabelle: ¡Hola, Marcelo!, ¿qué tal?
Marcelo: Bien, ¿y tú?
Isabelle: Muy bien. Mira, esta es Ulrike, una nueva compañera, es alemana.
Marcelo: ¡Hola! ¡Encantado!¿Eres de Berlín?
Ulrike: Sí, pero ahora vivo en Madrid.

EN UN HOTEL

Recepcionista: Su nombre, por favor.
Fernando: Yo me llamo Fernando Álvarez y ella es Carmen Hernández.
Recepcionista: ¿De dónde son ustedes?
Fernando: Somos argentinos, de Buenos Aires.
Recepcionista: Ah, Buenos Aires... Aquí están sus tarjetas, bienvenidos a Zacatecas.
Fernando: Gracias.

EN UNA OFICINA

Díaz: ¡Buenos días!, señor Álvarez, ¿cómo está?
Álvarez: Muy bien, gracias. Mire, le presento a Marta Rodríguez, la nueva directora.
Díaz: Encantado de conocerla, yo me llamo Gerardo Díaz, y soy el responsable de la administración.
Rodríguez: Mucho gusto, Gerardo.

3 Completa.

EN UNA CAFETERÍA

Luis: ¡Hola, Eva!, ¿____________________?
Eva: Bien, ¿____________________?
Luis: Muy bien. ____________________, este es Roberto, un nuevo compañero.
Eva: ____________ ________________
¿De dónde ________________?
Roberto: Soy de aquí, de Monterrey.

4 (8) Escucha y comprueba.

Comunicación

Informal

- *¡Hola!, ¿qué tal? / ¿cómo estás?*
- *Bien, ¿y tú?*

- *¿Cómo te llamas?*
- *Carmen, ¿y tú?*

- *Esta es Celia. / Este es Roberto.*

Formal

- *¡Buenos días, señor Prado, ¿cómo está usted?*
- *Muy bien, gracias.*

- *Le presento al señor Rodríguez.*
- *¡Encantado/a! / Mucho gusto.*

Hablar

5 Practica los saludos y las presentaciones con tus compañeros de clase, en grupos de dos o tres personas.

Gramática

GÉNERO DE LOS ADJETIVOS DE NACIONALIDAD	
masculino	femenino
ital**iano**	ital**iana**
españ**ol**	españ**ola**
estadouni**dense**	estadouni**dense**
marroq**uí**	marroq**uí**

6 Completa el cuadro.

	PAÍSES	NACIONALIDADES	
1	China	chino	
2		iraní	
3	Reino Unido	británico	
4	Turquía		turca
5	Sudáfrica		sudafricana
6		colombiano	
7		brasileño	
8	Francia		francesa
9	Polonia	polaco	
10	Suecia		sueca
11			alemana
12	Canadá		

7 (CD 9) Escucha y repite.

8 Practica con tus compañeros. Selecciona una nacionalidad distinta a la tuya.

- *¿De dónde eres?*
- *Soy colombiana, ¿y tú?*
- *Yo soy francés.*

Escuchar

9 (CD 10) Escucha y escribe en las tarjetas.

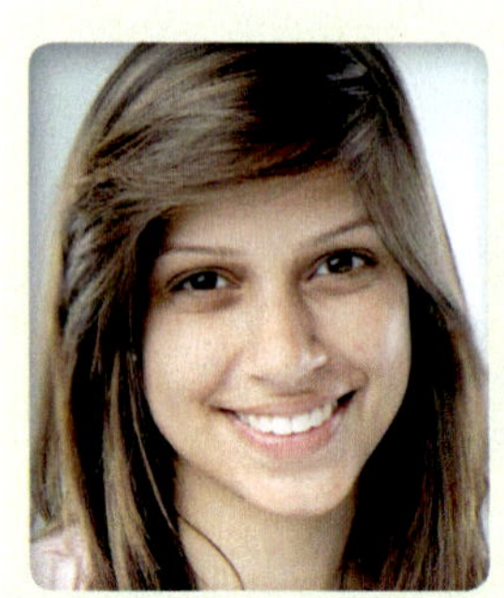

1

Nombre: ____________

Apellido: ____________

Nacionalidad: ____________

2

Nombre: ____________

Apellido: ____________

Nacionalidad: ____________

3

Nombre: ____________

Apellido: ____________

Nacionalidad: ____________

4

Nombre: ____________

Apellido: ____________

Nacionalidad: ____________

1B ¿A qué te dedicas?

- Profesiones: el género
- Tú y usted

Vocabulario

1 Escribe la letra correspondiente.

1 estilista	F		6 taxista	☐
2 profesor	☐		7 cartero	☐
3 doctora	☐		8 actriz	☐
4 mesero	☐		9 abogada	☐
5 ama de casa	☐		10 conserje	☐

A

B

C

D

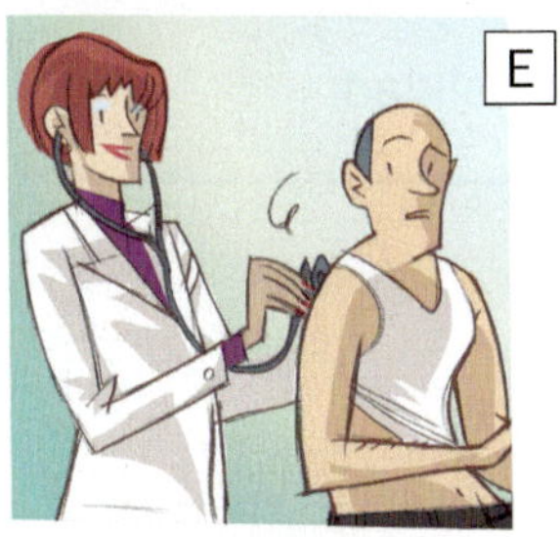
E

F

G

H

I

J

2 Escoge una profesión. Pregunta a tres compañeros.

- *¿A qué te dedicas?*
- *Soy doctor, ¿y tú?*
- *Yo soy abogada.*

Gramática

GÉNERO DE LOS NOMBRES DE PROFESIÓN	
masculino	femenino
mesero	mesera
doctor	doctora
estudiante	estudiante
presidente	presidenta
economista	economista

3 Escribe el femenino.

1 el vendedor la *vendedora*
2 el secretario la ______
3 el conductor la ______
4 el chef la ______
5 el futbolista la ______
6 el cantante la ______
7 el actor la ______
8 el jardinero la ______
9 el guía la ______
10 el pianista la ______

4 11 Escucha y lee.

Me llamo Manuel García. Soy doctor. Soy chiapaneco, pero vivo en Ciudad de México. Trabajo en un hospital. Mi esposa se llama Amelia, es maestra y trabaja en una preparatoria. Ella es oaxaqueña. Tenemos dos hijos, Sergio y Elena; los dos son estudiantes. Sergio estudia en la universidad, y Elena, en la preparatoria.

5 Responde.

1 ¿A qué se dedica Manuel? *Es doctor.*
2 ¿De dónde es Manuel?
3 ¿Dónde viven?
4 ¿Dónde trabaja Amelia?
5 ¿De dónde es Amelia?
6 ¿Cuántos hijos tienen?
7 ¿Qué hacen los hijos?

PRESENTE DE VERBOS REGULARES			
	trabajar	comer	vivir
yo	trabajo	como	vivo
tú	trabajas	comes	vives
él / ella / usted	trabaja	come	vive
nosotros/as	trabajamos	comemos	vivimos
vosotros/as	trabajáis	coméis	vivís
ellos / ellas / ustedes	trabajan	comen	viven

PRESENTE DE VERBOS IRREGULARES		
	ser	tener
yo	soy	tengo
tú	eres	tienes
él / ella / usted	es	tiene
nosotros/as	somos	tenemos
vosotros/as	sois	tenéis
ellos / ellas / ustedes	son	tienen

6 Completa las frases con la forma adecuada de los verbos anteriores.

1 Belén no ________ veracruzana, ________ regiomontana.
2 Rocío ________ en una agencia de viajes.
3 Gael García Bernal ________ un actor mexicano.
4 Nosotros ________ tres hijos.
5 Mi esposo________ muchas verduras.
6 ¿De dónde________ Fernando?
7 Yo no________ carne, ________ vegetariana.
8 Miguel y María ________ en una empresa sonorense.
9 ¿Tus papás ________ en una casa cerca de la playa?
10 Tú ________ más dinero que yo.
11 Nosotras no ________ maestras: Rosa ________ doctora y yo ________ periodista.
12 ¿Usted ________ colombiano?

7 Completa.

TÚ	USTED
¿Dónde vives?	¿Dónde *vive* usted?
¿Cómo ____________?	¿Cómo se llama usted?
¿Tienes hijos?	¿____________ hijos usted?
¿De dónde ____________?	¿De dónde ____________ usted?
¿A qué ____________?	¿A qué se dedica usted?

8 Practica las preguntas anteriores con *usted* con tu maestro.

Leer

9 Completa el texto siguiente con los verbos adecuados.

Me [1] llamo Elaine Araujo y [2] ________ arquitecta. [3] ________ brasileña, pero ahora [4] ________ en Guadalajara porque estudio una maestría en la universidad. También [5] ________ los fines de semana en un restaurante. Soy soltera, pero [6] ________ un novio mexicano: él [7] ________ en una empresa de sistemas computacionales.

Escribir

10 Escribe un párrafo sobre ti. Luego, léelo a tus compañeros.

Me llamo ____________________
____________, soy ____________
__________________________.

Pronunciación y ortografía

Entonación interrogativa

1  Escucha y repite.

1 ¿De dónde eres?
2 ¿De dónde son ustedes?
3 ¿Cómo te llamas?
4 ¿Quién es él?
5 ¿Dónde vives?
6 ¿Dónde trabaja usted?
7 ¿Dónde viven ustedes?
8 ¿Cómo se llama el esposo de Ana?

¿Cuál es tu número de celular?

■ *Preguntar y dar el número de teléfono y la dirección*

Vocabulario

1 Escribe los números.

seis • uno • ocho • tres • nueve

0 cero | 1 ________

2 dos | 3 ________ | 4 cuatro

5 cinco | 6 ________

7 siete | 8 ________

9 ________ | 10 diez

2 (13) Escucha y comprueba.

3 Practica con tu compañero.

2 + 3 = cinco
■ *¿Dos más tres?*
● *Cinco.*

8 - 6 = dos
■ *¿Ocho menos seis?*
● *Dos.*

3 + 5 = ________
4 + 4 = ________

9 - 4 = ________
1 - 0 = ________

Escuchar

4 (14) Escucha y escribe los números de teléfono.

1 María: 5546857698
2 Jorge: ________
3 Marina: ________, ________
4 Aeropuerto de Ciudad de México: ________
5 Cruz Roja: ________
6 Radio-taxi: ________

Hablar

5 Pregunta el número de teléfono a varios compañeros. Toma nota.

■ *Lars, ¿cuál es tu número de teléfono / celular?*
● *Es el 5580974678.*
■ *Gracias.*

6 Ahora pregúntale su dirección de correo electrónico.

■ *¿Cuál es tu correo electrónico?*
● *joseluis@gmail.com*

Vocabulario

7 (15) Escucha y aprende.

11 once
12 doce
13 trece
14 catorce
15 quince
16 dieciséis
17 diecisiete
18 dieciocho
19 diecinueve
20 veinte

8 En parejas escriban los números.

4 x 4 = dieciséis
Cuatro por cuatro dieciséis

9 x 2 = ________
3 x 6 = ________
5 x 3= ________
2 x 6 = ________

4 x 5 = ________
2 x 8 = ________
7 x 2 = ________
3 x 4 = ________

9 (16) Juega al bingo.

A Escoge una de las dos tablas.
B Escucha y señala los números que oyes. ¡Suerte!

1

B	I	N	G	O
1	4	7	13	16
2	5	8	14	18
3	6	11	15	19

2

3	7	10	13	16
4	8	11	14	17
5	9	12	15	20

Escuchar

10 17 Lee, escucha y completa.

EN UN GIMNASIO

Felipe: ¡Buenas tardes!
Rosa: ¡Hola!, [1] __________.
Felipe: Quiero inscribirme en el gimnasio.
Rosa: Tienes que darme tus datos. A ver, ¿[2] __________?
Felipe: Felipe Martínez.
Rosa: ¿Y el segundo apellido?
Felipe: Franco.
Rosa: ¿Dónde [3] __________?
Felipe: En la calle Reforma, número ochenta y siete, tercer piso, departamento 305.
Rosa: ¿Teléfono?
Felipe: [4] __________.
Rosa: ¿Profesión?
Felipe: [5] __________.
Rosa: Bueno, ya está; el precio es...

11 Completa la tarjeta con los datos de Felipe.

Gimnasio Praga

NOMBRE __________________ APELLIDOS __________________

DOMICILIO ACTUAL ______________________________

NÚMERO ______ PISO ________ DEPARTAMENTO ________ TELÉFONO ______________

PROFESIÓN __________________ CORREO ELECTRÓNICO femartinez@gmail.com

Gramática

INTERROGATIVOS

¿A **qué** te dedicas?
¿**Cómo** te llamas?
¿De **dónde** eres?
¿**Dónde** vives?
¿**Dónde** trabajas?
¿**Cuál** es tu número de teléfono?

12 Completa las frases con *qué*, *dónde*, *cómo*, *cuál*.

1 ■ ¿De dónde es Gloria Estefan?
● De Cuba.
2 ■ ¿__________ trabajas?
● En un banco.
3 ■ ¿__________ se llama tu compañero?
● Mariano.
4 ■ ¿__________ vive Julio?
● En Miami.
5 ■ ¿A __________ se dedica tu esposa?
● Es cantante.
6 ■ ¿De __________ son ustedes?
● Somos alemanes, de Bonn.
7 ■ ¿______ significa "saludo"?
● «Hola» es un saludo.
8 ■ ¿A __________ te dedicas?
● Soy pintor.
9 ■ ¿__________ es tu número de teléfono?
● 5524864796.

Hablar

13 Prepara cinco preguntas para un compañero y luego pregúntale. Anota las respuestas.

¿Dónde vives?
¿Cómo se llama tu papá?
¿De dónde eres?...

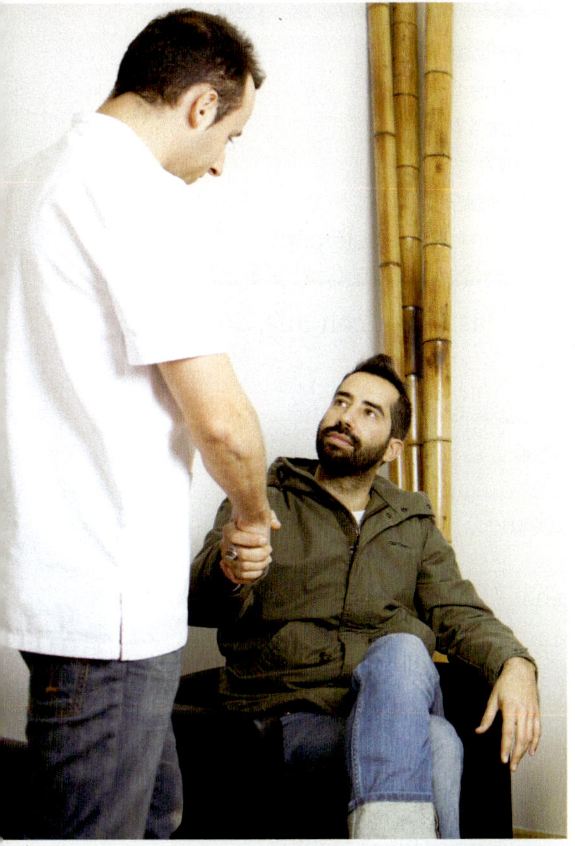

Leer

1 Lee el siguiente texto.

Saludos

En español podemos hablar en estilo formal o informal. En estilo formal usamos *usted (Ud.)* y *ustedes (Uds.)* para hablar con personas desconocidas, de mayor edad o superiores en el trabajo: un jefe, un profesor, un doctor. También en estilo formal utilizamos las fórmulas *señor (Sr.)* y *señora (Sra.)* con el apellido: *Sr. Pérez.*

En estilo informal usamos el nombre, y es muy habitual decir *¡hola!* para saludar y *¡hasta luego!,* para despedirse; pero también decimos *¡adiós!, ¡hasta mañana!* o *¡hasta pronto!*

En estilo formal es normal saludar también con *¡buenos días!,* por la mañana; *¡buenas tardes!,* por la tarde; y *¡buenas noches!,* por la noche.

2 Marca la forma adecuada.

	Tú	Usted
1 Hablo con un mesero.	☐	☐
2 Hablo con mi maestro.	☐	☐
3 Hablo con mi tío.	☐	☐
4 Hablo con la vendedora.	☐	☐
5 Hablo con un niño.	☐	☐
6 Hablo con una persona de 70 años desconocida.	☐	☐

3 Relaciona.

1 ¡Hola!, ¿qué tal?
2 ¡Adiós!
3 ¡Hola, amigo!, ¿cómo estás?
4 ¡Hola!, me llamo Javier.
5 Buenas noches, ¿cómo está usted?
6 Vos sos* Pablo, ¿no?

a ¡Hola!
b Sí, hola. Y vos Óscar, claro.
c Hola, yo soy Marisa.
d Bien, ¿y tú?, ¿qué tal?
e Bien, ¿y Ud.?
f ¡Adiós, hasta luego!

* En Argentina dicen *vos sos* en lugar de *tú eres*.

Escuchar

4 18 Escucha cómo se presentan cuatro personas y completa la tabla.

NOMBRE	PROFESIÓN	CIUDAD	CELULAR
	estudiante		
Sofía			
		Caracas	
Manuel			

Hablar

Alumno A (alumno B, ver «En parejas», pág. 172)

5 ¿Conoces a estos personajes famosos? Pregunta a B la información sobre los números 1, 3, 5 y 7.

¿Cómo se llama el número 1? ¿De dónde es? ¿A qué se dedica?

1

______
______
______

2

Benicio del Toro
puertorriqueño
actor

3

______
______
______

4

Gabriel Orozco
mexicano
artista

5

______
______
______

6

Salma Hayek
mexicana
actriz

7

______
______
______

8

Alejandro González Iñárritu
mexicano
director de cine

6 Responde a B la información sobre los números 2, 4, 6 y 8.

El número 2 se llama Benicio del Toro. Es puertorriqueño. Es actor.

Escribir

7 Completa una ficha con tus datos y otra con los de tu compañero.

Nombre:
Apellido:
Nacionalidad:
Profesión:
Domicilio:
Ciudad:
Teléfono:
Correo electrónico:

Nombre:
Apellido:
Nacionalidad:
Profesión:
Domicilio:
Ciudad:
Teléfono:
Correo electrónico:

AUTOEVALUACIÓN

1 Lee los textos y completa las preguntas.

A Me llamo Peter Tuck. Soy maestro de inglés. Vivo en Ciudad de México y trabajo en una escuela. Soy soltero.

B Yo me llamo Maria Rodrigues; soy brasileña, de Río de Janeiro. Mi esposo se llama Bruno y también es brasileño. Somos maestros.

C Yo me llamo Yoshie Kikkawa y soy japonesa, de Tokio. Soy casada. Mi esposo se llama Mitsuo y tenemos dos hijos, Kimiko y Ken. Los dos estudian en la escuela primaria.

1 ■ ¿Dónde vive Peter?
● En Ciudad de México.

2 ■ ¿_______________ Peter?
● En una escuela.

3 ■ ¿_______________ Maria?
● Es brasileña.

4 ■ ¿_______________ el esposo de Maria?
● Bruno.

5 ■ ¿_______________ Yoshie?
● De Tokio.

6 ■ ¿Qué _______________ los hijos de Yoshie?
● Estudian en la escuela primaria.

2 Completa los diálogos.

1 ■ Hola, me llamo Manuel, y _______________ mexicano. ¿Cómo _______________ tú?
● _______________ Marta.

2 ■ Buenos días, señor Jiménez, ¿cómo _______________ usted?
● Bien, gracias, ¿y _______________?

3 ■ Mire, señora Rodríguez, le _______________ al señor Márquez.
● _______________.
▼ Mucho gusto.

4 ■ Hola, Laura. ¿Qué _______________?
● Hola, Manu, muy _______________. Mira, _______________, es Marina, una nueva _______________.
■ Hola, ¿qué _______________?
▼ _______________, ¿y tú?
■ Muy bien.

3 (19) Escucha los apellidos y escribe el número de orden.

Díaz	☐	Martínez	☐
Vargas	☐	Díez	☐
Marín	☐	Martín	☐
Serrano	☐	López	☐
Moreno	☐	Romero	☐
Jiménez	☐	García	☐
Pérez	☐		

4 Lee y señala si hablan de tú o de usted.

	Tú	Usted
1 ¿Cómo te llamas?	☑	☐
2 ¿Dónde vive?	☐	☐
3 ¿De dónde es?	☐	☐
4 ¿Dónde trabaja?	☐	☐
5 ¿De dónde eres?	☐	☐
6 ¿Cuál es tu número de teléfono?	☐	☐
7 ¿A qué te dedicas?	☐	☐

¿Qué sabes?

	☺	😐	☹
• Saludar y presentar a alguien.	☐	☐	☐
• Decir la nacionalidad y la profesión.	☐	☐	☐
• Los números del 1 al 20.	☐	☐	☐
• Preguntar y decir el domicilio y el número de teléfono.	☐	☐	☐

Familias

- Presentar a la familia
- Dar información personal
- Decir dónde están las cosas
- Expresar posesión
- Preguntar y decir la hora
- **Cultura**: La familia hispana: celebraciones

¿Eres casado?

- Presentar a la familia
- Dar información personal

a) ______ b) ______ c) ______ d) ______

Hola, soy Jorge. Soy casado y esta es mi familia. Mi esposa se llama Rosa y tenemos dos hijos: Isabel, de doce años, y David, de diez. Vivimos en Querétaro, una ciudad a dos horas de la Ciudad de México. Soy maestro de computación.

Yo soy Luis. No tengo hermanos, no tengo novia, soy soltero y vivo en Mérida con mis papás y mi abuela. Mi papá se llama Manuel y tiene cincuenta y ocho años. Mi mamá se llama Rocío y tiene cincuenta y seis años. Mi abuela tiene setenta y nueve años y se llama Carmen. Soy estudiante de Medicina.

Vocabulario

1 Relaciona.

1 ¿Eres casado/a?
2 ¿Tienes hijos?
3 ¿Tienes hermanos?

a No, no tengo.
b Sí, un hermano y una hermana.
c No, soy soltero/a.

2 20 Jorge y Luis hablan de sus familias. Lee los textos y escucha.

3 Escribe el nombre de cada uno en las fotos.

4 Escribe las preguntas de estas respuestas.

1 Jorge vive a dos horas de la Ciudad de México.
¿Dónde vive Jorge?
2 Es maestro de computación.
3 Se llama Manuel.
4 Estudia Medicina.
5 Tiene setenta y nueve años.

5 Completa las frases siguientes con las palabras del recuadro.

~~esposa~~ • hermana • papá • hijo abuela • mamá • esposo

1 Rosa es la _esposa_ de Jorge.
2 David es ________________ de Jorge y Rosa.
3 Rosa es la ________________ de Isabel.
4 Isabel es ________________ de David.
5 Manuel es el ________________ de Luis.
6 Carmen es ________________ de Luis.
7 Manuel es el ________________ de Rocío.

Hablar

6 Haz estas preguntas a varios compañeros y luego completa la ficha.

1 ¿Eres casado/a o soltero/a?
2 ¿Tienes hijos?
3 ¿Tienes novio/a?
4 ¿Cómo se llama tu papá / mamá?
5 ¿Tienes hermanos?
6 ¿Tienes abuelos?

	NOMBRE
a Es soltero/a	
b Es casado/a	
c Tiene hijos	
d Tiene novio/a	
e No tiene hermanos	
f Tiene abuelos	

Escribir

7 Escribe algunas frases sobre tu familia y léeselas a tu compañero.

Mi papá se llama Toni y tiene sesenta años. Mi hermana es casada y tiene dos hijos. Mi papá es taxista y mi hermano estudia Arquitectura.

Gramática

PLURAL DE LOS NOMBRES	
un mapa	dos mapa**s**
un autobús	dos autobus**es**

8 Mira la imagen y señala si es verdadero (V) o falso (F).

En esta clase tienen:

a una televisión ☐
b dos mapas ☐
c cinco sillas ☐
d cinco libros ☐
e cinco estudiantes ☐
f un teléfono ☐
g tres mesas ☐
h dos plumas ☐

9 Escribe en plural.

1 un carro _dos carros_
2 un maestro ________
3 una ventana ________
4 una compañera ________
5 una ciudad ________
6 un cuaderno ________
7 un chavo ________
8 un hotel ________
9 un teléfono ________
10 una computadora ________

10 Completa.

SINGULAR	PLURAL
hermano / hermana	hermanos / _hermanas_
papá / ________	________ / mamás
________ / hija	hijos / ________
abuelo / ________	abuelos / ________

2B ¿Dónde están mis lentes?

- *Decir dónde están las cosas*
- *Expresar posesión*

Vocabulario

1 Mira el dibujo y escribe la letra correspondiente.

1	reloj	☐	7	silla	☐
2	paraguas	☐	8	mesa de centro	☐
3	tenis	*B*	9	lentes	☐
4	computadora	☐	10	teléfono	☐
5	cuadro	☐	11	sillón	☐
6	sofá	☐	12	lámpara	☐

Gramática

MARCADORES DE LUGAR

debajo de	**al lado de**	**encima de**
delante de	**a la derecha de**	**entre**
detrás de	**a la izquierda de**	**en**

*La planta está **debajo de** la ventana.*
*Los libros están **en** el portafolio.*

A + el = **al**
De + el = **del**

*El sofá está **al lado del** sillón.*

2 Mira la habitación anterior y completa las frases.

1 El reloj está *al lado* del cuadro.
2 Los tenis están ____________ de la mesa de centro.
3 El teléfono está ____________ de la computadora.
4 El sillón está ________________ del librero.
5 Los lentes están ____________ el teléfono y la computadora.
6 El gato está ______________________ de David.
7 La ventana está __________ de la planta.
8 El paraguas está __________ del teléfono.
9 El cuadro está __________ el librero y el reloj.
10 El gato está __________ del sofá.

3 Mira tu salón o tu habitación y escribe cinco frases.

El diccionario está al lado del cuaderno.
La silla está delante de la mesa.

ADJETIVOS POSESIVOS		
sujeto	singular	plural
yo	**mi** [primo / prima	**mis** [primos / primas
tú	**tu** [amigo / amiga	**tus** [amigos / amigas
él / ella / usted	**su** [hermano / hermana	**sus** [hermanos / hermanas
nosotros/as	**nuestro** tío **nuestra** tía	**nuestros** tíos **nuestras** tías
vosotros/as	**vuestro** hijo **vuestra** hija	**vuestros** hijos **vuestras** hijas
ellos / ellas / ustedes	**su** [abuelo / abuela	**sus** [abuelos / abuelas

4 Completa las frases con el posesivo correspondiente.

1 ¿Cuál es tu número de teléfono? (tú)
2 _______ gata se llama Bonita. (ella)
3 ¿Esta es _______ chamarra? (tú)
4 ¿Dónde está _______ diccionario? (él)
5 ¿Tienes _______ lentes? (yo)
6 _______ casa está cerca de aquí. (nosotros)
7 _______ primos viven en Guadalajara. (ellas)
8 ¿Dónde viven _______ papás? (usted)
9 ¿Dónde vive _______ hermano? (ustedes)
10 ¿Dónde trabaja _______ mamá? (él)

5 Completa la conversación con los adjetivos posesivos.

■ ¿Estos son (1) tus papás?
● Sí, (2) _______ mamá se llama Julia y (3) _______ papá, Miguel.
■ ¿Y estos?
● Son (4) _______ tíos, Carlos y Águeda.
■ ¿Esta es (5) _______ hija?
● Sí, esa es (6) _______ prima Carolina.
■ Pues es muy guapa (7) _______ prima.

PRONOMBRES DEMOSTRATIVOS

Este es Pedro.
Esta es Elena.
Estos son Pablo y Amanda.
Estas son Lucía y Graciela.

6 Completa.

Mira, (1) estos son mis amigos. (2) _________ es Celia, y (3) _________ es Gonzalo, su novio. (4) _________ de la derecha es Laura. (5) _________ de aquí son las hermanas de Gonzalo, Marisa y Pilar.

Hablar

7 Mira las imágenes y, con tu compañero, practica microdiálogos, como en el ejemplo.

1 ■ (Miguel / libros)
● ¿poesía?

■ (yo / cámara)
● ¿fotografía?
■ *Esta soy yo con mi cámara.*
● *¿Eres aficionada a la fotografía?*

2 ■ (nosotros / guitarras)
● ¿música?

3 ■ (Sara / cuadro)
● ¿arte?

4 ■ (María y Juan / bicicletas)
● ¿deporte?

5 ■ (mis hermanas / raquetas)
● ¿tenis?

¿Qué hora es?

Vocabulario

1 Mira los relojes. ¿Qué hora es?

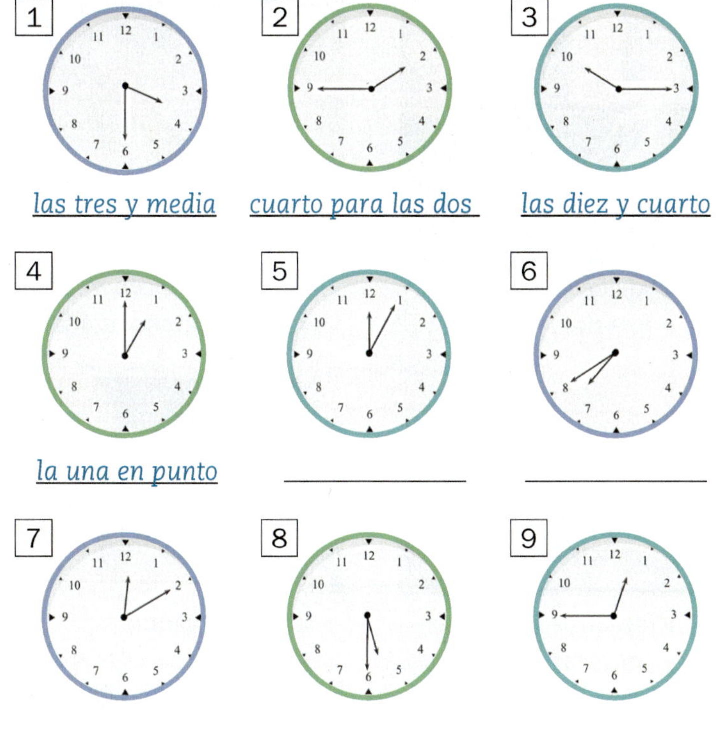

2 Escucha y repite.

3 Dibuja tres horas diferentes en tu cuaderno. En parejas, pregunta y di las horas.

- *Disculpe, ¿qué hora es?*
- *Son las siete veinte.*

Comunicación

- **Las comidas**
  desayunar - comer - cenar
- **Abrir / Cerrar**
  - *En México los bancos **abren** por la mañana, pero **cierran** por la tarde.*
  - *Los antros **abren** por la noche.*
  - *Muchos comercios no **cierran** a mediodía.*

Leer

4 Lee el texto y señala con V lo que es igual en tu país y con X lo que es diferente.

Horarios

1 En Noruega la gente come a las cinco de la tarde. ☐
2 En Senegal cenan a las ocho o las ocho y media de la noche. ☐
3 En México los bancos no abren por la tarde. ☐
4 En España la gente come a las dos de la tarde. ☐
5 Los españoles cenan a las diez de la noche. ☐
6 En Estados Unidos muchas tiendas abren por la noche. ☐
7 En Francia los restaurantes abren a mediodía. ☐
8 En Brasil los bancos abren a las diez de la mañana. ☐
9 En el Reino Unido las farmacias cierran a las cinco de la tarde. ☐
10 En España la mayoría de los comercios cierran de dos a cinco de la tarde. ☐

5 Habla con tu compañero y compara las afirmaciones anteriores con lo que ocurre en tu país.

- *En Noruega comen a las cinco de la tarde y en mi país también.*
- *En Noruega comen a las cinco de la tarde, pero en mi país comemos a la una.*

Vocabulario

6 Relaciona.

1 sesenta segundos
2 veinticuatro horas
3 siete días
4 doce meses
5 sesenta minutos
6 cien años
7 una década

a una hora
b una semana
c un minuto
d un día
e diez años
f un año
g un siglo

Escuchar

7 22 Escucha y completa con las palabras del recuadro.

cuarenta • noventa • setenta • seiscientos/as
cuatrocientos/as • trescientos/as • veinticuatro
cincuenta y dos • ciento once

21	veintiuno	90	______
22	veintidós	100	cien
23	veintitrés	103	ciento tres*
24	______	111	______
30	treinta	200	doscientos/as
31	treinta y uno	300	______
40	______	400	______
50	cincuenta	500	quinientos/as
52	______	600	______
60	sesenta	1000	mil
70	______	2000	dos mil**
80	ochenta	5000	cinco mil

* Cuando *cien* va seguido de unidades y decenas se dice *ciento, ciento uno, ciento dos...*

** No decimos *dos miles*.

8 23 Escucha y señala el número que oyes.

a 2 / 12
b 25 / 35
c 90 / 50
d 37 / 67
e 623 / 323
f 135 / 125
g 830 / 850
h 1589 / 1389
i 1988 / 1998
j 1975 / 1985

9 24 Escucha y escribe el número.

1 edad de la niña: 12 años.
2 precio de las naranjas: ______.
3 precio del paquete de café: ______.
4 año de nacimiento: ______.
5 distancia entre Monterrey y Guadalajara: ______ km.
6 precio del café y la cerveza: ______.
7 hora: ______.
8 páginas del libro: ______.
9 días del mes de marzo: ______.
10 número de la calle: ______.

Pronunciación y ortografía

Acentuación

1 25 Escucha.

teléfono lápiz ventana hotel
profesor hermano familia música

2 25 Escucha otra vez y repite. Observa las sílabas fuertes.

3 26 Escucha estas palabras y subraya la sílaba fuerte.

profesora español café gramática mesa
vivir hablar médico autobús Pilar alemán
brasileña familia libro examen

4 Escribe las palabras de la actividad anterior en la columna correspondiente.

música	ventana	hotel

Leer

1 Lee y señala verdadero (V) o falso (F).

La familia iberoamericana

Cuando una persona de España o Hispanoamérica habla de su familia, no habla solamente de sus padres y de sus hermanos, habla también de sus abuelos, de sus tíos, de sus primos y de otros parientes.

Además, las reuniones familiares son frecuentes. Todos se juntan para celebrar las fiestas más importantes, como los cumpleaños, la Navidad, el día del Padre y el día de la Madre. Ese día comen todos en una casa o en un restaurante.

Por otro lado, en algunos países de Hispanoamérica es normal celebrar el día en que las jóvenes cumplen quince años de una manera especial. Les hacen muchos regalos y toda la familia y amigos van a comer a un restaurante.

1 La familia iberoamericana está compuesta de padres e hijos. [F]
2 Las familias españolas e hispanoamericanas se reúnen muchas veces. ☐
3 Las celebraciones familiares siempre se hacen en un restaurante. ☐
4 El día de la Madre es una fiesta muy popular en México. ☐
5 Las jóvenes hispanoamericanas se casan a los quince años. ☐

2 Lee el siguiente texto.

Dos apellidos

En la mayoría de los países hispanoamericanos, todas las personas tienen dos apellidos. Normalmente el primero es el apellido del padre y el segundo es el de la madre. Estos dos apellidos aparecen en todos los documentos y no cambian al casarse, son para toda la vida.

¿Cuáles son los apellidos de Santiago?

Me llamo Santiago. Mi papá se llama Enrique Lozano Linares y mi mamá Luisa Pardo Pérez.

Santiago ____________ ____________

3 Lee los textos otra vez y contesta a las preguntas.

1 ¿Qué personas forman parte de una familia iberoamericana?
2 ¿Para qué se reúnen las familias iberoamericanas? ¿Cómo son sus celebraciones?
3 ¿Cómo se celebra en algunos países hispanoamericanos el cumpleaños de las niñas de quince años?
4 ¿Qué apellidos tienen las personas en la mayoría de los países hispanoamericanos?

Hablar

4 Comenta con tus compañeros.

- ¿Cuántos apellidos tienes?
- ¿Cambia en tu país el apellido de las mujeres cuando se casan?
- ¿Te parece bien la costumbre de tener dos apellidos?

Yo tengo un apellido y...

Escribir

5 Dibuja el árbol genealógico de tu familia. Después escribe un pequeño texto y comenta cómo se llaman, quiénes son, cuántos años tienen, dónde viven y en qué época del año se reúnen para las celebraciones familiares.

Escuchar

6 (27) Escucha y completa.

Dos de los actores españoles más famosos en el mundo son Penélope Cruz y su [1] __________, Javier Bardem. Mónica, la [2] __________ de Penélope, y Pilar y Carlos, la [3] __________ y el [4] ________ de Javier, también son actores.

La familia Alcántara celebra la primera comunión de su [5] ________ María. Junto a la niña están sus [6] ________, Antonio y Merche, sus [7] ________, Carlitos y Toni, y su [8] ________, Herminia.

Carolina Herrera, diseñadora de moda, es reconocida internacionalmente. Con su segundo [9] ________, Reinaldo, tiene dos [10] ________. La más pequeña, Adriana, trabaja con ella diseñando vestidos.

Hablar

Alumno A (alumno B, ver «En parejas», pág. 172)

7 Pregunta a B dónde están los objetos del recuadro.

¿Dónde están los lentes?

8 Responde a B dónde están sus objetos.

El celular está al lado de la computadora.

2 AUTOEVALUACIÓN

1 Relaciona.

1 ¿Dónde está mi pluma?
2 ¿Eres casado?
3 ¿Tienes hijos?
4 ¿Cuántos hermanos tienes?
5 ¿Qué hora es?
6 ¿A qué hora comen en tu país?

a No, soy soltero.
b Tres.
c Encima de la mesa.
d Sí, una niña.
e A la una.
f Cuarto para las dos.

2 Escribe los números.

a 27 *veintisiete*
b 52 ______
c 116 ______
d 238 ______
e 456 ______
f 510 ______
g 1987 ______
h 2003 ______
i 2999 ______
j 4100 ______

3 Escribe en plural.

1 Este hotel es muy caro.
Estos hoteles son muy caros.
2 Mi hermana es casada.
______
3 Mi hermano tiene un hijo.
______ dos ______
4 Mi compañero es japonés.
______
5 Esta maestra es simpática.
______
6 Este libro no es interesante.
______
7 Este maestro no es mexicano.
______
8 Esta joven es soltera.
______
9 Mi gato es joven.
______
10 ¿Tu padre es mexicano?
______

4 Completa con los verbos *estar* o *tener*.

1 Los tenis *están* debajo de la silla.
2 Marieli ______ dos hijos.
3 Mi hermano ______ novia.
4 Yo no ______ abuelos.
5 ¿Carmen y Ana ______ hermanos?
6 ¿Dónde ______ la carpeta roja?
7 Mi esposo no ______ en casa.
8 Nosotros no ______ carro.
9 Luis y Pepe ______ trabajo.

5 28 Escucha y escribe las horas de salida y llegada de los autobuses.

SALIDAS			
autobús	andén	destino	hora
ADO	3	Michoacán	______
Del Norte	6	Ciudad de México	______
ETN	2	Guadalajara	______
LLEGADAS			
autobús	andén	procedencia	hora
ETN	11	Guadalajara	______
Flecha Roja	8	Querétaro	______
Del Norte	4	Colima	______

¿Qué sabes?

- Hablar de la familia.
- Formar el plural de los nombres.
- Decir dónde están las cosas.
- Preguntar y decir la hora.
- Contar hasta 5000.

El trabajo

·· Hablar de rutinas diarias

·· Hablar del trabajo: lugar, profesión y horario

·· Pedir un desayuno

·· **Cultura**: El trabajo y los horarios

Rosa se levanta a las siete

Vocabulario

1 Relaciona las frases con los dibujos.

1 Carlos y Ana se casan. [C]
2 Roberto se afeita todos los días. [ ]
3 Rosa se levanta a las siete. [ ]
4 Mercedes se baña. [ ]
5 Mis vecinos se acuestan temprano. [ ]

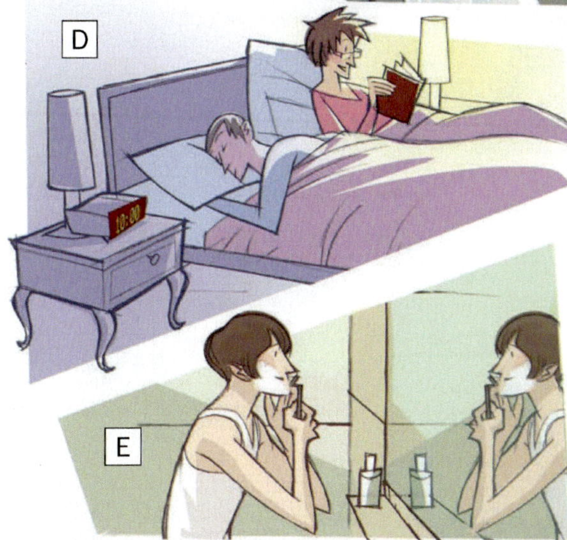

Comunicación

Temprano / Tarde

■ *Los lunes me levanto muy **temprano**, a las seis de la mañana.*
● *¿Y los domingos?*
■ *Los domingos me levanto muy **tarde**, a las 11 o las 12.*

2 Responde.

1 ¿A qué hora te levantas?
2 ¿A qué hora te acuestas?

Gramática

VERBOS REFLEXIVOS

		levantarse	acostarse*
yo	**me**	levanto	acuesto
tú	**te**	levantas	acuestas
él / ella / Ud.	**se**	levanta	acuesta
nosotros/as	**nos**	levantamos	acostamos
vosotros/as	**os**	levantáis	acostáis
ellos / ellas / Uds.	**se**	levantan	acuestan

* Verbo irregular

3 Completa la siguiente conversación con los verbos del recuadro.

levantarse • acostarse • bañarse

■ Y tú, Juan, ¿a qué hora *te levantas*?
● Bueno, yo ____ ________ temprano, a las seis, más o menos, ____ ________ rápidamente y tomo café.
■ Y tu esposa, ¿a qué hora ____ ________?
● Pues a las siete. Ella también ____ ________ más tarde, como a las doce de la noche.
■ ¿Y tus hijos?
● Ellos cenan, ven un poco la tele y ____ ________ temprano, a las diez.
■ ¿Y a qué hora ____ ________?
● A las siete, porque entran a la escuela a las ocho.
■ ¿Y los fines de semana también ________ ________ todos temprano?
● ¡Ah, no!, claro que no, los domingos ________ ________ más tarde, a las nueve, porque, claro, también ____ ________ más tarde.

4 29 Escucha y comprueba.

PRESENTE DE VERBOS IRREGULARES			
empezar	volver	ir	salir
empiezo	vuelvo	voy	salgo
empiezas	vuelves	vas	sales
empieza	vuelve	va	sale
empezamos	volvemos	vamos	salimos
empezáis	volvéis	vais	salís
empiezan	vuelven	van	salen

5 Forma frases.

1 Carmen / empezar / su trabajo / a las ocho.
Carmen empieza su trabajo a las ocho.
2 ¿A qué hora / empezar / la película?
3 Mi papá / ir / al trabajo / en carro.
4 Yo / volver / a mi casa / a las siete.
5 ¿Cuándo / volver / de vacaciones tus hermanos?
6 ¿Ir (ustedes) / a casa de la abuela?
7 ¿Cómo / ir (tú) / al trabajo?
8 ¿Ir (ustedes) / a la escuela / en transporte escolar?
9 ¿A qué hora / salir (tú) / de casa?
10 ¿A qué hora / empezar / las clases?

PREPOSICIONES DE TIEMPO

Días

El lunes Hoy El sábado	**en**	la mañana la tarde la noche

Yo solo trabajo ***en*** *la mañana.*
Julia se baña ***en*** *la tarde.*
Los sábados ***en*** *la noche vamos al antro.*

Horas

Son A	las diez las cinco las tres	**de**	la mañana la tarde la noche la madrugada

Se levanta ***a*** *las seis* ***de*** *la mañana.*
Ella trabaja ***desde*** *las ocho* ***hasta*** *las cinco.*
Ella trabaja ***de*** *ocho* ***a*** *tres.*
Hoy ***en*** *la tarde no tengo clase.*
El sábado ***en*** *la noche vamos* ***a*** *la disco.*

Comunicación

Cuantificadores

- *Todos los meseros del hotel hablan inglés.*
- *La mayoría de los españoles se acuesta tarde.*
- *Muchas personas en el mundo estudian español.*
- *Algunos alumnos van a la escuela en camión.*

6 Lee el artículo y contesta a las preguntas.

Escuela Provincial de *Ballet* Alejo Carpentier (La Habana, Cuba)

En esta escuela estudian los alumnos desde los nueve hasta los catorce años. El ritmo de trabajo es muy duro, tienen clase en la mañana y en la tarde. En la mañana, las clases empiezan a las siete y cuarto todos los días, y algunos alumnos se levantan a las cinco de la mañana. Las clases de baile terminan a las doce, y a esa hora los alumnos van a otra escuela que está cerca. Allí estudian las mismas asignaturas (Lengua, Matemáticas, Geografía, etc.) que los demás niños de su edad. Terminan las clases a las seis de la tarde y a veces vuelven otra vez a la escuela de *ballet*, hasta las ocho.

(Texto adaptado de «El milagro cubano», de Mauricio Vicent para *El País*).

1 ¿Cuántas horas de *ballet* tienen cada día?
2 ¿Estudian en la misma escuela otras asignaturas?
3 ¿Qué edad tienen los alumnos de esta escuela?
4 ¿A qué hora terminan las clases por la tarde?

7 Lee el texto otra vez y completa las frases con las preposiciones del recuadro.

a • de • desde • hasta • en

1 En esta escuela estudian los niños ________ los nueve ________ los catorce años.
2 Algunos alumnos se levantan muy temprano, ________ las cinco ________ la mañana.
3 ________ la mañana, los niños están en la escuela de *ballet* ________ las siete y cuarto ________ las doce.
4 En la escuela de *ballet* los alumnos tienen clase ________ la mañana y ________ la tarde.
5 Los alumnos de *ballet* van a otra escuela ____ las doce ____ las seis de la tarde.
6 Por la tarde, las clases de *ballet* son ____ las ocho.

¿Estudias o trabajas?

- *Hablar del trabajo: lugar, profesión y horario*

Leer

1 Escribe los días de la semana en el orden adecuado.

martes **lunes** **jueves** **sábado** **viernes** **domingo** **miércoles**

1. ________ 2. ________ 3. ________ 4. ________ 5. ________ 6. ________ 7. ________

¿Qué día es hoy?

2 30 Lee y escucha los textos de Lucía y Carlos.

Lucía es técnica de sonido y trabaja en una emisora de radio, la Cadena Día. Tiene veintinueve años y no es casada. Vive en Querétaro, y habla inglés y francés perfectamente. Todos los días trabaja de ocho a cinco, menos los sábados y domingos. Los días laborables se levanta a las seis y sale de casa a las siete y media. Va al trabajo en camión. Los sábados en la noche sale con sus amigos a cenar y a bailar, por eso se acuesta muy tarde, a las tres o cuatro de la mañana.

Carlos es bombero. Trabaja en el municipio de Xochimilco. Vive lejos del trabajo, por eso toma el metro todos los días. Tiene treinta y cuatro años, es casado y no tiene hijos. Trabaja en turnos de veinticuatro horas, un día sí y otro no. Si trabaja el sábado o el domingo, después tiene dos días libres. Siempre se levanta muy temprano, a las seis o a las siete de la mañana, por eso normalmente no sale en las noches. Cena a las ocho, después ve la tele y a las diez y media se acuesta.

3 Lee otra vez y completa las frases.

Lucía

1 Lucía *es* técnica de sonido.
2 Trabaja _____ ocho _____ cinco.
3 Normalmente ________________ a las seis.
4 ________ al trabajo ________ camión.
5 Los sábados ________ la noche ________ con sus amigos.
6 Los sábados ________ muy tarde.

Carlos

1 Carlos *vive* lejos del trabajo.
2 No ______________ hijos.
3 Se levanta muy ______________, ____ las seis o ______ las siete ____ la mañana.
4 Carlos normalmente no ____________ en las noches y ______________ a las diez y media.

Hablar

4 Escribe las siguientes preguntas y luego pregunta a tu compañero. Toma nota de sus respuestas.

1 ¿Hora / levantarse / normalmente?
¿A qué hora te levantas normalmente?
2 ¿Hora / empezar las clases o el trabajo?
3 ¿Hora / terminar las clases o el trabajo?
4 ¿Hora / llegar a casa?
5 ¿Cómo / ir a la escuela o al trabajo?
6 ¿Hacer / después de cenar?
7 ¿Cuándo / ver / la televisión?
8 ¿Bañarse en la mañana o en la noche?
9 ¿Hora / acostarse / normalmente?
10 ¿Hora / levantarse / los domingos?
11 ¿Hora / acostarse / los sábados?
12 ¿Salir / los sábados en la noche?

Escribir

5 Escribe un párrafo sobre la vida de tu compañero.

Michael es ____________,
trabaja en ____________.
Va al trabajo en ____________.

Vocabulario

6 ¿Dónde trabajan? Escribe cada profesión en la columna correspondiente.

doctor/a • estudiante • enfermero/a • cajero/a
ingeniero en sistemas computacionales • chef
secretario/a • maestro/a • vendedor/a • mesero/a

hospital	universidad	oficina

supermercado	restaurante

7 ¿Qué hace? Relaciona las dos columnas.

1 El / La vendedor/a
2 El / La recepcionista
3 El / La auxiliar de vuelo
4 El / La enfermero/a
5 El / La profesor/a
6 El / La chef
7 El / La mesero/a
8 El / La cajero/a

a hace la comida.
b cuida enfermos.
c cobra a los clientes.
d atiende a los clientes.
e enseña a los alumnos.
f atiende a los pasajeros.
g recibe a los turistas.
h vende ropa.

Hablar

8 Piensa en tres o cuatro personas conocidas y comenta con tus compañeros a qué se dedican, dónde trabajan, qué hacen...

Ángel es vendedor, trabaja en una tienda departamental, vende muebles...

9 En grupos de cuatro. Uno representa con mímica una profesión y el resto adivina de qué profesión se trata.

3c ¿Qué desayunas?

▪ *Pedir un desayuno*

Vocabulario

1 ¿Qué tomas en el desayuno?

- ☐ leche
- ☐ café (con leche)
- ☐ té (con limón)
- ☐ chocolate
- ☐ jugo de frutas
- ☐ ________________

2 Ahora escribe la letra correspondiente.

1 té ☐
2 café con leche ☐
3 jugo de naranja ☐
4 mantecadas ☐
5 cereales ☐
6 leche ☐
7 huevo ☐
8 queso ☐
9 pan con mermelada ☐

Escuchar

3 31 Escucha a estas cuatro personas de diferentes países hablar de su desayuno y completa la tabla.

	NACIONALIDAD	DESAYUNO
1 Philip	*alemán*	*pan con mantequilla y salami y un huevo, o muesli con yogur, y té o café*
2 Claudia		
3 Elizabeth		
4 Manuel		

4 En grupos. Cada uno cuenta qué desayuna normalmente y qué los domingos.

Yo, normalmente, solo desayuno café con leche y pan dulce, pero los domingos almuerzo huevos con jamón y tomo jugo de naranja, además del café con leche, claro.

Vocabulario

Escuchar

5 Ordena el siguiente diálogo.

Mesera:	Buenos días, ¿qué desean?	☐
Hijo:	Yo solo quiero un jugo.	☐
Mamá:	Yo quiero un desayuno ranchero, ¿y tú, hijo?	☐
Hijo:	No, mamá, solo quiero un jugo de naranja.	☐
Mamá:	Come algo más: un pan dulce o un pan tostado.	☐
Mamá:	Bueno, pues un desayuno ranchero y un jugo de naranja.	☐
Mesera:	Muy bien.	☐

6 (32) Escucha y comprueba.

Hablar

7 En grupos de tres. Fíjate en la carta de la Cafetería Tía Chole y practica otras conversaciones. Uno es el mesero y los otros dos van a desayunar o merendar.

- ■ *¿Qué desean?*
- ● *Un desayuno continental, por favor.*
- ▼ *Yo, un café con leche y pan tostado con mantequilla y mermelada.*

Pronunciación y ortografía

g / gu

1  (33) Escucha y repite.

gato agua gota guerra guion

¿Qué sonido se repite en todas las palabras?

> El sonido /g/ se escribe **g** antes de **a**, **o** y se escribe ***gu*** antes de **e**, **i**.

2 Completa con *g* o *gu*.

1 __uapo
2 ci__arrillos
3 __itarra
4 __astar
5 pa__ar
6 __erra
7 __uatemala
8 __oma

3 (34) Escucha y repite.

- ¿Cuántas horas al día trabajan las personas en tu país?
- ¿Cuántos días a la semana trabajan?
- ¿Cuánto tiempo tienen de vacaciones?

Leer

1 Lee este texto.

EL TRABAJO Y LOS HORARIOS

El desayuno de los mexicanos normalmente es fuerte en comparación con otros países. Consiste en un platillo de huevos preparados de distintas formas, frijoles refritos, tortillas y salsa. También son comunes los tacos de diferentes tipos de guisos; los chilaquiles (totopos guisados con salsa de tomate, acompañados con queso), los molletes (mitades de bolillo con mantequilla, frijoles refritos y queso derretido) y el menudo. Algunos prefieren un desayuno ligero con café, leche o chocolate con pan dulce, pan tostado o cereal.
La comida se hace normalmente entre la una y las tres de la tarde, como en la mayoría de los países latinoamericanos.
Para la comida principal del día, algunos restaurantes tienen "menús ejecutivos", que resultan más baratos que pedir a la carta, aunque mucha gente se lleva su propia comida al trabajo. A diferencia de otros países, algunas empresas grandes tienen sus propios comedores, ahí proporcionan a sus empleados una comida gratis o a un costo muy bajo.
La cena se hace entre las siete y las nueve de la noche aproximadamente.
La mayoría de las tiendas y los negocios tienen horario corrido, están abiertas todo el día. Abren a las nueve de la mañana y cierran a las ocho de la noche. Algunos supermercados, farmacias y tiendas de conveniencia están abiertos 24 horas al día.

2 Ahora contesta verdadero (V) o falso (F).

1 Los mexicanos nunca desayunan ligero. ☐
2 La mayoría de los mexicanos come en restaurantes. ☐
3 El horario de las comidas de los mexicanos es igual que el de los demás países latinoamericanos. ☐
4 Los mexicanos cenan bastante tarde. ☐
5 La mayoría de los negocios mexicanos tienen horario corrido. ☐
6 Algunos mexicanos comen en sus centros de trabajo. ☐

Hablar

3 Comenta con tu compañero.

1 ¿A qué hora se levanta la gente en tu país?
2 ¿A qué hora se acuesta?
3 ¿Cuál es el desayuno típico?
4 ¿Cuál es la comida más importante del día?
5 ¿A qué hora cenan?
6 ¿Qué horario tienen las tiendas?

Escuchar

4 (35) Adriana es argentina y nos habla de la vida en Buenos Aires. Escucha y contesta a las preguntas.

1 ¿A qué hora se levantan en Buenos Aires?
2 ¿A qué hora almuerzan* normalmente?
3 ¿Qué horario tienen las tiendas?
4 ¿Abren los bancos por la tarde?
5 ¿A qué hora cenan?
6 ¿Estudian los niños por la mañana y por la tarde?

* En Argentina el almuerzo equivale a la comida en México (el almuerzo en México es una comida ligera en la mañana, consiste en huevo o platillos regionales. Se acompaña con café, jugo o leche).

Escribir

5 Escribe un párrafo sobre tu rutina diaria. Para ello, utiliza los verbos del recuadro.

levantarse • bañarse • desayunar
empezar • terminar • comer • volver
cenar • acostarse • salir

Yo me levanto a las ________. Me baño ________. Salgo de casa ________.

Escuchar

6 (36) Escucha y completa.

Susana [1] se levanta normalmente a las siete, [2] ____ ________, se viste, [3] ________ algo rápido y sale de casa a las [4] ________.
Su trabajo empieza a las nueve. Primero va al súper y después prepara la [5] ________ para unas treinta personas.

¿Sabes a qué se dedica?

Es [6] ____________.

Emilio [7] ____ ________ tarde porque no trabaja en la mañana. Desayuna café con leche y dos [8] ________ mientras lee el periódico. Come temprano porque [9] ________ de casa a las tres.
Va a la [10] ________ en metro. Sus clases [11] ________ a las cuatro y terminan a las ocho de la noche.

¿Sabes a qué se dedica?

Es [12] ____________.

Jaime se levanta [13] ________ temprano porque prepara el [14] ________ de sus hijos y los lleva a la escuela. Después va en [15] ________ a su trabajo, que está a las afueras de la ciudad. [16] ________ en una gran tienda departamental atendiendo a los clientes. Su [17] ________ es de ocho de la mañana a seis de la tarde.
Cuando sale del trabajo, recoge a los [18] ________ y los lleva a casa.

¿Sabes a qué se dedica?

Es [19] ____________.

Hablar

Alumno A (alumno B, ver «En parejas», pág 173)

7 Pregunta a B y completa la siguiente ficha.

NOMBRE:	________
EDAD:	________
TRABAJO:	________
PAÍS:	________
CIUDAD:	________
LUGAR DE TRABAJO:	________
TRANSPORTE:	________
FAMILIA:	________

8 Responde a las preguntas de B.

NOMBRE:	Elena Boschmonar
EDAD:	28 años
TRABAJO:	Azafata
PAÍS:	Uruguay
CIUDAD:	Montevideo
LUGAR DE TRABAJO:	Aerolíneas
TRANSPORTE:	Camión de la empresa
FAMILIA:	Soltera. Vive con sus padres

3 AUTOEVALUACIÓN

1 Relaciona.

1 ¿A qué te dedicas?
2 ¿Qué horario tienes?
3 ¿Tienes algún día libre?
4 ¿Dónde trabajas?
5 ¿Cómo vas al trabajo?
6 ¿Eres casado?
7 ¿Cuántos años tienes?

a Soy bombero.
b En el Municipio.
c Sí, los domingos.
d No, soy soltero.
e Trabajo de 8 a 5.
f 37.
g Voy en metro.

2 Escribe el verbo.

1 empezar (él): *empieza*
2 volver (yo): ____________________
3 ir (nosotros): ____________________
4 empezar (ustedes): ____________________
5 ir (ellos): ____________________
6 volver (usted): ____________________
7 volver (tú): ____________________

3 Completa con el verbo entre paréntesis en presente de indicativo.

1 Pepe *se baña* con agua fría. (bañarse)
2 Celia ____ ____________ a las once y media. (acostarse)
3 ■ ¿Tú ____ ____________ todos los días? (afeitarse)
● No, solo los domingos.
4 Ana ____ ____________ todos los días. (maquillarse)
5 Mi hija tiene seis años y ya ____ ____________ sola. (vestirse)
6 ¿A qué hora ____ ____________ ustedes los domingos? (acostarse)
7 Luis y Rosa ____ ____________ muy temprano. (levantarse)
8 ¿A qué hora ____ ____________ tú? (levantarse)
9 Yo ____ ____________ en la noche. (bañarse)

4 Completa con la preposición adecuada (*a, de, desde, en, hasta*).

1 Yo empiezo a trabajar *a* las ocho *de* la mañana.
2 José no trabaja ________ la tarde.
3 Paloma trabaja ________ las ocho ________ las tres.
4 Los domingos ________ la mañana voy al parque.
5 Los sábados ______ la noche voy al antro.
6 Mi esposo regresa ______ casa ______ las ocho ______ la noche.
7 Mi hija va ______ la escuela ______ la mañana y ______ la tarde.

5 Ordena el siguiente diálogo.

[1] ■ Buenos días, ¿qué desean?
[ ] ◆ No, no, no me gusta.
[ ] ◆ Yo un jugo de naranja y un sándwich de jamón y queso.
[ ] ● ¿No quieres café?
[ ] ● Yo quiero un café con leche y pan tostado, ¿y tú?
[ ] ■ Muy bien.

6 Completa con el verbo entre paréntesis en presente de indicativo.

Los horarios de los mexicanos que viven en las zonas rurales (1) _______ (ser) diferentes de aquellos que viven en la ciudad. La mayoría (2) _______ (levantarse) entre las seis y las siete de la mañana y (3) _______ (acostarse) entre las once y las doce de la noche. Muchos de ellos dicen que no (4) _______ (dormir) lo necesario porque apenas superan las seis horas de sueño.

En las grandes ciudades la distancia entre la casa y el trabajo (5) _______ (ser) bastante grande, por eso la mayoría (6) _______ (ir) al trabajo en transporte público (metro o camión). En general, los mexicanos (7) _______ (perder) entre noventa y ciento veinte minutos al día solo para ir al trabajo y regresar a casa.

Los niños mexicanos (8) _______ (tener) muchas veces los mismos problemas que sus padres porque también (9) _______ (acostarse) más tarde y (10) _______ (dormir) menos horas de las necesarias. Los escuelas públicas mexicanas normalmente (11) _______ (empezar) a las siete treinta de la mañana, (12) _______ (tener) una pausa para comer algo ligero a las diez, y (13) _______ (terminar) las clases a las doce treinta.

¿Qué sabes?

	😊	😐	☹
• Hablar de rutinas.	☐	☐	☐
• Hablar de horarios.	☐	☐	☐
• Pedir un desayuno.	☐	☐	☐
• Hablar de profesiones y del lugar de trabajo.	☐	☐	☐
• Los verbos reflexivos.	☐	☐	☐
• Las preposiciones *en / de / a / hasta / desde*.	☐	☐	☐

La casa

- Describir las partes de una casa
- Nombres de los muebles y electrodomésticos
- Indicar el lugar y la existencia
- Hacer una reservación en un hotel
- **Cultura**: Tipos de vivienda en México

4A ¿Dónde vives?

- *Describir las partes de una casa*

Vocabulario

1 ¿Dónde vives?

- ☐ En un departamento.
- ☐ En una casa.
- ☐ En un estudio.
- ☐ En un loft.
- ☐ En un penthouse.
- ☐ ____________________

2 37 Lee y escucha.

Rosa y Miguel tienen una tienda de ropa en el centro de la Ciudad de México. Tienen dos hijos y viven en las afueras de la ciudad en una casa de dos plantas.

En la planta baja hay un recibidor, una cocina con un pequeño comedor, una sala grande y un medio baño.

En la planta de arriba hay tres recámaras y un cuarto de baño. La casa tiene también un jardín pequeño.

3 Lee las frases y escribe verdadero (V) o falso (F).

1. Rosa y Miguel trabajan en las afueras de la Ciudad de México. F
2. Viven al lado de su tienda. ☐
3. La cocina está en la planta baja. ☐
4. La sala es muy grande. ☐
5. La casa tiene una cochera. ☐
6. En la planta baja hay tres recámaras. ☐
7. Las recámaras están en el piso de arriba. ☐
8. No hay jardín. ☐
9. Hay un medio baño en la planta baja. ☐
10. La sala está en la planta de arriba. ☐

4 38 Completa la siguiente conversación de Rosa con su amiga Laura. Después, escucha y comprueba.

Laura: ¿Cuántas [1] ____________ tiene tu casa?
Rosa: Dos. Es una vivienda unifamiliar.
Laura: ¿Dónde está el [2] ____________?
Rosa: En la planta de arriba. Y en la planta baja hay un medio baño.
Laura: ¿Tiene [3] ____________?
Rosa: Sí, uno pequeño, al lado de la cocina.
Laura: ¿Cuántas [4] ____________ tiene?
Rosa: Tres, están todas en la planta de arriba.
Laura: ¿Tienen [5] ____________?
Rosa: No, nos estacionamos en la calle.

5 🔘39 Escucha a Manuel hablar de su casa. Contesta a las preguntas.

1 ¿Cómo es el departamento de Manuel?
2 ¿Cuántas recámaras tiene?
3 ¿Dónde está el cuarto de baño?
4 ¿Tiene terraza? ¿Cómo es?

6 En parejas. Habla con tu compañero sobre tu casa: cuántas habitaciones tiene, dónde están... Dibuja en tu cuaderno el plano.

7 Escribe la descripción de la casa de tu compañero y utiliza el vocabulario del recuadro.

sala • comedor • cocina • jardín
cuarto de baño • recámara • cochera

La casa de ____________ es pequeña / grande. Tiene ____________ recámaras.

Gramática

8 🔘40 Escucha y repite.

NÚMEROS ORDINALES			
1.º / 1.ª	primero/a	6.º / 6.ª	sexto/a
2.º / 2.ª	segundo/a	7.º / 7.ª	séptimo/a
3.º / 3.ª	tercero/a	8.º / 8.ª	octavo/a
4.º / 4.ª	cuarto/a	9.º / 9.ª	noveno/a
5.º / 5.ª	quinto/a	10.º / 10.ª	décimo/a

Comunicación

Los ordinales **primero** y **tercero** pierden la *-o* delante de un nombre masculino singular.

piso primero / primer piso
piso tercero / tercer piso

■ *¿Es la primera vez que estudias en esta facultad?*
● *No... Es el **tercer** año que repito este curso.*

■ *Vivo en el **primer** piso.*
● *Y yo en el **tercero**.*

9 Completa las frases con un adjetivo del recuadro.

primera • tercera • quinto • segundo • ~~primer~~

1 El elevador está en el *primer* piso.
2 ■ ¿Luis, tú qué estudias?
● Estoy en ____________ de Economía.
3 ¡Qué impresionante! Es la ____________ vez que veo el mar.
4 Nosotras somos tres hermanas, yo soy la ____________.
5 El departamento de contabilidad está en el ____________ piso.

10 🔘41 Escucha y completa.

	PISO	PUERTA
1 Sr. González	*4.º*	*derecha*
2 Sra. Rodríguez		
3 Srta. Herrero		
4 Sr. Acedo		
5 Sr. de la Fuente		
6 Sres. Barroso		

11 Pregunta y contesta a cuatro compañeros, según el modelo.

■ *¿En qué departamento vives?*
● *En el cuarto a la derecha.*

- *Nombres de los muebles y electrodomésticos*
- *Indicar el lugar y la existencia*

a vitrocerámica
b lavavajillas
c fregadero
d lavadora
e gabinete
f refrigerador
g horno
h microondas
i mesa
j silla

a sofá
b sillón
c mesa de centro
d librero
e equipo de música
f televisión (TV)
g lámpara
h cojín
i tapete

a lavabo
b gabinete
c espejo
d toalla
e tina

Vocabulario

1 Fíjate en las fotos y completa con las palabras de los recuadros.

Esta es mi casa

Mi cocina es grande y luminosa y tenemos un (1) refrigerador nuevo. Al lado hay un (2) __________ y debajo de este hay un (3) __________. Hay muchos (4) __________ y una (5) __________ con (6) __________ para desayunar.

En la sala-comedor tenemos un (7) sofá muy cómodo y dos (8) __________ pequeños. Los libros están en un (9) __________ de madera que hay junto a una planta. En el centro de la sala hay una (10) __________ y un (11) __________ blanco.

El cuarto de baño es bastante grande también. Hay una (12) tina y un gabinete. El (13) __________ está encima del (14) __________.

2 Completa las frases con la forma correcta de los verbos del recuadro.

escuchar • guardar • ver • lavarse
bañarse • dormir • calentar
comer • ~~hacer~~ • leer

1 En la cocina tú haces la comida.
2 En el cuarto de baño tú ___ __________.
3 En la sala tú __________ la televisión.
4 En el comedor tú __________.
5 En la recámara tú __________.
6 En la sala tú __________ música.
7 En los gabinetes de la cocina tú __________ los platos y las tazas.
8 En el cuarto de baño tú ___ __________ los dientes.
9 En la sala tú __________ los libros de lectura.
10 En el microondas tú __________ la comida.

ARTÍCULOS

Determinados: el / la / los / las

- Para algo que conocemos.
  *¿Dónde está **el** gato?*

Indeterminados: un / una / unos / unas

- Para algo que mencionamos por primera vez.
  *Hay **un** gato en el jardín.*

3 Señala el artículo más adecuado.

1 *La* / *Una* computadora está en mi recámara.
2 En mi clase hay *un* / *el* mapa del mundo.
3 ¿Hay *la* / *una* película buena en la tele?
4 *Los* / *Unos* libros están en mi mochila.
5 En el patio hay *unos* / *los* niños.
6 *Las* / *Unas* llaves están en la mesa de la cocina.
7 *La* / *Una* tina está en el cuarto de baño.
8 En la cocina hay *el* / *un* fregadero.

HAY Y ESTÁ(N)

HAY + un, una, unos, unas + nombre
*En el cuarto de baño **hay** una toalla.*

HAY + muchos/as, pocos/as, algunos/as... + nombre
***Hay** muchos gabinetes en la cocina.*

HAY + dos, tres, cuatro ... + nombre
*En la sala **hay** dos sillones.*

HAY + nombre
*¿**Hay** café en la cocina?*

el, la, los, las + nombre + ESTÁ(N)
*El café **está** en el gabinete de la cocina.*

ESTÁ(N) + preposición
*El espejo **está** encima del lavabo.*

ESTÁ + nombre propio
- *¿**Está** Juan?*
- *No, está en casa de sus abuelos.*

4 Completa las frases con *hay* / *está* / *están*.

1 Disculpe, ¿*hay* un supermercado cerca de aquí?
2 Por favor, ¿dónde ________ los cines Ideal?
3 Mañana no ________ clase, es fiesta.
4 No ________ agua en la botella.
5 El comedor ________ al lado de la cocina.
6 ¿Dónde ________ las llaves?
7 ¿________ Jesús en la oficina?
8 ¿________ leche en el refrigerador?

5 Describe qué hay en tu cocina, tu cuarto de baño y tu sala. Compara la descripción con la de tu compañero.

6 (42) Escucha la información sobre las casas en venta y completa la tabla.

	metros	recámaras	baños
1			
2			
3			

7 Observa la fotografía durante treinta segundos.

Ahora cierra el libro y escribe qué cosas hay en la sala y dónde están. Compara tus resultados con los de tus compañeros. ¿Quién tiene más aciertos?

Hay una planta. Está encima de la mesa de centro.

Visita a Cuernavaca

■ *Hacer una reservación en un hotel*

Vocabulario

1 Relaciona las siguientes palabras con los símbolos de las instalaciones del hotel.

1 alberca [e]
2 habitación individual [ ]
3 habitación doble [ ]
4 restaurante [ ]
5 tarjetas de crédito [ ]
6 estacionamiento [ ]

2 43 Escucha y completa el siguiente diálogo.

Recepcionista: Quinta Margarita, ¿dígame?
Carlos: Buenas tardes. ¿Puede decirme si hay habitaciones libres para el próximo fin de semana?
Recepcionista: Sí. ¿Qué desea, una habitación [1] ______________ o [2] ________________ ?
Carlos: Una doble, por favor. ¿Qué precio tiene?
Recepcionista: [3] ________________ por noche más IVA.
Carlos: De acuerdo. ¿Puede hacerme una reservación, por favor?
Recepcionista: ¿Cuántas noches?
Carlos: [4] ______________ y [5] ______________, si es posible.
Recepcionista: No hay problema.
Carlos: ¿Hay [6] ________________?
Recepcionista: Sí, señor, hay una.
Carlos: ¿Admiten tarjetas de crédito?
Recepcionista: Sí, por supuesto.

3 Practica este diálogo con tu compañero.

4 44 Escucha el final del diálogo anterior y completa la ficha de reservación.

HOTEL

Nombre:	*Carlos*
Apellidos:	
Dirección:	
Ciudad:	
N.° de teléfono:	
Sencilla o doble:	
N.° de noches:	

Leer

5 45 Lee y escucha.

Los patios

Los patios son lugares comunes para encontrarse, para jugar, para platicar, para descansar.

Hay muchos tipos de patios: el patio de la escuela, donde los niños pasan el recreo; el patio andaluz, en el sur de España, lleno de macetas con flores, que en verano protege del calor y es un lugar de descanso y de conversación.

En las ciudades hay patios interiores, donde la gente tiende la ropa y habla con los vecinos de enfrente.

En Hispanoamérica muchas casas coloniales conservan bellos patios llenos de plantas tropicales que ayudan a pasar las horas más calurosas del día.

En la ciudad andaluza de Córdoba, el segundo fin de semana de mayo se celebra el Festival de los Patios. Los vecinos abren sus casas, y vecinos y turistas pueden visitar sus hermosos patios.

6 ¿Verdadero (V) o falso (F)?

1 En las escuelas hay un patio. [V]
2 En las ciudades no hay patios. [ ]
3 En los patios coloniales hay plantas tropicales. [ ]
4 Córdoba está en España. [ ]
5 El Festival de los Patios de Córdoba es el 1 de mayo. [ ]
6 Los turistas siempre pueden visitar los patios cordobeses. [ ]

Pronunciación y ortografía

c / qu

1 46 **Escucha y repite.**

queso cuarto **cuanto**
quinto **casa** **comedor**

2 **¿Qué sonido se repite en todas las palabras?**

El sonido /**k**/ se escribe **qu** antes de **e, i** y se escribe **c** antes de **a, o, u**.

3 **Completa con *qu* o *c*.**

1 __uando
2 __ién
3 __uatro
4 tran__ilo
5 __ocina
6 __erer
7 __ímica
8 __omer
9 médi__o
10 E__uador
11 pe__eño
12 __inientos
13 __ampo
14 a__ostarse
15 pelu__ero
16 __uince

A

B

C

D

Hablar

1 ¿En qué lugar puedes encontrar las viviendas que aparecen en las fotos? Coméntalo con tu compañero.

1 En un pueblo. ☐
2 En una ciudad. ☐
3 En la montaña. ☐
4 En la playa. ☐

Leer

2 Lee los textos y relaciónalos con las fotos.

¿En el norte o en el sur?

1 En Guanajuato, en el centro de México, hay casas con arquitectura de la época colonial. Las habitaciones están alrededor de un patio interior, en los pasillos hay columnas con arcos. ☐

2 En el norte de México hay climas áridos, pero también bellas playas. Hay ciudades industriales grandes y modernas. La mayoría de la población vive en casas, pero los jóvenes profesionistas prefieren vivir en departamentos. Los departamentos son modernos, están en edificios con espacios y servicios compartidos, tales como gimnasios, salas para eventos y alberca. ☐

3 En las costas mexicanas hay muchas viviendas destinadas al turismo: pequeñas urbanizaciones de casas y departamentos y grandes hoteles se mezclan con las viviendas tradicionales. ☐

4 En Yucatán y otras partes de México, hay casas tradicionales indígenas, de paja o de adobe, que tienen su origen en las antiguas culturas prehispánicas. Estas casas son sencillas y no intervienen especialistas en su construcción. ☐

3 Completa las frases.

1 Guanajuato está ______________________.
2 En el norte de México hay ______________________.
3 En el norte de México muchos edificios ______________________.
4 En las costas mexicanas hay ______________________.
5 En las ciudades muchos jóvenes profesionistas ______________________.

4 Contesta a las siguientes preguntas.

1 ¿En qué zona de México muchas casas tienen patio?
2 ¿De qué material son las casas del sureste de México?
3 ¿Dónde hay muchos departamentos, casas y hoteles?
4 ¿Dónde vive la mayoría de la población?
5 ¿Dónde se encuentran las casas tradicionales indígenas?

Hablar

5 Imagina que estás de vacaciones en alguna de las diferentes zonas de México. Contesta a las preguntas de tu compañero.

1 ¿En qué parte de México estás?
2 ¿En qué tipo de casa?
3 Describe la casa.

Escribir

6 Escribe un correo electrónico a tu familia o a algún amigo y describe la casa en la que pasas tus vacaciones. Utiliza las ideas de la actividad anterior.

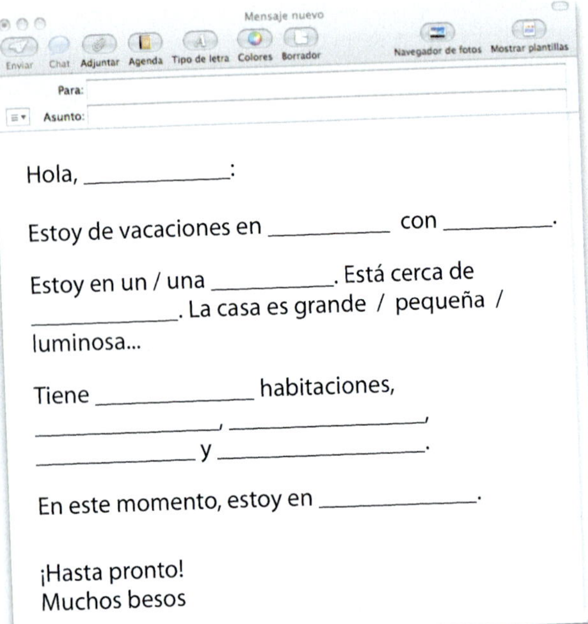

Escuchar

7 47 Escucha la entrevista con Patricia y elige la opción correcta.

1 ¿Con quién pasa Patricia las vacaciones?
   a) Con su esposo y sus hijos.
   b) Con su amigo Juan y su esposa.
   c) Con su esposo, su amigo Juan y su esposa.
2 ¿Dónde se aloja?
   a) En un hotel.
   b) En un campamento.
   c) En su casa.
3 Su casa es:
   a) un unifamiliar.
   b) un departamento.
   c) un estudio.
4 ¿Dónde pasa las vacaciones?
   a) En la montaña.
   b) En la playa.
   c) En un crucero en el mar.
5 Su casa tiene:
   a) tres recámaras y dos baños.
   b) dos baños y dos recámaras.
   c) tres recamaras y un baño.
6 También tiene:
   a) cochera y terraza.
   b) jardín y cochera.
   c) jardín y terraza.

Hablar

Alumno A (alumno B, ver «En parejas», pág. 174)

8 Pregunta a B la información que falta en el anuncio del Hotel Miramar.

1 ¿En qué piso están: *el restaurante, la recepción, la estética, el estacionamiento?*
2 Pregunta el precio de la habitación individual: *¿Cuánto cuesta …?*
3 Pregunta el horario del desayuno: *¿A qué hora se puede desayunar?*

9 Responde a las preguntas de B.

AUTOEVALUACIÓN

1 ¿En qué parte de la casa están normalmente las siguientes cosas?

1 cama: *en la recámara*
2 microondas: ________________
3 sillones: ________________
4 equipo de música: ________________
5 espejo: ________________
6 lavavajillas: ________________
7 tina: ________________
8 televisión: ________________

2 ¿Qué hay en cada habitación?

1 sala-comedor	*sillones,*
2 cocina	
3 recámara	
4 cuarto de baño	

3 Completa la siguiente serie de ordinales.

Primero, ________________ **, tercero,**
________________ , ________________ ,
sexto, ________________ **, octavo, noveno,**
________________ .

4 Elige la forma correcta.

1 En la clase *hay / están* muchos estudiantes.
2 En mi casa la televisión no *hay / está* en la sala.
3 *Hay / Está* una cafetería aquí cerca.
4 ¿Dónde *hay / están* las llaves?
5 En el refrigerador *hay / está* carne.
6 La información *hay / está* en internet.
7 ¿Dónde *hay / está* la pluma roja?

5 Completa con *un / una / unos / unas / el / la / los / las*.

1 Esta noche no salimos. Nos quedamos en casa y vemos *una* película.
2 En _____ cocina hay cosas para comer. Podemos hacer _____ tortas.
3 ■ ¿Tienes queso?
● Sí, hay _____ paquete en _____ refrigerador.
4 ■ ¿Hay jamón?
● No, pero tengo _____ quesos muy ricos.
5 ■ ¿Ponemos _____ poco de tomate?
● Sí, aquí hay _____ tomate bastante grande.
6 ■ ¿Dónde están _____ servilletas?
● En _____ cajón de la derecha.
7 ■ ¿Quieres _____ cerveza?
● No, prefiero _____ refresco.
8 Aquí están _____ vasos pequeños.

6 Relaciona cada pregunta con su respuesta.

1 ¿Qué tipo de habitación desea? — c
2 Buenas tardes, ¿hay habitaciones libres?
3 ¿Admiten tarjetas de crédito?
4 ¿Para cuántas noches?
5 ¿Cuál es el precio de la habitación?

a Para el fin de semana.
b Sí, por supuesto.
c Una doble.
d Con desayuno, 1,200 pesos.
e Sí, tenemos una individual y dos dobles.

7 Ordena en tu cuaderno el diálogo del ejercicio anterior.

¿Qué sabes?

	☺	😐	☹
• Describir las partes de la casa.	☐	☐	☐
• Los números ordinales del 1.° al 10.°.	☐	☐	☐
• La diferencia entre *hay* y *está*.	☐	☐	☐
• Reservar una habitación en un hotel.	☐	☐	☐
• Escribir sobre las vacaciones.	☐	☐	☐

Comer

- Pedir la comida en un restaurante
- Hablar de gustos
- Actividades de tiempo libre
- Comprender una receta de cocina
- **Cultura**: Comidas de México

Vocabulario

1 ¿Conoces algún platillo mexicano? Escribe los nombres junto a la fotografía correspondiente.

guacamole • tacos de carne asada
sopa de tortilla • pollo en mole

2  Observa el menú del restaurante La Morenita, después escucha el diálogo y completa la tabla.

	TERESA	JUAN
entrada	*ensalada mixta*	
plato fuerte		
bebida		
postre		

3 Mira la carta del menú y elige qué quieres comer de entrada, plato fuerte, bebida y postre. Luego, en grupos de tres, practica varias veces. Uno hace de mesero y los otros, de clientes.

Comunicación

- ■ *¿Qué van a desear de entrada?*
- ● *Yo de entrada quiero...*
- ▲ *Pues yo...*
- ■ *¿Y de plato fuerte?*
  (...)
- ■ *¿Qué quieren de beber?*
  (...)
- ■ *¿Y de postre?*
  (...)
- ● *¿Me trae la cuenta, por favor?*
- ■ *Sí, ahora mismo.*

Restaurante
La Morenita

Entradas
- Guacamole
- Sopa del día
- Queso fundido
- Ensalada mixta
- Tostadas de mariscos

180 pesos incluido pan, bebida y café

Plato fuerte
- Chiles rellenos
- Carne asada
- Pescado frito
- Milanesa de pollo a la plancha

Postres
- Helado de vainilla, chocolate o fresa
- Flan
- Arroz con leche

Bebidas
- Limonada de la casa
- Refresco
- Cerveza
- Agua mineral

Av. Cuauhtémoc 2015 Sur -
Tel. (81)83057555 - PUEBLA

4 Relaciona.

1 taza	☐	7 cuchara	☐
2 tenedor	☐	8 vaso	☐
3 cucharita	☐	9 servilleta	☐
4 copa	☐	10 jarrón	☐
5 cuchillo	☐	11 plato	☐
6 mantel	☐	12 jarra	☐

A

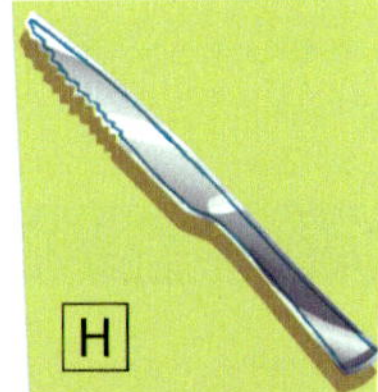

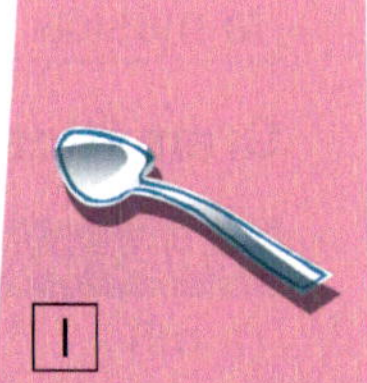

5 Completa con la palabra adecuada.

1 una copa de vino
2 una ______________ de café
3 una ______________ para la sopa
4 un ______________ de agua
5 un ______________ de flores
6 una ______________ de agua
7 un ______________ para la sopa
8 un ______________ para la mesa

Hablar

6 Practica con tu compañero.

- *¿Me trae una servilleta, por favor?*
- *Sí, ahora mismo.*

Leer

7 49 Lee y escucha.

Hoy comemos fuera

En Latinoamérica, comer es algo que nos gusta compartir con amigos, familiares, compañeros de trabajo o estudio. Para la mayoría de los latinos es más importante la compañía que el tipo de restaurante.

Al escoger un restaurante preocupa la higiene, la calidad de los alimentos, pero no siempre la dieta equilibrada. En países con un clima agradable, de largos días con luz, el comer o cenar fuera de casa es un hábito extendido.

Es durante los días festivos cuando más se visitan bares y restaurantes.

8 Di si estas afirmaciones son verdaderas (V) o falsas (F).

1 A los latinos les gusta comer solos. F
2 Cuando comen fuera de casa, les gusta hacerlo con familiares y amigos. ☐
3 Para los latinos lo más importante es el tipo de restaurante. ☐
4 Los restaurantes están más llenos los días laborables. ☐
5 Los latinos con frecuencia cenan fuera de casa. ☐

Hablar

9 Responde a estas preguntas y luego pregunta a tu compañero.

1 ¿Te gusta comer fuera de casa?
2 ¿Qué comes habitualmente fuera de casa: tortas, tacos, comidas completas, comida rápida (hamburguesa, salchichas...)?
3 ¿Cuántas veces al mes sales a comer o cenar?
4 ¿Meriendas todos los días? ¿Qué meriendas?

¿Te gusta el cine?

- Hablar de gustos
- Actividades de tiempo libre

Vocabulario

1 ¿Te gusta el cine? ¿Qué tipo de películas te gustan? Coméntalo con tus compañeros.

a) las comedias
b) los dramas
c) los musicales
d) las películas románticas
e) las películas policíacas
f) las películas de terror
g) las películas de ciencia-ficción
h) las películas de aventuras

- *A mí me gustan las películas de terror y de ciencia-ficción.* ☺
- *Pues a mí no me gustan las películas de terror.* ☹

2 Relaciona las siguientes actividades con los dibujos.

1 bailar ☐
2 andar en bicicleta ☐
3 caminar ☐
4 ir de compras ☐
5 escribir un *blog* ☐
6 pintar ☐
7 navegar por internet ☐
8 nadar ☐
9 jugar futbol ☐
10 escuchar música ☐
11 leer ☐
12 viajar ☐

3 (CD 50) Escucha a Elena hablar de sus gustos y de los de su esposo. Señala Sí o No.

	ELENA	LUIS
el cine		
pasear por el campo		
ir de compras		
navegar por internet		
leer		
el futbol		
la música		

Gramática

VERBO *GUSTAR*		
(a mí)	**me**	gusta(n)
(a ti)	**te**	
(a él / ella / Ud.)	**le**	
(a nosotros/as)	**nos**	
(a vosotros/as)	**os**	
(a ellos / ellas / Uds.)	**les**	
*A Elena **le gusta** viajar.*		
*A Jaime **le gustan** los deportes.*		
*A nosotros no **nos gusta** el futbol.*		

4 Completa las frases con un pronombre (*me, te, le...*) y *gusta* o *gustan*.

1 A María le gusta mucho nadar.
2 A mi esposo ____ ____________ ir al cine.
3 A mí no ____ ____________ las películas de terror.
4 A los latinos ____ ____________ mucho salir y hablar con los amigos.
5 A nosotros ____ ____________ los animales.
6 ¿A ustedes ____ ____________ la música tecno?
7 ¿A Ud. ____ ____________ el guacamole?
8 ¿A ti ____ ____________ los deportes de riesgo?
9 A mis papás no ____ ____________ el teatro, prefieren el cine.
10 A Jorge no ____ ____________ nada estudiar.

GUSTAR

+ Me **encanta** escuchar música.
Me gusta **mucho** cocinar.
Me gusta **bastante** leer.
No me gustan **mucho** los deportes.
No me gusta bailar.
– **No** me gusta **nada** ir de compras.

5 Escribe tres frases sobre tus gustos.

Me gusta mucho...

TAMBIÉN / TAMPOCO - SÍ / NO

- ● *Me encanta el cine.* ☺
- ■ *A mí **también**.* ☺
- ▲ *Pues a mí **no**.* ☹
- ● *No me gusta andar en bicicleta.* ☹
- ■ *A mí **tampoco**.* ☹
- ▲ *Pues a mí **sí**.* ☺

6 Pregunta a dos compañeros sobre sus gustos. Utiliza el vocabulario de la actividad 2.

- ■ *¿Les gusta el cine?*
- ● *A mí no mucho, me gusta más leer.*
- ▲ *A mí tampoco.*

7 Escribe unas frases con las respuestas de tus compañeros.

A Peter no le gusta mucho el cine, pero le gusta / encanta leer.
A Nadia no le gusta nada caminar, prefiere ir al antro.

Leer

8 Lee los anuncios de la derecha y responde a las preguntas.

1. ¿Quién estudia en la universidad?
2. ¿A quién le gusta la fotografía?
3. ¿Quién es de Argentina?
4. ¿A quiénes les gustan los videojuegos?
5. ¿Cómo se llama el queretano?
6. ¿Quién va a la playa habitualmente?

9 Escribe un anuncio en una hoja, pero sin poner tu nombre, y dáselo a tu profesor. Tienes que descubrir de quién son los anuncios que el profesor les enseña.

Me llamo **Marisol**, tengo 26 años y soy soltera. Estudio Economía y trabajo en un gimnasio de mi colonia. Me gusta viajar, conocer lugares nuevos y chatear. Busco amigos para viajar juntos por México. **Chiapas.**

Me llamo **Miguel**, tengo 25 años. Estudio Artes Gráficas en una escuela técnica. Me encanta jugar futbol, jugar con videojuegos, ir al antro... Busco chavos y chavas con aficiones similares. **Querétaro.**

Me llamo **Tiago**, soy brasileño, de Río de Janeiro. Soy profesor de surf. Me gusta ir a la playa, navegar por internet, jugar con videojuegos... También me gusta ver partidos de baloncesto en la tele. ¿Por qué no me escribes? **Río de Janeiro.**

Me llamo **Olga**, tengo 32 años y soy periodista Trabajo en el periódico local de mi pueblo. Me gusta el cine, salir de copas, bailar tangos y tomar fotografías de las ciudades que visito. Escríbeme. **Buenos Aires.**

5C Receta del Caribe

■ *Comprender una receta de cocina*

Vocabulario

1 ¿Te gusta cocinar? ¿Qué sabes hacer?

2 Completa la lista de ingredientes para hacer un licuado de plátano con las palabras del recuadro.

azúcar • hielo • limón • leche • vainilla • plátanos

Licuado de plátano

Ingredientes:

3 ______________

1 vaso de ______________

1/4 de taza de ______________

1/4 de taza de jugo de ______________

1/2 cucharadita de ______________

8 cubitos de ______________

3 Ordena las instrucciones para su preparación.

a Añade los cubitos de hielo y mézclalos con los otros ingredientes. ☐

b Pela los plátanos y córtalos en rodajas. 1

c Reparte la mezcla en cuatro vasos. ☐

d Mezcla los plátanos, la leche, el azúcar, el jugo de limón y la vainilla en una licuadora. ☐

e Invita a tus amigos. ☐

4 51 Escucha y comprueba.

Gramática

IMPERATIVO	cortar	comer	abrir
tú	corta	come	abre
usted	corte	coma	abra

El **imperativo** se utiliza para dar órdenes, dar instrucciones, pedir un favor y recomendar.

5 Completa las siguientes instrucciones para llevar una vida sana. Utiliza los verbos del recuadro en imperativo.

caminar • tomar • descansar
comer • evitar • ~~beber~~

Si quieres llevar una vida sana, sigue estas instrucciones.

Todos los días

1 *Bebe* más de un litro de agua.

2 ______________ tres piezas de fruta.

3 ______________ durante media hora.

4 ______________ más de siete horas.

5 ______________ fumar.

6 ______________ bebidas sin alcohol.

6 Escribe en forma de órdenes (*tú* y *usted*) y practica en voz alta.

1 Hablar más bajo.
Habla más bajo, por favor. (tú)
Hable más bajo, por favor. (usted)

2 Escribir tu / su nombre.

3 Terminar el trabajo.

4 Abrir la puerta.

5 Cerrar la ventana.

6 Escuchar lo que digo.

7 Comer más verduras.

8 Ordenar tu / su cuarto.

9 Añadir azúcar al jugo.

10 Limpiar la mesa.

7 Escribe en tu cuaderno la receta de tu ensalada preferida. Después, explícasela a tu compañero.

Escuchar

8 ¿De dónde crees que son originalmente estos productos?

¿Productos de América?

Muchos de los alimentos que se comen hoy en el mundo proceden de América: el maíz, el cacao, el aguacate... Pero también hay productos que se consumen en América y que son de origen europeo: la uva, la naranja, el limón... ¿De dónde son originarios estos productos?

1 **la piña**
- ☐ Hawái
- ☐ Cuba y Puerto Rico

2 **el cacahuate (maní)**
- ☐ Georgia (Estados Unidos)
- ☐ Bolivia y Perú

3 **el tomate**
- ☐ México
- ☐ Italia

4 **el plátano**
- ☐ Ecuador
- ☐ África

5 **el café**
- ☐ África
- ☐ Brasil

6 **la papa**
- ☐ Perú y Ecuador
- ☐ Irlanda

9 52 Escucha y comprueba.

Pronunciación y ortografía

b / v

1 53 Escucha y repite.

Isabel vivir vino bueno Ávila viajar botella abuelo hablar muy bien beber

La ***b*** y la ***v*** se pronuncian igual.

2 54 Escucha y repite.

1 ¿Dónde vive Isabel?
2 Cuba es una isla preciosa.
3 Vicente es abogado y trabaja en Puebla.
4 Las bebidas están en el refri.
5 Este vino es muy bueno.
6 Valeriano viaja mucho en avión.
7 Beatriz es de Venezuela.
8 Esta bicicleta es muy barata.
9 En Taxco no hay bastantes ambulancias.
10 La abuela de Bibiana está muy bien.

3 Completa con *b* o *v*.

1 Yo ___i___o en ___arcelona.
2 Este licuado tiene ___ainilla.
3 Mesero, un ___aso de agua, por fa___or.
4 A Isa___el le gusta ___iajar y ___ailar tangos.
5 ___e___er agua es muy ___ueno.
6 ¿Este ___erano ___as de ___acaciones?
7 La ___otella está ___acía.
8 El ___anco a___re a las nue___e.

4 55 Escucha y repite.

5 56 Escucha y subraya la palabra que oyes.

1 pala / bala
2 poca / boca
3 parra / barra
4 peso / beso
5 pino / vino
6 pera / vera
7 paca / vaca
8 pisa / visa
9 pata / bata
10 pez / vez

Leer

1 Lee estos anuncios de los restaurantes y después contesta a las preguntas.

1 ¿En qué estación de metro está el restaurante peruano?
2 ¿En qué restaurante podemos celebrar una reunión con nuestra familia o de negocios?
3 ¿Qué tipo de comida ofrece el restaurante Vida natural?
4 ¿Dónde podemos comer carne argentina?
5 ¿Dónde podemos comer tapas?
6 ¿Dónde podemos comer pescado?
7 ¿Qué restaurantes tienen servicio de estacionamiento?
8 ¿Cuánto cuesta el menú en Casa Pepe?
9 ¿Dónde podemos comer pizza?
10 ¿Qué restaurante tiene platillos mexicanos?

RESTAURANTE PERUANO
LA LLAMA
Probablemente la mejor comida peruana en la Ciudad de México

sabrosos platillos peruanos

Insurgentes Sur, 240 (atrás del Hotel Estrella) Metro Insurgentes
Teléfonos: 55 67 62 36 91 / 55 24 30 78 61
63400 Ciudad de México www.restaurante_lallama.com

La Estancia
Asador restaurante

Único sabor criollo en México

Carnes elaboradas al estilo autóctono de la campiña argentina

Cabrito Carnes Argentinas Lechón
Carnes gallegas Pescados a la brasa

Servicio de estacionamiento

Av. Constituyentes 101, Pte. Tel.: 442 234 3440
Querétaro www.asadorlaestancia.com

Vida natural
Restaurante vegetariano
Cocina vegetariana con productos ecológicos de la región
Nuestras especialidades:
sopas, ensaladas, pasta, pizzas y gran variedad de postres.

Av. Cupules 61 Tel. 999 920 1126 (Mérida, Yucatán)
www.vidanatural.com

Escuchar

2 57 Mira los mapas, escucha y relaciona.

1 México
2 Perú
3 Argentina
4 Colombia y Venezuela
5 Uruguay
6 España
7 Brasil
8 Costa Rica

a paella
b ceviche
c arepas
d gallo pinto
e carne asada
f feijoada
g guacamole
h chivito

Escribir

3 Escribe un párrafo sobre la comida típica de tu país o ciudad.

En mi ciudad, los platillos más típicos son: ...
Este platillo está elaborado con estos ingredientes: ...

Hablar

Alumno A (alumno B, ver «En parejas», pág. 174)

4 Pregunta a B sobre sus gustos.

¿Te gusta el chocolate?
¿Te gustan las piñas?

5 Responde a B las preguntas sobre tus gustos.

Sí, mucho. / Sí, bastante. / No, no mucho. / No, nada.

	MUCHO	BASTANTE	NO MUCHO	NADA
el chocolate				
las piñas				
la carne asada				
el café con leche				
las papas				
la carne				
el queso				
la fruta				
las ensaladas				

1 ¿Cuáles son los ingredientes principales de los platillos de este menú? Vamos a completarlo.

huevos • ~~caldo de pollo~~ • mole • pollo • leche
chile chipotle • garbanzos • chocolate • azúcar
aceite • zanahoria • aguacate • queso • arroz

MENÚ

Entrada

CALDO TLALPEÑO: caldo de pollo, ______, ______, ______, ______, ______, ______.

Plato fuerte

POLLO EN MOLE: ______, ______, ______, ______.

Postre

FLAN: ______, ______, ______.

2 Elabora un menú con platillos típicos de tu país y haz la lista de ingredientes que necesitas para su elaboración.

3 Escribe el pronombre correcto (*me, te, le, nos, les*).

1 A ellos les gusta la música clásica.
2 A nosotros ______ gusta salir de noche.
3 A su hermana ______ gusta el guacamole.
4 A mí no ______ gustan los toros.
5 ¿A ti ______ gusta el futbol?
6 ¿A ustedes ______ gustan las ensaladas?
7 A Luisa no ______ gusta viajar.

4 Haz frases como en el ejemplo.

1 Rosa / no gustar / animales
A Rosa no le gustan los animales.
2 Ellos / gustar / salir
3 Nosotros / gustar / ver la tele
4 Yo / no gustar / futbol
5 ¿Tú / gustar / flan?
6 Pepe / no gustar / la fruta
7 ¿Ustedes / gustar / nadar?

5 Escribe en imperativo las órdenes que da Maribel a su hijo.

1 ¡Baja la tele! (bajar)
2 ¡______ más verdura! (comer)
3 ¡______ la ventana de tu recámara! (abrir)
4 ¡______ una nota para tu profesor! (escribir)
5 ¡______ cuando te hablo! (escuchar)
6 ¡______ a tu hermana! (ayudar)
7 ¡______ más leche! (beber)

6 Relaciona cada pregunta con su respuesta.

1 ¿Qué desea para beber? [d]
2 ¿ Y de plato fuerte? [ ]
3 ¿Me permite la carta, por favor? [ ]
4 ¿Y de postre? [ ]
5 ¿Qué quiere el señor de entrada? [ ]
6 ¿Desea algo más? [ ]

a Sí, ahora mismo. Un momento.
b Una sopa de fideos, por favor.
c Un helado de vainilla.
d Agua mineral.
e No, muchas gracias.
f Pollo con papas.

7 Ahora ordena en tu cuaderno el diálogo anterior.

¿Qué sabes?

- Pedir en un restaurante.
- Hablar de gustos.
- Hablar del tiempo libre.
- Comprender y dar instrucciones sencillas.

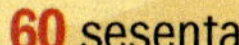

La colonia

- Pedir información para viajar en transporte público
- Dar instrucciones
- Pedir favores
- Describir la colonia donde vivimos
- **Cultura**: Ciudades mexicanas

¿Cómo se llega a Garibaldi?

Pedir información para viajar en transporte público

Escuchar

1 Mira el dibujo y responde. ¿Qué están haciendo Sergio y Beatriz?

a Están llamando un taxi.
b Están comprando un boleto de metro.
c Están sacando su carro del estacionamiento.

2 Completa la conversación con las expresiones del recuadro.

¿Cuánto es? • cómo se llega • Puede darme séptima estación • dos boletos de metro

Sergio: Disculpe, queremos (1) ________, por favor.
Taquillero: ¿Sencillos o quiere una tarjeta recargable?
Sergio: Sencillos. (2) ________
Taquillero: 10 pesos.
Sergio: Aquí tiene. Disculpe, ¿puede decirme (3) ________ de Terminal Aérea a Garibaldi?
Taquillero: Pues desde aquí es muy fácil: tome usted la línea cinco hacia Politécnico. En la primera estación, cambie a la línea verde hacia Buenavista y la (4) ________ es Garibaldi.
Sergio: Muchas gracias. ¿(5) ________ un plano del metro?
Taquillero: Sí, claro.

3 58 Escucha y comprueba.

4 58 Escucha otra vez y marca el recorrido en el plano del metro de Ciudad de México.

5 Lee de nuevo el diálogo de la actividad 2 y completa el siguiente cuadro.

FORMAL *(USTED)*
■ (1) ____________, ¿cómo se llega de Terminal Aérea a Garibaldi? ● (2) ____________ la línea 5 hacia Politécnico. En la primera estación (3) ____________ a la línea verde hacia Buenavista y la séptima estación es Garibaldi.
INFORMAL *(TÚ)*
■ Disculpa, ¿cómo voy / se llega de Terminal Aérea a Garibaldi? ● Toma la línea 5 hacia Politécnico. En la primera estación cambia a la línea verde hacia Buenavista y la séptima estación es Garibaldi.

6 Observa la diferencia entre las formas *tú* y *usted*.

Hablar

7 Mira otra vez el plano, fíjate en las estaciones destacadas en amarillo y practica con tu compañero.

- De Terminal Aérea a Chapultepec
- De Coyoacán a Terminal Aérea
- De Terminal Aérea a Bellas Artes
- De Tacubaya al Zócalo
- De Polanco a la Villa Basílica

■ *Disculpa, ¿cómo se llega de Terminal Aérea a Chapultepec?*
● *Toma la línea cinco hacia Pantitlán. Cambia a la línea 1 hacia Observatorio. La estación número 16 es Chapultepec.*

Leer

8 Lee el texto y responde a las preguntas.

El metro
en la Ciudad de México

El Metro de la Ciudad de México brinda servicio los 365 días del año a 3.9 millones de pasajeros al día. Consta de 12 líneas y 195 estaciones. En la CDMX hay 184 y 11 estaciones están en el Estado de México.

El horario de servicio en días laborales es de 5:00 a 24:00 horas. Los sábados de 6:00 a 24:00 horas y los domingos y días festivos de 7:00 a 24:00 horas.

El costo del boleto es de $5.00 MXN y puedes transbordar de una línea a otra, sin necesidad de pagar otro boleto. También hay tarjetas recargables y se recargan con un mínimo de $5.00 MXN y un máximo de $120.00 MXN. El acceso es gratuito para niños menores de 5 años, adultos mayores de 60 años con credencial del INSEN (Instituto Nacional de las Personas Adultas Mayores) y de Jóvenes del INJUVE (Instituto Nacional de la Juventud) discapacitados y policías uniformados.

Existe una tarifa de $3.00 MNX para mujeres jefas de familia, estudiantes de escasos recursos y personas desempleadas. Los usuarios pueden ingresar con perros guía a todas las estaciones de la red del Metro.

1 ¿Qué días da servicio el metro de la CDMX? ¿A cuántas personas?
2 Son las seis y media, tienes que ir al trabajo, ¿está abierto ya el metro? ¿Desde qué hora?
3 Son las dos de la madrugada, ¿puedes volver a casa en metro? ¿Por qué?
4 ¿Qué costo tiene un boleto? ¿Cuánto cuesta la tarjeta recargable?
5 ¿Quiénes tienen acceso gratuito al metro?
6 ¿Hay tarifas especiales? ¿Para quiénes?

Cierra la ventana, por favor

- *Dar instrucciones*
- *Pedir favores*

Gramática

1 59 Escucha y relaciona los dibujos con las frases.

1 ■ Carlos, siéntate en tu lugar, por favor.
● Voy. [h]

2 ■ Venga a mi oficina, quiero hablar con usted.
● Ahora mismo. ☐

3 ■ Pon la televisión, empieza el partido de futbol.
● Sale. ☐

4 ■ Cierra la ventana, por favor, tengo frío.
● Sí, claro. ☐

5 ■ Tome la primera a la derecha y después siga derecho.
● Muchas gracias. ☐

6 ■ Da vuelta a la derecha, esa es la calle.
● Ah, sí, tienes razón. ☐

7 ■ Haz las tareas antes de cenar.
● Sí, mamá. ☐

8 ■ Por favor, siéntese. Ahora lo atiende el doctor.
● Bien, gracias. ☐

9 ■ ¿Dígame?
● ¿Está el señor López? ☐

10 ■ Alejandro, contesta al teléfono, por favor.
● Claro. ☐

a

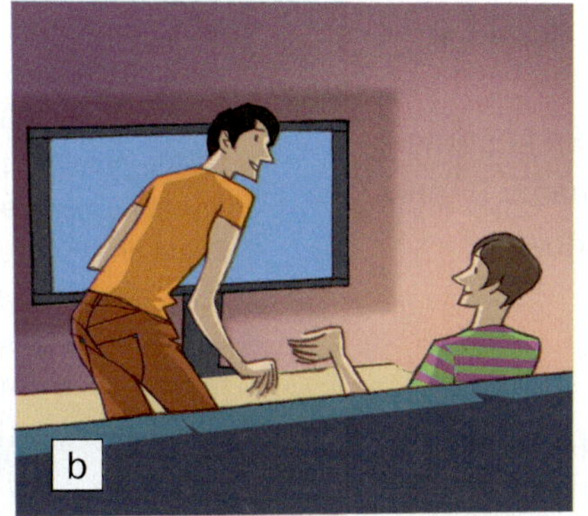
b

c

d

e

f

g

h

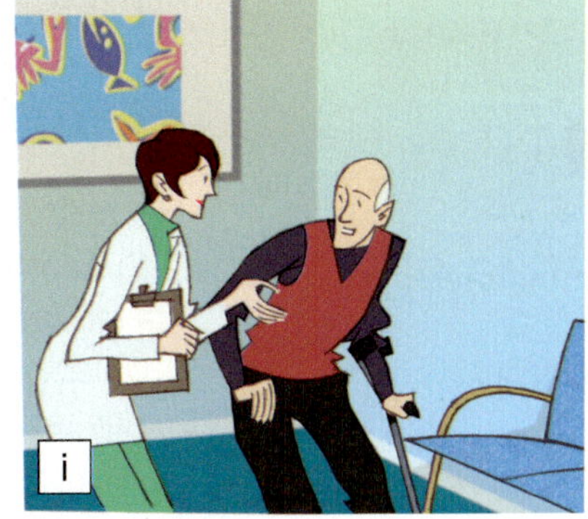
i

j

IMPERATIVOS IRREGULARES			
hacer	poner	venir	seguir
haz haga	pon ponga	ven venga	sigue siga
despertarse	cerrar	sentarse	decir
despiértate despiértese	cierra cierre	siéntate siéntese	di diga

2 Completa con el verbo en imperativo.

1 El hospital está muy cerca, da vuelta a la derecha por esa calle y luego (seguir, tú) *sigue* todo derecho.
2 (Hacer) __________ tú la ensalada, mientras yo pongo la mesa.
3 ¡Carlos! (Ir, tú) __________ a tu habitación ahora mismo.
4 (Cerrar, tú) __________ la puerta, por favor, hay mucho ruido.
5 Pedro, (decir, tú) __________ la verdad. No me gustan las mentiras.
6 (Sentarse, usted) __________ un momento, ahora vuelvo.
7 Señor Ramírez, (poner) __________ el informe en la carpeta roja.
8 (Despertarse, tú) __________ mañana antes de las 7, por favor.

3 Completa con los verbos del recuadro.

hacer • sentarse • poner • ~~pasar~~ • cerrar

Jefe: Señor Hernández, ¿puede venir a mi oficina, por favor?
Señor Hernández: Sí, claro.
[...]
Señor Hernández: ¿Se puede?
Jefe: Sí, sí, (1) *pase* y (2) __________ la puerta, por favor... (3) __________. Tengo una reunión en el banco el próximo lunes y necesito la información de su departamento.
Señor Hernández: No hay problema, está todo preparado.
Jefe: Bien, (4) __________ el informe antes del lunes y (5) __________ todos los datos de este año.

4 60 Escucha y comprueba.

Comunicación

+ DIRECTO	– DIRECTO
Ven un momento. Haga ya la comida.	¿Puedes venir un momento? ¿Puede hacer ya la comida?

5 Transforma las frases como en el ejemplo.

1 Venga a mi oficina.
¿Puede venir a mi oficina?
2 Pon la televisión, empieza la película.
3 Cierre la ventana, por favor.
4 Hoy haz tú la cena.
5 Dime la hora, por favor.
6 Pase al pizarrón, por favor.
7 Pásame la sal. Está al fondo del gabinete.
8 Prenda la computadora. Hay mucha información en internet.
9 Despiértese a las 8, por favor.
10 Llame a Luis la semana próxima.

Escribir

6 Piensa en un compañero sentado lejos de ti en la clase y escribe una petición en un papel. Luego léelo en voz alta.

Para Svieta:
Préstame tu diccionario, por favor.
Olga.

Puedes pedirle:

Abrir / Cerrar la ventana.

Prestar dinero / una pluma / un lápiz / un diccionario.

Sentarse más cerca de ti.

Prender / Apagar la luz.

Esperar a la salida de clase.

6c Mi colonia es tranquila

■ *Describir la colonia donde vivimos*

Leer

1 ¿Cómo es tu colonia? ¿Es tranquila o ruidosa? ¿Está cerca de tu trabajo o del lugar donde estudias español? ¿O está lejos?

2 Lee los mensajes.

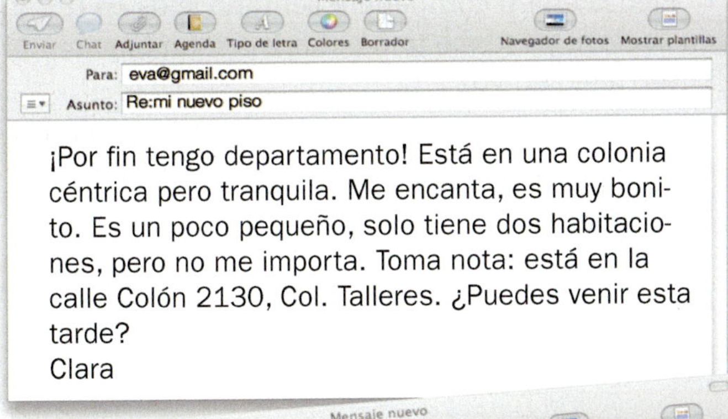

Mensaje nuevo

Enviar Chat Adjuntar Agenda Tipo de letra Colores Borrador Navegador de fotos Mostrar plantillas

Para: eva@gmail.com

Asunto: Re:mi nuevo piso

¡Por fin tengo departamento! Está en una colonia céntrica pero tranquila. Me encanta, es muy bonito. Es un poco pequeño, solo tiene dos habitaciones, pero no me importa. Toma nota: está en la calle Colón 2130, Col. Talleres. ¿Puedes venir esta tarde?

Clara

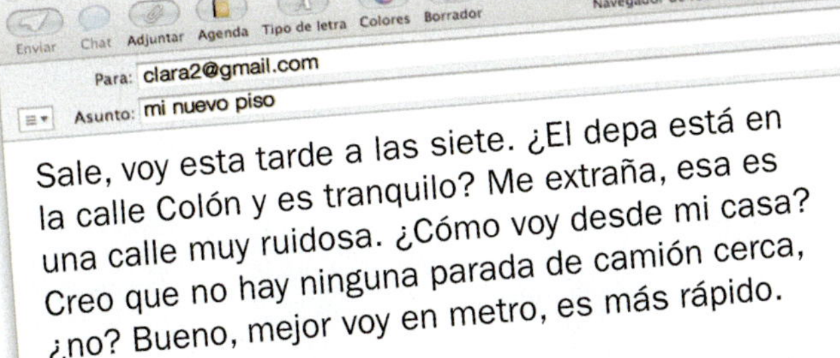

Mensaje nuevo

Enviar Chat Adjuntar Agenda Tipo de letra Colores Borrador Navegador de fotos Mostrar plantillas

Para: clara2@gmail.com

Asunto: mi nuevo piso

Sale, voy esta tarde a las siete. ¿El depa está en la calle Colón y es tranquilo? Me extraña, esa es una calle muy ruidosa. ¿Cómo voy desde mi casa? Creo que no hay ninguna parada de camión cerca, ¿no? Bueno, mejor voy en metro, es más rápido.

Eva

3 Contesta a las preguntas.

1 ¿Cómo es el departamento de Clara?
2 ¿Dónde está?
3 ¿Qué piensa Eva de la calle Colón?
4 ¿Cómo va a ir Eva a visitar a Clara?

Gramática

VERBO *SER*	
es / son	grande(s) – pequeño(s) tranquilo(s) – ruidoso(s) rápido(s) – lento(s)
es	bueno / malo

VERBO *ESTAR*	
está / están	abierto(s) – cerrado(s) a la izquierda a la derecha cerca – lejos en la calle… enfrente de…
está	bien / mal

4 Subraya la forma adecuada.

1 El departamento ***es / está*** en una colonia céntrica y ***es / está*** pequeño, solo tiene dos habitaciones.
2 Su casa ***es / está*** en la calle Insurgentes, enfrente de la estación del metro.
3 El metro ***es / está*** más rápido que el camión.
4 Fumar no ***es / está*** bueno.
5 El hospital ***es / está*** lejos de mi casa, en una colonia que ***es / está*** muy tranquila porque ***es / está*** a las afueras de la ciudad.
6 Este ejercicio ***es / está*** mal.
7 Esta escuela ***es / está*** al lado de la parada del camión.
8 Mi casa no ***es / está*** muy grande.
9 ¿***Son / Están*** tus hijos en la escuela?
10 El banco ***está / es*** enfrente de mi oficina. Por las tardes no ***es / está*** abierto.

5 Haz frases con los elementos de cada columna.

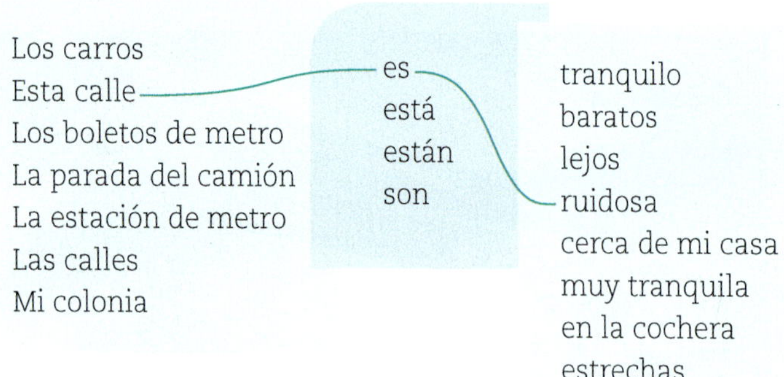

Hablar

6 En parejas. Habla con tu compañero sobre tu colonia.

- ¿Te gusta?
- ¿Es tranquila o animada?
- ¿Tiene mucho tráfico?
- ¿Está bien comunicada (camión, metro, etc.)?
- ¿Tiene tiendas?

Pronunciación y ortografía

r / rr

1 Escucha y repite.

rey arroz perro reloj rojo arriba caro pero diario soltera para

El sonido /rr/ (fuerte) se escribe simple *(r)* a principio de palabra y doble *(rr)* en medio de dos vocales. El sonido /r/ (suave) se escribe siempre simple *(r)*.

2 Escucha y completa con *r* o *rr*.

1 ___oma
2 Inglate___a
3 Pe___ú
4 carte___o
5 compañe___o
6 ___osa
7 piza___ón
8 te___aza
9 ca___o
10 ___uido

3 Dicta a tu compañero estos trabalenguas.

El perro de san Roque no tiene rabo porque Ramón Rodríguez se lo ha cortado.

Erre con erre, guitarra; erre con erre, barril; rápido ruedan las ruedas del ferrocarril.

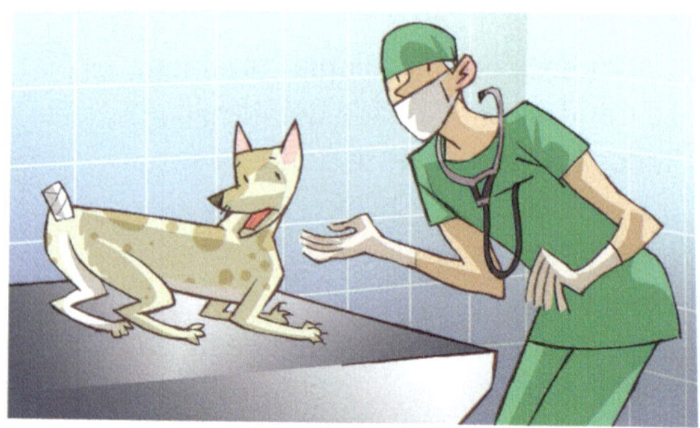

La Condesa

1 Esta colonia es muy famosa por su ambiente bohemio y su vida cultural y nocturna. Es tan popular como el barrio de Malasaña en Madrid, el Barrio Alto de Lisboa o el East Village en Nueva York.

2 Está situada de 4 a 5 km al oeste del Zócalo en la Ciudad de México y en las construcciones modernas predomina el arte decó.

3 Por las noches, las calles de la Condesa, así como sus múltiples cafés, bares, restaurantes y galerías se llenan de gente. Por eso muchos vecinos se quejan del ruido y la suciedad que originan los visitantes.

4 La colonia debe su nombre a la familia de la Condesa de Miravalle, que tuvo ahí su hacienda. El desarrollo de esta zona comenzó a principios del siglo XX con la construcción de bulevares, camellones, glorietas y dos grandes parques.

5 Desde su fundación en la Condesa ha vivido gente de la clase media alta de la ciudad y personajes famosos en la historia de México como la actriz y diva Dolores del Río, el compositor Agustín Lara, el actor Mario Moreno "Cantinflas", el compositor Francisco Gabilondo Soler y el escritor Juan José Arreola entre muchos más.

Leer

1 Lee el texto «La Condesa» y relaciona los párrafos 1-5 con los siguientes temas.

- **a** vida nocturna ☐
- **b** barrios famosos ☐
- **c** personajes famosos ☐
- **d** su historia ☐
- **e** localización ☐

2 ¿Verdadero o falso?

1 La Condesa es una colonia tranquila. ☐
2 La Condesa está al lado del Zócalo. ☐
3 Todos los vecinos de la Condesa se quejan del ruido. ☐
4 La Condesa es famosa desde inicios del siglo XX. ☐
5 En la Condesa no vive gente de la clase media alta. ☐

Escuchar

3 (63) Escucha y completa la conversación sobre Cozumel entre Andrés y Pilar.

1 Pilar está muy ______________ en Cozumel.
2 Cozumel es una ciudad ______________ y ______________.
3 Cozumel está rodeada de ______________.
4 Hay ______________, ______________ y ______________.
5 Pilar se mueve por la ciudad en ______________ y en ______________.
6 Habitualmente hace ______________.
7 Pilar vive con ______________.
8 Algunos sábados Pilar ______________ para hacer ejercicio.
9 Otros días va con sus amigos a conocer ______________ y a la ______________.
10 Andrés no va ahora a Cozumel porque ______________.

Escribir

4 Lee el texto y observa el uso de *y*, *pero*, *porque*.

San Miguel de Allende

San Miguel de Allende es una ciudad colonial del estado de Guanajuato **y** está situada en el centro de la República Mexicana. Tiene clima templado y la temperatura promedio es de los 16° a los 18 °C. En 2008 fue nombrada Patrimonio Cultural de la Humanidad por la Unesco por su cultura, su arquitectura **y** su importancia en la lucha de la Independencia de México.

Me gusta San Miguel de Allende **porque** es una ciudad muy acogedora con muchos lugares interesantes para visitar. Tiene muchas iglesias con fachadas de cantera, **pero** la más bonita es la Parroquia de San Miguel Arcángel, símbolo de la ciudad. Si quieres comprar artesanías, tienes que visitar el Mercado de Artesanías **porque** tiene una gran variedad de objetos típicos hechos con metales, papel maché, vidrio soplado **y** más.

No tiene metro, **pero** hay taxis **y** camiones locales que recorren toda la ciudad a una tarifa muy económica. Caminar por sus calles pequeñas **y** empedradas es lo más recomendable para admirar la riqueza arquitectónica de la ciudad.

5 Completa las siguientes frases con *y*, *pero*, *porque*.

1 Me gustan sus iglesias ______ sus mercados de artesanías.
2 Tiene camiones, ______ no tiene metro.
3 Voy a ir al Mercado de Artesanías ______ quiero comprar objetos de papel maché.
4 Mi ciudad es acogedora ______ tiene muchos lugares turísticos.
5 Puedes tomar un taxi, ______ es mejor caminar.
6 Tiene una cultura ______ una arquitectura muy interesantes.
7 San Miguel de Allende me gusta ______ tiene mucha historia.

6 Escribe una descripción de una ciudad. Puedes utilizar las frases del recuadro.

- Es una ciudad situada en el norte / sur / oeste / este de...
- Tiene una población de...
- Lo que más me gusta es...
- Hay muchos / pocos músicos, teatros, cines, discotecas...
- Es (muy) tranquila / pequeña / grande...

Hablar

7 En grupos de tres, cada alumno elige una profesión del recuadro. Los otros dos compañeros elaboran una lista de consejos para ser un buen profesional, utilizando imperativos.

deportista • maestro/a • doctro/a
estilista • taxista • bailarín/a

Para ser un buen deportista:

- *haz ejercicio todos los días*
- *come pasta todos los días*
- *bebe mucha agua*
- *duerme ocho horas diarias*
- ...

6 AUTOEVALUACIÓN

1 Completa esta nota que Juan escribe para un compañero del trabajo. Utiliza los verbos del recuadro.

guardar • ~~sacar~~ • conectar
apagar • cerrar

Carlos:
Me voy dentro de diez minutos. El informe está en mi mesa, por favor (1) saca las fotocopias y (2)__________ todo en el primer cajón. Después (3)__________ la oficina con llave y (4)__________ la alarma. Ah, antes de salir, (5)__________ todas las luces.
Gracias por todo,
Juan

2 Relaciona los adjetivos contrarios.

1 ruidoso	a antiguo
2 bueno	b caro
3 barato	c tranquilo
4 bonito	d pequeño
5 rápido	e malo
6 nuevo	f viejo
7 grande	g lento
8 moderno	h feo

3 Completa las frases con *ser* o *estar*.

1 Mi departamento nuevo es bastante grande.
2 Esa oficina __________ bastante lejos de aquí.
3 Las fotocopias no __________ bien.
4 La catedral __________ en el centro.
5 Mi colonia __________ antigua.
6 Este restaurante __________ muy ruidoso, no me gusta nada.
7 Las llaves __________ en el cajón.
8 Federico no __________ en su casa.
9 Luisa __________ muy amable.
10 Esta colonia __________ muy céntrica.

4 Lee este correo y contesta verdadero (V) o falso (F).

Vacaciones
Enviar Chat Adjuntar Agenda Tipo de letra Colores Borrador
Para: Gloria@hotmail.com
Cc:
Asunto: Vacaciones
Cuenta: YOLANDA <Yolanda@wanadoo.es>

Querida Gloria:
Te escribo desde La Habana. Esta ciudad es fantástica. Mi hotel está en un barrio muy bonito que se llama El Vedado. Se puede pasear tranquilamente por sus calles, hay mercados de artesanías, algunas tiendas y restaurantes, y está al lado del mar. La mayoría de las casas son de una o dos plantas y de muchos colores: azules, amarillas, de color rosa... Otro barrio interesante es La Habana Vieja, que es la zona más antigua. Tiene algunos edificios (la catedral, el hotel Inglaterra, el Capitolio) muy bien conservados. Las calles son más estrechas y hay bastante tráfico, pero es muy agradable pasear por ahí, tomar un helado y sentarse en cualquiera de las plazas.
¡Tengo muchas fotos!
Besos,
Yolanda

1 El hotel de Yolanda está en La Habana Vieja. ☐
2 El Vedado está al lado del mar. ☐
3 En El Vedado hay muchos edificios altos. ☐
4 La catedral está en La Habana Vieja. ☐
5 En la zona antigua no hay tráfico. ☐

5 Escribe un párrafo sobre tu colonia.

¿Es grande / pequeña / no muy grande?
¿Tiene mucho / poco tráfico?
¿Hay muchas / pocas / bastantes tiendas?
¿Cómo son los edificios: nuevos / antiguos?

¿Qué sabes?

- Preguntar cómo ir en metro o camión de un lugar a otro. ☐ ☐ ☐
- Dar instrucciones y pedir favores. ☐ ☐ ☐
- Describir una colonia. ☐ ☐ ☐
- La diferencia entre *ser* y *estar*. ☐ ☐ ☐
- Escribir sobre una ciudad. ☐ ☐ ☐

Salir con los amigos

- Hablar por teléfono
- Concertar una cita
- Hablar de acciones en desarrollo
- Descripciones físicas y de carácter
- **Cultura**: El tiempo libre de los jóvenes hispanos

¿Dónde nos vemos?

- *Hablar por teléfono*
- *Concertar una cita*

Hablar

1 ¿Te gusta salir con los amigos? ¿Adónde vas? Coméntalo con tus compañeros.

al futbol **al antro**
al cine **a casa de otros amigos**

Cuando salgo con mis amigos voy a...

2 64 Lee y escucha.

Mamá: ¿Sí, dígame?
Pedro: ¿Está Antonio?
Mamá: Sí, ¿de parte de quién?
Pedro: Soy Pedro.
Mamá: Enseguida contesta.
(...)
Antonio: ¿Pedro?
Pedro: ¡Hola, Antonio! ¿Qué haces?
Antonio: Nada, estoy viendo la tele.
Pedro: ¿Vamos al cine esta tarde?
Antonio: Ok, sale, ¿y qué película está?
Pedro: Podemos ver la última película de Alejandro González Iñárritu, ¿no?
Antonio: ¡Perfecto! ¿A qué hora y dónde nos vemos?
Pedro: ¿A las siete en la entrada del cine?
Antonio: No, mejor a las ocho. ¿De acuerdo?
Pedro: Sale. ¡Hasta luego!

3 Ahora contesta a las preguntas.

1 ¿Qué van a hacer Antonio y Pedro?
2 ¿Dónde quedan de verse?
3 ¿A qué hora?

4 Completa los diálogos. Utiliza las expresiones de los recuadros.

Lo siento • Te parece bien
Vienes conmigo • no puedo

- ¿Sí?
- ¿Está Alicia?
- Sí, soy yo.
- ¡Hola! Soy Mónica.
- ¡Hola! ¿Qué onda?
- Voy a salir de compras esta tarde. ¿(1) ________?
- (2) ________, hoy (3) ________, tengo mucho trabajo. Mejor mañana.
- Bueno, sale. ¿A qué hora? ¿(4) ________ a las seis?
- Sí, de acuerdo.
- Hasta mañana.

¿Te parece bien? • lo siento • ¿por qué no vienes?

- ¿Bueno?
- Hola, Ángel, soy Rosa.
- Hola, ¿qué tal?
- Muy bien. Te llamo porque Luis y yo vamos a ir el sábado a Puebla, (5) ________
- ¿El sábado? No puedo, (6) ________, es el cumpleaños de mi mamá y voy a comer en su casa. Pero podemos vernos después. ¿Por qué no vienen a casa a cenar?
- ¿A cenar el sábado? Sale, le digo a Luis y, si podemos, luego te llamo. (7) ________
- Perfecto. Espero tu llamada.
- Hasta luego.
- Hasta luego.

5 65 Escucha y comprueba.

6 Señala en los diálogos de la actividad 4 las expresiones para aceptar una propuesta y completa el cuadro.

INVITAR	ACEPTAR
¿Nos vemos mañana?	*Bueno, sale.*
¿Te parece bien a las seis?	
¿Por qué no vienen a casa a cenar?	
¿Te parece bien?	

Comunicación

Rechazar una propuesta

– *Lo siento, no puedo, tengo mucho trabajo.*
– *No puedo, ¿te parece bien mañana?*
– *No, mejor a las ocho.*

Hablar

7 Imagina que vives en Monterrey. Practica con tus compañeros con estos datos.

PROPUESTA	¿CUÁNDO?
a ir al teatro	mañana
b comer	el sábado
c tomar una copa	esta noche
d jugar billar	esta tarde
e ir al cine	este domingo

¿DÓNDE?	¿HORA?
a Macroplaza	18:00 h
b Barrio Antiguo	14:30 h
c Cinemex	23:15 h
d Museo MARCO	20:30 h
e Paseo Santa Lucía	17:45 h

- ■ *¿Vamos al teatro mañana?*
- ● *Ok. ¿Dónde nos vemos?*
- ■ *En la Macroplaza. ¿Te parece bien?*
- ● *Sí, ¿a qué hora?*
- ■ *A las seis.*
- ● *Sale. ¡Hasta luego!*
- ■ *¡Hasta luego!*

8 Ordena la siguiente conversación telefónica.

- ■ No está en este momento. ¿Quiere dejarle un recado? ☐
- ■ Muy bien, le dejo una nota. ☐
- ■ Inmobiliaria Miramar. Buenos días. ☐
- ● Muchas gracias. Adiós. ☐
- ■ Adiós. ☐
- ● Sí, por favor, dígale que la señora García va mañana a las once y media para hablar con él. ☐
- ● Buenos días. ¿Puedo hablar con el señor Álvarez? ☐

9 66 Escucha y comprueba.

Comunicación

Dejar recados

■ *No está en este momento. ¿Quiere dejarle un recado?*
● *Sí, por favor, dígale que...*

Hablar

10 Practica con tu compañero las siguientes conversaciones telefónicas.

Estudiante A:
1 Llamas a Pepe para ir al cine.
2 Llamas a Julia para ir al cine.
3 Llamas a Luis y se ponen de acuerdo para ir al cine.

Estudiante B:
1 Eres el papá de Pepe, y Pepe no está en su casa.
2 Eres Julia, no puedes ir al cine.
3 Eres Luis, tienes ganas ir al cine y te pones de acuerdo con tu compañero.

¿Qué estás haciendo?

- *Hablar de acciones en desarrollo*

Gramática

1 Mira el dibujo y señala si las siguientes frases son verdaderas (V) o falsas (F).

1 El chavo del traje de baño amarillo está dándose un regaderazo. ☑ V
2 El señor con lentes de sol está leyendo el periódico. ☐
3 La señora del traje de baño verde está abriendo la sombrilla. ☐
4 Los chavos de la toalla blanca están jugando a las cartas. ☐
5 La joven del sombrero rojo está paseando. ☐
6 Una señora está durmiendo sobre el camastro. ☐
7 Dos señoras están hablando en la orilla. ☐
8 Un grupo de chavas está jugando a la pelota. ☐
9 La chava del traje de baño rosa está secándose el pelo. ☐
10 La señora pelirroja está peinándose. ☐

ESTAR + GERUNDIO	
estoy	hablando
estás	
está	
estamos	
estáis	
están	

Infinitivo	Gerundio
llorar	llorando
comer	comiendo
escribir	escribiendo

GERUNDIOS IRREGULARES	
leer	leyendo
dormir	durmiendo

2 Mira los dibujos y di qué están haciendo los personajes. Fíjate en el ejemplo.

1 dormir / escuchar
No está durmiendo, está escuchando música.

2 escribir / pintar

3 hablar / cantar

4 estudiar / ver la tele

5 leer / navegar por internet

6 discutir / hablar

ESTAR + GERUNDIO (VERBOS REFLEXIVOS)
Estoy lavándo**me**. / **Me** estoy lavando.
Estás lavándo**te**. / **Te** estás lavando.
Está lavándo**se**. / **Se** está lavando.
Estamos lavándo**nos**. / **Nos** estamos lavando.
Estáis lavándo**os**. / **Os** estáis lavando.
Están lavándo**se**. / **Se** están lavando.

3 Completa las frases con el pronombre reflexivo adecuado.

1 ■ Rosa, ¿qué estás haciendo?
● ¿Ahora mismo? Estoy peinándo*me* porque voy a salir.
2 ■ ¡Luis, al teléfono!
● ¡No puedo, estoy bañándo_____!
3 ■ Niños, ¿qué hacen?
● ¡Nada, mamá, _____ estamos lavando las manos!
4 ■ ¡Qué ruido hacen los vecinos!
● Sí, están levantándo_____ ahora porque salen de viaje.
5 ■ ¡Hola! ¿Está Roberto?
● Sí, pero está afeitándo_____ , llama más tarde.
6 ■ ¿Y Clara? ¿Dónde está?
● En el baño, está bañándo_____.
7 ■ Joana, ¿qué haces?
● _____ estoy pintando para salir.
8 Pero hija, ¿todavía _____ estás vistiendo? Vas a llegar tarde a la escuela.
9 ■ ¿Está libre el baño?
● No, Jordi _____ está bañando.
10 ■ ¿Qué haces, Laura?
● _____ estoy pintando para salir, enseguida acabo.

4 67 Escucha y comprueba.

Pronunciación y ortografía

Entonación exclamativa

1 68 Escucha y repite.

¡Sale! ¡Hasta luego! ¡Qué bien!
¡Para nada! ¡Qué bonita!
¡Es horrible! ¡Perfecto! ¡Ok!

2 69 **Escucha las siguientes frases y reacciona con una de las exclamaciones anteriores.**

1 *¡Para nada!*
2 _____________
3 _____________
4 _____________
5 _____________
6 _____________
7 _____________
8 _____________

3 70 **Ahora, escucha y comprueba.**

Vocabulario

1 Señala en estos personajes las siguientes características físicas.

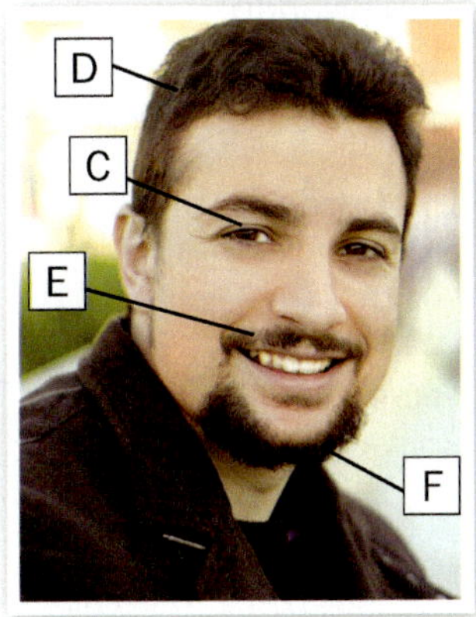

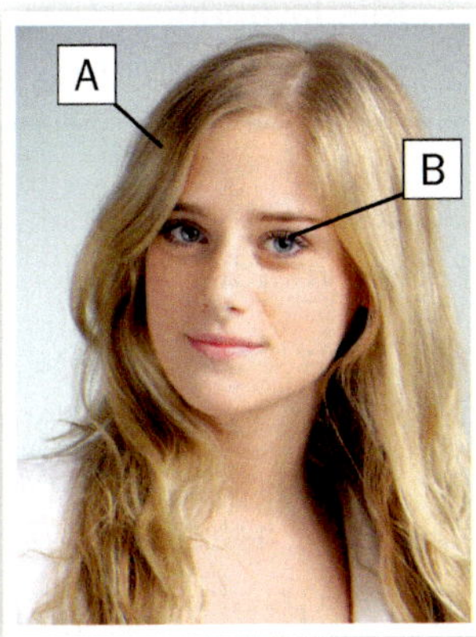

1 pelo largo y rubio ☐
2 pelo corto y negro ☐
3 ojos claros ☐
4 ojos oscuros ☐
5 bigote ☐
6 barba ☐

2 71 Ahora completa con las características físicas anteriores las siguientes descripciones de los personajes del ejercicio 1. Después, escucha y comprueba.

1 Tiene el ________ largo y rubio. Tiene los ________ verdes. ¡No tiene ________!
2 Tiene los ________ oscuros. Tiene el ________ corto y la ________ negra.

Comunicación

es	joven ≠ grande / viejo alto/a ≠ bajo/a delgado/a ≠ gordo/a calvo
tiene	el pelo largo / corto / rubio / negro / castaño el pelo liso / rizado los ojos azules / café / oscuros ≠ claros
trae / tiene	lentes / barba / bigote

4 Describe a estas dos personas. ¿Sabes quiénes son?

3 72 Escucha las descripciones y relaciónalas con las siguientes fotografías.

A

B

C

D

5 Piensa en un compañero de clase y toma nota sobre su físico sin escribir su nombre.

1. *Es alto/a*
2. *Es delgado/a*
3. *Es rubio/a y tiene el pelo corto*
4. *(No) Trae...*

6 Utiliza esas notas para describir a esa persona en voz alta. ¿Saben tus compañeros quién es?

Vocabulario

7 Relaciona.

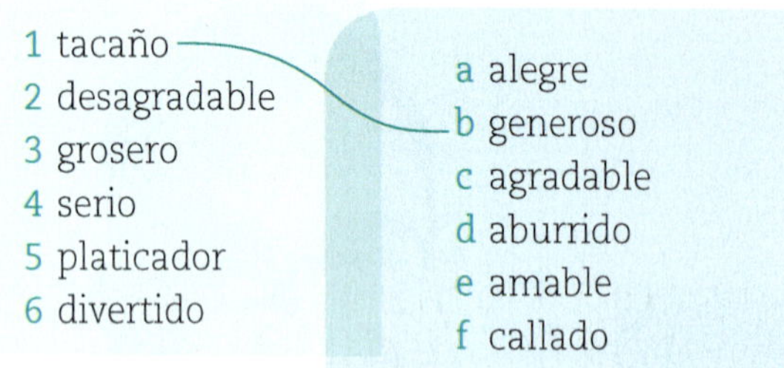

1 tacaño
2 desagradable
3 grosero
4 serio
5 platicador
6 divertido

a alegre
b generoso
c agradable
d aburrido
e amable
f callado

8 ¿Qué palabra utilizas para describir el carácter de estas personas?

1 Nunca gasta dinero.
2 Nunca habla.
3 Siempre está hablando.
4 Siempre está sonriendo.
5 Actúa con mucha amabilidad.
6 Hace muchos regalos.

9 Completa el párrafo con las palabras del recuadro.

gusta • gustan (x2)
~~es~~ • favorita • odia • generosas

Dolores Fuentes es periodista. Ella dice que (1) es agradable, alegre y muy platicadora. Le gustan las personas (2) __________. En su tiempo libre le (3) __________ mucho pasear por la playa y mirar el mar. Su comida (4) __________ es el mole poblano, que normalmente acompaña con una cerveza fría.
Dos de sus aficiones son el cine y la música clásica. Le (5) __________ mucho las películas antiguas, su favorita es *Tiempos modernos*, de Charlie Chaplin.
(6) __________ las guerras y tampoco le (7) __________ nada las personas desagradables y groseras.

Hablar

10 Primero lee las preguntas y luego haz la encuesta a tu compañero. Utiliza el vocabulario que has aprendido.

1 ¿Cómo eres tú? *Agradable y platicador.*
2 ¿Cómo te gustan las personas?
3 ¿Qué tipo de personas no te gustan?
4 ¿Qué prefieres hacer en tu tiempo libre?
5 ¿Cuál es tu comida preferida?
6 ¿Cuál es tu bebida preferida?
7 ¿Cuál es tu deporte favorito?
8 ¿Qué tipo de música prefieres?
9 ¿Cuál es tu película favorita?

Escribir

11 Escribe un párrafo parecido al de la actividad 9 sobre tu compañero.

Fátima es agradable y generosa.
Le gustan las personas alegres...

Escuchar

12 73 Escucha la descripción que hace Ana de ella y de su amiga Mónica. Señala verdadero (V) o falso (F).

1 Mónica es la mejor amiga de Ana. ☐
2 Mónica no es inteligente. ☐
3 Mónica y Ana no estudian música. ☐
4 A Mónica y Ana les gusta mucho la música ☐
5 Ana toca el violín. ☐
6 Mónica toca el violín. ☐
7 El compositor preferido de Ana es Beethoven. ☐
8 Ana y Mónica se parecen físicamente. ☐
9 Mónica tiene el pelo largo y negro. ☐
10 Ana es rubia y tiene ojos pequeños. ☐

Los sábados por la noche

Para los jóvenes la noche del sábado es muy especial. No tienen que estudiar, no tienen que trabajar, no tienen que aprender los verbos irregulares... Entonces, ¿qué hacen los sábados por la noche? Depende. No todos tienen los mismos gustos.

Tomás

DIECIOCHO AÑOS, COSTA RICA

Conozco a muchas chavas de mi edad, pero normalmente prefiero salir con mis amigos. Hay muchas cosas que nos gusta hacer juntos. Cuando tenemos suficiente dinero vamos al cine o a una cafetería. Si no, vamos a la casa de otro amigo y escuchamos música.

Carolina

DIECISIETE AÑOS, PERÚ

Yo no salgo mucho porque mis papás son muy estrictos. Casi nunca me dan permiso para salir de noche. Así que me quedo en casa viendo la televisión.

Rafael

VEINTITRÉS AÑOS, MÉXICO

Yo siempre salgo con mi novia y mis amigos. Normalmente vamos al cine y a tomar algo. A veces nos reunimos en casa de alguien y jugamos con los videojuegos.

Leer

1 Lee el texto anterior y señala verdadero (V) o falso (F).

1 Los jóvenes tienen que estudiar los sábados por la noche. ☐
2 No todos los jóvenes tienen los mismos gustos. ☐
3 Tomás, algunas veces, va al cine. ☐
4 Carolina se queda en casa, viendo la televisión. ☐
5 Rafael sale solo con sus amigos. ☐

Hablar

2 En grupos de cuatro, habla con tus compañeros.

- ¿Sales a menudo los sábados por la noche?
- ¿Con quién sales?
- ¿Adónde te gusta ir?
- ¿Sales los domingos?
- ¿Sales solo/a o con tus amigos?

Escuchar

3 (74) Un programa de radio quiere saber qué hacen los mexicanos los fines de semana. Escucha las dos entrevistas y marca con una cruz quién hace las siguientes actividades.

	ELLA	ÉL
1 Los sábados por la tarde va al cine.	☐	☐
2 Los sábados por la mañana juega futbol.	☐	☐
3 Los viernes por la noche sale con sus amigas.	☐	☐
4 Los viernes por la noche va al cine.	☐	☐
5 Los domingos va al Parque Fundidora o visita una exposición.	☐	☐
6 El domingo duerme casi todo el día.	☐	☐

Escribir

4 Señala las actividades de tiempo libre que haces normalmente.

- ir al cine / teatro ☐
- bailar ☐
- ver la tele ☐
- cenar fuera de casa ☐
- salir con los amigos ☐
- leer ☐
- ver una película en internet ☐
- practicar algún deporte ☐
- jugar con los videojuegos ☐
- invitar a amigos a mi casa ☐
- tocar un instrumento musical ☐
- conectarme a internet ☐

5 ¿Cuáles de ellas haces los días laborables y cuáles los fines de semana?

DÍAS LABORABLES	FINES DE SEMANA

6 ¿Con quién las haces?

con mi familia
con mis compañeros
con mis amigos
yo solo

7 Con toda la información anterior, escribe un texto sobre las actividades que realizas en tu tiempo libre. Utiliza las palabras del recuadro.

> los días laborables • siempre
> los fines de semana • normalmente
> nunca • además • también

1 Mira la sección de espectáculos del periódico y busca la siguiente información.

	ESPECTÁCULOS			
	TELEVISIÓN	CINE	TEATRO	MÚSICA
viernes	Canal de las Estrellas, 20h: *Noticiero.*	Cinépolis, 22:30h: *La Cumbre Escarlata*, de Guillermo del Toro.	Teatro Versalles, 22:30 h: *Un mal día*, de Renan Moreno.	Aula Magna, 21h: *Romance de un Cellista.* Espectáculo de música, danza y literatura.
sábado	Imagen Televisión, 22:30 h: *¡Qué madre tan padre!*	Cinemex, 20 h: *El Renacido*, de Alejandro González Iñárritú.	Teatro de la Ciudad, 20 h: *El Fantasma de la Ópera* (musical), de Gaston Leroux.	Teatro Telcel, 21:30 h: *El Rey León.*
domingo	TV Azteca,20:30 h: *Futbol, América-Rayados.*	Cinemax, 21:30 h: *Gravedad*, de Alfonso Cuarón.	Teatro Blanquita, 21 h: *El Mercader de Venecia*, de William Shakespeare.	Gran Teatro Moliere, 22h: *Siddhartha.*

a ¿Qué pasan en la tele el viernes?
b ¿Dónde presentan *El fantasma de la Ópera*?
c ¿Qué podemos ver en el Teatro Telcel?
d ¿A qué hora empieza el programa de televisión *¡Qué madre tan padre!*?
e ¿Qué equipos juegan futbol el domingo por la tarde?
f ¿Qué película podemos ver el domingo?
g ¿Qué obra presentan en el Teatro Blanquita?
h ¿Qué musical hay en el Gran Teatro Moliere?

2 Lee esta conversación y completa.

▪ El hermano de Luisa me cae muy bien, siempre está sonriendo y puedo hablar con él de todo.
• Es verdad. Luisa dice que hace regalos a todo el mundo y que tiene muchos amigos.
▪ Sin embargo, su novio es completamente distinto, no le gusta nada gastar dinero y tampoco habla mucho.
• Sí, es muy serio, pero siempre se comporta con mucha amabilidad y a ella eso le gusta.

El hermano de Luisa es (1) ________, (2) ________ y (3) ________.
El novio de Luisa es (4) ________, (5) ________ y (6) ________.

3 Describe lo que están haciendo los personajes del dibujo. Utiliza los verbos del recuadro.

~~reírse~~ • comer • discutir • escuchar • hablar

Ana se está riendo.

¿Qué sabes?

	☺	😐	☹
• Hablar por teléfono.	☐	☐	☐
• Concertar una cita.	☐	☐	☐
• Hablar de acciones en desarrollo.	☐	☐	☐
• Describir personas.	☐	☐	☐

De vacaciones

- Preguntar y dar instrucciones para llegar a un lugar
- Hablar del pasado
- Hablar del clima
- Los meses y las vacaciones del año
- **Cultura**: De vacaciones por España

Disculpe, ¿para ir a la catedral?

Preguntar y dar instrucciones para llegar a un lugar

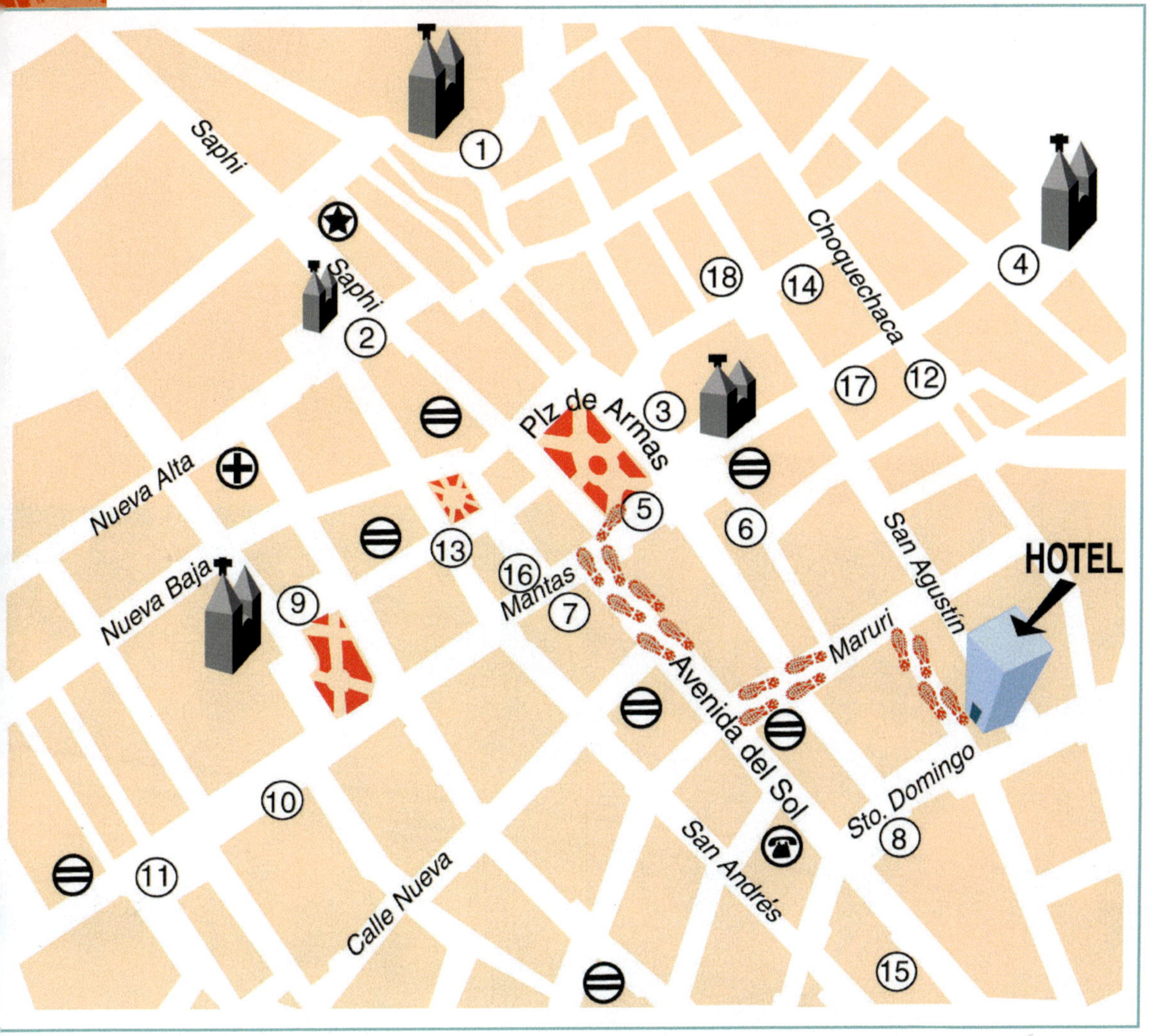

1 San Cristóbal
2 Santa Teresa
3 Catedral
4 San Blas
5 La Compañía
6 Santa Catalina
7 La Merced
8 Santo Domingo
9 San Francisco
10 Santa Clara
11 San Pedro
12 Piedra de los 12 Ángulos
13 Casa de Garcilaso
14 Monasterio de Nazarenas
15 Centro de Arte Nativo
16 Oficina de Correos
17 Museo de Arte
18 Museo Arqueológico

Farmacia
Central telefónica
Posta sanitaria*
Estación de policía

*Centro de salud

Hablar

1 Mira el plano de Cuzco y encuentra:

una farmacia | una posta sanitaria | la iglesia de San Francisco | la oficina de correos | el Museo de Arte

2 Escribe frases como en el ejemplo.

Hay una farmacia en la calle…
La iglesia de San Francisco está en la calle…

Comunicación

sigue / siga (todo) derecho

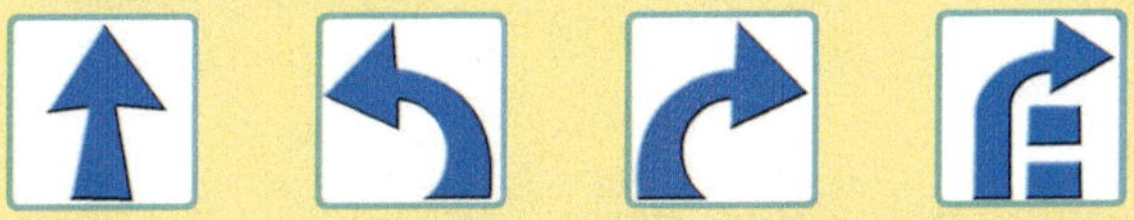

da / dé vuelta a la izquierda

da / dé vuelta a la derecha

toma / tome la segunda calle a la derecha

3 75 Luis está en el hotel y quiere ir a la plaza de Armas. Lee y escucha el diálogo. Sigue el recorrido en el plano.

Luis: Buenos días, disculpe, ¿puede decirme cómo se llega a la plaza de Armas?

Recepcionista: Sí, ¡claro! Es muy sencillo. Al salir del hotel dé vuelta a la derecha y siga todo derecho hasta el final de la calle. Entonces dé vuelta a la izquierda. Siga derecho y tome la tercera calle a la derecha, la avenida del Sol, y al final de la avenida, a la derecha, se encuentra la plaza de Armas.

Luis: Entonces, salgo a la derecha, doy vuelta a la izquierda y en la avenida del Sol doy vuelta a la derecha. La plaza está al final de la calle, a la derecha, ¿verdad?

Recepcionista: Así es, señor. En quince minutos puede estar allí.

Luis: Muchas gracias. ¡Hasta luego!

4 Mira el plano y completa los diálogos.

1 Desde el hotel:

■ Disculpe, ¿puede decirme dónde está la farmacia más cercana?

● ________________ la calle Santo Domingo, dé vuelta la primera __________ y, después, la primera ______________.

2 Desde la iglesia de San Francisco:

■ Por favor, ¿puede decirme cómo se llega a la iglesia de Santa Teresa?

● Dé vuelta ____________, después tome la segunda calle ____________, la calle Nueva Alta, y al final de la calle, ____________, está la iglesia de Santa Teresa.

5 (CD 76) Escucha y comprueba.

6 Ustedes están en la iglesia de Santa Teresa. Mirando el plano de Cuzco, haz las siguientes preguntas a tu compañero. Luego él te hará otras.

1 Disculpe, por favor, ¿para ir a la catedral?
2 ¿Puede decirme cómo se llega a la plaza de Armas, por favor?
3 ¿La iglesia de San Francisco, por favor?
4 Disculpe, ¿el Centro de Salud, por favor?

Vocabulario

7 Mira los dibujos y escribe la letra correspondiente.

1 medicinas [c]
2 fruta y carne [ ]
3 periódico [ ]
4 cartas [ ]
5 policía [ ]

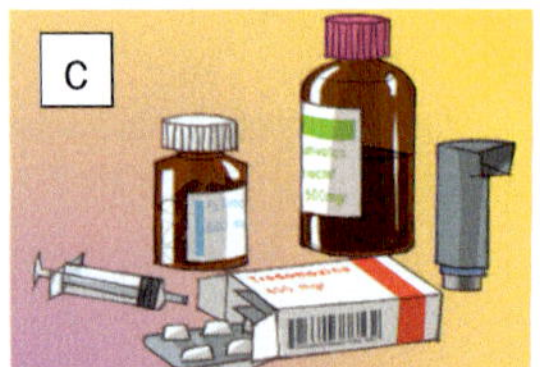

8 Relaciona los establecimientos con el vocabulario anterior.

1 correos [ ]

2 puesto de periódicos [ ]

3 farmacia [ ]

4 mercado [ ]

5 comandancia de policía [ ]

¿Qué hizo Rosa ayer?

■ *Hablar del pasado (ayer)*

Gramática

1 ¿Adónde fuiste el sábado?

■ *Yo fui a…*
● *Yo no salí, me quedé en la casa.*

2 ¿Qué hizo la doctora Ramírez ayer? Relaciona las frases con las imágenes.

1 Salió de la casa a las ocho de la mañana. [d]
2 Empezó a trabajar a las ocho y media. [ ]
3 Comió en la cafetería del hospital. [ ]
4 Terminó de trabajar a las seis de la tarde. [ ]
5 Por la tarde, fue al supermercado. [ ]
6 Compró algo de fruta para la cena. [ ]

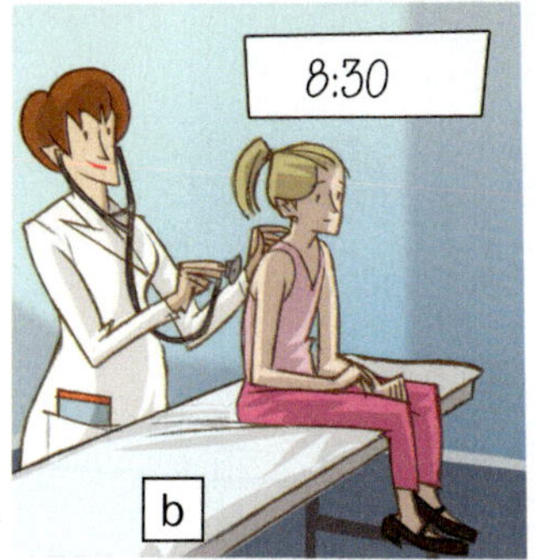

PRETÉRITO

Verbos regulares

	trabajar	comer	salir
yo	trabaj**é**	com**í**	sal**í**
tú	trabaj**aste**	com**iste**	sal**iste**
él / ella / Ud.	trabaj**ó**	com**ió**	sal**ió**
nosotros/as	trabaj**amos**	com**imos**	sal**imos**
vosotros/as	trabaj**asteis**	com**isteis**	sal**isteis**
ellos / ellas / Uds.	trabaj**aron**	com**ieron**	sal**ieron**

3 Escribe las siguientes frases en pretérito.

1 Ayer / no leer / el periódico. (yo)
Ayer no leí el periódico.
2 El lunes / Juan y yo / comer / en un restaurante nuevo.
3 Anoche / cenar / con María. (nosotros)
4 Mis amigos / no trabajar / el sábado en la noche.
5 ¿Comprar / ayer / el periódico? (tú)
6 Eduardo / llevar / al niño a la escuela.
7 ¿Salir / el viernes por la noche? (ustedes)
8 La semana pasada / conocer / a los papás de Juan. (yo)
9 ¿Hablar / a Juan / ayer? (tú)
10 El sábado pasado / ver / una película. (nosotros)

4 Completa las frases con la forma correcta de los verbos del recuadro.

comer • nacer • salir • cambiar • viajar

1 ■ ¿Dónde _________ (tú)?
● En Córdoba, Veracruz.
2 Ayer _________ (nosotros) en un restaurante peruano.
3 El año pasado _________ (yo) en avión por primera vez.
4 ■ ¿Cuándo _________ (ustedes) de casa?
● A las ocho de la mañana.
5 El mes pasado _________ (ellos) de carro.

5 ¿Qué hizo Rosa ayer? Llena los espacios en blanco con el pretérito de los verbos.

acabar • cenar • visitar
pasar • llegar • ~~atender~~ • invitar

Ayer, como todos los días, me levanté a las siete de la mañana y me preparé para ir a trabajar. Al llegar al hospital, (1) atendí a los enfermos de la consulta y (2)__________ a los pacientes de las habitaciones. A las cinco de la tarde, (3)__________ de trabajar y (4)__________ por el supermercado a comprar algo para la cena. A las seis de la tarde (5)__________ por fin a casa, muy cansada, como todos los días. Pero ayer fue diferente: mi marido me (6)__________ a un concierto y después (7)__________ en mi restaurante favorito.

6 77 Escucha y comprueba.

PRETÉRITO

Verbos irregulares

	ir / ser	estar
yo	fui	estuve
tú	fuiste	estuviste
él / ella / Ud.	fue	estuvo
nosotros/as	fuimos	estuvimos
vosotros/as	fuisteis	estuvisteis
ellos / ellas / Uds.	fueron	estuvieron

7 Elige la forma correcta.

1 Juan y María ***estuvieron / fueron*** en el parque ayer.
2 Mi hermano ***estuvo / fue*** el capitán del equipo el año pasado.
3 ¿***Fuiste / Estuviste*** a la oficina de correos ayer?
4 Ayer ***fue / estuvo*** mi cumpleaños.
5 ¿Dónde ***estuvieron / fueron*** los últimos Juegos Olímpicos?

Escuchar

8 78 Soledad y Federico son dos ejecutivos. Escúchalos y completa el cuadro con las ciudades en las que estuvieron la semana pasada.

	Soledad	Federico
lunes		
martes		
miércoles		
jueves		
viernes		

- Lima
- Madrid
- Buenos Aires
- Río de Janeiro
- Caracas

Hablar

9 Completa las preguntas con el pretérito.

1 ¿A qué hora (levantarse) *te levantaste* ayer?
2 ¿A qué hora (empezar) __________ a trabajar?
3 ¿A qué hora (salir) __________?
4 ¿Dónde (ir) __________ a comer?
5 ¿Con quién (comer) __________?
6 ¿Dónde (estar) __________ después de comer?
7 ¿Cuándo (llegar) __________ a casa?
8 ¿Qué (cenar) __________?
9 ¿Qué (ver) __________ en la televisión?
10 ¿A qué hora (acostarse) __________?

10 Haz las preguntas anteriores a tu compañero y escribe lo que te dice.

Ayer mi compañero se levantó a las…

Pronunciación y ortografía

Acentuación

1 79 Escucha y señala lo que oyes.

1 a) Uso lentes. ☐
 b) Usó lentes. ☐
2 a) Como mucho. ☐
 b) Comió mucho. ☐
3 a) ¿Abro la puerta? ☐
 b) ¿Abrió la puerta? ☐
4 a) ¿Hablo más alto? ☐
 b) ¿Habló más alto? ☐
5 a) Entro a las ocho. ☐
 b) Entró a las ocho. ☐
6 a) Trabajo en la mañana. ☐
 b) Trabajó en la mañana. ☐
7 a) Estudio Geografía. ☐
 b) Estudió Geografía. ☐

2 79 Escucha otra vez y repite.

¿Cómo está el clima hoy?

- *Hablar del clima*
- *Los meses y las estaciones*

a

b

c

d

e

f

Vocabulario

1 Relaciona las siguientes expresiones con las fotos.

	HOY	AYER	
1	hace frío	hizo frío	a
2	hace calor	hizo calor	
3	hace aire	hizo aire	
4	está nublado	estuvo nublado	
5	llueve	llovió	
6	nieva	nevó	

2 Contesta a las siguientes preguntas.

1 ¿Cómo está el clima hoy?
2 ¿Cómo estuvo el clima ayer?
3 ¿Hizo frío el fin de semana pasado?
4 ¿Cómo es el clima en tu país en primavera / verano / otoño / invierno?
5 ¿Qué clima te gusta más? *Me gusta cuando…*

Comunicación

primavera — verano — otoño — invierno

3 Completa el siguiente calendario con el clima que suele hacer en tu ciudad en los distintos meses del año.

enero		julio	
febrero		agosto	
marzo		septiembre	
abril		octubre	
mayo		noviembre	
junio		diciembre	

Hablar

4 Pregunta a tu compañero.

1 ¿Cuándo es tu cumpleaños?
Mi cumpleaños es el…
2 ¿Cuándo es el cumpleaños de tu mamá?
3 ¿Cuándo es el cumpleaños de tu papá?
4 ¿Cuándo es el cumpleaños de tu mejor amigo?

Escuchar

5 Completa el texto con las palabras del recuadro.

nunca • mucho • hace (x2) • primavera
altas • enero • noviembre • julio

En Taxco, durante los meses de invierno (diciembre, (1) ________ y febrero) (2) ________ mucho frío, pero (3) ________ nieva. Durante la (4) ________ (marzo, abril y mayo), suben las temperaturas y empieza a hacer buen clima. En verano (junio, (5) ________ y agosto), hace (6) ________ calor: todos los días hace mucho sol y las temperaturas son muy (7) ________. En otoño (septiembre, octubre y (8) ________), los días son más cortos, el cielo está nublado y a veces llueve y (9) ________ aire.

6 (80) Ahora escucha y comprueba.

Escribir

7 Escribe un párrafo sobre el clima en tu país.

8 (81) Escucha el informe del clima y completa la tabla.

	BRASIL	CARIBE	MÉXICO
clima			
temperatura			

Leer

9 Lee el texto de México y contesta a las preguntas.

¿En qué celebraciones...
1 ... reciben regalos los niños?
2 ... las fiestas duran dos semanas?
3 ... se prenden velas?
4 ... se utilizan trajes regionales?
5 ... se baila en las calles?
6 ... se representa la muerte de Jesucristo?

Ven a disfrutar de tus vacaciones en México y participa con nosotros en nuestras fiestas tradicionales

Carnaval: Los festejos de Carnaval se celebran en febrero. Empiezan el viernes y terminan el martes de la semana siguiente. Durante estos días la gente baila en las calles, en los hoteles y en las casas de la ciudad, en un ambiente muy alegre. Las mujeres se visten con hermosos trajes regionales y bailan sus danzas tradicionales.

Semana Santa: La Semana Santa se celebra en marzo o en abril. Los habitantes de los pueblos hacen procesiones, llevan velas y ofrecen flores. También se realizan representaciones de los principales hechos de la pasión y muerte de Jesucristo.

Día de muertos: El 1 y 2 de noviembre pueblos enteros van a las tumbas de sus muertos, llevándoles dulces, comida y flores. El espectáculo es impresionante por la noche cuando se prenden las velas en los cementerios.

Fiestas de Navidad y Año Nuevo: Estas fiestas empiezan el 24 de diciembre y terminan el 6 de enero, cuando los tres Reyes Magos dejan juguetes y golosinas en los zapatos de los niños.

Vacaciones en ESPAÑA

Hay tantas cosas que ver en España que es difícil seleccionar las más interesantes. Si empezamos por el noroeste, podemos visitar Galicia y allí pararnos a ver Santiago de Compostela y su catedral. Siguiendo por la costa cantábrica, el viajero descubre paisajes inolvidables de praderas suaves y pequeñas playas entre acantilados. Desde el País Vasco nos dirigimos a Cataluña, que mira al Mediterráneo. La ciudad catalana más importante es Barcelona, puerto de mar y punto de partida y llegada de barcos de todo el mundo. Podemos seguir nuestro viaje por la costa mediterránea para disfrutar de las ciudades y playas que llegan hasta Almería y Málaga, en Andalucía. También la comunidad andaluza merece una atención especial por los restos de cultura árabe que se pueden ver en Córdoba, Sevilla y Granada, especialmente. Desde Córdoba podemos ir a Madrid, atravesando la Mancha, la tierra de Don Quijote, el héroe de Cervantes. Aquí acaba nuestro viaje por esta vez, pero aún nos quedan por ver muchos otros paisajes y ciudades.

Leer

1 Con tu compañero elabora una lista de ciudades y monumentos españoles.

2 (82) Lee el texto «Vacaciones en España» y después escucha.

3 Señala verdadero (V) o falso (F).

1 La catedral de Santiago está en Galicia. ☐
2 Barcelona está en la costa cantábrica. ☐
3 En Córdoba hay restos árabes. ☐
4 Almería no tiene playa. ☐
5 La Mancha está al sur de Madrid. ☐

4 Señala en el mapa el recorrido del viaje propuesto en el texto.

Escribir

5 Lee el blog de Sara. ¿Dónde estuvo de vacaciones? ¿Con quién fue? ¿Qué clima hace en esa zona de España?

EL BLOG DE SARA

La Semana Santa pasada fui con mis amigos a Granada, en el sur de España. El viaje fue muy interesante. Es una ciudad de origen árabe. Visitamos La Alhambra. Sus edificios y jardines forman el conjunto más importante de arte musulmán en Europa. Por la noche cenamos en el barrio del Sacromonte y vimos un espectáculo flamenco. Al día siguiente subimos a Sierra Nevada. Pasamos el día esquiando con un excelente clima. Otro día estuvimos en la costa. Sus habitantes dicen que ahí hace sol más de 320 días al año. Nos bañamos en las playas de Almuñécar y comimos un arroz riquísimo en un restaurante junto al mar. Fueron unos días fantásticos. Les recomiendo a todos este viaje.

6 Prepara unas notas sobre tus últimas vacaciones.

- ¿Dónde estuviste?
- ¿Con quién viajaste?
- ¿Qué actividades realizaste?
- ¿Qué lugares visitaste?
- ¿Qué comiste?
- ¿Qué clima hace en esa zona?

7 Ahora escribe una descripción del lugar donde pasaste tus últimas vacaciones.

Escuchar

8 (83) Escucha este programa de radio sobre Barcelona. ¿Las frases siguientes son verdaderas (V) o falsas (F)? Corrige las falsas.

1. Barcelona está en el interior de España. ☐
2. Montserrat Caballé es una cantante de rock. ☐
3. Montserrat Caballé grabó con Freddie Mercury la canción «Barcelona». ☐
4. Podemos ver las mejores obras de Miró en Palma de Mallorca. ☐
5. Joan Manuel Serrat es muy conocido en los países de habla hispana. ☐
6. Arancha Sánchez Vicario ganó una vez el torneo de tenis de Roland Garros. ☐

Hablar

Alumno A (alumno B, ver «En parejas», pág 175)

9 Tú y tu compañero se encuentran en la esquina de la calle Argentina con la calle Ecuador. Pregunta a B cómo se llega a los siguientes lugares.

la escuela • la tienda de conveniencia
el súper • el hotel • el restaurante

■ *¿Puedes decirme cómo se llega a la escuela?*
● *Ve por la calle Argentina y toma la primera a la derecha, la calle Mayor. Sigue derecho y, después de cruzar la calle Colombia, a la izquierda, junto a la parada del camión, está la escuela.*

10 Tú y tu compañero se encuentran en la esquina de la calle Argentina con la calle Ecuador. Escucha a B y dile cómo se llega a los lugares que te pregunta.

11 Encuentra en la clase a alguien que hizo ayer estas cosas. Pregunta a varios compañeros.

1. Se levantó antes de las ocho.
   ¿Te levantaste antes de las ocho?
2. Desayunó café con leche.
   ¿Desayunaste café con leche?
3. Fue al súper.
   ¿Fuiste al súper?
4. Comió fuera de su casa.
5. Fue al gimnasio.
6. Vio una película.
7. Navegó por internet.
8. Habló por teléfono con sus papás.
9. Cenó una ensalada.
10. Se acostó antes de las once.

1 ¿Dónde se puede(n) encontrar...

1 ... refrescos? *En la tienda de conveniencia*.
2 ... revistas? ______________
3 ... aspirinas? ______________
4 ... carne y pescado? ______________
5 ... un médico? ______________
6 ... un policía? ______________

2 ¿Verdadero (V) o falso (F)?

1 En el desierto llueve mucho. [F]
2 Cuando hace calor, no uso abrigo. ☐
3 Siempre nieva en verano. ☐
4 En otoño caen las hojas de los árboles. ☐
5 Cuando hace mucho aire, es difícil abrir el paraguas. ☐
6 Cuando llueve, está nublado. ☐

3 Ordena los párrafos de la postal que Carolina escribe a Rosa.

Querida Rosa:

☐ a) Después ellos fueron a la plaza Mayor a tomar un aperitivo y yo me fui de compras con Ana, mi compañera de departamento.

☐ b) Segovia es una ciudad bellísima. Ayer estuve ahí de excursión con unos amigos.

☐ c) Al final del día, Ana y yo tomamos unas fotos del acueducto. El tiempo se pasó muy rápido, pero fueron unas horas inolvidables.

☐ d) Por la mañana visitamos la catedral y el Alcázar.

☐ e) Por la tarde, todos bajamos al río. Dimos un paseo muy agradable.

¡Hasta pronto!
Carolina

CORREOS ESPAÑA 2,40€
SEGOVIA
CONSIGNE EN SUS ENVÍOS EL CÓDIGO POSTAL

Rosa García Iglesias
c/ Príncipe, 15 - 1.º izda.
28080 Madrid

4 Completa el siguiente texto con el pretérito de los verbos.

Ayer me (1) *levanté* (levantar) a las seis y media de la mañana. Mi esposo y yo (2) __________ (desayunar) juntos y después él se (3) __________ (ir) a trabajar en camión y yo me (4) __________ (ir) en carro. Mis hijos (5) __________ (estar) en la escuela hasta las tres. Luego, todos (6) __________ (comer) juntos. Por la tarde, mi esposo (7) __________ (preparar) la cena y yo (8) __________ (ayudar) a mi hijo menor con las tareas. A las once nos (9) __________ (ir) todos a dormir.

5 84 Escucha a Sara, Lucía y Carlos hablar de sus últimas vacaciones y completa el cuadro.

1 ¿Dónde estuvieron?
2 ¿Qué transporte utilizaron?
3 ¿Con quién estuvieron?
4 ¿Cuánto tiempo estuvieron?

Sara
1
2
3
4
Lucía
1
2
3
4
Carlos
1
2
3

¿Qué sabes?

	☺	😐	☹
• Preguntar y dar instrucciones sobre cómo se llega a un lugar.	☐	☐	☐
• Nombres de establecimientos.	☐	☐	☐
• Hablar del pasado.	☐	☐	☐
• Hablar del clima.	☐	☐	☐
• Los meses y las estaciones del año.	☐	☐	☐

Compras

- Recursos para ir de compras
- Los colores
- Describir la ropa
- Hacer comparaciones
- **Cultura**: Ciudades y arte español e hispanoamericano

¿Cuánto cuestan estos zapatos?

Hablar

1 Pregunta a tus compañeros.

1 ¿Te gusta ir de compras?
2 ¿Dónde compras, en tiendas pequeñas o en centros comerciales?

2 Celia y Álvaro van de compras. Completa el diálogo con las palabras del recuadro.

cuánto cuestan • No están mal • Gracias • muy bonitos

Celia: Mira estos zapatos, Álvaro, son (1) ____________.
Álvaro: (2) _________________, pero a mí me gustan más aquellos café.
Celia: Disculpe, ¿(3) __________ estos zapatos negros?
Dependiente: Quinientos pesos.
Celia: ¿Y aquellos café?
Dependiente: Novecientos pesos.
Celia: ¿Novecientos pesos? (4) ____________, tengo que pensarlo.

a mí tampoco • talla • Sale • qué te parece • me la llevo

Álvaro: Celia, ¿(5) ____________ esta camisa para mí?
Celia: Bien, ¿cuánto cuesta?
Álvaro: Solo seiscientos pesos. Voy a probármela.
Celia: (6) ____________.
(...)
Celia: A ver... pues no te queda bien, ¿eh?
Álvaro: No, (7) ____________ me gusta.
Celia: Toma, pruébate esta chamarra, es muy bonita.
Álvaro: A ver... Pues sí, parece que me queda bien, ¿no?
Celia: Muy bien, es tu (8) ____________.
Álvaro: ¿Cuánto cuesta?
Celia: Mil quinientos pesos, es un poco cara.
Álvaro: Bueno, pero me gusta mucho, (9) ____________.

me lo llevo • En efectivo • ¿Cómo me queda?

Celia: Mira, ¿qué te parece este gorro? (10) ____________
Álvaro: Bien, muy bien.
Celia: Pues (11) ____________, solo cuesta doscientos pesos.
(...)
Dependiente: Una chamarra y un gorro de lana... Muy bien, son mil setecientos pesos. ¿Pagan en efectivo o con tarjeta?
Álvaro: (12) ____________.

3 85 Escucha y comprueba.

Comunicación

Pedir opinión sobre ropa

- *¿Cómo me queda esta falda?*
- *(No) Te queda bien / mal.*
- *Pues yo creo que me queda muy larga / corta / ancha / ajustada.*
- *¿No te la llevas?*

4 En parejas. Practica con tu compañero la conversación anterior: uno es el vendedor y el otro es el cliente. Pueden comprar una bolsa, un pantalón de mezclilla, un anillo, unos zapatos, una camisa, una chamarra, un gorro...

Gramática

PRONOMBRES DE OBJETO DIRECTO (3.ª PERSONA)

- ¿Conoces a Ismael?
- No, no **lo** conozco.
- ¿Conoces a mi esposa?
- No, no **la** conozco.
- ¿Conoces a los vecinos de arriba?
- No, no **los** conozco.
- ¿Conoces a mis hermanas?
- No, no **las** conozco.

Lo compro (el suéter)
La compro (la chamarra)
Los compro (los pantalones)
Las compro (las blusas)

- El pronombre va detrás del imperativo: *pruebatelo*
- Puede ir delante o detrás de perífrasis de infinitivo o gerundio:
  *Quiero comprar**lo**. / **Lo** quiero comprar.*
  *Estoy probándome**lo**. / Me **lo** estoy probando.*

5 Responde afirmativamente, usando el pronombre de objeto directo.

1 ¿Te gusta esta camisa?
Sí, me la llevo.
2 ¿Te gustan estos zapatos?
3 ¿Te gusta esta falda?
4 ¿Te gustan estos pantalones?
5 ¿Te gusta este anillo?
6 ¿Te gusta la cartera negra de piel?

6 Completa las frases con los pronombres *lo, la, los, las*.

1 Me gusta mucho este suéter, me lo llevo.
2 ¿Sabes dónde están mis lentes? No _______ veo.
3 ■ ¿Quién es él?
● No lo sé, no _______ conozco.
■ ¿Y aquella de pelo negro?
● Tampoco _______ conozco.
4 ■ Y tus amigos Pepa y Jaime, ¿qué tal están?
● No sé, hace tiempo que no _______ veo.
5 ■ ¿Te quedan bien los pantalones de mezclilla?
● Sí, me _______ llevo.
6 ■ Ahí está Rosa, ¿____ invitas a un café?
● Sale.

PRONOMBRES PERSONALES DE OBJETO DIRECTO

singular		plural	
yo	**me**	nosotros/as	**nos**
tú	**te**	vosotros/as	**os**
él	**lo / le**	ellos	**los / les**
ella	**la**	ellas	**las**
Ud.	**la / lo / le**	Uds.	**las / los / les**

*Yo **te** quiero, ¿tú **me** quieres?*
*¿Ismael **los** quiere?*

7 Construye frases con los pronombres.

1 Yo / invitar / a ti
Yo te invito.
2 ¿Tú / invitar / a mí?
3 Ellos / invitar / a nosotros
4 Nosotros / invitar / a ellas
5 ¿Ustedes / invitar / a mí?
6 Ella / invitar / a Belén y Jorge
7 Mario / invitar / a ustedes
8 Diego / invitar / a ti
9 ¿Uds. / invitar / a Irene?
10 Alberto / no invitar / a mí

9B Mi novio trae corbata

- *Los colores*
- *Describir la ropa*

Vocabulario

1 Responde.

a ¿De qué color traes hoy la playera / camisa?

b ¿De qué color son los camiones en tu ciudad?

2 Mira el dibujo, ¿a qué persona corresponde cada una de las descripciones?

1 Trae un vestido verde y unos zapatos blancos.
2 Trae unos pantalones rojos, una camisa blanca y unos tenis amarillos.
3 Trae una camisa azul, muy elegante, y una corbata blanca. También trae un traje oscuro.
4 Trae unos pantalones verdes, una playera roja y un collar que combina con los aretes.
5 Trae unos pantalones de mezclilla, una camisa de puntos y unos tenis café.

3 86 Escucha y comprueba.

ADJETIVOS

singular		plural	
masculino	**femenino**	**masculino**	**femenino**
blanco	blanca	blanco**s**	blanca**s**
verde	verde	verde**s**	verde**s**
azul	azul	azul**es**	azul**es**

Hay colores que son nombres de plantas, flores y frutos que normalmente no cambian en género ni en número:

pantalones ***rosa*** *zapatos (de color)* ***naranja***

Hablar

4 Elige dos compañeros y describe qué ropa traen. Lee el texto en voz alta. El resto de la clase tiene que adivinar quiénes son.

5 Responde al cuestionario «Tu ropa y tú».

Tu ropa y tú

1 ¿Cómo prefieres la ropa?
- a Cómoda. ❍
- b Elegante. ❍
- c Moderna. ❍

2 ¿Con quién vas a comprarla?
- a Con mi mamá. ❍
- b Solo/a. ❍
- c Con un amigo/a. ❍

3 ¿Cuándo compras ropa?
- a Todos los meses. ❍
- b Una vez al año. ❍
- c Cuando necesito algo. ❍

4 Si vas a una entrevista de trabajo, ¿qué te pones?
- a Algo formal: un traje, por ejemplo. ❍
- b Algo cómodo: pantalones de mezclilla. ❍
- c Algo informal, pero elegante: una falda bonita / una chamarra moderna. ❍

5 Cuando vas a la fiesta de cumpleaños de un/a amigo/a, ¿qué usas?
- a Algo cómodo: playera y pantalón de mezclilla. ❍
- b Algo elegante: un vestido largo / camisa y pantalón negros. ❍
- c Me da igual: lo primero que encuentro. ❍

6 ¿Qué color es el más elegante?
- a Negro ❍
- b Rojo ❍
- c Blanco ❍
- d Otro: ____________

7 ¿Cuál es tu color preferido para la ropa? ______________

6 Compara tus respuestas con las de tu compañero.

7 Relaciona los adjetivos contrarios.

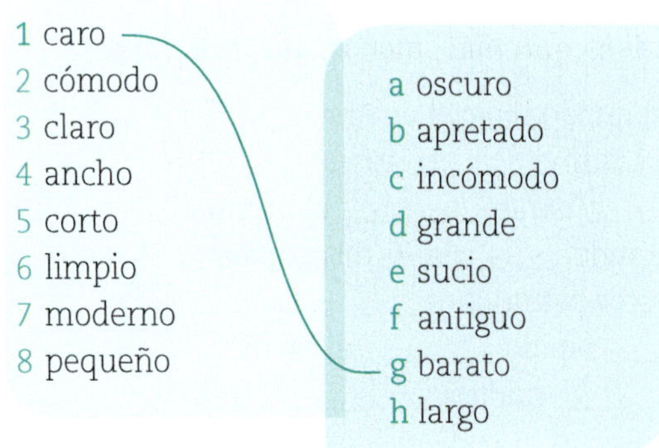

1 caro
2 cómodo
3 claro
4 ancho
5 corto
6 limpio
7 moderno
8 pequeño

a oscuro
b apretado
c incómodo
d grande
e sucio
f antiguo
g barato
h largo

Escribir

8 Escribe cinco frases utilizando los adjetivos anteriores. Fíjate en el modelo.

Rosa trae una falda larga.

9 En parejas. Lee las frases anteriores a tu compañero, que tiene que decidir si las frases son correctas o no.

Pronunciación y ortografía

g / j

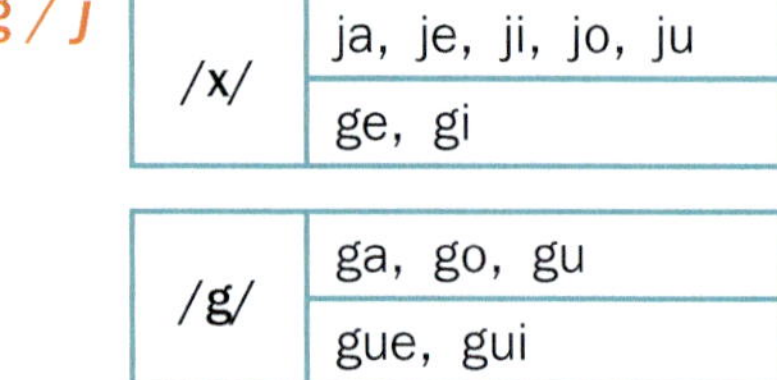

/x/	ja, je, ji, jo, ju
	ge, gi
/g/	ga, go, gu
	gue, gui

1 87 Escucha y repite.

jamón jugar rojo julio joven
gimnasia jefe jirafa geranio
genio gato goma agua guerra
guitarra guapo águila
Guadalajara gota

2 88 Escucha y señala lo que oyes.

9c Buenos Aires es más grande que Toledo

▪ *Hacer comparaciones*

Vocabulario

1 ¿Vives en un pueblo o en una ciudad? Subraya los adjetivos que describen tu pueblo o ciudad.

moderno/a • ruidoso/a • tranquilo/a • grande • antiguo/a
limpio/a • pequeño/a • interesante • aburrido/a

2 Mira las fotos de Buenos Aires y Toledo, lee las frases y señala si las afirmaciones son verdaderas (V) o falsas (F).

1 Buenos Aires es más antigua que Toledo. ☐
2 Toledo es más pequeña que Buenos Aires. ☐
3 Las calles de Buenos Aires son más anchas que las calles de Toledo. ☐
4 Toledo es más ruidosa que Buenos Aires. ☐
5 Buenos Aires está más contaminada que Toledo. ☐
6 Los edificios de Buenos Aires son tan modernos como los de Toledo. ☐

Gramática

COMPARATIVOS
más + adjetivo + que *Juan es **más agradable que** Pedro.*
menos + adjetivo + que *Pedro es **menos agradable que** Juan.*
tan + adjetivo + como *Juan (no) es **tan alto como** Pedro.*

3 Completa las frases con *más, menos, que, tan, como.*

1 Tu carro no es tan rápido como el de Ana.
2 Ese vestido es más caro ________ este.
3 El taxi no es ________ barato ________ el metro.
4 ¿Su casa es tan grande ______ la de mis papás?
5 ¿Te gustan más estos pantalones _____ esos?
6 El avión es ________ rápido ________ el carro.
7 La bicicleta es ________ ruidosa ________ el tren.

COMPARATIVOS IRREGULARES	
bueno	**mejor / mejores + que** *Esta película es **mejor que** esa.*
malo	**peor / peores + que** *Esos pasteles son **peores que** estos.*
grande	**mayor / mayores + que** *Yo soy **mayor que** ella.*
pequeño	**menor / menores + que** *Cinco es **menor que** ocho.*

4 Completa el diálogo con los comparativos *peor(es)*, *mejor(es)*.

Luis: Voy a hacer mi maleta para el viaje, a ver... ¿qué llevo? Mira, estos zapatos están bien, ¿no?

Carla: No, para ir a la montaña, las botas son (1) ________ que los zapatos.

Luis: Tienes razón. ¿Llevo los pantalones de mezclilla?

Carla: No, para el frío son (2) ________ los pantalones de pana.

Luis: Bueno, llevo los dos y listo.

Carla: ¿Por qué llevas la maleta azul?

Luis: Pues porque es (3) ________ que la gris, tiene ruedas.

Carla: Yo prefiero la gris, le caben más cosas. Toma el paraguas, guárdalo.

Luis: ¿El rojo? No, este es (4) ________ que el negro.

Carla: Lo siento, el negro ya está en mi maleta.

5 89 Escucha y comprueba.

6 Observa la imagen y elige la opción correcta.

1 Carlos es *mayor* / *menor* que Clara.
2 Clara es *mayor* / *menor* que Carlos.
3 Clarita es *mayor* / *menor* que Carlitos.
4 Carlitos es *mayor* / *menor* que Clarita.

7 Relaciona. Hay más de una opción.

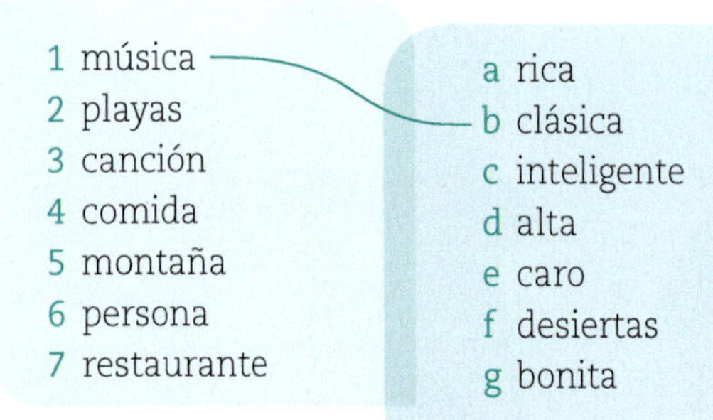

1 música	a rica
2 playas	b clásica
3 canción	c inteligente
4 comida	d alta
5 montaña	e caro
6 persona	f desiertas
7 restaurante	g bonita

8 Escribe frases, comparando.

1 El tren y el avión. (*rápido* / *lento*)
El avión es más rápido que el tren.
2 Nueva York y París. (*grande* / *pequeño*)
3 Los carros y las motos. (*seguros* / *inseguros*)
4 Vivir en el campo y vivir en la ciudad. (*aburrido* / *divertido*)
5 La comida casera y la comida rápida. (*buena* / *mala*)
6 En verano y en invierno. (*bueno* / *malo*)

Hablar

9 Pregunta a tu compañero por las respuestas de la actividad anterior.

- *¿Qué ciudad es más grande, Nueva York o París?*
- *Nueva York es más grande que París.*

Gramática

DEMOSTRATIVOS (ADJETIVOS Y PRONOMBRES)			
singular		plural	
masculino	**femenino**	**masculino**	**femenino**
este	esta	estos	estas
ese	esa	esos	esas
aquel	aquella	aquellos	aquellas

PRONOMBRES DEMOSTRATIVOS (NEUTROS)		
esto	eso	aquello

10 Subraya el demostrativo adecuado.

1 ¿Te gustan *estos* / *estas* lentes de sol?
2 ¿Cuánto cuesta *este* / *esto* anillo?
3 ¿De quién es *esta* / *esto*?
4 ¿De quién es *esta* / *este* cartera?
5 Luis, trae *aquel* / *aquella* bolsa.
6 ¿Qué es *aquellos* / *aquello*?
7 Dame *esa* / *ese* caja de ahí.
8 *Eso* / *Esos* no me gusta.

Escuchar

1 (90) María y Jordi nos cuentan cómo es su ciudad favorita. Escucha y completa los textos.

A María le gusta vivir en una ciudad (1) __________ porque tiene (2) __________ oferta cultural y de actividades de tiempo libre. Sin embargo, no le gusta el ruido ni la (3) __________. Piensa que, para tener una ciudad más limpia, lo mejor es usar transporte (4) __________.

Jordi prefiere vivir en una ciudad pequeña porque tiene más (5) __________ y sus hijos viven más en contacto con la (6) __________. Probablemente cambie de ciudad en el (7) __________ si sus hijos van a la (8) __________.

Hablar

2 Habla con tu compañero sobre cómo es la ciudad que te gusta.

moderna • antigua • tranquila • ruidosa grande • pequeña • bien comunicada turística • limpia • segura

parques • espectáculos • transporte público playa • contaminación • museos bibliotecas • vida nocturna

- *A mí me gustan las ciudades turísticas porque siempre hay mucha gente y tienen muchos lugares interesantes y mucha vida nocturna.*
- *Pues yo prefiero las ciudades tranquilas...*

- *En México a mí me gusta Guadalajara, por ejemplo...*
- *Pues a mí me gusta más una ciudad como Querétaro.*

Escribir

3 Escribe un texto de unas 100 palabras sobre cómo es tu ciudad favorita. Utiliza todo el vocabulario que ya conoces.

Leer

4 Antes de leer el texto de la página siguiente contesta a las preguntas.

1 ¿Conoces algún cuadro o pintor español o hispanoamericano?
2 ¿Conoces algún museo famoso en México o en algún país latinoamericano?

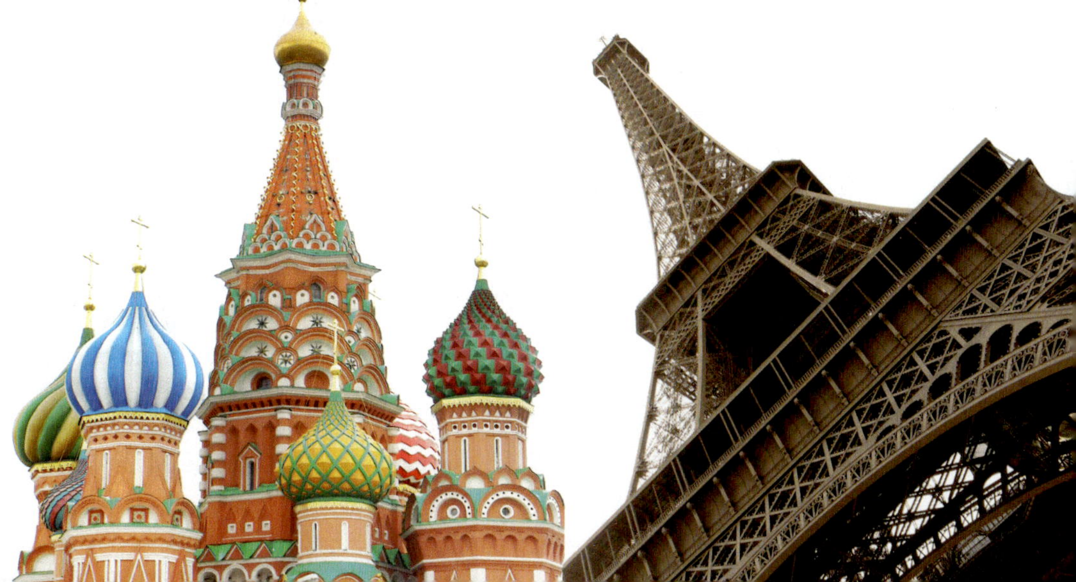

Los murales de Diego Rivera

Diego Rivera (Guanajuato/1886 — Ciudad de México/1957) fue un destacado muralista mexicano que realizó obras de alto contenido social en edificios públicos.

Sueño de una tarde dominical en la Alameda Central, mural de 1947, mide 4.70 m. x 15.60 m. y tiene un peso de 35 toneladas. En la actualidad es la principal pintura en la exhibición permanente del Museo Mural Diego Rivera, lugar creado especialmente para esta obra.

En él Rivera ilustró momentos importantes de la vida política y social en la historia de México, como la conquista, la época colonial, la independencia, la invasión norteamericana y la intervención europea.

Incluyó personajes que ya no existían, pintó con muchos colores y no dejó casi nada sin colorear. Este mural es como una gran película que habla de la historia de la ciudad y la cultura mexicana.

Benito Juárez, José Martí, Sor Juana Inés de la Cruz, Emiliano Zapata y demás personajes clave en la historia de México aparecen plasmados en el mural.

5 Lee el texto y señala verdadero (V) o falso (F).

1. Diego Rivera fue un famoso artista mexicano. [V]
2. La obra no es de gran tamaño. [ ]
3. Plasmó los momentos claves de la historia de México. [ ]
4. Este mural se colocó en el Museo de Bellas artes de la Ciudad de México. [ ]
5. La pintura sirve para decoración de una casa particular. [ ]
6. Los más importantes personajes de la historia mundial aparecieron en el mural. [ ]
7. La obra de Rivera es muy romántica. [ ]

6 Comenta con tus compañeros.

- ¿Te gusta la pintura?
- ¿Qué cuadro te gusta más?
- ¿Cuál te gusta menos?
- ¿Vas a museos con frecuencia?

9 AUTOEVALUACIÓN

1 Completa las descripciones con los adjetivos del recuadro.

negro • negros • ~~café~~
blanca • café

Rafael viene hoy muy elegante. Trae unos pantalones (1) café, una camisa (2) ___________ y una corbata a rayas. La chamarra es (3) ____________, del mismo color que los pantalones. Los zapatos son (4) __________ y trae un sombrero también (5) ___________.

moderno • negros (x2)
azul • roja • negra

Marina viene hoy a clase con ropa deportiva. Trae unos pantalones de color (6) ____________, una playera (7) __________ con un estampado muy (8) ____________, unos calcetines (9) ___________, unos tenis (10) __________ y, en el pelo, una cinta también (11) ____________.

2 Relaciona.

1 Buenos días, ¿puedo ayudarle? [f]
2 ¿Puedo probarme estos pantalones? ☐
3 ¿Cómo paga, con tarjeta o en efectivo? ☐
4 Álvaro, ¿te gustan estos zapatos? ☐
5 ¿No tiene otro más barato? ☐
6 ¿Cómo le queda la falda? ☐

a Bien, me la llevo.
b No mucho, me gustan más aquellos.
c Sí, claro, ahí están los probadores.
d Con tarjeta.
e Sí, este solo cuesta treinta euros.
f Sí, ¿cuánto cuestan estos lentes?

3 Completa con los pronombres *lo, la, los, las*.

Julia: ¿Qué llevas en esa bolsa?
Cristina: Los regalos de Navidad.
Julia: ¿Puedo (1) verlos?
Cristina: Bueno: estos paquetes son para los abuelos.
Julia: ¿Y esas cajas blancas?
Cristina: Son para mamá y papá.
Julia: ¿Puedo (2) abrir______?
Cristina: No, es una sorpresa.
Julia: ¿Y ese carro rojo? ¿Es para Raúl?
Cristina: Sí, tengo que (3) envolver______ primero. ¿Tienes papel de regalo?
Julia Sí, (4) ______ tengo en el primer cajón del escritorio. ¿Para quién es esta raqueta? ¿Para mí?
Cristina: No, es para Raúl, (5) ______ voy a envolver también.
Julia: ¿Y para mí?
Cristina: Es este paquete, ¿(6) ______ quieres ver ahora? ¿No prefieres esperar?
Julia: No, ahora, (7) ábre______, por favor.
Cristina: No, mejor (8) ábre______ tú.
Julia: ¡Un cinturón negro! Me encanta. ¿Puedo (9) ponérme______ hoy?

4 Selecciona la opción correcta.

1 ■ ¿Qué es **esto** / **este**?
● Es un cuaderno, ¿te gusta?
2 ■ ¿Quién es **eso** / **ese** chavo?
● Es mi hermano **mayor** / **más grande**.
3 ■ ¡Mira! Están robando una moto del estacionamiento.
● ¿Cuál?
■ **Esta** / **Aquella** moto del fondo, la azul.
4 ■ ¿Cuánto cuestan **estas** / **aquellas** bolsas de dulces, las de ahí?
● Ochenta pesos, pero **estas** / **esas** otras de aquí son **más** / **menos** baratas, cuestan sesenta pesos.

5 Escribe el adjetivo contrario.

1 antiguo ______ 3 tranquilo ______ 5 barato ______
2 sucio ______ 4 claro ______ 6 largo ______

¿Qué sabes?

- Ir de compras.
- Describir la ropa.
- Concordancia de nombres y adjetivos de color.
- Hacer comparaciones.
- Algunas obras de pintores hispanos.

Salud y enfermedad

- Las partes del cuerpo
- Hablar de enfermedades
- Hablar de hábitos en el pasado
- Expresar planes e intenciones
- Escribir un blog sobre un viaje
- **Cultura**: El imperio inca

- *Las partes del cuerpo*
- *Hablar de enfermedades*

Vocabulario

1 ¿Vas mucho al doctor? ¿Cuándo? ¿En verano, en invierno, en primavera...?

2 91 Mira la imagen, escucha y repite.

3 92 Escucha, fíjate en las fotos y relaciona cada personaje con su problema de salud.

1 A Pedro 2 A Daniel 3 A Carmen 4 A Julia 5 A Victoria 6 Ana 7 A Ricardo	le duele le duelen tiene	a los oídos b el estómago c la espalda d la cabeza e la garganta f las muelas g fiebre

Leer

4 (93) Escucha y luego lee los siguientes diálogos.

A

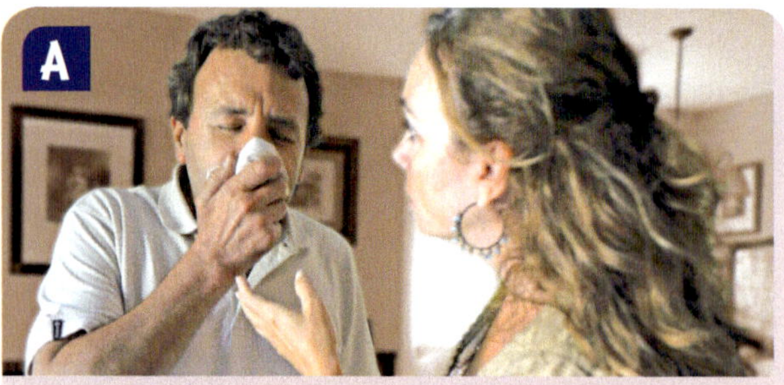

Sara: ¡Hola, Ángel!, ¿cómo estás?
Ángel: No muy bien.
Sara: ¿Qué te pasa?
Ángel: Tengo una gripa muy fuerte.
Sara: ¿Y qué tomas cuando estás así?
Ángel: De momento, nada.
Sara: ¿Por qué no te tomas una aspirina con un vaso de limonada caliente con miel y te acuestas?
Ángel: Sí, creo que es lo mejor.

B

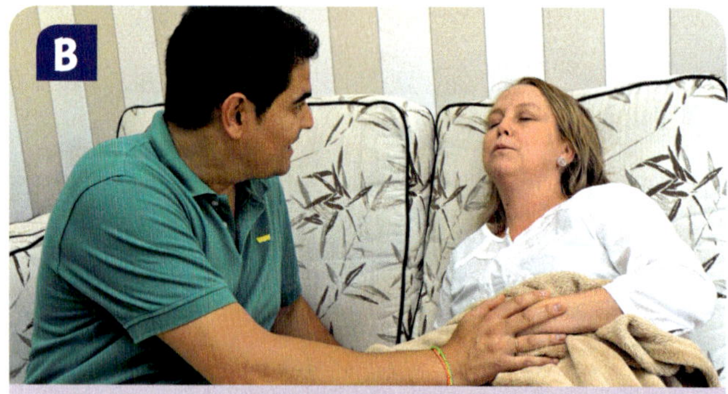

Raúl: ¡No te ves bien! ¿Qué te pasa?
Luisa: Me duele muchísimo el estómago.
Raúl: ¿Por qué no vas al doctor?
Luisa: Sí, voy a ir mañana.
Raúl: Mira, tómate un té y acuéstate sin cenar.
Luisa: Sí, creo que es lo mejor.

5 Ahora contesta a las preguntas.

1 ¿Qué le pasa a Ángel?
2 ¿Qué le aconseja Sara?
3 ¿Qué le pasa a Luisa?
4 ¿Qué le aconseja Raúl?

Gramática

VERBO *DOLER*

(a mí)	me	
(a ti)	te	
(a él / ella / Ud.)	le	**duele** la cabeza
(a nosotros/as)	nos	**duelen** los oídos
(a vosotros/as)	os	
(a ellos / ellas / Uds.)	les	

6 Completa con el pronombre y la forma adecuada del verbo *doler*.

1 A mi hermano le duelen las piernas.
2 A mí ________________ las muelas.
3 Carmen y Vanessa son estilistas y ________________ la espalda.
4 ¿A ti ________________ algo?
5 ¡No hagan tanto ruido! Al abuelo y a mí ________________ la cabeza.
6 ¿A usted no ________________ el estómago con esa comida tan fuerte?

7 Relaciona estos problemas de salud con su remedio.

1 dolor de cabeza
2 dolor de garganta
3 dolor de espalda
4 dolor de muelas
5 fiebre
6 dolor de oídos

a tomar una aspirina
b ir al quiropráctico
c ir al doctor
d ir al dentista
e tomar limonada con miel
f acostarse y descansar

Escuchar

8 (94) Escucha y completa las siguientes conversaciones.

- El paciente n.° 1 tiene la gripa.
  Consejo del doctor: tomar ________________ y ________________.
- Al paciente n.° 2 le duele ________________.
  Consejo del doctor tomar ________________ y ________________.
- Al paciente n.° 3 le duele ________________.
  Consejo del doctor: no tomar ________________ ni ________________, comer ________________ y ________________, y tomar ________________.

Hablar

9 En parejas, practica diálogos como en el ejemplo, dando consejos para los problemas de salud de tu compañero (mira la actividad 7).

- *¿Qué te pasa?*
- *Me duele la cabeza.*
- *¿Por qué no tomas una aspirina?*

10B Antes salíamos con los amigos

- *Hablar de hábitos en el pasado*

Gramática

1 «Antes la gente era más feliz que ahora». ¿Estás de acuerdo?

No estoy de acuerdo porque antes no había televisión.

2 95 Escucha y después lee el siguiente texto.

Elena y Emilio ya son papás. Su vida cambió cuando, de repente, se encontraron con... dos bebés en los brazos.

Elena: Antes de ser papás teníamos una vida social muy activa: viajábamos, íbamos al cine, salíamos con amigos, teníamos mucho tiempo libre. Emilio jugaba *hockey*, yo estudiaba alemán...

Emilio: Ahora todo es distinto. Dedicamos todo nuestro tiempo a Álvaro y Adrián, que son maravillosos.

3 ¿Verdadero (V) o falso (F)?

1 Elena y Emilio tienen un bebé. ☐
2 Antes viajaban mucho. ☐
3 Emilio no practicaba deportes. ☐
4 Emilio estudiaba idiomas. ☐
5 Ahora están muy ocupados con sus hijos. ☐

IMPERFECTO

Verbos regulares

	viajar	tener	salir
yo	viaj**aba**	ten**ía**	sal**ía**
tú	viaj**abas**	ten**ías**	sal**ías**
él / ella / Ud.	viaj**aba**	ten**ía**	sal**ía**
nosotros/as	viaj**ábamos**	ten**íamos**	sal**íamos**
vosotros/as	viaj**abais**	ten**íais**	sal**íais**
ellos / ellas / Uds.	viaj**aban**	ten**ían**	sal**ían**

4 Elige la forma correcta del verbo.

1 Antes Elena y Emilio no ***tenían / tienen*** hijos.
2 Cuando no tenían hijos, Elena y Emilio ***viajan / viajaban*** por todo el mundo.
3 Ahora Elena no ***estudiaba / estudia*** alemán.
4 Emilio ya no ***juega / jugaba*** *hockey*.
5 Antes de ser padres, ***salían / salen*** los fines de semana con sus amigos.
6 Antes les ***gustan / gustaba*** mucho el cine.

IMPERFECTO

Verbos irregulares

	ir	ser	ver
yo	iba	era	veía
tú	ibas	eras	veías
él / ella / Ud.	iba	era	veía
nosotros/as	íbamos	éramos	veíamos
vosotros/as	ibais	erais	veíais
ellos / ellas / Uds.	iban	eran	veían

5 Completa el siguiente texto sobre la vida de Emilio.

Yo antes (1) era jugador de un equipo de *hockey*. (2) ________ (entrenar) tres días a la semana. Los domingos mis compañeros y yo (3) ________ (jugar) un partido de liga. Cada dos semanas nos (4) ________ (ir) en autobús al campo del equipo contrario. A veces, Elena me (5) ________ (acompañar) y después de los partidos (6) ________ (ir) a cenar todos juntos. Todo (7) ________ (ser) maravilloso. Pero ahora es más divertido porque somos cuatro.

Hablar

6 ¿Cómo era tu vida cuando tenías diez o doce años? En parejas, pregunta y responde a tu compañero.

1 ¿Cómo era tu escuela?
2 ¿A qué hora entrabas y a qué hora salías?
3 ¿Qué hacías cuando salías de la escuela?
4 ¿Comías en la escuela o en tu casa?
5 ¿Qué hacías los domingos por la mañana?, ¿y por la tarde?
6 ¿Cómo era tu maestro favorito o maestra favorita?
7 ¿Qué hacías durante las vacaciones de verano?
8 ¿Cómo se llamaba tu mejor amigo/a?
9 ¿Qué deporte practicabas?
10 ¿Cuál era tu materia favorita? ¿Por qué?

Escuchar

8 96 Escucha la historia de Martina y elige la respuesta correcta.

1 Martina tiene:
a casi cien años.
b menos de ochenta años.

2 Cuando era niña, vivía:
a con sus papás.
b con sus hermanos y su mamá

3 Trabajaba en el campo:
a cuando era niña.
b después de terminar sus estudios.

4 Trabajaba:
a ocho horas diarias.
b doce horas diarias.

5 A los diecinueve años tenía:
a dos hijos.
b un hijo.

6 Los sábados y domingos:
a compraba en el tianguis.
b trabajaba en el tianguis.

7 ¡Federico se sacó la lotería! Comenta con tu compañero cómo era su vida antes de ser millonario. Utiliza los verbos del recuadro.

tener • desayunar • regalar • navegar • comer • ~~vivir~~

Antes no vivía en una mansión.

10C Voy a trabajar en un hotel

▪ *Expresar planes e intenciones*

Leer

1 Lee este correo y completa las frases.

Voy a trabajar en un hotel

Enviar · Chat · Adjuntar · Dirección · Tipo de letra · Colores · Borrador

Para: fernando@mail.com
Cc:
Asunto: Voy a trabajar en un hotel
Cuenta: Santiago <santiago@yahoo.es>

¡Hola, Fernando!
¡Por fin terminaron las clases! Tengo muchos planes para este verano: en julio voy a trabajar en un hotel en Cancún durante un mes, porque quiero ahorrar dinero para viajar por Europa. Quiero ir a Londres con María, vamos a estudiar un poco de inglés. De regreso, voy a visitar París con mi hermano, que está ahí estudiando francés. Como ves, tengo un verano muy ocupado. Y tú, ¿qué vas a hacer? Cuéntame.
Un abrazo,
Santiago

1 Santiago __________ muchos planes para este verano.
2 En julio __________ a trabajar en un hotel.
3 Después __________ por Europa.
4 Santiago y María __________ a ir a Londres.
5 Después de Londres __________ visitar París.

2 Relaciona los planes de Santiago con las siguientes situaciones, como en el ejemplo.

1 Santiago va a trabajar en un hotel. [c]
2 Va a viajar por Europa. [ ]
3 Él y María van a ir a Londres. [ ]
4 Va a visitar París. [ ]
5 Su hermano está en París. [ ]

a Quiere aprender francés.
b Quieren mejorar su inglés.
c Quiere ahorrar dinero.
d Tiene un mes de vacaciones.
e Quiere estar unos días con su hermano.

Santiago va a trabajar en un hotel porque quiere ahorrar dinero.

3 ¿Qué van a hacer? Fíjate en las fotos y utiliza los verbos del recuadro.

ver una obra de teatro • comprar un carro
darse un beso • tener un hijo • casarse • ~~nadar~~

1 *Van a nadar.*

2

3

4

5

6

Hablar

4 En parejas, di lo que vas a hacer este fin de semana. Utiliza las siguientes ideas:

levantarme tarde | hacer ejercicio | reunirme con amigos | ir a pasear | limpiar la casa | salir a cenar | navegar por internet | ver televisión

5 ¿Qué va a hacer Federico con el dinero que se ganó en la lotería? Relaciona las preguntas con las respuestas.

1 ¡Felicidades, Federico! ¿Cómo te sientes? ☐
2 ¿Vas a organizar una fiesta? ☐
3 ¿Qué es lo primero que te vas a comprar? ☐
4 ¿Te vas a comprar un barco? ☐
5 ¿Te vas a ir de vacaciones? ☐
6 ¿Qué le vas a regalar a tu esposa? ☐

a No, no sé navegar.
b Sí, voy a dar una vuelta alrededor del mundo.
c Muchas joyas.
d ¡De maravilla! ¡Como nunca!
e Sí, con todos mis amigos.
f Una casa muy grande en el campo.

Escribir

6 Imagina que eres periodista. Escribe una pequeña noticia sobre los planes de Federico.

Federico tiene grandes planes para el futuro.
Dice que va a...
Dice que no va a...

Pronunciación y ortografía

1 (97) Escucha las siguientes palabras y escríbelas en el lugar correspondiente según el acento.

alemán café teléfono cantante
árbol canción examen estudiar
computadora ventana periódico
celular pintura música

ESDRÚJULAS
teléfono

LLANAS
cantante

AGUDAS
alemán

Reglas de acentuación

a Las palabras agudas llevan tilde cuando terminan en vocal, ***n*** o **s**.
b Las palabras llanas o graves llevan tilde cuando terminan en consonante diferente de ***n*** o **s**.
c Las palabras esdrújulas llevan tilde siempre.

2 (98) Escucha y escribe las tildes que faltan.

1 Andres me habló por telefono para saludarme.
2 Barbara trabaja en una empresa de informatica en Mexico.
3 Yo estudie decoracion en Milan.
4 Antes Raul vivia cerca de aqui, pero ahora esta viviendo en Chiapas.
5 Aqui hace mas calor que ahi.
6 Ella es mas guapa que el.
7 Los telefonos celulares son muy comodos.
8 Esta casa es mas centrica que tu departamento.

Leer

1 Lee el texto y relaciona los títulos 1-6 con los párrafos A-F.

1 El imperio inca. [A]
2 Constructores de carreteras. [ ]
3 Casas sencillas. [ ]
4 Un pueblo religioso. [ ]
5 Campesinos y artesanos. [ ]
6 La ciudad imperial. [ ]

A En el siglo xv, los incas, antes de la llegada de los españoles a Perú, vivían en la montaña, en el corazón de los Andes. Hablaban una lengua llamada quechua y tenían un gran imperio.

B Cuzco, la capital del imperio, se levantaba a 3200 m de altitud. Estaba rodeada de montañas y protegida por una fortaleza. Para los incas, Cuzco era el centro del mundo.

C Los incas creían en dioses como el Sol, la Luna y el Trueno. Pero también adoraban montañas, lagos y plantas.

D Las casas eran de piedra, con tejados de hierba seca y una sola habitación. Dentro, los incas comían en cuclillas. Por la noche dormían envueltos en mantas.

E Los incas construyeron una importante red de caminos empedrados. En las laderas abruptas tallaban escalones en la roca. Y para cruzar los precipicios, hacían puentes colgantes con cuerdas vegetales.

F Se calcula que en el imperio vivían ocho millones de personas. Los campesinos cultivaban la tierra y cuidaban rebaños de llamas. Los artesanos fabricaban objetos de cerámica y tejidos.

2 Corrige las siguientes afirmaciones.

1 Los incas hablaban español.
Los incas hablaban quechua.
2 Los campesinos vivían del comercio.
3 Los incas adoraban a un solo dios.
4 Vivían en grandes casas de madera.
5 En la época de los incas, no había vías de comunicación.
6 Cuzco está al nivel del mar.

Escribir

3 Lee el blog de Carlos sobre su viaje a la Sierra Tarahumara. ¿Qué expresan los verbos en azul? ¿Y los verbos en verde?

http://aventura.blogspot.com/

BARRANCAS DEL COBRE

Viernes, 1 de julio
La semana que viene me voy a ir de vacaciones con tres amigos. Vamos a acampar en las Barrancas del Cobre. Me voy a llevar mi computadora portátil para continuar con mi blog.

Viernes, 8 de julio
Ayer armamos la tienda de campaña junto a un río. Hacía muy buen clima y nadamos en el río. Voy a tomar muchas fotos porque las vistas de las montañas son espectaculares. Mañana vamos a navegar en canoa por el río.

Sábado, 9 de julio
Ayer nos la pasamos muy bien con la canoa, pero el agua estaba muy fría. Me caí al agua varias veces. Hoy vamos a hacer senderismo por la montaña. Me voy a llevar la brújula y el botiquín.

4 Escribe un blog sobre un viaje. No olvides utilizar los tiempos apropiados.

- Piensa en los detalles del viaje: ¿dónde?, ¿cuándo?, ¿con quién?, ¿qué vas a llevar?...
- Describe el clima y el lugar.
- ¿Qué actividades vas a hacer?
- ¿Qué hiciste el primer día?
- ¿Cómo fueron las actividades del segundo día?

Escuchar

5 99 Escucha la entrevista con la alpinista Elisa Urrutia y contesta a las preguntas.

1 ¿Elisa va a escalar la próxima semana?
2 ¿Por qué Elisa necesita un poco de descanso?
3 ¿Qué trabajo va a realizar en el centro de alpinismo?
4 ¿Qué acontecimiento importante sucedió en su vida el año pasado?
5 ¿Qué acontecimiento importante va a suceder en su vida el otoño próximo?

Hablar

Alumno A (alumno B, ver «En parejas», pág. 175)

6 Imagina que sacaste la lotería. Prepara respuestas para la entrevista que te hará B.

a ¿Con quién lo vas a celebrar?
b ¿Qué vas a comprar?
c ¿Adónde vas a ir de vacaciones?
d ¿Con quién vas a ir?
e ¿Qué vas a hacer al regreso del viaje?

7 Prepara preguntas para entrevistar a B, que se va a ir a estudiar a otro país. Puedes añadir otras preguntas.

a A qué país / ir
b Qué / estudiar
c Dónde / quedarse
d Con quién / vivir
e En qué / trabajar

10 AUTOEVALUACIÓN

1 Relaciona.

1 Estos zapatos son nuevos, por eso ☑ c
2 Juan usa dos aretes ☐
3 Los futbolistas cuidan especialmente ☐
4 Uso guantes ☐
5 Ana lleva varios anillos ☐
6 Cuando subo mucho de peso, ☐

a me duelen los brazos.
b sus piernas.
c me duelen los pies.
d porque tengo frío en las manos.
e en cada oreja.
f en los dedos.

2 Completa el texto con el imperfecto de los verbos entre paréntesis.

Marisa y Alfredo se casaron la semana pasada. Ahora viven juntos en Ciudad de México, pero antes de conocerse, cuando ellos (1) eran (ser) jóvenes, los dos (2) ________ (vivir) en distintas ciudades. Marisa (3) ________ (trabajar) con un grupo de teatro infantil y (4) ________ (estudiar) en la universidad. Alfredo (5) ________ (filmar) películas con un grupo de aficionados y (6) ________ (escribir) excelentes guiones. Un día, cuando los dos (7) ________ (ir) a un festival de cine, se conocieron y, desde entonces, son inseparables.

3 Subraya el verbo más adecuado.

1 Ayer ***fui / iba*** a ver a Jacinto.
2 Cuando Luis ***tenía / tuvo*** diez años, ***jugaba / jugó*** futbol todos los sábados.
3 Antes me ***gustaba / gustó*** la música rock, pero ahora me ***gustaba / gusta*** la música romántica.
4 Elena y Emilio antes no ***tuvieron / tenían*** hijos y ahora tienen dos.
5 Elena y Emilio ***iban / fueron*** a París en el año 2002.
6 Mi esposo ***jugó / jugaba*** al básquetbol cuando ***era / fue*** joven.
7 Yo no fumo, pero antes ***fumé / fumaba*** mucho.
8 Mi hermana de niña ***era / fue*** rubia.
9 ¿***Viste / Veías*** a Sara el sábado pasado?
10 Ayer me ***acostaba / acosté*** muy tarde.

4 Escribe las preguntas sobre planes para el próximo fin de semana.

1 ¿Tú / estudiar?
¿Vas a estudiar?
2 ¿Ustedes / ir al cine?
3 ¿Lorenzo / escuchar música?
4 ¿Tu novio / comprar ropa?
5 ¿Tú / navegar por internet?
6 ¿Ustedes / hacer los ejercicios de español?
7 ¿Ellos / ir al futbol?
8 ¿Tus papás / ir a la ópera?
9 ¿Tú / viajar en barco?
10 ¿Nosotros / verse con Alba?

5 100 **Escucha al grupo de música Los Escorpiones hablando con su mánager y contesta a las preguntas.**

1 ¿Cuándo va a estar listo el nuevo disco de Los Escorpiones en el mercado?
2 ¿Cuándo van a empezar la gira?
3 ¿Van a hacer su propia página web?
4 ¿Qué van a hacer en septiembre?
5 ¿Quién va a cantar con ellos en el concierto?

¿Qué sabes?

- Las partes del cuerpo.
- Hablar de enfermedades (verbo *doler*).
- Hablar de hábitos en el pasado.
- Expresar planes e intenciones (*ir a* + infinitivo).
- Las reglas de acentuación.

GRAMÁTICA

VERBOS *SER* Y *TENER*. PRESENTE

	ser	tener
yo	soy	tengo
tú	eres	tienes
él / ella / Ud.	es	tiene
nosotros/as	somos	tenemos
vosotros/as	sois	tenéis
ellos / ellas / Uds.	son	tienen

→ Usamos el verbo ***ser*** para identificarnos, hablar de la nacionalidad y de la profesión.

*Esta **es** Edith Edith **es** mexicana. Edith **es** azafata.*

GÉNERO DE LOS NOMBRES

→ Los nombres de las cosas tienen género masculino o femenino:

el libro *la ventana*

→ Los nombres de las personas y animales tienen género masculino y femenino.

el gato *la gata*
el maestro *la maestra*
el hombre *la mujer*

→ En el caso de los nombres de profesión:

a Si el masculino termina en **-o**, cambia por **-a**:
el abogado *la abogada*

b Si el masculino termina en consonante, añade **-a**:
pintor *pintora*

c Si el masculino termina en **-e**, puede quedar igual o cambiar por **-a**.
el estudiante *la estudiante*
el presidente *la presidenta*

d Si el masculino termina en **-ista**, no cambia.
el taxista *la taxista*

GÉNERO DE LOS ADJETIVOS

→ Los adjetivos tienen el mismo género que el nombre al que se refieren.

*El maestro es **divertido**. La maestra es **divertida**.*

→ En el caso de los adjetivos de nacionalidad:

a Si el masculino termina en **-o**, el femenino termina en **-a**.
brasileño *brasileña*

b Si el masculino termina en consonante, el femenino añade **-a**.
alemán *alemana*

c Si el masculino termina en **-a**, **-e**, **-í**, no cambia.
belga / belga *cretense / cretense* *iraní / iraní*

VERBOS REGULARES. PRESENTE

Tenemos tres conjugaciones (1.ª, 2.ª, 3.ª), según la terminación del infinitivo: **-ar**, **-er**, **-ir**.

trabajar	comer	vivir
trabaj**o**	com**o**	viv**o**
trabaj**as**	com**es**	viv**es**
trabaj**a**	com**e**	viv**e**
trabaj**amos**	com**emos**	viv**imos**
trabaj**áis**	com**éis**	viv**ís**
trabaj**an**	com**en**	viv**en**

PRONOMBRES PERSONALES SUJETO

→ Tenemos 10 pronombres (*vosotros* y *vosotras* solo se usan en España):

yo • tú • él • ella • usted (Ud.) • nosotros
nosotras • ellos • ellas • ustedes (Uds.)

→ Estos pronombres no se utilizan siempre, solo cuando queremos distinguir bien entre diferentes sujetos.

TÚ / USTED, VOSOTROS / USTEDES

→ En América Latina usamos ***tú*** y ***ustedes*** cuando hablamos con conocidos, amigos y personas de igual o inferior rango.

→ Usamos ***usted*** y ***ustedes*** cuando hablamos con desconocidos, personas mayores y de mayor rango.

→ En España se usa ***vosotros/as*** en lugar de ***ustedes*** y, en algunos países, ***vos*** en lugar de ***tú***.

VOCABULARIO

GENTILICIOS

alemán/a • tapatío/a • brasileño/a
regiomontano/a • estadounidense • francés/a
inglés/a • japonés/a • marroquí • mexicano/a

PROFESIONES

ciclista • actriz • mesero/a • cantante
cartero/a • escritor/a • estudiante • futbolista
doctor/a • policía • estilista • maestro/a
contador/a • taxista • vendedor/a

NÚMEROS

0 cero 1 uno 2 dos 3 tres 4 cuatro 5 cinco 6 seis
7 siete 8 ocho 9 nueve 10 diez 11 once 12 doce
13 trece 14 catorce 15 quince 16 dieciséis
17 diecisiete 18 dieciocho 19 diecinueve 20 veinte

GRAMÁTICA

PLURAL DE LOS NOMBRES

→ Si el singular termina en vocal (excepto **í**), el plural se forma añadiendo una **-s**.

un libro *dos libros*

→ Si el singular termina en consonante, se añade **-es**.

un hotel *dos hoteles* *un lápiz* *dos lápices*

ADJETIVOS POSESIVOS

sujeto	Posesivos	
	singular	plural
yo	mi	mis
tú	tu	tus
él / ella / Ud.	su	sus
nosotros/as	nuestro/a	nuestros/as
vosotros/as	vuestro/a	vuestros/as
ellos/as / Uds.	su	sus

→ Los adjetivos posesivos concuerdan en número con el nombre al que acompañan.

*Esta es **mi** hermana y estos son **mis** papás.*

VERBO *ESTAR*. PRESENTE

Presente del verbo *estar*	
yo	estoy
tú	estás
él / ella / Ud.	está
nosotros/as	estamos
vosotros/as	estáis
ellos / ellas / Uds.	están

→ Usamos el verbo ***estar*** para expresar ubicación.

*Pedro **está** en casa.*

DEMOSTRATIVOS

→ Los pronombres demostrativos ***esta, este, estas, estos*** se refieren a algo o alguien cercano.

	singular	plural
masculino	este	estos
femenino	esta	estas

***Esta** es mi prima.*
***Este** es mi perro Miko.*
***Estas** son las bicicletas de mis hermanos.*
***Estos** son mis compañeros de clase.*

VOCABULARIO

MARCADORES DE LUGAR

El celular está...

al lado del libro

debajo del libro

encima del libro

delante de los libros

detrás de los libros

entre el libro y la lámpara

a la derecha

a la izquierda

FAMILIA

abuelo/a • papá • mamá • hijo/a
primo/a • esposo/a • hermano/a

ESTADO CIVIL

soltero/a • casado/a • divorciado/a

LA CLASE

pluma • cuaderno • diccionario • lápiz • libro
mapa • mesa • silla • televisión • ventana

NÚMEROS

20 veinte
21 veintiuno
22 veintidós
23 veintitrés
24 veinticuatro
25 veinticinco
26 veintiséis
27 veintisiete
28 veintiocho
29 veintinueve
30 treinta
31 treinta y uno
40 cuarenta
50 cincuenta
60 sesenta
70 setenta
80 ochenta
90 noventa

100 cien
101 ciento uno
200 doscientos/as
300 trescientos/as
400 cuatrocientos/as
500 quinientos/as
600 seiscientos/as
700 setecientos/as
800 ochocientos/as
900 novecientos/as
1 000 mil
1 105 mil ciento cinco
1 500 mil quinientos
1 940 mil novecientos cuarenta
2 001 dos mil uno
5 000 cinco mil

GRAMÁTICA

VERBOS REFLEXIVOS. PRESENTE

		levantar(se)	acostar(se)
yo	**me**	levanto	acuesto
tú	**te**	levantas	acuestas
él / ella / Ud.	**se**	levanta	acuesta
nosotros/as	**nos**	levantamos	acostamos
vosotros/as	**os**	levantáis	acostáis
ellos / ellas / Uds.	**se**	levantan	acuestan

→ Los pronombres reflexivos se usan con verbos que expresan acciones que el sujeto realiza sobre sí mismo: *lavarse, bañarse, peinarse, afeitarse*, etcétera.

→ Cuando la acción del sujeto no se realiza sobre sí mismo estos verbos no llevan pronombre.

*María **se lava** la cara.*
*María **lava** la ropa.*

→ Tenemos otros verbos que se utilizan con estos pronombres, aunque no son reflexivos: *llamarse, quedarse, casarse*, etcétera.

VERBOS IRREGULARES. PRESENTE

Verbos con irregularidades vocálicas	
empezar (e>ie)	volver (o>ue)
empiezo	vuelvo
empiezas	vuelves
empieza	vuelve
empezamos	volvemos
empezáis	volvéis
empiezan	vuelven

Otros verbos irregulares		
ir	venir	salir
voy	vengo	salgo
vas	vienes	sales
va	viene	sale
vamos	venimos	salimos
vais	venís	salís
van	vienen	salen

PREPOSICIONES DE TIEMPO

Días		
El lunes Hoy El sábado	en	la mañana la tarde la noche

Horas			
Son A	las diez las cinco las tres	de	la mañana la tarde la noche la madrugada

*Rosa se levanta **a** las siete.*
*Carlos sale de casa **a** las ocho.*
*Yo trabajo **desde** las ocho **hasta** las tres.*
*Yo no trabajo **por** la tarde.*
*Ella termina su trabajo **a** las cinco **de** la tarde.*
*Rosa vuelve a su casa **a** las cuatro.*
*Mi jefe trabaja **de** ocho **de** la mañana **a** ocho **de** la noche.*

VOCABULARIO

VERBOS DE ACCIONES COTIDIANAS

levantarse • acostarse • lavarse
bañarse • peinarse • afeitarse
desayunar • comer • cenar • almorzar
estudiar • trabajar • empezar • terminar

VERBOS DE MOVIMIENTO

salir • ir • venir • entrar • llegar • volver

PROFESIONES

doctor/a • enfermero/a • contador/a • mesero/a
ingeniero/a en sistemas computacionales • chef
cajero/a • maestro/a • vendedor/a • mesero/a
estudiante • recepcionista • azafato/a

DESAYUNOS

leche • té • mantequilla • mermelada
jugo • huevo • queso • pan dulce
café • torta • pan tostado

DÍAS DE LA SEMANA

lunes • martes • miércoles • jueves
viernes • sábado • domingo

GRAMÁTICA

ORDINALES

1.º / 1.ª primero/a	6.º / 6.ª sexto/a
2.º / 2.ª segundo/a	7.º / 7.ª séptimo/a
3.º / 3.ª tercero/a	8.º / 8.ª octavo/a
4.º / 4.ª cuarto/a	9.º / 9.ª noveno/a
5.º / 5.ª quinto/a	10.º / 10.ª décimo/a

→ Los ordinales se usan, por ejemplo, para nombrar los pisos de una casa y el número de orden en un grupo.

*Mi amigo vive en el **cuarto** piso.*

*Luis siempre llega **primero**.*

→ Los ordinales concuerdan en género y número con el sustantivo al que acompañan.

*Mi clase está en la **segunda** planta.*

*Yo tengo los **primeros** discos de este grupo.*

→ Los ordinales **primero** y **tercero** pierden la **-o** delante de un nombre masculino singular.

*Estudio **tercer**(o) curso de Inglés.*

*Vivo en el **primer**(o) piso.*

ARTÍCULOS

	Determinados		Indeterminados	
	Para algo que conocemos		Para algo que mencionamos por primera vez	
	masc.	fem.	masc.	fem.
singular	el	la	un	una
plural	los	las	unos	unas

→ Los artículos determinados se usan:

- Cuando hablamos de algo que conocemos.
  *Cierra **la** ventana.*
- Con la hora.
  *Son **las** cinco.*
- Con los días de la semana.
  ***Los** viernes vamos al cine.*

→ Los artículos indeterminados se usan:

- Cuando mencionamos algo por primera vez.
  *Tengo **un** carro nuevo.*
- Con el verbo *haber*.
  *¿Dónde hay **una** silla?*

HAY / ESTÁ(N)

→ Se utiliza ***hay*** para hablar de la existencia o no de personas, animales, lugares y objetos.

***Hay** vasos en la cocina.*

→ Con ***hay***, a los nombres nunca les pueden acompañar los artículos determinados.

*En mi pueblo no **hay** (la) universidad.*

→ Se utiliza ***está(n)*** para indicar un lugar.

*La leche **está** en el refrigerador.*

*¿Dónde **están** mis libros?*

VOCABULARIO

COSAS DE LA CASA

closet • elevador • refrigerador
espejo • sillón • lavabo • lámpara • llave
microondas • cocina • cuarto de baño
recámara / habitación • sala / comedor
cochera • jardín • alberca • patio

¿DÓNDE?

derecha • izquierda • arriba • abajo

GRAMÁTICA

VERBO *GUSTAR*. PRESENTE

(a mí)	me	gusta	el cine la música viajar
(a ti)	te		
(a él / ella / Ud.)	le		
(a nosotros/as)	nos	gustan	los museos los deportes las plantas
(a vosotros/as)	os		
(a ellos / ellas / Uds.)	les		

→ El verbo *gustar* se utiliza en la tercera persona del singular o del plural, dependiendo del sujeto gramatical.

*A mí **me gusta** el cine.*
*A mí **me gustan** las películas de terror.*

*A ti **te gusta** la música clásica.*
*A ti **te gusta** bailar.*
*¿A ti **te gustan** los videojuegos?*

*A él **le gusta** el chocolate.*
*A ella no **le gustan** los deportes.*
*¿A usted **le gusta** el pescado?*

*A nosotros **nos gusta** el futbol.*
*A nosotras **nos gustan** los pasteles.*

*A ellas **les gusta** el arte.*
*A ellos **les gustan** los animales.*
*¿A ustedes **les gusta** pescar?*

GUSTAR
+ Me **encanta** escuchar música.
Me gusta **mucho** cocinar.
Me gusta **bastante** leer.
No me gustan **mucho** los deportes.
No me gusta bailar.
– **No** me gusta **nada** ir de compras.

TAMBIÉN / TAMPOCO - SÍ / NO
● *Me encanta el cine.* ☺
■ *A mí **también**.* ☺
▲ *Pues a mí **no**.* ☹
● *No me gusta andar en bicicleta.* ☹
■ *A mí **tampoco**.* ☹
▲ *Pues a mí **sí**.* ☺

VERBO *QUERER*. PRESENTE

Presente del verbo *querer*	
yo	quiero
tú	quieres
él / ella / Ud.	quiere
nosotros/as	queremos
vosotros/as	queréis
ellos / ellas / Uds.	quieren

*Mamá, **quiero** un helado.*
*Mamá, hoy no **quiero** sopa, **quiero** pasta.*

→ Utilizar el verbo *querer* en presente para expresar deseo normalmente no es cortés: así, para suavizar, se suele utilizar el verbo en imperfecto (*quería…*). Pero en este caso concreto, en un restaurante, sí es habitual el uso de *quiero…*

IMPERATIVO (VERBOS REGULARES)

	cortar	comer	abrir
tú	corta	come	abre
usted	corte	coma	abra

→ El imperativo se usa para dar instrucciones, órdenes y pedir favores.

***Corta** la lechuga en trozos pequeños.*
***Come** la sopa, por favor.*
***Abre** el libro, Peter.*

VOCABULARIO

COMIDA BÁSICA

arroz • pan • carne • ensalada
pescado • fruta • huevos • queso
papas • sal • azúcar

BEBIDAS

agua • cerveza • refresco • vino • jugo

ACTIVIDADES DE TIEMPO LIBRE

bailar • escuchar música
navegar por internet • ir al teatro
ir de compras • ir al antro
andar en bicicleta • viajar
hacer deporte • caminar

GRAMÁTICA

IMPERATIVOS IRREGULARES

→ Los verbos en imperativo tienen la misma irregularidad que en presente.

Infinitivo	Presente	Imperativo
cerrar	cierro	cierra, cierre
dormir	duermo	duerme, duerma
sentarse	me siento	siéntate, siéntese
poner	pongo	pon, ponga
decir	digo	di, diga
venir	vengo	ven, venga
hacer	hago	haz, haga
irse	voy	vete, váyase
salir	salgo	sal, salga
hervir	hiervo	hierve, hierva
tener	tengo	ten, tenga
dar (la vuelta)	doy	da, dé
seguir	sigo	sigue, siga

→ Se usa el imperativo:

- Para dar instrucciones o consejos.
  *Primero **eche** una cucharada de sal, luego **hierva** el arroz durante…*
  *Si te duele la cabeza, **toma** una pastilla y **acuéstate**.*
- Hacer peticiones o dar órdenes, especialmente seguido de *por favor*.
  ***Habla** más despacio, por favor.*
  ***Siéntese**, por favor.*
  *¡**Ven** aquí ahora mismo!*

SER / ESTAR

Ser

→ Se usa para describir características o cualidades de algo o de alguien: tamaño, color, carácter…

*Luis **es** alto y delgado.*
*Su casa **es** pequeña.*
*Su carro **es** rojo.*
*Luis **es** muy agradable.*

→ Expresa también nacionalidad, profesión, posesión…

*Mary **es** inglesa.*
*¿Ellos **son** doctores?*
*Ese libro no **es** mío.*

Estar

→ Expresa lugar o posición.

*La escuela **está** en la c/ Velázquez.*
*La parada del camión **está** enfrente de mi casa.*

→ Sirve para expresar también estados de salud o de ánimo.

*Clara **está** enferma, tiene gripa.*
*Hoy **estoy** muy contenta.*

→ Con los adverbios *bien* y *mal* siempre usamos **estar**.

*Este ejercicio **está** (~~es~~) mal.*

VOCABULARIO

TRANSPORTES

boleto • camión • metro • tren
línea de metro • viaje • estación • parada

ADJETIVOS

tranquilo • ruidoso • céntrico • rápido • frío
lento • malo • pequeño • fácil • difícil • bueno

ADVERBIOS

cerca • lejos • bien • mal

GRAMÁTICA

GERUNDIO DE VERBOS REGULARES

Infinitivo	Gerundio
llorar	llor**ando**
comer	com**iendo**
escribir	escrib**iendo**

GERUNDIO DE VERBOS IRREGULARES

Infinitivo	Gerundio
leer	leyendo
dormir	durmiendo

ESTAR + GERUNDIO

Estar + gerundio		
yo	estoy	
tú	estás	
él / ella / Ud.	está	
nosotros/as	estamos	hablando
vosotros/as	estáis	
ellos / ellas / Uds.	están	

→ *Estar* + gerundio suele expresar acciones que se desarrollan en el momento en que se habla.

- *¿Qué **estás haciendo**?*
- ***Estoy leyendo** el periódico.*

ESTAR + GERUNDIO (VERBOS REFLEXIVOS)

Estoy lavándome. / Me estoy lavando.
Estás lavándote. / Te estás lavando.
Está lavándose. / Se está lavando.
Estamos lavándonos. / Nos estamos lavando.
Están lavándose. / Se están lavando.

VOCABULARIO

HABLAR POR TELÉFONO

¿Sí? • No está en este momento
¿Quiere dejar un recado? • Bueno

VERBOS DE ACTIVIDADES

leer el periódico

jugar a las cartas

lavarse

pintar

ir al cine

bañarse

bailar

pasear

jugar futbol

DESCRIPCIÓN DE PERSONAS

- PELO: rubio / negro / largo / corto
- OJOS: claros / oscuros / café / verdes
- ES: grande / joven / alto / bajo / delgado / gordo
- TRAER: barba / bigote / lentes

CARÁCTER

agradable • desagradable • tacaño/a
generoso/a • platicador/a • serio/a
alegre • amable • callado/a

GRAMÁTICA

PRETÉRITO (VERBOS REGULARES)

Trabajar	Comer	Salir
trabajé	comí	salí
trabaj**aste**	com**iste**	sal**iste**
trabaj**ó**	com**ió**	sal**ió**
trabaj**amos**	com**imos**	sal**imos**
trabaj**asteis**	com**isteis**	sal**isteis**
trabaj**aron**	com**ieron**	sal**ieron**

→ El pretérito expresa acciones acabadas en un momento determinado del pasado.

*Ayer **trabajé** mucho.*

*El verano pasado **estuve** en Cancún.*

PRETÉRITO (VERBOS IRREGULARES)

Hacer	Ir / Ser	Estar
hice	fui	estuve
hiciste	fuiste	estuviste
hizo	fue	estuvo
hicimos	fuimos	estuvimos
hicisteis	fuisteis	estuvisteis
hicieron	fueron	estuvieron

VOCABULARIO

ESTABLECIMIENTOS

farmacia • oficina de correos • iglesia
comandancia de policía • puesto de periódicos
mercado • tienda de conveniencia

OBJETOS

medicinas • cartas • periódicos
refrescos • botanas

ESTACIONES DEL AÑO

el invierno

la primavera

el verano

el otoño

MESES DEL AÑO

enero • febrero • marzo • abril • mayo
junio • julio • agosto • septiembre • octubre
noviembre • diciembre

EL CLIMA

llover • llueve • está lloviendo • nevar • nieva
está nevando • hace frío • hace (mucho) calor
hace aire • está nublado

está lloviendo

está nevando

hace mucho calor

hace aire

hace frío

está nublado

GRAMÁTICA

DEMOSTRATIVOS (ADJETIVOS Y PRONOMBRES)

	Demostrativos (adjetivos y pronombres)	
	singular	plural
masculino	este / ese / aquel	estos / esos / aquellos
femenino	esta / esa / aquella	estas / esas / aquellas

Pronombres demostrativos (neutro)		
esto	eso	aquello

→ Los adjetivos demostrativos van delante del nombre y concuerdan con él en género y número.

Este carro es de mi vecino.

Esas chavas son muy agradables.

→ Los pronombres demostrativos *esto, eso, aquello* nunca van con el nombre. Se refieren a una idea o a algo de lo que no sabemos el género.

Esto no me gusta nada.

*¿Qué es **aquello** que se ve en el cielo?*

→ El uso de un pronombre u otro nos indica la cercanía o lejanía del objeto señalado.

Este carro. (cerca del hablante, aquí)

Ese carro. (cerca del oyente, ahí)

***Aquel** carro.* (lejos de los dos, allí)

PRONOMBRES PERSONALES DE OBJETO DIRECTO

sujeto	objeto
yo	me
tú	te
él / ella / Ud.	lo / la / le
nosotros/as	nos
vosotros/as	os
ellos / ellas / Uds.	los / las / les

*¿Compramos las flores? = ¿**Las** compramos?*

*Hoy no vi a tu papá. = Hoy no **lo** vi.*

*¿Sabes que vendo mi casa? = ¿Sabes que **la** vendo?*

→ Normalmente, los pronombres personales de objeto directo van delante del verbo y separados.

Te quiero.

→ Pero con el imperativo afirmativo van detrás y unidos al verbo.

¡Mírame!

Cómpralo, por favor.

→ Con algunas construcciones pueden ir delante o detrás.

La puerta está abierta, ¿puedes cerrarla? = ¿la puedes cerrar?

CONCORDANCIA DEL NOMBRE Y LOS ADJETIVOS DE COLOR

→ Los adjetivos concuerdan en género y número con el nombre al que se refieren.

*¿Puedo agarrar la pluma **roja**?*

*Tengo unos pantalones **grises**.*

	singular	plural
masculino	blanco / verde / azul	blanco**s** / verde**s** / azul**es**
femenino	blanca / verde / azul	blanca**s** / verde**s** / azul**es**

→ Hay colores que son nombres de plantas, flores y frutos que normalmente no cambian en género ni en número:

*pantalones **rosa*** *zapatos (de color) **naranja***

COMPARATIVOS

más + adjetivo + que
*Juan es **más agradable que** Pedro.*
menos + adjetivo + que
*Pedro es **menos agradable que** Juan.*
tan + adjetivo + como
*Juan (no) es **tan alto como** Pedro.*

COMPARATIVOS IRREGULARES

bueno	mejor / mejores + que
*Esta película **es mejor que** esa.*	
malo	**peor / peores + que**
*Esos pasteles **son peores que** estos.*	
grande	**mayor / mayores + que**
*Yo soy **mayor que** ella.*	
pequeño	**menor / menores + que**
*Sus hijos son **menores que** los míos.*	

→ Cuando hablamos de hermanos usamos *mayor* y *menor*:

*Mi hermano **mayor** es arquitecto.*

→ Cuando nos referimos a personas viejas usamos *grande*:

*Su abuela es **más grande que** la mía.*

VOCABULARIO

ROPA Y COMPLEMENTOS

anillo • camisa • playera • cartera
collar • corbata • falda • lentes • suéter
medias • aretes • zapatos
pantalón de mezclilla • tenis

GRAMÁTICA

VERBO *DOLER*. PRESENTE

(a mí)	me	
(a ti)	te	
(a él / ella / Ud.)	le	**duele** la cabeza
(a nosotros/as)	nos	**duelen** los oídos
(a vosotros/as)	os	
(a ellos / ellas / Uds.)	les	

→ El verbo ***doler***, al igual que el verbo ***gustar***, se utiliza en la tercera persona del singular o del plural, según sea el sujeto.

*¿Te **duele** la cabeza?*

*A Ana **le duelen** los oídos.*

PRETÉRITO IMPERFECTO (VERBOS REGULARES)

viajar	tener	salir
viaj**aba**	ten**ía**	sal**ía**
viaj**abas**	ten**ías**	sal**ías**
viaj**aba**	ten**ía**	sal**ía**
viaj**ábamos**	ten**íamos**	sal**íamos**
viaj**abais**	ten**íais**	sal**íais**
viaj**aban**	ten**ían**	sal**ían**

→ Usamos el pretérito imperfecto para expresar acciones habituales en el pasado.

*Cuando éramos jóvenes, **íbamos** a la disco.*

*Ahora no salimos, pero antes **salíamos** mucho.*

→ También se usa para describir en el pasado.

*Mi profesor de matemáticas **era** simpático y nunca nos **castigaba**.*

PRETÉRITO IMPERFECTO (VERBOS IRREGULARES)

ir	ser	ver
iba	era	veía
ibas	eras	veías
iba	era	veía
íbamos	éramos	veíamos
ibais	erais	veíais
iban	eran	veían

IR A + INFINITIVO

Ir a + infinitivo		
yo	voy a	
tú	vas a	
él / ella / Ud.	va a	estudiar
nosotros/as	vamos a	
vosotros/as	vais a	
ellos / ellas / Uds.	van a	

VOCABULARIO

EL CUERPO HUMANO

brazo • cabeza • cara • cuello
dedo • espalda • estómago • garganta
hombro • mano • oído • oreja
pecho • pie • pierna • rodilla

NUEVO

ESPAÑOL EN MARCHA

CUADERNO DE EJERCICIOS

Francisca Castro Viúdez
Pilar Díaz Ballesteros
Ignacio Rodero Díez
Carmen Sardinero Francos
María Elena Arévalo Alvarado
Alma Edith Bautista Alférez
Elena Jiménez Martín

Español Lengua Extranjera

1 Saludos

A Mucho gusto

1 Relaciona.

1 ¡Hola!, ¿cómo estás?
2 ¿De dónde eres?
3 ¿Cómo te llamas?
4 Este es Rubén.
5 Mucho gusto.
6 ¿Eres mexicano?

a Encantado.
b Soy japonesa.
c Me llamo Mayumi.
d Bien, ¿y tú?
e ¡Hola!, Rubén, ¿qué tal?
f No, soy cubano.

2 Escribe las preguntas.

1 A *¿De dónde eres?*
B Soy yucateco.
2 A ¡Hola!, ¿______?
B Bien, ¿y usted?
3 A ¿______?
B No, soy mexicana.
4 A ¿______?
B Soy francesa.
5 A ¿______?
B Renata, ¿y tú?

3 Completa la tabla.

TÚ	USTED
¿Cómo te llamas?	*¿Cómo se llama usted?*
	¿De dónde es usted?
¿Cómo estás?	

4 Completa los diálogos con los elementos del recuadro.

soy • eres • ~~cómo~~ • y tú

1 A Hola, *¿cómo* te llamas?
B Anil, ¿y tú?
A Safiya.
B ¿______ francesa?
A No, ______ nigeriana. ¿______?
B Yo soy paquistaní.

pero • en • ~~esta~~ • gracias • dónde

2 PABLO: María, mira, *esta* es Susanne.
MARÍA: Hola, Susanne, ¿cómo estás?
SUSANNE: Bien, ______ .
MARÍA: ¿De ______ eres?
SUSANNE: Soy francesa, ______ ahora vivo ______ Madrid.

presento • gracias • buenos • mucho gusto

3 SUSANA: Buenos días, Sr. López.
SR. LÓPEZ: ______ días, Susana.
SUSANA: Mire, le ______ a la nueva directora, Julia Linares.
SR. LÓPEZ: ______ de conocerla.
JULIA: ______, igualmente.

5 Completa la tabla.

PAÍS	NACIONALIDAD	
	masculino	**femenino**
Francia	francés	francesa
Portugal		portuguesa
Marruecos		marroquí
Brasil	brasileño	
		peruana
Canadá	canadiense	
	alemán	
Polonia	polaco	
Bielorrusia		bielorrusa
	irlandés	
México		

6 Escribe los nombres que se deletrean. Cinco son apellidos y cinco son ciudades.

1 Ese – a – ene – che – e – zeta
Sánchez

2 Erre – o – de – erre – i – ge – u – e – zeta

3 Zeta – o – erre – erre – i – doble ele – a

4 Eme – a – erre – te – i – ene – e – zeta

5 Hache – u – e – erre – te – a

6 Be – o – ge – o – te – a

7 Uve – a – ele – e – ene – ce – i – a

8 Uve – a – erre – ese – o – uve – i – a

9 Te – u – ene – e – zeta

10 A – ene – ce – a – erre – a

B ¿A qué te dedicas?

1 Busca en esta sopa de letras los nombres de ocho profesionales.

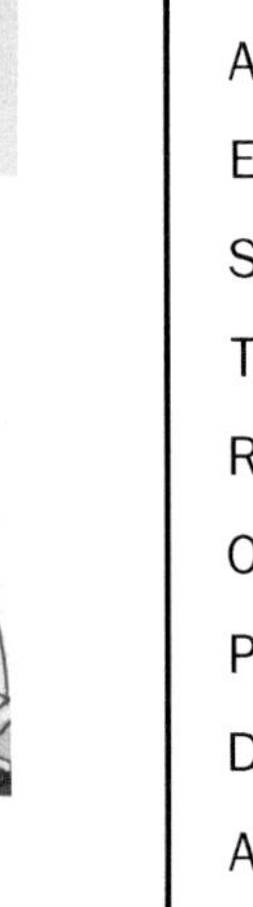

2 Forma frases, como en el modelo.

1 Él / hablar por teléfono / todos los días.
Él habla por teléfono todos los días.
2 Rosa / tener / tres hijos.
____
3 Ignacio / hablar / inglés y francés.
____
4 Nosotros / comer / en casa los domingos.
____
5 ¿Usted / hablar / ruso?
____
6 ¿Ustedes / vivir / en México?
____
7 Ellos / vivir / en París.
____
8 Layla / estudiar / en la universidad.
____
9 Yo / no trabajar / ni estudiar.
____
10 ¿Usted / trabajar / aquí?
____

3 Completa la tabla.

SER	TENER
soy	tengo
	tienes
somos	
son	

4 Completa las frases con *tener* o *ser*.

1 Elena *tiene* dos hijos.
2 Roberto _______ de Buenos Aires.
3 ¿De dónde _______ Jorge y Claudia?
4 A ¿_______ ustedes estadounidenses?
B No, _______ ingleses.
5 Yo _______ un novio español.
6 Mi amiga Gisela _______ brasileña.
7 A ¿_______ novio (ustedes)?
B Ella sí, pero yo no _______.
8 A ¿Tú _______ peruana?
B No, _______ boliviana.
9 A Julia _______ mi hermana, _______ maestra.
B Yo también _______ maestra.
10 Mi hija _______ una casa en Cancún.
11 A (Nosotros) _______ argentinos. Y ustedes, ¿de dónde _______?
B _______ chilenos.
12 A ¿(Tú) _______ hijos?
B No, no _______ hijos.

5 Forma frases tomando un elemento de cada columna.

Luis y yo	habla	Derecho
Renata	trabajo	traductora
Yo	estudiamos	regiomontanos
Ángel y Rosa	es	cuatro idiomas
	tienen	en un restaurante
	somos	dos hijos
		chefs

C ¿Cuál es tu número de celular?

1 Relaciona los números con su transcripción en letras.

a 5567870300
b 8442308296
c 9988272010
d 9616187200
e 8114280321
f 3321600321

1 nueve, nueve, ocho, ocho, dos, siete, dos, cero, uno, cero
2 nueve, seis, uno, seis, uno, ocho, siete, dos, cero, cero
3 tres, tres, dos, uno, seis, cero, cero, tres, dos, uno
4 cinco, cinco, seis, siete, ocho, siete, cero, tres, cero, cero
5 ocho, uno, uno, cuatro, dos, ocho, cero, tres, dos, uno
6 ocho, cuatro, cuatro, dos, tres, cero, ocho, dos, nueve, seis

2 Escribe los números de teléfono.

a 9988404637
nueve, nueve, ocho, ocho, cuatro, cero, cuatro, seis, tres, siete

b 9515067080
____

c 9737025787
____

d 8444380111
____

e 8111086753
____

3 Completa.

once		trece
		dieciséis
		diecinueve

4 101 Escucha y completa las fichas.

NOMBRE: Manuel
APELLIDOS:
NACIONALIDAD:
PROFESIÓN:
CIUDAD: TEL.:
CORREO ELECTRÓNICO: manuel.romero@gmail.com

NOMBRE: Isabel
APELLIDOS:
NACIONALIDAD:
PROFESIÓN:
CIUDAD: TEL.:
CORREO ELECTRÓNICO:

5 Completa la tarjeta con tus datos.

NOMBRE:
APELLIDOS:
NACIONALIDAD:
PROFESIÓN:
CIUDAD: TEL.:
CORREO ELECTRÓNICO:

6 Completa las frases con la información correspondiente a las fichas.

NOMBRE: **José**
APELLIDOS: **Martínez López**
TRABAJO: **contador**
DOMICILIO: **Bogotá**
NACIONALIDAD: **colombiano**

NOMBRE: **Noelia**
APELLIDOS: **Montoro Ruiz**
TRABAJO: **pianista**
DOMICILIO: **La Habana**
NACIONALIDAD: **cubana**

1 Se llama José Martínez ______. Es ______. ______ en Bogotá y es ______.

2 ______ Noelia ______ ______. Es ______. ______ en La Habana y es ______.

7 Completa con los verbos del recuadro. Cada uno se repite varias veces.

llamarse • estudiar • vivir • ser
tener • trabajar • hablar

A
Hola, (1) *me llamo* Antonio Rodríguez, (2)______ taxista. (3)______ con mi familia en Tlaxcala. Soy casado y (4)______ un hijo de quince años. Mi esposa (5)______ Susana y (6)______ estilista, (7)______ en una estética cerca de nuestra casa. Mi hijo (8)______ en la preparatoria, (9)______ un buen estudiante. En mi casa (10)______ también mi mamá, tiene 68 años y (11)______ viuda. Ella nos ayuda en el trabajo de la casa.

B
Yo (12)______ Luisa y (13)______ enfermera. (14)______ veracruzana, pero (15)______ en Querétaro. (16)______ en un hospital, claro. (17)______ soltera, pero tengo una familia muy grande. Mis hermanos y mis papás (18)______ en Veracruz.

C
Mira esta foto, (19)______ Javier, mi novio. (20)______ 23 años y (21)______ ingeniero en sistemas computacionales, (22)______ en una empresa de computadoras. (23)______ inglés y francés, (24)______ muy inteligente.

2 Familias

A ¿Eres casado?

1 Relaciona.

1 ¿Tienes hermanos?
2 ¿Eres casada?
3 ¿Cuántos hijos tienen ustedes?
4 ¿Cómo se llama tu mamá?
5 ¿Eres casado o soltero?
6 ¿Tienes abuelos?
7 ¿De dónde es tu papá?
8 ¿Cuántos años tiene tu mamá?
9 ¿Dónde vives?
10 ¿Dónde trabaja tu papá?

a No, soy soltera.
b Rocío.
c Yo soy casado, ¿y tú?
d Sí, una abuela.
e Dos, un niño y una niña.
f Sí, uno mayor que yo.
g Cincuenta.
h Es de Veracruz.
i En un departamento en la Ciudad de México.
j En un restaurante.

2 Completa la descripción de las familias con el verbo *ser, tener* o *llamarse*.

LAURA

Yo vivo con mi familia. Mi papá (1)________ Jaime y (2)________ abogado. Mi mamá, Paloma, (3)________ 45 años y (4)________ bibliotecaria. Mi hermano Víctor (5)________ estudiante, (6)________ mayor que yo, (7)________ 20 años.
Además (8) ________ dos hermanas pequeñas. (9) ________ Elena y Estrella. (10) ________ muy simpáticas.

PABLO

Yo vivo en Ciudad de México y mi familia en un pueblo. (1)________ dos hermanas, María (2)________ la mayor, (3)________ 21 años y estudia medicina. Isabel (4)________ la menor, (5)________ 18 años y estudia en la preparatoria. Las dos (6) ________ muchos amigos.
Mi mamá (7)________ Rosa, (8)________ doctora y mi papá (9)________ Francisco y (10)________ economista.

3 Mira el árbol genealógico y completa las frases.

José Luis ⚭ Mercedes
Miguel ⚭ Marisa — Jorge ⚭ Adela
Irene, Celia — Álvaro

CELIA: Mercedes es mi *abuela.*
MARISA: Miguel es mi ________
MERCEDES: Jorge es mi ________
IRENE: Jorge es mi ________
IRENE: Marisa es mi ________
MIGUEL: Marisa es mi ________
ÁLVARO: José Luis es mi ________
CELIA: Miguel y Marisa son mis ________
ÁLVARO: José Luis y Mercedes son mis ________
ADELA: Celia es mi ________

4 Escribe el plural.

1 Juan es colombiano.
Rosa y María *son colombianas.*
2 Mi papá es profesor.
Mis papás ________ .
3 Yo tengo un gato.
Nosotros ________ .
4 Él es casado.
Ellos ________ .
5 Este hotel es caro.
Estos ________ .
6 ¿Tu compañero es mexicano?
¿Tus ________ ?
7 Este chavo es estudiante.
Estos ________ .
8 ¿Tu pluma es nueva?
¿________ ?
9 La ventana está abierta.
________ .
10 Esta es la amiga de mi hermana.
________ .

B ¿Dónde están mis lentes?

1 Encuentra el nombre de los objetos en la sopa de letras.

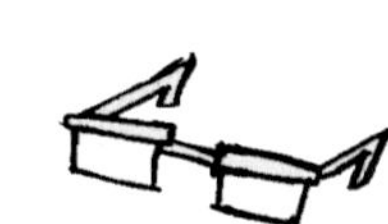

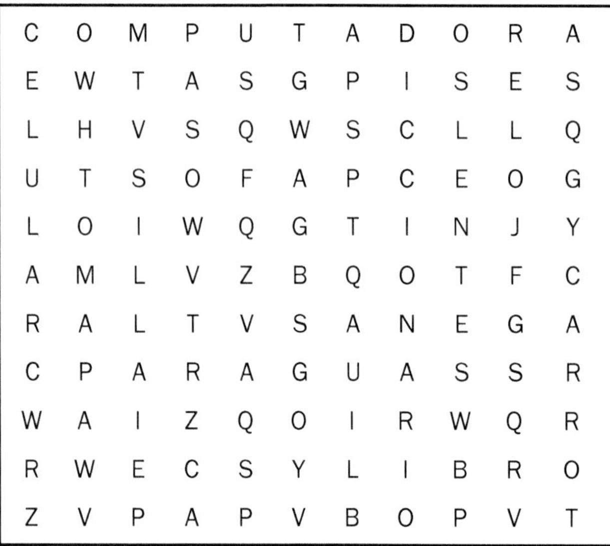

C	O	M	P	U	T	A	D	O	R	A
E	W	T	A	S	G	P	I	S	E	S
L	H	V	S	Q	W	S	C	L	L	Q
U	T	S	O	F	A	P	C	E	O	G
L	O	I	W	Q	G	T	I	N	J	Y
A	M	L	V	Z	B	Q	O	T	F	C
R	A	L	T	V	S	A	N	E	G	A
C	P	A	R	A	G	U	A	S	S	R
W	A	I	Z	Q	O	I	R	W	Q	R
R	W	E	C	S	Y	L	I	B	R	O
Z	V	P	A	P	V	B	O	P	V	T

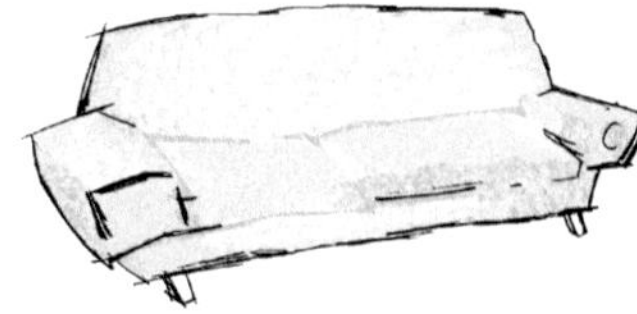

2 Esta es la clase de idiomas, pero el maestro no está. Responde a las preguntas con ayuda de los marcadores de lugar del recuadro.

al lado de (x2) • encima de (x3) • debajo de • entre • detrás • delante • en

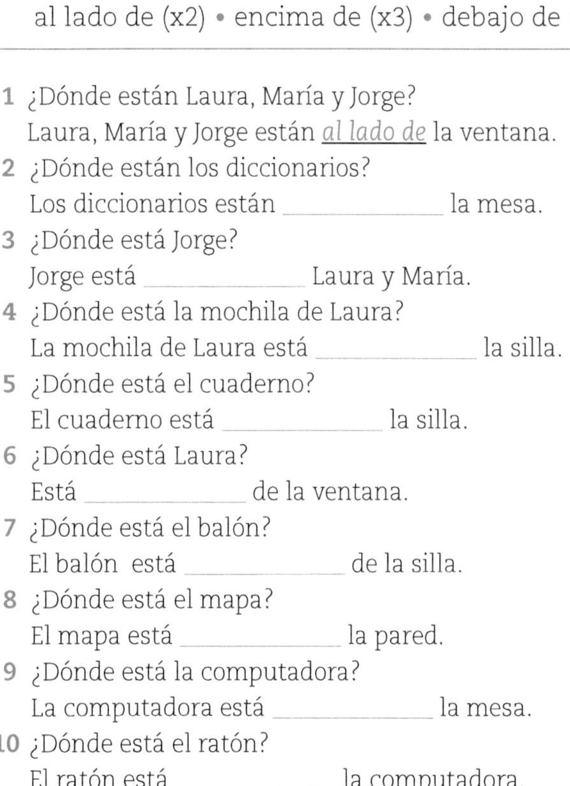

1. ¿Dónde están Laura, María y Jorge?
   Laura, María y Jorge están _al lado de_ la ventana.
2. ¿Dónde están los diccionarios?
   Los diccionarios están ______________ la mesa.
3. ¿Dónde está Jorge?
   Jorge está ______________ Laura y María.
4. ¿Dónde está la mochila de Laura?
   La mochila de Laura está ______________ la silla.
5. ¿Dónde está el cuaderno?
   El cuaderno está ______________ la silla.
6. ¿Dónde está Laura?
   Está ______________ de la ventana.
7. ¿Dónde está el balón?
   El balón está ______________ de la silla.
8. ¿Dónde está el mapa?
   El mapa está ______________ la pared.
9. ¿Dónde está la computadora?
   La computadora está ______________ la mesa.
10. ¿Dónde está el ratón?
    El ratón está ______________ la computadora.

3 Sigue el modelo.

1 hermano (yo)
Este es mi hermano.
2 papás (yo)
Estos ______.
3 mamá (tú)
¿______?
4 tíos (él)
______.
5 libros (tú)
______.
6 hermanas (yo)
______.
7 abuelos (ella)
______.
8 teléfono (Ud.)
¿______?
9 celular (yo)
______.
10 carro (ella)
¿______?

C ¿Qué hora es?

1 Escribe la hora correcta debajo de cada reloj.

1 ______

2 ______

3 ______

4 ______

5 ______

6 ______

7 ______

8 ______

2 Completa.

a 25 *veinticinco.*
b 87 ______ y siete.
c 94 noventa ______.
d 103 ______ tres.
e 115 ______ quince.
f 230 doscientos ______.
g 321 trescientos ______.
h 446 ______ cuarenta y seis.
i 535 ______ treinta y cinco.
j 1212 mil ______.
k 1936 ______ treinta y seis.
l 1998 mil novecientos ______.
ll 2550 dos mil ______.

3 102 Escucha a esta persona hablar de los horarios de su país y escribe la hora.

Desayuno: desayunan a las ______.
Comida: a la ______ o a las ______.
Cena: a las ______ de la noche.
Los niños empiezan las clases a las ______ de la mañana.
Los bancos abren a las ______ y cierran a las ______ de la tarde.
Las tiendas abren a las ______ y cierran a las ______ de la noche.

4 Escribe sobre los horarios en tu país.

En mi país la gente desayuna a las ______, come a las ______ y cena a las ______.
Los niños empiezan las clases a las ______.
Los bancos abren a las ______ y cierran a las ______.
Las tiendas abren a las ______ y cierran a las ______.

5 Lee el texto y señala verdadero (V) o falso (F).

HIJOS ADOPTADOS

Manuel y Nuria son regiomontanos, viven en Monterrey. Manolo es gerente y tiene 36 años. Su esposa, Nuria, tiene 34 años y es estilista. Tienen dos hijos: Marcos y Benito. Pero los hijos no son regios, ni mexicanos. Marcos es ecuatoriano, tiene 8 años, y Benito, de 7 años, es colombiano. Los dos son adoptados. Ahora forman una familia feliz.

1 Manuel y Nuria no son mexicanos. ☐
2 La familia vive en Ciudad de México. ☐
3 Nuria es estilista. ☐
4 Manuel y Nuria tienen tres hijos. ☐
5 Marcos y Benito son hijos adoptados. ☐

6 Ordena las frases.

1 simpática / es / hermana / mi / muy.
Mi hermana es muy simpática.
2 ¿vives / tus / tú / papás / con?
______
3 ¿papás / tus / viven / dónde?
______
4 mayor / hermano / mi / doctor / es.
______
5 esposo / alemana / empresa / trabaja / una / en / mi.
______
6 vive / papás / abuelo / mi / con / mis.
______
7 ¿estudian / hijos / universidad / en / tus / la?
______

7 103 Escucha y completa los datos.

	VUELO	HORA	Puerta embarque
Lima		7:55	6C
Santiago	064	12:05	
Buenos Aires	1289		5B
España	576	18:35	
Roma		23:10	10A

8 Corrige los errores.

1 Mis papás es italianos.
Mis papás son italianos.
2 ¿Dónde está mis lápices?
______
3 Enrique tiene dos reloj.
______
4 El diccionario está encima de mesa.
______
5 Mi hermano estudio Medicina.
______
6 Son la una y cuarto.
______
7 Esta sofá es muy cómodo.
______
8 En mi país la gente cena las diez.
______

9 Completa las frases con las palabras del recuadro.

> tu • sus • este • esta (x2) • estos
> estas • mi • tus • su • mis

1 *Esta* no es mi mesa.
2 _____ hijo tiene un perro.
3 ¿De qué color es _____ carro, Juan?
4 ¿Son _____ los libros de _____ compañeros, Laura?
5 María no vive en casa de _____ papás.
6 _____ son mis amigas, Marta y Nieves.
7 A Mi esposa y yo tenemos un hijo.
B ¿Y cuántos años tiene _____ hijo?
8 _____ chavo no es mi hermano, es mi primo.
9 En _____ foto estamos mi hermano y yo con _____ papás en la playa.

3 El trabajo

A Rosa se levanta a las siete

1 Forma frases.

1 María / bañarse / en la mañana.
María se baña en la mañana.
2 Jorge / levantarse / muy tarde.
____
3 ¿Tú / acostarse / antes de las 12?
¿__________?
4 Mi novio no / afeitarse / todos los días.
____
5 Clarita / peinarse / sola.
____
6 Yo / acostarse / antes que mi esposa.
____
7 Mis papás / levantarse / temprano.
____
8 Peter / sentarse / en la última fila.
____

2 Completa con la preposición adecuada.

a (al) de desde hasta en

1 El lunes próximo vuelvo a mi país.
2 La farmacia está abierta ______ las diez ______ la mañana ______ las ocho ______ la noche.
3 Rebeca sale ______ casa ______ las 8.
4 Yo voy ______ trabajar ______ metro y vuelvo ______ casa a pie.
5 ¿______ qué hora te levantas?
6 Los bancos abren ______ nueve ______ cuatro.
7 Los sábados ______ la mañana voy ______ gimnasio.
8 Raúl y Luisa vuelven ______ las vacaciones mañana.
9 En esta escuela hay clases ______ la mañana y ______ la tarde.
10 Yo trabajo ______ casa.
11 No he visto ______ Juan ______ el verano pasado.

3 Relaciona.

1 ir	a despertarse
2 dormir	b salir
3 abrir	c volver
4 entrar	d terminar
5 acostarse	e levantarse
6 empezar	f cerrar

4 Completa la tabla.

Acostarse	Volver	Ir
me acuesto		
	vuelves	
		va
	volvemos	
os acostáis		
		van

5 Busca en la sopa de letras estas formas verbales.

~~ir, yo~~ • cerrar, ella • empezar, nosotros
salir, yo • venir, nosotros • cerrar, yo
venir, yo • empezar, usted • salir, ellos

C	E	M	P	E	Z	A	M	O	S
I	W	R	V	O	Y	Ñ	E	M	A
E	C	I	E	R	R	A	M	H	L
R	V	E	N	G	O	B	P	X	G
R	M	Q	I	Z	M	Ñ	I	K	O
O	U	Z	M	S	A	L	E	N	C
Z	W	R	O	M	B	O	Z	Q	L
V	B	R	S	T	U	M	A	X	L

6 Completa con el verbo en presente.

1 A Hola, María, ¿de dónde (venir) _vienes_?
  B (venir) ________ de comprar unos regalos y (ir) ________ ahora mismo al súper, que (cerrar) ________ a las 9.

2 A ¿(ir, nosotros) ________ mañana a la playa?
  B Si (acostarse, nosotros) ________ temprano hoy, sí.

3 A ¿A qué hora (empezar) ________ la película?
  B A las 12, pero yo (acostarse) ________ ya, estoy muy cansada.

4 A Es tarde, ¿(volver, nosotros) ________ a casa?
  B Sí, ¿(ir, nosotros) ________ en metro o en taxi?

5 ¿Tú (levantarse) ________ muy temprano?

B ¿Estudias o trabajas?

1 Une estas fichas correctamente y encontrarás los días de la semana.

~~LU~~	SÁ	NES	CO	BA	GO
MIN	DO	NES	JUE	VIER	
MIÉR	TES	MAR	VES	LES	DO

1 _LU_ ________
2 ________ ________
3 ________ ________ ________
4 ________ ________
5 ________ ________
6 ________ ________ ________
7 ________ ________ ________

3 Relaciona.

1 músico/a	a oficina
2 estudiante	b aeropuerto
3 mesero/a	c orquesta
4 enfermero/a	d restaurante
5 vendedor/a	e universidad
6 azafato/a	f hospital
7 secretario/a	g supermercado

4 Escribe algunas frases sobre estas personas. Utiliza el vocabulario del ejercicio anterior.

1 Paloma es azafata y trabaja en un ____________ .
2 Celia es vendedora y ________________________ .
3 Ana y Luisa ________ enfermeras y ____________ .
4 Mi hermana ____________ y ________________ una oficina.
5 Jaime y Pedro ______________________________ restaurante.

2 Relaciona las imágenes con las profesiones.

1 músico ☐
2 conductor ☐
3 policía ☐
4 pintor ☐
5 estudiante ☐
6 mesero ☐
7 enfermera ☐

a b c d e f g

5 Nuria vive en Cuernavaca con su hija. Mira los dibujos y escribe frases sobre su vida. Utiliza los verbos del recuadro.

ir a nadar • bañarse • leer • cenar • trabajar • llevar a la escuela
desayunar • recoger • ~~levantarse~~

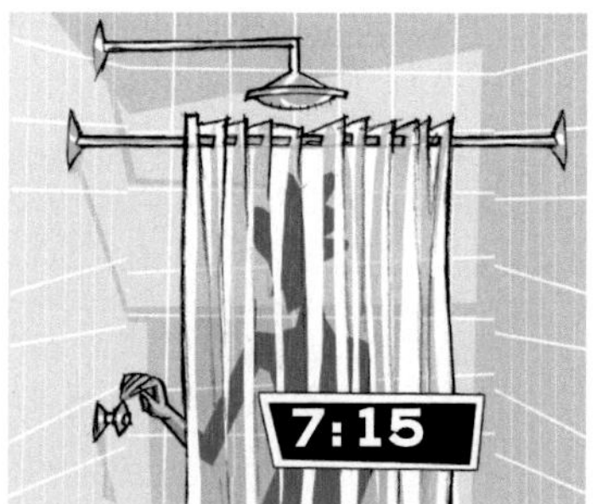

1 Nuria *se levanta* a las 7:00.
2 Nuria ________________ a las 7:15.
3 Nuria ________________ con su hija a las 7:30.
4 ________________ a la niña a las 8.
5 ________________ en la escuela desde las 9 hasta las 2 de la tarde.
6 ________________ a su hija a las 2:30 p.m.
7 ________________ a la alberca a las 6:00 p.m.
8 ________________ con su hija a las 8:00 p.m.
9 ________________ un libro antes de dormirse.

6 Completa el texto con las palabras del recuadro.

soy muy trabajo porque salgo fines el cine y semanas cantantes ~~de~~

Hola, me llamo Paula y soy *de* Ciudad de México. Tengo 28 años y ________ periodista. ________ en la redacción de la revista *Clarita*. Mi trabajo es ________ interesante ________ conozco a mucha gente: artistas, políticos, ________... Todas las ________ hago un reportaje ________ una entrevista. Los ________ de semana ________ con mis amigos. El sábado vamos a bailar y ________ domingo, al ________ .

C ¿Qué desayunas?

1 104 Cuatro personas están en una cafetería. Escucha y completa qué desayuna cada una.

¿Están listos para ordenar?

	A	B	C
A	________ y pan tostado.	________ de queso	________ una mantecada
B	________ .	________ .	y ________ .

2 Relaciona las palabras de la columna de la izquierda con las de la derecha. Hay más de una posibilidad.

1 jugo
2 pan
3 café
4 aceite
5 sándwich
6 té

a con mermelada
b de jamón
c con leche
d de oliva
e con limón
f con mantequilla
g de queso
h de frutas

3 Responde a las siguientes preguntas.

1 ¿A qué hora desayunas?
____

2 ¿Qué desayunas normalmente?
____

3 ¿A qué hora comes normalmente? ¿Y los domingos?
____

4 ¿Tomas café después de comer?
____

5 ¿Meriendas? ¿Qué meriendas?
____

6 ¿A qué hora cenas?
____

4 Completa con g o gu.

1 __itarra
2 para__ayo
3 re__alo
4 __oma
5 Uru__ay
6 cole__io
7 __erra
8 domin__o
9 pa__ar
10 Norue__a

4 La casa

A ¿Dónde vives?

1 Mira las fotos y escribe debajo en qué lugar de la casa están. En el recuadro tienes el lugar de la casa donde tienes que situarlo.

recámara • cocina • comedor • ~~jardín~~ • sala • cochera • cuarto de baño

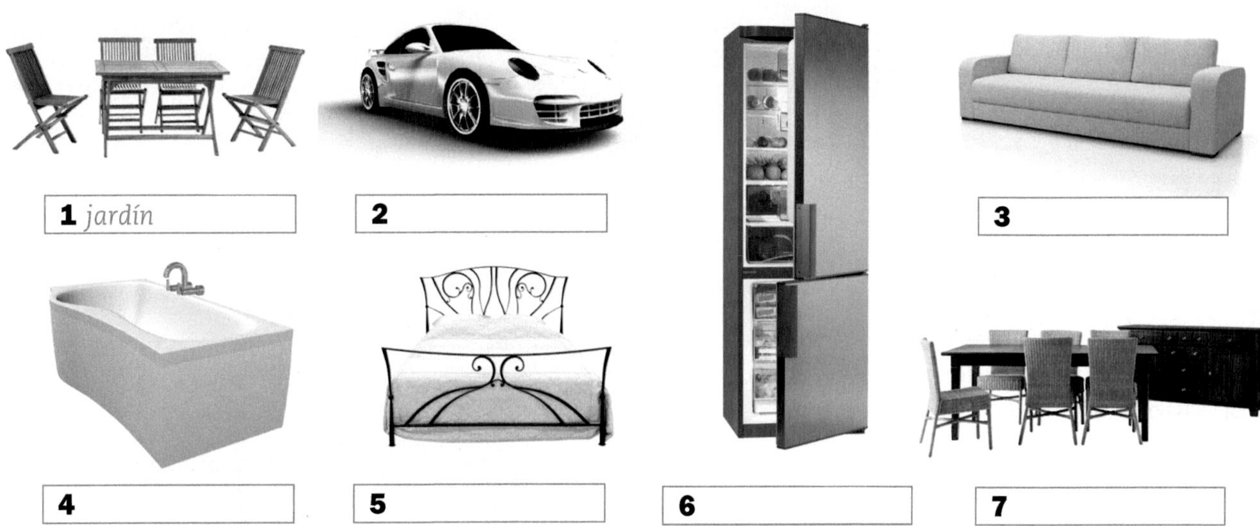

1 *jardín*
2
3
4
5
6
7

2 ¿En qué departamento vive cada personaje?

1 Doña Matilde en el 1.° a la izda.
En el primero izquierda.
2 Don Federico en el 4.° a la dcha.
____
3 Juan y Manuel en el 3.° C.
____
4 Mi hermana en el 2.° izda.
____
5 La señora González en el 10.° dcha.
____
6 El señor Vergara en el 1.° dcha.
____

3 Lee el anuncio de *venta de departamentos* y completa las frases.

1 El departamento de Valle Soleado tiene dos habitaciones y un __________ completo. La __________ está amueblada.
2 Las __________ del departamento de San Miguel de Allende tienen mucha luz.
3 La única casa que tiene __________ es la de Vergel.
4 Por 2,500,000 pesos tenemos un departamento en Polanco con un __________ pequeño.
5 El departamento de Pirámides tiene una gran __________.

Venta de departamentos

- **Valle Soledado:** 2 recámaras, cocina amueblada, baño completo: **1,800,000 pesos.**
- **San Miguel de Allende:** 90 m², 3 recámaras, muy luminoso: **3,500,000 pesos.**
- **VERGEL:** 70 m², 2 recámaras, estacionamiento, cerca del metro: **1,500,000 pesos.**
- **Polanco:** 3 recámaras, planta baja, pequeño jardín: **2,500,000 pesos.**
- **Pirámides:** departamento, 60 m², una recámara, sala muy grande, junto a la central de autobuses: **2,000,000 pesos.**

B Interiores

1 ¿En qué parte de la casa pueden estar las siguientes cosas? Hay varias opciones.

sillones lavabo lavavajillas
~~gabinetes~~ espejo equipo de música
mesa tina microondas

Sala	Cocina	Cuarto de baño
	gabinetes	

2 Completa los espacios con el artículo determinado (*el / la / los / las*).

1 Compro *el* periódico todas las mañanas.
2 _____ casa de Isidro es muy grande.
3 _____ amigos de Juan son muy jóvenes.
4 Yo vivo en _____ centro de Monterrey.
5 Trabajo con _____ hermanas de Ángela.
6 _____ metro está cerca de _____ Macroplaza.
7 _____ comedor de mi casa tiene dos ventanas.
8 ¿Están _____ platos en _____ lavavajillas?
9 Tengo _____ entradas para _____ concierto.
10 _____ mesa y _____ sillas de madera están en _____ jardín.

3 Completa los espacios con el artículo indeterminado (*un / una / unos / unas*).

1 Este hotel tiene *una* alberca espectacular.
2 ¿Trabajas en _____ empresa de sistemas computacionales?
3 Este es _____ restaurante muy bueno.
4 Tengo _____ libros de arte preciosos.
5 Este departamento tiene _____ cuarto de baño muy grande.
6 Tengo _____ pantalones nuevos.
7 Rosa vive en _____ casa pequeña.
8 Estudio en _____ escuela bilingüe.
9 ¿Quieres _____ vaso de leche?
10 ¡Hace _____ día excelente!
11 Al lado de la habitación hay _____ cuarto de baño.
12 En la habitación hay _____ hombre y _____ mujer.
13 En el frutero hay _____ naranjas y _____ manzana.

4 Completa los espacios con el artículo determinado o indeterminado correspondiente.

1 *El* libro está en mi portafolio pero no sé dónde están _____ lentes.
2 Cerca de mi casa hay _____ mercado.
3 _____ pizarrón está en _____ pared.
4 _____ campos de futbol están al final del parque.
5 Allí está _____ tienda de fotografía.
6 Me levanto a _____ seis todos los días.
7 Pablo tiene _____ carro muy viejo.
8 Cerca de mi casa hay _____ central de autobuses.
9 Iván es _____ esposo de _____ amiga de mi hermana.

5 Ordena las siguientes frases.

1 dos restaurantes / mi casa / cerca de / hay.
Cerca de mi casa hay dos restaurantes.
2 Barcelona / el Museo Picasso / está / en.
_____
3 Saltillo / cerca de / está / Monterrey.
_____
4 hay / de tren / mi casa / una estación / junto a.
_____
5 lavabo / espejo / está / encima / del / el.
_____
6 está / computadora / habitación / la / hermano / la / en / mi / de.
_____
7 ¿banco / aquí / hay / cerca / dónde / de / un?
_____
8 cine / niños / está / los / Andrés / el / con / en
_____

6 Completa las frases con:

hay • está • están • tiene • tienen

1 La recámara *está* al final del pasillo.
2 ¿_____ una farmacia por aquí cerca?
3 ¿Dónde _____ los sanitarios, por favor?
4 En la plaza _____ un museo.
5 El librero _____ a la derecha de la tv.
6 ¿_____ unas tiendas departamentales cerca de tu casa?
7 Mis abuelos _____ una casa en el campo.
8 ¿Dónde _____ la calle Pino Suárez?
9 ¿_____ tu madre microondas en la cocina?
10 El espejo _____ en el cuarto de baño.

7 Escucha a Carmen hablar de su casa y di si las frases son verdaderas (V) o falsas (F). Corrige las falsas.

1 La casa de Carmen está en la ciudad. ☐
2 La casa de Carmen es muy bonita. ☐
3 La casa tiene dos cuartos de baño. ☐
4 La sala tiene chimenea. ☐
5 La cocina está cerca de la sala. ☐
6 La casa no tiene cochera. ☐
7 El jardín es pequeño. ☐
8 Tiene muchos árboles y flores. ☐
9 En la casa no hay alberca. ☐

____

____

____

____

____

8 Completa el texto con las palabras del recuadro.

está • en • recámaras • quinto • librero • ~~grande~~ • porque • cocina • hay • televisión • la

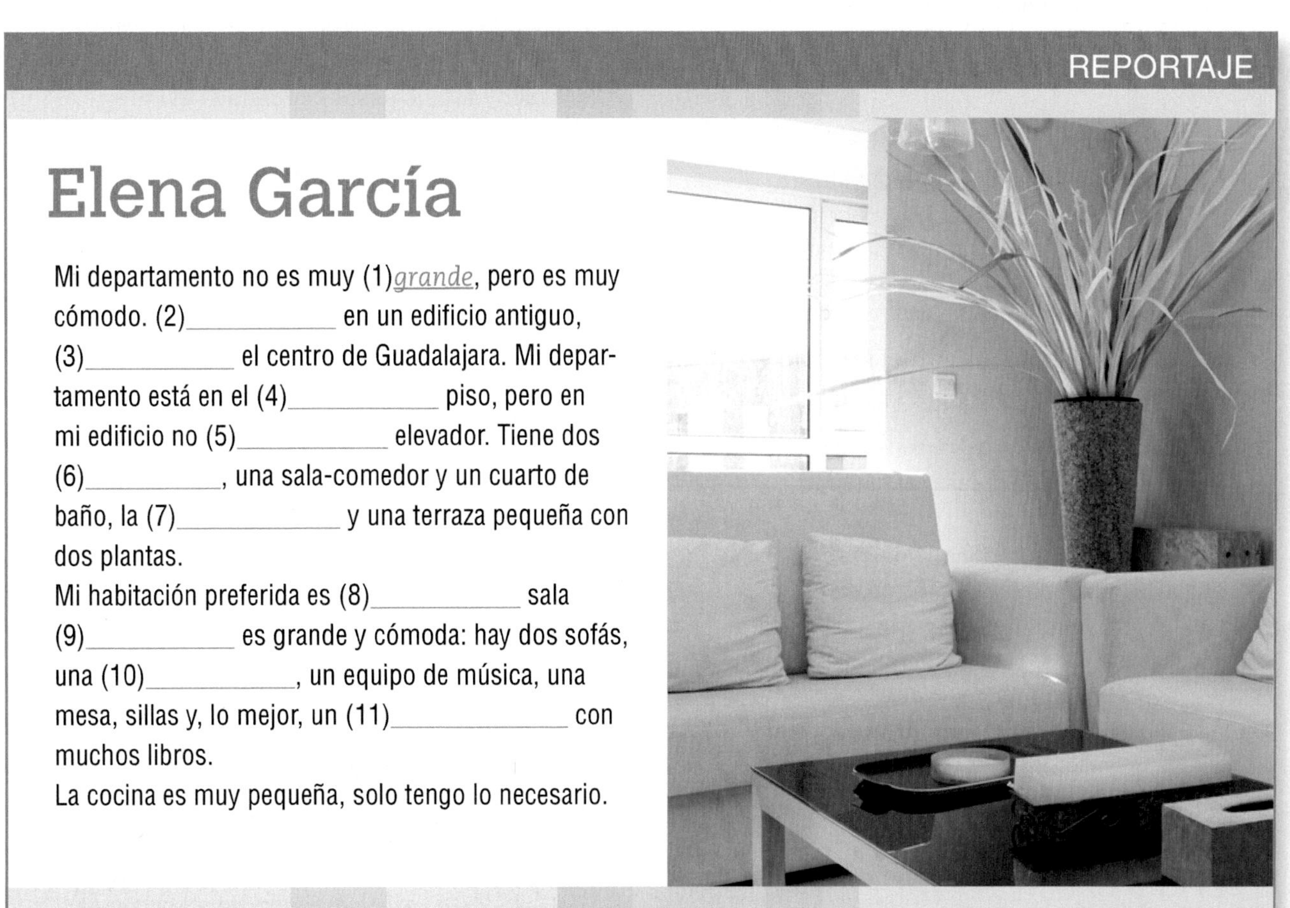

REPORTAJE

Elena García

Mi departamento no es muy (1)*grande*, pero es muy cómodo. (2)__________ en un edificio antiguo, (3)__________ el centro de Guadalajara. Mi departamento está en el (4)__________ piso, pero en mi edificio no (5)__________ elevador. Tiene dos (6)__________, una sala-comedor y un cuarto de baño, la (7)__________ y una terraza pequeña con dos plantas.

Mi habitación preferida es (8)__________ sala (9)__________ es grande y cómoda: hay dos sofás, una (10)__________, un equipo de música, una mesa, sillas y, lo mejor, un (11)__________ con muchos libros.

La cocina es muy pequeña, solo tengo lo necesario.

C Visita a Cuernavaca

1 Pon las siguientes frases en un orden lógico.

a Pago la cuenta. ☐
b Lleno la ficha en la recepción. ☐
c Paso la noche en el hotel. ☐
d Subo a mi habitación. ☐
e Llego al hotel. 1
f Desayuno. ☐
g Salgo del hotel. ☐

2 ¿Qué se dice en estas situaciones?

1 Quieres pasar el próximo fin de semana en un hotel con tu amigo/a. Telefoneas al hotel. ¿Qué preguntas?

______

2 Quieres saber cuánto cuesta la habitación.

______

3 Quieres saber si el uso de la alberca está incluido en el precio.

______

4 Quieres saber si el IVA está incluido en el precio.

______

5 Quieres saber si se puede pagar con tarjeta de crédito.

______

3 Lee el correo de María y contesta a las preguntas.

Querido Roberto:

Te escribo esta carta desde la habitación de mi hotel en Cuernavaca. Mis amigos y yo estamos de viaje por el centro de México. El hotel es muy bonito, tiene de todo: restaurante, alberca, canchas de tenis... y unas vistas preciosas.
Mañana vamos de excursión por el Palacio de Cortés y visitamos la Catedral y exconvento de La Asunción. Al día siguiente vamos a Tepoztlán, y el último día tenemos una cena de despedida en el restaurante del hotel.
Nos vemos a la vuelta.
Besos.
María

1 ¿En qué ciudad está María?

______

2 ¿Qué opina María del hotel?

______

3 ¿Qué instalaciones tiene el hotel?

______

4 ¿Qué otra ciudad piensan visitar?

______

5 Comer

A Comer fuera de casa

1 Mira las fotografías y escribe las comidas favoritas de Amalia y Juan.

Amalia

1 ejotes
2 ______
3 ______
4 ______

Juan

1 ______
2 ______
3 ______
4 ______

2 Localiza la palabra que no pertenece a su grupo.

1 sopa, gazpacho, merluza, ensalada.
2 milanesa de res, chuletas, pescado, flan.
3 arroz con leche, ejotes, fruta, helado.
4 espárragos, vino, cerveza, agua.
5 plátano, naranja, manzana, milanesa de res.

3 Ordena las siguientes frases. Después utilízalas para completar la conversación en el restaurante.

1 postre / de / fruta de temporada / dos / los / para.
De postre, fruta de temporada para los dos.
2 quiero / de / yo / entrada / sopa de fideos.
______
3 merluza / plato fuerte / quiero / de.
______
4 ensalada / yo / y.
______
5 yo / pues / pollo asado.
______
6 agua / beber / para / por favor.
______

MESERO: Buenas, ¿qué van a ordenar de entrada?
JORGE: ______
ANA: ______
MESERO: ¿Y de plato fuerte?
JORGE: ______
ANA: ______
MESERO: ¿Qué quieren para beber?
JORGE: ______
MESERO: ¿Y de postre?
ANA: ______
MESERO: Gracias, señores.

B ¿Te gusta el cine?

1 Observa las habitaciones de Carmen y de Pablo. ¿Qué actividades les gusta realizar en su tiempo libre?

esquiar • escuchar música clásica • escuchar rock
andar en bicicleta • navegar por internet • ver la televisión
tomar fotos • estar con animales • leer
cuidar las plantas • ir al cine

Carmen

Pablo

1 A Carmen *le gusta la música clásica.*
2 A Pablo ____________
3 A los dos ____________
4 ____________
5 ____________
6 ____________
7 ____________
8 ____________
9 ____________
10 ____________
11 ____________

2 ¿Qué aficiones compartes y no compartes con Pablo y Carmen?

1 A mí ____________
2 A mí no ____________
3 ____________
4 ____________

3 Ordena las siguientes preguntas. Después, contéstalas.

1 ¿a tus amigos / gusta / computación / les / la?
¿A tus amigos les gusta la computación?
Sí, les gusta mucho. / No, no les gusta.
2 ¿ciclismo / a ti y a tu compañero / gusta / les / el?
____
____
3 ¿animales / te / los / gustan?
____
____
4 ¿ver / le / televisión / gusta / la / a tu amigo?
____
____
5 ¿el / terror / gusta / te / cine / de?
____
____
6 ¿mole / te / el / gusta?
____
____

4 Escribe frases con el verbo "gustar" y expresa tus gustos como en el ejemplo.

1 jugo de naranja
Me gusta / No me gusta el jugo de naranja.
2 los plátanos
3 las verduras
4 la leche
5 los cacahuates
6 las papas
7 el café
8 el té

5 Reacciona según tus gustos con : a mí *también/tampoco* o *a mí sí/no.*

1 Me gusta mucho ir al cine.
2 No me gusta nada la música latina.
3 Me gustan las películas de ciencia ficción.
4 No me gusta bailar.
5 Me gusta leer libros de viajes.
6 Me gusta ver partidos de futbol en la tele.
7 No me gusta comer en restaurantes.
8 Me gusta ir de compras.

C Receta del Caribe

1 Completa la tabla con el imperativo de los verbos.

INFINITIVO	IMPERATIVO	
	tú	**usted**
Hablar	*habla*	*hable*
Trabajar		
Comer		
Abrir		
Beber		

ENSALADA MEDITERRÁNEA

Ingredientes
- Una lechuga.
- Dos tomates.
- Una cebolla pequeña.
- Una lata de atún.
- Aceite, vinagre y sal.

2 Completa la receta con el imperativo de los verbos del recuadro.

añadir ~~*lavar*~~ *servir* *mezclar* *cortar*

1 *Lava* la lechuga y los tomates.
2 __________ las verduras en trozos pequeños.
3 __________ el atún a las verduras troceadas.
4 __________ el aceite, el vinagre y la sal en una taza.
5 __________ la ensalada mezclada con el aderezo anterior.

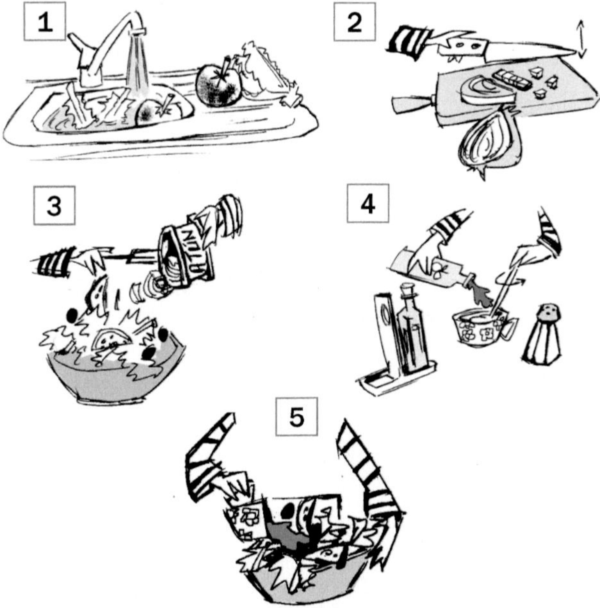

3 Completa las frases con el imperativo de los siguientes verbos entre paréntesis.

CONSEJOS

Aprender a cocinar puede ser fácil y divertido, pero recuerda siempre lo siguiente:

1 Prepara (preparar) todos los ingredientes, antes de empezar.
2 ________ (comprar) siempre productos de primera calidad.
3 ________ (elaborar) siempre un menú equilibrado.
4 ________ (usar) siempre aceite de oliva.
5 ________ (añadir) algún detalle imaginativo a tus platillos.
6 ________ (recoger) bien la cocina, una vez terminado tu trabajo.

4 Clasifica estos platillos en la carta del Menú.

helado • sopa de fideos • aguas frescas
fruta • ensalada mixta • cerveza
merluza a la plancha • milanesa de res
pollo asado • agua mineral • flan
chuletas de cerdo • vino tinto
sopa de verduras • ejotes con jamón

Restaurante Miramar

Menú del día 120 pesos

Entrada

____
____
____
____

Plato fuerte

____
____
____
____

Postre

____
____
____

Bebidas

____
____
____

5 106 Lee y escucha el siguiente texto y contesta a las preguntas.

LA DIETA MEDITERRÁNEA

¿En qué se basa esta cultura gastronómica? Se basa, principalmente, en el aceite de oliva, el pan y el vino. Con estos productos básicos se alimentan los pueblos mediterráneos desde hace más de cinco mil años.

Los países mediterráneos consumen como grasa principal el aceite de oliva, que favorece la disminución del colesterol. También consumen gran cantidad de pescados azules, legumbres y frutas, y menos carne.

Las primeras investigaciones sobre esta dieta se centran en Grecia y en España, donde se estudian las características de su cocina, sus ingredientes, técnicas de cocción, etc., y se llega a la conclusión de que la dieta de estos países es la ideal para mantener una buena salud.

1 ¿Cuáles son los alimentos básicos de la dieta mediterránea?
____
2 ¿Desde cuándo utilizan estos alimentos los pueblos mediterráneos?
____
3 ¿Por qué es bueno para la salud el aceite de oliva?
____
4 ¿Qué alimentos sustituyen a la carne en la dieta mediterránea?
____
5 ¿En qué países se basan las primeras investigaciones sobre esta dieta?
____

6 La colonia

A ¿Cómo se llega a Garibaldi?

1 Completa los diálogos con los verbos del recuadro en el tiempo adecuado.

ser • cambiar • tomar • bajar • llegar

1 A Disculpa, ¿cómo se *llega* de Terminal Aérea a Garibaldi?
B Mira, _________ la línea cinco hacia Politécnico. En la primera estación _________ a la línea verde hacia Buenavista y la séptima estación _________ Garibaldi.

2 A Disculpe, ¿cómo se _________ de Bellas Artes al Zócalo?
B _________ la línea dos en dirección Tasqueña, _________ en la segunda estación, ahí está el Zócalo.

3 A Disculpa, ¿cómo se _________ de Bellas Artes a Coyoacán?
B Es muy fácil, _________ la línea dos hacia Cuatro Caminos y _________ en la primera estación, Hidalgo, _________ a la línea tres en dirección a Universidad. _________ en la décima estación, esa es Coyoacán.

2 Completa con las siguientes preposiciones.

a (al) de en desde hasta

1 Las estaciones *de* metro abren *a* las 6 _________ la mañana.
2 Quiero una tarjeta recargable _________ diez viajes.
3 ¿Cómo se llega _________ Zócalo?
4 _________ Observatorio _________ Chapultepec hay tres estaciones.
5 Yo voy _________ casa _________ trabajo _________ metro.
6 Maribel va _________ su trabajo _________ carro.
7 Luis, ¿puedes venir _________ mi oficina, por favor?
8 Mis vecinos salen _________ su casa _________ las 7.
9 Trabajo _________ las siete _________ la tarde.
10 _________ mi casa _________ la oficina tardo una hora.

3 107 Escucha la conversación y señala verdadero (V) o falso (F).

1 Beatriz está en su hotel. ☐
2 Marta trabaja lejos del Zócalo. ☐
3 Marta espera a Beatriz en su trabajo. ☐

4 107 Escucha otra vez y marca en el plano el recorrido del que están hablando.

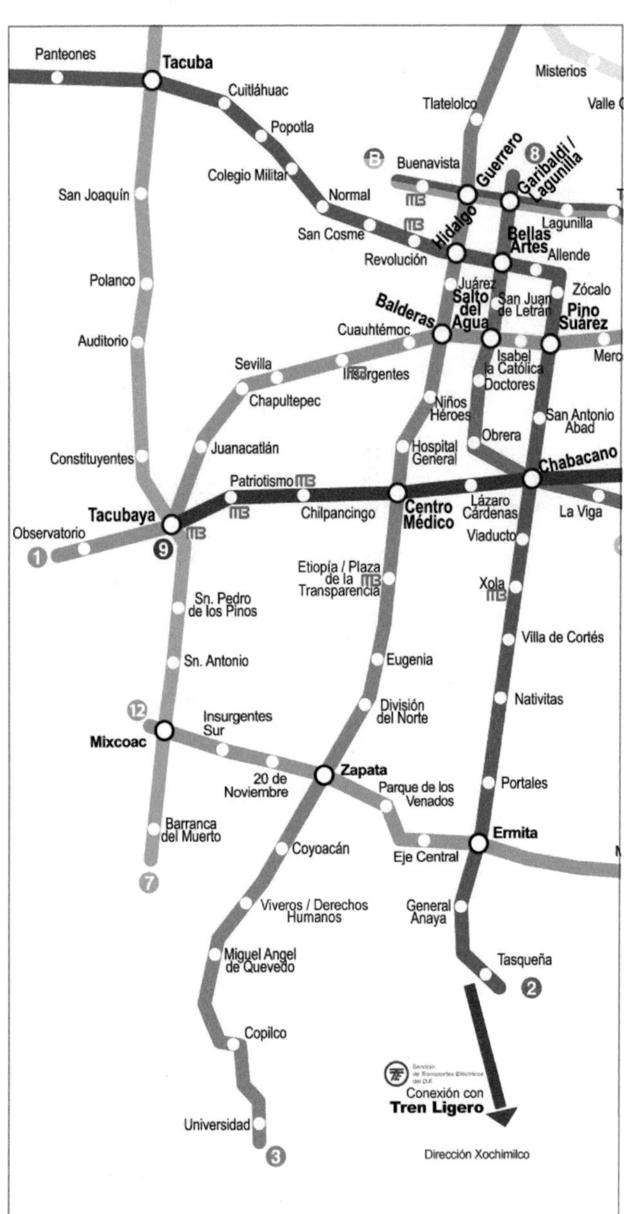

B Cierra la ventana, por favor

1 Relaciona.

1 Pon	a más despacio
2 Habla	b la cuenta
3 Ven	c la luz
4 Haz	d la puerta
5 Cierra	e todo derecho
6 Pide	f aquí
7 Prende	g la televisión
8 Recoge	h los ejercicios
9 Da vuelta	i la mesa
10 Sigue	j a la derecha

2 Transforma las frases anteriores.

1 *¿Puedes poner la televisión?*
2 ______
3 ______
4 ______
5 ______
6 ______
7 ______
8 ______
9 ______
10 ______

3 Completa la tabla.

INFINITIVO	PRESENTE	IMPERATIVO
cerrar	cierro	cierra
empezar		
prender		
seguir	sigo	sigue
pedir		
guardar	guardo	

4 Forma el imperativo.

1 Cerrar / el libro.
Cierra el libro.
2 Empezar / a trabajar.
______
3 Prender / la computadora.
______
4 Christian / sentarse ahí.
______
5 Seguir / por aquí (Ud.).
______
6 Pedir / dinero / a tus papás.
______
7 Acostarse / pronto.
______
8 Levantarse ya / son las diez.
______
9 Darme / un vaso de agua.
______
10 Prestarme / tu carro.
______
11 Mostrarme / su pasaporte (Ud.).
______

5 Jaime tiene que ordenar la habitación. Escribe las instrucciones que le da su mamá.

Guardar la ropa limpia en el closet
Poner la ropa sucia en la lavadora.
Hacer la cama.
Colocar los libros en los estantes.
Poner los CD en su lugar.

1 *Guarda la ropa limpia en el closet.*
2 ______
3 ______
4 ______
5 ______

C Mi colonia es tranquila

1 Escribe la letra adecuada.

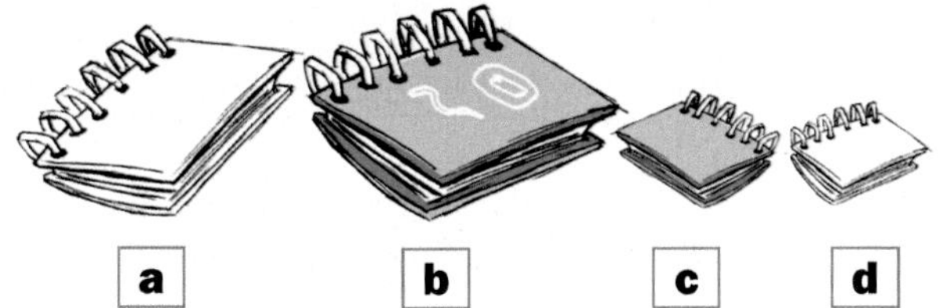

1 Está al lado del cuaderno gris grande y es de otro color. ☐
2 Está a la izquierda de otro cuaderno que también es pequeño. ☐
3 Es grande y está entre un cuaderno grande y uno pequeño. ☐
4 Es blanco y está a la derecha de un cuaderno gris. ☐

2 Completa con *es / está*.

ROSA: ¿Tu departamento (1) es grande?
ANDRÉS: No, solo tiene 40 m^2, (2)________ muy pequeño, pero me gusta porque (3)________ en una colonia muy céntrica.
ROSA: ¿(4)________ cerca del trabajo?
ANDRÉS: Sí, muy cerca. Solo tiene un problema: que mi calle (5)________ muy ruidosa y no duermo bien por las noches. ¿Y tu departamento, cómo (6)________?
ROSA: Pues (7)________ muy tranquilo y tiene mucha luz, me encanta. Pero tengo un problema: (8)________ muy lejos del trabajo. Tardo casi una hora en llegar todos los días.

3 Escribe el adjetivo contrario.

1 largo corto
2 rápido ________
3 alto ________
4 grande ________
5 fácil ________
6 ruidoso ________
7 barato ________
8 bonito ________
9 ancho ________
10 claro ________
11 delgado ________

4 De estas frases solo dos son correctas. Busca los errores en las frases incorrectas y corrígelas.

1 Guanajuato está una ciudad muy bonita, tiene muchos monumentos importantes. es
2 Mi casa es en una colonia muy tranquila y silenciosa. ________
3 Este problema de matemáticas es muy difícil. ________
4 Roberto está rubio, delgado y bastante alto, está ahora en la escuela. ________
5 Fumar está malo para la salud. ________
6 Esa estación de metro es al lado de mi casa y la parada del camión está enfrente. ________
7 Los alumnos son en la clase de historia. ________
8 ¿Está cerca de aquí la estación del metro? ________
9 Estos ejercicios no son bien. ________
10 ¿Es tu hermano en tu casa? ________
11 Mi correo electrónico es lleno. ________
12 La taza es vacía. ________
13 Mi hermano es en cama, porque es enfermo. ________
14 Este ejercicio no es bien. ________
15 Este libro está muy bueno. ________

5 Relaciona.

a	metro	puerto
b	avión	aeropuerto
c	barco	parada
d	taxi	estación

6 Haz la encuesta.

ENCUESTA

1 ¿Qué medio de transporte utilizas normalmente?
- a metro ☐
- b camión ☐
- c carro ☐
- d otro ☐

2 ¿Cuánto dinero gastas aproximadamente en transporte durante un mes?
- a 0-200 pesos ☐
- b 201-400 pesos ☐
- c más de 401 pesos ☐

3 ¿Qué medio de transporte prefieres para hacer viajes largos?
- a avión ☐
- b carro ☐
- c tren ☐
- d barco ☐

4 ¿Crees que el transporte público es...?
- a barato ☐
- b sucio ☐
- c cómodo ☐
- d rápido ☐

5 ¿Cuántos kilómetros caminas al día aproximadamente?
- a 0-1 km ☐
- b 2-4 km ☐
- c 5-7 km ☐
- d más de 7 km ☐

7 108 ¿Te gusta la música latina? Escucha estos cuatro ritmos musicales. ¿Puedes relacionarlos con sus nombres?

a tango ______ b ranchera ______ c flamenco ______ d salsa ______

8 Completa el texto con estas palabras.

ritmos ~~*cultura*~~ *cantantes* *baila* *salsa* *canciones* *popular*

MÚSICA LATINA

La música es un elemento muy importante de la (1) cultura hispanoamericana. En América se mezclan los (2)________ indígenas con los africanos y con los que trajeron los españoles.

Además del tango, la ranchera o la (3)________, son famosos el merengue, la cumbia, el bolero y, sobre todo, la bachata, que se (4)________ en la República Dominicana y en muchos otros lugares del mundo. La bachata aparece en los pueblos pero en los años 70 se hace también muy (5)________ en las ciudades.

Los temas de estas (6)________ hablan casi siempre de amor y se acompañan de instrumentos de cuerda y percusión. Uno de los (7)________ más famosos es Juan Luis Guerra.

9 Después de completar el texto, contesta verdadero (V) o falso (F).

1 El tango, la salsa y el flamenco son ritmos típicos de Hispanoamérica. ☐
2 La bachata nace en las ciudades. ☐
3 Las canciones de bachata suelen tratar de amor. ☐
4 La bachata se toca solo con un instrumento. ☐

7 Salir con los amigos

A ¿Dónde nos vemos?

1 109 Ordena las siguientes conversaciones. Después escucha y comprueba.

1

MARÍA: ¿A qué hora te parece bien?
RICARDO: De acuerdo. ¡Hasta mañana!
MARÍA: No, mejor a las seis y media.
RICARDO: Lo siento, hoy no puedo, tengo que ir de compras con mi hermano. ¿Te parece bien mañana?
MARÍA: ¿Por qué no vamos a tomar algo después de trabajar?
RICARDO: ¿A las seis?

MARÍA: *¿Por qué no vamos a tomar algo después de trabajar?*

RICARDO:

2

DANIEL: ¿Y si nos tomamos un café antes?
CARMEN: No puedo, lo siento. Voy a cenar con unos amigos.
DANIEL: ¿Vamos al cine esta noche?
CARMEN: Bueno, de acuerdo. ¿Vamos al Café Central?
DANIEL: Perfecto. Nos vemos ahí a las cinco.

DANIEL:

2 Imagínate que eres Ricardo o Carmen. Escribe diferentes razones por las que no puedes salir con ellos.

3 110 Carolina y Pedro están en Radio Centro hablando sobre sus espectáculos favoritos. Escucha sus comentarios y di si las frases siguientes son verdaderas (V) o falsas (F).

1 A Pedro le gusta ir a los conciertos de rock. V
2 A Carolina le gusta la música moderna. ☐
3 No les gusta volver a casa caminando. ☐
4 A Pedro le gustan los espectáculos musicales. ☐
5 A Carolina no le gusta la ópera. ☐
6 A ellos no les gusta ir al cine. ☐

4 Completa las siguientes conversaciones telefónicas con las frases del recuadro.

Ahora contesta   *No está en este momento*   *¿De parte de quién?*

1 A ¿Bueno?
B Buenas tardes, ¿está Ramón?
A (1) ____________
B Soy Arturo.

2 A ¿Sí?
B ¿Está Manuel?
A Un momento. (2) ____________

3 A ¿Diga?
B ¿Está Vicente, por favor?
A (3) ____________ ¿De parte de quién?

5 Relaciona cada pregunta con su respuesta.

1 ¿Y el domingo? ☐
2 Entonces, ¡hasta el domingo! ¿De acuerdo? ☐
3 ¿A qué hora quedamos de vernos? ☐
4 ¿Está Enrique? ☐
5 Sale. ¿Vamos en mi carro o en el tuyo? ☐
6 Soy Pilar. Te llamaba para ver si vienes este fin de semana a la sierra. ¿Qué te parece el sábado? *d*

a Pues, podemos quedar de vernos a las 11.
b Sí, soy yo.
c Podemos ir en el mío.
d No, ese día no puedo. Viene mi hermano a comer a casa.
e De acuerdo, nos vemos el domingo.
f Sí, ese día me parece bien.

6 Escribe las preguntas para las siguientes respuestas.

1 *¿Está Pilar?*
No, Pilar no está. Está trabajando.
2 ____________
Puedes hablarle a las 3 de la tarde.
3 ____________
Lo siento, mañana no puedo ir al cine.
4 ____________
No, las seis es un poco temprano; mejor a las ocho.
5 ____________
(Quedamos de vernos) a las cinco.
6 ____________
(Quedamos de vernos) en la puerta de mi casa.

7 Lee el texto y di si las frases siguientes son verdaderas (V) o falsas (F).

La noche en el Barrio Antiguo

Cerca de la Macroplaza nos encontramos con una de las zonas más populares de Monterrey: el Barrio Antiguo. Lugar de artistas, músicos y pintores. En la actualidad es una zona en la que se pueden encontrar al mismo tiempo teatros, bares, antros y restaurantes que están abiertos hasta altas horas de la noche.

Su ambiente es una mezcla de edades y procedencias, y es una buena opción si lo que quieres es disfrutar de una noche bohemia. El Barrio Antiguo es el punto de encuentro de gran cantidad de personas que generalmente se reúnen en la calle Mina, denominada Corredor del Arte, y después se reparten por los alrededores.

Macroplaza, Monterrey

1 El Barrio Antiguo está en Monterrey. ☐
2 El Corredor del Arte está en la calle Mina. ☐
3 Artistas, músicos y pintores no se encuentran en el Barrio Antiguo. ☐
4 Los restaurantes en el Barrio Antiguo cierran muy temprano. ☐
5 En esta zona de Monterrey se reúnen personas de todas las edades. ☐
6 La gente queda de verse en la calle Mina. ☐

B ¿Qué estás haciendo?

1 Mira el cuadro de *Las meninas*. ¿Qué están haciendo los personajes?

1 Velázquez está pintando (pintar).
2 Las meninas __________ (jugar) con la princesa.
3 La princesa __________ (mirar) al perro.
4 El perro __________ (descansar).
5 Los reyes __________ (ver) la escena.
6 Un hombre __________ (salir) de la habitación.

2 Subraya la forma apropiada del verbo.

1 Soy vegetariano. No como / estoy comiendo carne.
2 ¿Dónde está Juan? *Hace / Está haciendo* la comida.
3 ¿Qué periódico *lees / estás leyendo* últimamente?
4 Todas las mañanas *hago / estoy haciendo* deporte.
5 No te entiendo, no *hablo / estoy hablando* francés.
6 ¿Cuántos años *tienes / estás teniendo?*
7 Lo siento, no puede contestar en este momento porque *duerme / está durmiendo.*
8 No podemos hablar con él ahora. *Trabaja / Está trabajando* en este momento.
9 Juan no está en la biblioteca. *Estudia / Está estudiando* en casa de una amiga.

3 Completa el texto con la forma correcta del verbo (presente o *estar* + gerundio).

Pepa (1) *vive* (vivir) en Cuernavaca, pero en este momento (2)__________ (pasar) unos días en Cancún con unos amigos. Esta semana Pepa y sus amigos (3)__________ (visitar) la zona arqueológica de Tulum.

Hoy, como hay buen clima, sus amigos (4)__________ (bañarse) en la playa. Cancún (5)__________ (tener) unas playas preciosas, pero a Pepa no te (6)__________ (gustar) la playa. Ella y su amiga Lara (7)__________ (ver) las pirámides. Luego, por las noches todos juntos (8)__________ (cenar) en algún restaurante del puerto.

4 Pon las palabras en el orden correcto.

1 para / me / un / preparando / examen / estoy.
Me estoy preparando para un examen.
2 ¿haciendo / qué / ahora / estás?
____
3 unos / comiendo / tacos / están.
____
4 haciendo / cena / estamos / la.
____
5 está / esposo / trabajando / mi.
____
6 semana / mucho / esta / lloviendo / está.
____
7 están / película / mis / viendo / amigos / una.
____
8 estamos / y / Claudia / proyecto / nuevo / yo / trabajando / en / un.
____
9 cuarto / bañándose / las / en / niñas / el / están / de / baño / grande.
____
10 ¿qué / haciendo / los / están / su / niños / habitación / en?
____

5 ¿Qué están haciendo? Utiliza la forma correcta del verbo con el pronombre reflexivo correspondiente.

1 María / lavarse la cara.
María se está lavando la cara.
2 Luis / afeitarse.
______
3 Mi hermano / bañarse.
______
4 (yo) / peinarse.
______
5 Susana y Rosa / pintarse los labios.
______
6 Yo / bañarse.
______
7 Mi hijo / peinarse.
______
8 (él) / cepillarse los dientes.
______
9 Mi mamá / secarse el pelo en el cuarto de baño.
______
10 Mis hermanos / vestirse para ir al concierto.
______

C ¿Cómo es?

1 ¿Son verdaderas (V) o falsas (F) estas frases sobre el cuadro *Las meninas* de Velázquez?

1 El pintor tiene el pelo corto. [F]
2 La infanta trae lentes. ☐
3 Las meninas son rubias. ☐
4 Una menina es rubia. ☐
5 El pintor tiene barba y bigote. ☐
6 El pintor es calvo. ☐
7 La infanta es alta. ☐

2 Describe, utilizando las palabras del recuadro, a los siguientes personajes del cuadro.

pelo largo • pelo rubio • barba
pelo negro • bigote
joven • jóvenes • mayor • alto

Velázquez ______
______
______

La infanta Margarita ______
______
______

Las meninas ______
______
______

3 Escribe los contrarios.

1 tacaño ______
2 ______ platicador
3 agradable ______
4 serio ______
5 ______ amable

4 ¿Cómo crees que son estas personas? Utiliza los adjetivos de los ejercicios anteriores.

El hombre: ______
______
______

La mujer: ______
______
______

8 De vacaciones

A Por favor, ¿para ir a la catedral?

1 Relaciona las preguntas con las respuestas.

1 ¿Para qué vas a correos? ☐
2 ¿Para qué vas a la farmacia? ☐
3 ¿Para qué vas a la estación? ☐
4 ¿Para qué vas a la tienda de conveniencia? ☐
5 ¿Para qué vas al mercado? ☐
6 ¿Para qué vas al puesto de periódicos? ☐

a Para comprar medicinas.
b Para comprar el periódico.
c Para tomar el camión.
d Para comprar carne y pescado.
e Para enviar una carta.
f Para comprar refrescos.

2 Mira el plano de calles y completa las conversaciones.

1 **A** Por favor, ¿para ir a la iglesia?
B Dé vuelta la primera a la derecha y después tome la ______________.

2 **A** ¿Puede decirme cómo se llega a la central de autobuses, por favor?
B Siga todo derecho y tome ______________ y después dé vuelta por la segunda calle a la izquierda.

3 **A** ¿El hotel Colón, por favor?
B Siga todo derecho y tome ______________ y ______________ ______________.

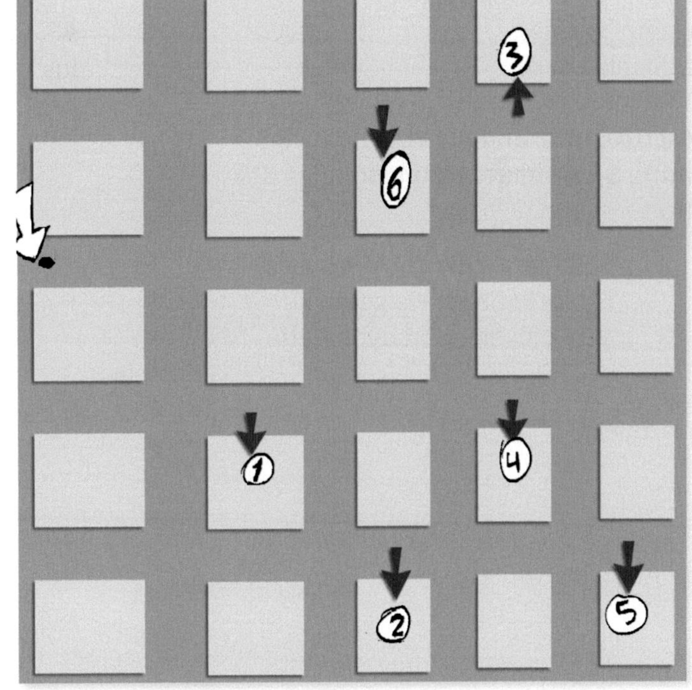

1 Iglesia **2** Central de autobuses **3** Hotel Colón **4** Restaurante **5** Parque **6** Teatro

3 Escribe tres conversaciones más como las del ejercicio 2.

1 A quiere ir al parque.
A ______________
B ______________
____

2 A quiere ir al teatro.
A ______________
B ______________
____

3 A quiere ir al restaurante.
A ______________
B ______________
____

4 Completa las frases con las preposiciones del recuadro.

a (x4) en (x3) de (x6) hasta (x2)
al (x2) por (x2)

1 Hay una farmacia *en* la calle Santa Marta.
2 Para encontrar la estación de metro, siga _____ el final _____ la calle.
3 El cine está _____ la derecha del restaurante.
4 La iglesia _____ San Juan es un edificio muy bonito.
5 Hay un hotel _____ la primera calle _____ la izquierda.
6 _____ Observatorio hay una estación _____ metro.
7 El mercado está _____ lado _____ la estación _____ metro.
8 ¿Cómo se llega _____ la Macroplaza?
9 Vaya _____ la calle _____ Santo Domingo _____ llegar _____ cine Avenida.
10 Dé vuelta _____ la segunda calle _____ la derecha.

5 Lee esta poesía y relaciona los dibujos con los nombres.

La plaza tiene una  ,
la  tiene un  ,
el  tiene una  ,
la  , una blanca  .
Ha pasado un  ,
–¿quién sabe por qué pasó?–
y se ha llevado la plaza,
con su  y su  ,
con su  y su  ,
su  y su blanca  .

ANTONIO MACHADO

a Dama b Caballero c Torre d Balcón e Flor

1  ☐ 2 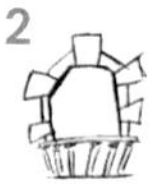 ☐ 3  ☐ 4  ☐ 5  ☐

B ¿Qué hizo Rosa ayer?

1 Completa la tabla.

INFINITIVO	PRETÉRITO	
	yo	él / ella
ver	*vi*	*vio*
ir	fui	
		comió
escuchar		
	leí	
empezar		
	estuve	
	jugué	
salir		
	viví	
nacer		
		trabajó

2 Relaciona las frases. Pon el verbo de A en presente y el de B en pretérito.

A.
1 Normalmente *trabajo* (trabajar) ocho horas al día, pero [c]
2 Ana, normalmente, _______ (ir) en carro al trabajo, pero ☐
3 Mateo _______ (ver) la televisión por las noches, pero ☐
4 Ana y Mateo _______ (ir) a la playa los fines de semanas, pero ☐
5 Normalmente _______ (llover) mucho en invierno, pero ☐
6 Mateo y yo normalmente _______ (ir) a acampar en agosto, pero ☐

B.
a el verano pasado _______ (estar) en un hotel.
b el fin de semana pasado _______(jugar) al tenis.
c ayer *empecé* (empezar) a las 9 de la mañana y terminé a las 9 de la noche.
d el año pasado _______ (nevar) mucho.
e ayer _______ (ir) en camión.
f ayer en la noche _______ (escuchar) música.

3 Completa la conversación con el pretérito de los verbos señalados.

A Ayer fue mi cumpleaños. ¡Ya tengo 30 años!
B ¡Órale, felicidades! ¿Adónde (1) fuiste (ir, tú)?
A (2)______ (ir) a un restaurante italiano con mis amigos.
B ¿Qué (3)______ (comer / ustedes)?
A Todos (4)______ (pedir) pasta.
B ¿Qué tal la (5)______ (pasar)?
A Nos la (6) ______ (pasar) muy bien y nos (7)______ (reír) mucho. ¿Cuándo es tu cumpleaños?
B (8)______ (ser) ayer.
A ¡Mira! ¡Qué casualidad! ¡Muchas felicidades!
B ¡Gracias!

4 Mira la agenda de Guillermo. Ordena las preguntas y contéstalas.

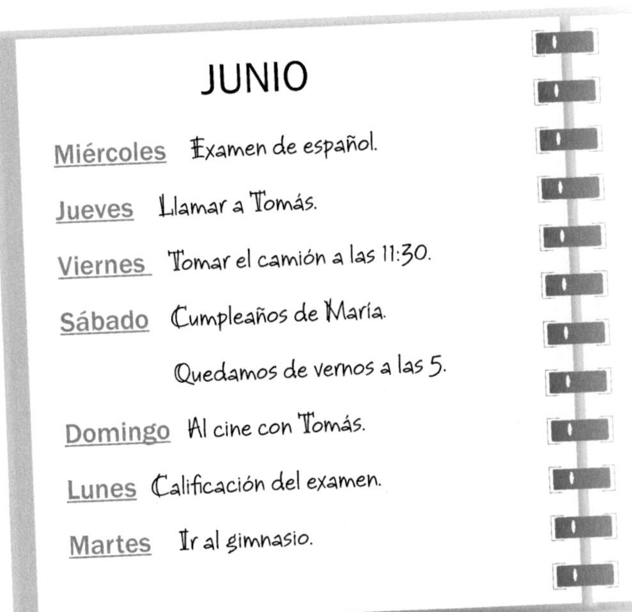

1 ¿por / llamó / a / teléfono / quién / jueves / el?
______
2 ¿tomó / qué / camión / el / día?
______
3 ¿hora / camión / a / salió / qué / el?
______
4 ¿fue / el / sábado / de / cumpleaños / quién / el?
______
5 ¿hora / quedaron de verse / qué / a?
______
6 ¿fue / el / quién / cine / domingo / al / con?
______
7 ¿la / examen / calificación / cuándo / del / vio?
______
8 ¿el / adónde / martes / fue?
______

C ¿Cómo está el clima hoy?

1 111 Completa con las palabras del recuadro. Después, escucha y comprueba.

vuelo • Más tarde • despedí • río • salieron • ~~estuve~~ • Después • Finalmente • tomé (x2)

UN PAÍS MARAVILLOSO

Desde niña, siempre deseé conocer la selva. Este verano (1) estuve en Perú, un país maravilloso.

Al día siguiente de mi llegada a Lima, (2)______ un (3)______ a Iquitos, bellísima ciudad tropical, como sacada de una película: los mototaxis, los mercados de fruta, las casas, y el (4)______ Amazonas.

(5)______ entramos en la selva, dispuestos a pescar pirañas, nadar en el Amazonas, comer plátano frito…

(6)______ , nos detuvimos en un pueblo en medio de la selva. En unos segundos un montón de niños (7)______ de sus casas y me rodearon con sus rostros sonrientes.

(8)______, me (9)______ unas fotos con ellos y me (10)______ muy contenta de llevarme un recuerdo auténtico del Amazonas.

2 Corrige las frases a partir de la información del texto anterior.

1 Nunca deseé conocer la selva.

____

2 Al tercer día salimos para Iquitos.

____

3 En Iquitos vimos el río Paraná.

____

4 En el Amazonas se pescan tiburones.

____

5 En la selva no nadamos en el río Amazonas.

____

6 En el pueblo de la selva conocimos a un grupo de jóvenes.

____

7 No me llevé ningún recuerdo del Amazonas.

____

8 No me tomé fotos con los niños.

____

3 ¿Qué clima hizo ayer en Sudamérica? ¿Y hoy, qué clima hace?

	Perú	México	Argentina	Brasil
Ayer	aire y lluvia	calor y nublado	frío	nublado y lluvia
Hoy	frío y nieve	lluvia	aire	frío y aire

Ayer en Perú hizo aire y llovió. Hoy hace frío y nieva.

1 ______________________________

2 ______________________________

3 ______________________________

4 Lee el siguiente anuncio de una revista de viajes y contesta a las preguntas.

Datos básicos

Población: unos 118 millones de habitantes.
Moneda: peso mexicano (1 € = 17 pesos).
Documentación: pasaporte.

Cuándo ir

Los mejores meses del año son de octubre a mayo.

Cómo llegar

Vuelos directos diarios con Iberia y Aeroméxico.

Visitas imprescindibles

Ciudad de México: el Museo Nacional de Antropología y las cercanas pirámides de Teotihuacán.
Oaxaca: ruinas de Monte Albán.
Chiapas y Yucatán: pirámides mayas.
Playas de Cancún.

Información: www.visitmexico.com

1 ¿Cuántos habitantes tiene México?

____

2 ¿Cuántos pesos mexicanos puedes comprar con 300 €?

____

3 ¿Qué compañías tienen vuelo directo todos los días desde España?

____

4 Menciona seis buenos meses para ir a México.

____

5 ¿Dónde está el Museo Nacional de Antropología? ¿Y las pirámides mayas?

____

6 ¿Si vas a México tienes que llevar el traje de baño? ¿Para qué?

____

9 Compras

A ¿Cuánto cuestan estos zapatos?

1 Completa estas conversaciones con las palabras que faltan.

1

A ¿En qué puedo ayudarla?
B Sí, ¿(1) *cuánto* cuestan estos aretes?
A 600 pesos.
B ¿Y esos de ahí, los azules?
A Esos tienen descuento, (2)__________ 500 pesos.
B Me los (3)__________ .
A ¿Va a pagar en efectivo o (4)__________________?

2

A Buenos días. ¿Cuánto (1)__________ la falda roja del aparador?
B (2)__________ 1,000 pesos.
A ¿Puedo (3)__________?
B Sí, claro, los probadores están al final del pasillo.
(...)
B ¿Qué tal le (4)__________?
A Pues no me (5)__________ mucho, lo siento, no me la (6)__________.

3

A Mira esa playera verde, solo (1)__________ 200 pesos.
B Me (2)__________ más esta, ¿por qué no te la pruebas?
A Sale... A ver... ¿Cómo se me (3)__________?
B Superbien.
A ¿(4)__________ cuesta?
B No te preocupes, yo te la regalo.

2 112 Escucha y comprueba tus respuestas.

3 Haz preguntas como en el ejemplo con los pronombres *la, lo, las, los.*

1 Yo no traigo el diccionario.
¿Tú lo traes?
2 Yo no veo esas películas.
¿Tú ______________________________?
3 Yo no compro esos libros.
¿Tú ______________________________?
4 Yo no conozco a la tía de David.
¿Tú ______________________________?
5 Yo no leo el periódico.
¿Tú ______________________________?
6 Yo no uso la computadora de la escuela.
¿Tú ______________________________?
7 Yo no utilizo el transporte público.
¿Tú ______________________________?

4 Completa las frases con los pronombres del recuadro.

~~me~~ te lo (x2) la los (x3) nos las

1 ¿Por qué no *me* escuchas?
2 Ahí está María, ¿______ ves?
3 ¿Dónde están mis zapatos? No ______ veo.
4 A ¿Conoces al nuevo maestro?
B No, no ______ conozco.
5 A ¿Dónde están los niños?
B No ______ sé.
6 ¿Vienen a la cafetería? Yo ______ invito.
7 Isabel, ______ (a ti) espero en la puerta del cine.
8 A ¿______ (a nosotros) invitas a tu cumpleaños?
B Sí, ______ espero a las 7.
9 A ¿Cómo están tus hermanas?
B Muy bien, ______ vi ayer.

B Mi novio trae corbata

1 Busca el nombre de esta ropa en la sopa de letras.

R	W	S	U	E	T	E	R	P	O
R	P	P	L	A	Y	E	R	A	Z
E	C	V	B	E	R	T	D	N	M
A	S	R	A	M	O	S	Z	T	A
S	O	P	B	F	A	L	D	A	N
I	T	V	M	S	W	C	X	L	X
M	A	X	A	B	R	I	G	O	M
A	P	X	W	E	T	R	Y	N	U
C	A	L	C	E	T	I	N	E	S
B	Z	B	R	E	T	G	H	S	M

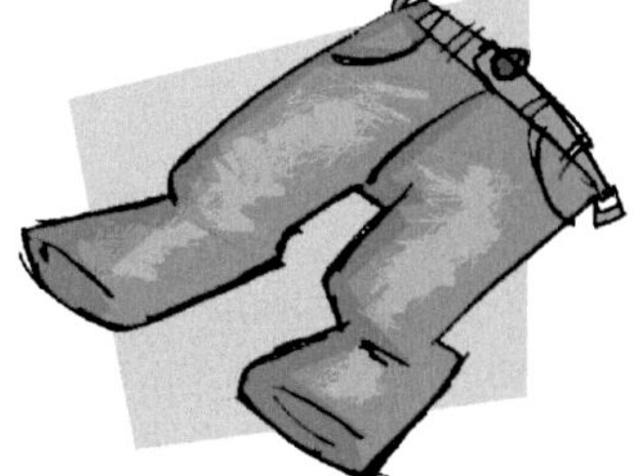

2 Completa.

En el departamento de objetos perdidos de esta tienda departamental tenemos:

1 una carter__ café,
2 una carpet__ negr__,
3 unos guantes gris__ __,
4 unos lentes roj__ __, muy modern__ __,
5 una pelot__ amarill__,
6 unas plumas azul__ __,
7 un paraguas ros__,
8 unos calcetines verd__ __ y
9 una bufand__ naranj__.

3 Escribe los adjetivos contrarios.

1 barato ________	3 corto ________	5 sucio ________	7 oscuro ________
2 antiguo ________	4 cómodo ________	6 ancho ________	8 grande ________

4 Completa con las palabras del recuadro.

de mezclilla *gasta* *favorito* *cómoda* *compras* *zapatos* *elegante* *bonitos*

Carmen tiene 46 años y trabaja en la Secretaría de Relaciones Exteriores. No (1) ________ mucho dinero en comprar ropa. Generalmente va de (2) ________ dos veces al año, una antes de las vacaciones de verano y otra al principio del invierno. Le gusta la ropa (3) ________ y moderna, no muy formal. Prefiere usar pantalones (4) ________, playeras o camisas de algodón y (5) ________ muy cómodos. Cuando va a una fiesta, prefiere algo más (6) ________: un vestido o unos pantalones de vestir (7) ________. Su color (8) ________ es el negro, aunque también le gustan mucho el rojo y el naranja.

C Buenos Aires es más grande que Toledo

1 Escribe una frase con el mismo significado.

1 Estos pantalones de mezclilla son más caros que aquellos.
Aquellos pantalones de mezclilla son más baratos que estos.
2 Juanjo es mayor que yo.
____
3 El carro de Ramón es peor que el de Miguel.
____
4 El sillón es más cómodo que la silla.
____
5 Trae la falda más larga que el abrigo.
____
6 Raquel tiene menos libros que nosotras.
____
7 Mi carro es más viejo que el tuyo.
____

2 Completa las frases.

1 Est*e* vestido es muy cort______.
2 Es______ clase es pequeñ______.
3 Es______ carros son nuev______.
4 Aquell______ chavas están cansad______.
5 ¿Cuánto cuesta est______ falda roj______?
6 ¿De quién es est______ libro?
7 A ¿Es______ botas son car______?
B Sí, pero mira, aquell______ son más barat______.
8 A Es______ pantalones son muy lar______.
B Sí, aquell______ son más cort______.
9 Est______ aretes están con descuento.
10 Es______ bolsa es bonit______ y barat______, pero aquella es car______ y bastante fe______.

3 Completa este texto utilizando los comparativos del recuadro.

menos ***tan*** *mayor* ~~*mejor*~~ ***más*** *(x2)*

¿DÓNDE TE GUSTA IR DE VACACIONES?

ÁNGEL: Es (1) mejor ir a la playa que a la montaña.
SUSANA: ¿Por qué? Yo prefiero la montaña, así las vacaciones son (2)__________ tranquilas.
ÁNGEL: Sí, en la montaña hay (3)__________ gente pero también es mucho (4)__________ aburrido. ¿Adónde vas en las noches? ¿Y qué haces durante el día? No hay nada (5)__________ relajante como broncearse un día entero al sol y bañarse en el mar de vez en cuando.
SUSANA: Dormir poco y broncearse es muy malo para la piel. ¿Sabes?, creo que por eso tú pareces mucho (6)__________ que yo. Mira, no tengo ni una arruga.

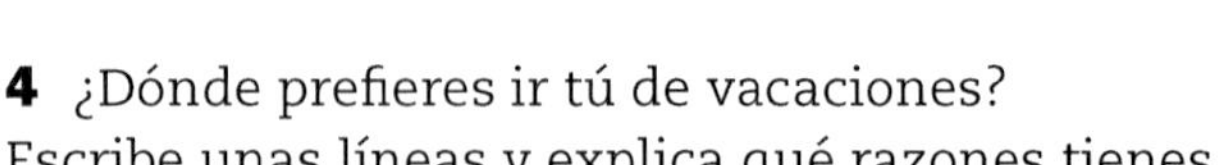

4 ¿Dónde prefieres ir tú de vacaciones?
Escribe unas líneas y explica qué razones tienes.

A mí me gusta mucho ir a la playa porque...
Yo prefiero ir a la montaña...

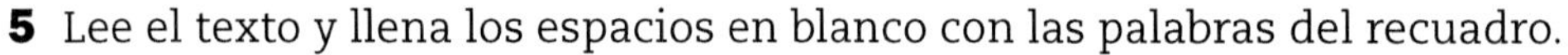

5 Lee el texto y llena los espacios en blanco con las palabras del recuadro.

Patrimonio de la Humanidad • ~~centro~~ • conquista • convento • barrocos destacado • diseñó y fundó • inversión • asentamiento • acueducto

QUERÉTARO

Querétaro es la capital del Estado de Querétaro y una de las ciudades más bellas de México. Situada en el (1) centro de la república, en la época prehispánica fue un (2)________ purépecha muy importante. Despúes de la (3)________, Don Fernando de Tapia (4)________ la ciudad el 25 de julio de 1531. Este personaje también construyó el (5)________ de San Francisco, primera edificación religiosa de la ciudad. Otro de los más relevantes monumentos de Querétaro es el (6)________ (1726), ahora considerado el símbolo de la ciudad. Desde 1996, el centro histórico de Santiago de Querétaro es (7)________ por sus extraordinarios edificios (8)________.
Hoy en día es un (9)________ centro turístico y uno de los estados con mayor crecimiento económico debido a la (10)________ nacional y extranjera que recibe.

10 Salud y enfermedad

A La salud

1 Mira el dibujo y escribe el nombre de las distintas partes del cuerpo.

pecho • cuello • pelo • oreja • ojo
cara • hombro • brazo • mano • dedo
~~rodilla~~ • pie • pierna

1 rodilla
2 ____
3 ____
4 ____
5 ____
6 ____
7 ____
8 ____
9 ____
10 ____
11 ____
12 ____
13 ____

2 ¿Qué palabra no pertenece a su grupo?

1 ojo, diente, bigote, dedo.
2 hombro, mano, oreja, dedo.
3 rodilla, cara, pierna, pie.
4 pie, cara, cuello, pelo.
5 brazo, mano, dedo, ojo.
6 pecho, hombro, rodilla, cuello.

3 Escribe las respuestas. La número 1 es la palabra vertical.

CRUCIGRAMA

1 Oyes con ellas: ____
2 Te lo puedes afeitar: ____
3 Los usas para abrazar: ____
4 Te los lavas después de comer: ____
5 Los cierras cuando duermes: ____
6 Te las lavas antes de comer: ____
7 En ellos te pones los anillos: ____

4 Ordena la siguiente conversación entre Sonia y Alfonso.

SONIA: Seguro que mañana te sientes mejor. ☐
SONIA: ¿Estás tomando alguna medicina? ☐
SONIA: ¿Qué te sucede, Alfonso? ¿Te sientes bien? 1
SONIA: ¿Por qué no te tomas una aspirina y descansas? ☐
ALFONSO: Sí, es lo mejor, porque mañana tengo mucho trabajo. ☐
ALFONSO: No, no muy bien. Tengo fiebre. ☐
ALFONSO: No, de momento no. ☐

5 113 Escucha y comprueba.

6 Completa las siguientes frases con el verbo *doler*.

1 ¡Baja el volumen! A papá *le duele* la cabeza.
2 A Juan y a Carmen ________ la espalda.
3 No puedo cenar porque ________ el estómago.
4 Mi hermana va mañana al dentista porque ________ las muelas.
5 ¿Y a ti qué ________?
6 Caminamos mucho y ahora ________ las piernas.

B Antes salíamos con los amigos

1 Relaciona las frases y completa con el imperfecto.

1 Ahora trabajo en una oficina, [d]
2 Ahora vamos al cine, [ ]
3 Ahora Juan viene los martes a clase, [ ]
4 Ahora compro el periódico, [ ]
5 Ahora me gusta la música clásica, [ ]
6 Ahora haces la comida, [ ]

a antes ________ los jueves.
b antes ________ la cena.
c antes ________ revistas.
d antes *trabajaba* en un restaurante.
e antes ________ el rock.
f antes ________ al teatro.

2 Completa las frases con el imperfecto de los verbos del recuadro.

~~*vivir*~~ *tener (x2)* *ir (x2)* *trabajar* *tocar (x2)* *ser (x2)* *escalar* *leer* *existir*

1 Antes de venir a Monterrey, *vivíamos* en Ciudad de México.
2 Cuando Mercedes ________ 14 años, siempre ________ en bicicleta.
3 Ahora es recepcionista, antes ________ como mesero.
4 Antes ________ muy mal la guitarra, ahora tengo un maestro privado y lo hago mejor.
5 Julia y Jorge, cuando ________ jóvenes, ________ el piano.
6 De niño ________ a la escuela en el transporte escolar.
7 Cuando ________ jóvenes, mi esposo y yo ________ con un grupo de montañismo.
8 Antes, mi hijo ________ una moto y ________ muchas revistas de motociclismo.
9 Hace cincuenta años no ________ los celulares.

3 Completa la siguiente entrevista con el imperfecto de los verbos entre paréntesis.

MARCOS CURIEL cumple 95 años el próximo 14 de noviembre.

ENTREVISTADOR: ¿Tiene amigos de su edad?
MARCOS: Tengo algunos amigos más jóvenes. (1) *Tenía* (tener) uno de mi edad, pero murió a los 90 años.
ENTREVISTADOR: ¿Es el mundo ahora muy diferente?
MARCOS: Todo está muy cambiado. Antes todos nosotros (2)________ (vivir) más tranquilos y ahora la gente corre demasiado.
ENTREVISTADOR: Cuando (3)________ (ser) niño, no (4)________ (haber) televisión, ni radio…
MARCOS: No, nosotros no (5)________ (tener) nada de eso.
ENTREVISTADOR: ¿Qué es lo que más recuerda de su infancia?
MARCOS: Me acuerdo de cuando yo (6)________ (ir) a ayudar a mi papá. Él (7)________ (ser) peluquero y (8)________ (atender) a mucha gente.
ENTREVISTADOR: ¿Cuál es el secreto para llegar a los noventa y cinco años?
MARCOS: Cuando mi familia y yo (9)________ (vivir) en Querétaro, (10)________ (tomar) muchos alimentos naturales, leche recién ordeñada y papas recogidas del campo.

4 Vuelve a leer la entrevista con Marcos y contesta a las preguntas.

1 ¿Cuántos años tenía su amigo cuando murió?

____

2 Según Marcos, ¿cómo vivía la gente antes?

____

3 ¿Qué cosas no tenía Marcos cuando era niño?

____

4 ¿Dónde vivía Marcos con su familia?

____

5 ¿En qué trabajaba el papá de Marcos?

____

6 ¿Qué comían Marcos y su familia?

____

C Voy a trabajar en un hotel

1 Relaciona las preguntas con sus respuestas.

1 ¿Para qué vas a aprender español? [c]
2 ¿Cuándo se va a casar Pedro? ☐
3 ¿Cuántos días van a estar? ☐
4 ¿A qué hora vamos a vernos? ☐
5 ¿Qué carrera vas a estudiar? ☐
6 ¿Adónde van a ir de viaje de novios? ☐

a A las ocho y media.
b En abril.
c Porque quiero viajar a México.
d A la isla de Cozumel.
e Tres o cuatro.
f Medicina.

2 ¿Qué planes tienen para el fin de semana?

1 Juan / lavar el carro.
Juan va a lavar el carro.

2 Yo / hablar por teléfono con mis amigos.

____

3 Ana / cenar con Pedro.

____

4 María y Alberto / pintar su casa.

____

5 Tomás y yo / reparar nuestras bicicletas.

____

6 ¿(Tú) / ir a la alberca?

____

7 ¿(Ustedes) / venir a comer?

____

8 ¿Tu hermano / correr el maratón de Ciudad de México?

____

9 Mis tíos / no ver el partido en casa. (ellos) / ver en un bar.

____

10 ¿(Tú) / remodelar la cocina?

____

3 Completa la conversación.

ROSA: ¡Hola, Pablo! Soy Rosa. ¿Qué vas a hacer este sábado?
PABLO: Tenemos un examen el lunes, y Elena (1)__________ (venir) a estudiar a mi casa.
ROSA: ¿Y el domingo?
PABLO: El domingo por la mañana Ángel y yo (2)__________ (ver) una exposición y por la tarde (3)__________ (jugar) boliche. ¿Nos acompañas?
ROSA: El domingo por la mañana yo no (4)__________ (poder) porque (5)__________ (lavar) el carro, pero nos vemos por la tarde.
PABLO: ¡Excelente! ¡Hasta el domingo!

4 Relaciona cada país o ciudad con una actividad.

1 Estados Unidos ☐
2 Moscú ☐
3 Egipto ☐
4 España ☐
5 Río de Janeiro ☐
6 Kenia ☐
7 Grecia ☐
8 París ☐
9 Roma ☐
10 Londres ☐

a Escuchar flamenco.
b Visitar las pirámides.
c Pasear por la plaza Roja.
d Nadar en las playas de Copacabana.
e Tomar fotos a los leones.
f Navegar por el Támesis.
g Volar sobre el Gran Cañón.
h Conocer las islas griegas.
i Conocer el Coliseo.
j Admirar la Gioconda.

5 Di qué van a hacer las siguientes personas en sus vacaciones.

1 David / Kenia
David va a tomar fotos a los leones.

2 Pedro / Estados Unidos.

3 Alberto y Pablo / Moscú

4 Yo / Egipto

5 Tú / España

6 Tu novia y tú / Río de Janeiro

7 Nosotros / Grecia

8 Mis papás / París

9 Pablo y María / Roma

10 Tu amigo Pedro / Londres

6 Lee el texto y di si las frases siguientes son verdaderas (V) o falsas (F).

¡REMODELE SU CASA!

¿Necesita su casa una remodelación? Todas las semanas la revista *Su Casa al Día* va a sortear un premio de 100 000 pesos entre nuestros lectores para remodelar su casa y su mobiliario. Esta semana la ganadora es la señora Ruiz, que nos va a contar sus planes de remodelación.

ENTREVISTADORA: **¿Qué va a hacer con el dinero, señora Ruiz?**

SRA. RUIZ: Lo primero que voy a hacer es pintar toda la casa. Voy a poner distintos colores en cada habitación.

ENTREVISTADORA: **¿Qué piensa su familia?**

SRA. RUIZ: Están todos de acuerdo. Ellos van a elegir el color de cada habitación.

ENTREVISTADORA: **¿Y qué va a hacer con los muebles?**

SRA. RUIZ: Voy a cambiar los muebles viejos y también uno o dos electrodomésticos.

ENTREVISTADORA: **¿Va a hacer algo más?**

SRA. RUIZ: Si me sobra dinero, vamos a comprar una pantalla grande plana, como de cine.

ENTREVISTADORA: **Es una idea excelente. ¡Que lo disfruten, Sra. Ruiz!**

1 La Sra. Ruiz va a recibir una herencia de 100 000 pesos. F
2 Se va a gastar el dinero en un viaje. ☐
3 Va a pintar las paredes de colores. ☐
4 La familia no está de acuerdo con la remodelación. ☐
5 Los hijos van a elegir los colores de las habitaciones. ☐
6 Con el dinero restante van a comprar una pantalla. ☐

V Vocabulario

Abreviaturas

adj. = adjetivo
adv. = adverbio
conj. = conjunción
prep. = preposición
pron. = pronombre
n. m. = nombre masculino
n. f. = nombre femenino
v. = verbo
v. r. = verbo reflexivo

Repasa las palabras más importantes de cada unidad. Puedes incluir notas o una traducción a tu idioma.

UNIDAD 0

abrir (v.) ____________
alumno/a (n.) ____________
buenas noches ____________
buenas tardes ____________
buenos días ____________
compañero/a (n.) ____________
completar (v.) ____________
cuaderno (n. m.) ____________
diccionario (n. m.) ____________
empezar (v.) ____________
escribir (v.) ____________
escuchar (v.) ____________
estudiante (n.) ____________
estudiar (v.) ____________
hablar (v.) ____________
hola ____________
lápiz (n. m.) ____________
leer (v.) ____________
libro (v.) ____________
llamarse (v. r.) ____________
maestro/a (n.) ____________
mirar (v.) ____________
muy bien ____________
palabra (n. f.) ____________
pluma (n. f.) ____________
practicar (v.) ____________
preguntar (v.) ____________
repetir (v.) ____________
responder (v.) ____________
ser (v.) ____________
y (conj.) ____________

UNIDAD 1

actriz (n. f.) ____________
ama de casa (n.) ____________
bailar (v.) ____________
cafetería (n. f.) ____________
calle (n. f.) ____________
cantante (n.) ____________
cartero/a (n.) ____________
casado/a (adj.) ____________
celular (n. m.) ____________
ciclista (n.) ____________
clase (n. f.) ____________
comer (v.) ____________
conocer (v.) ____________
contador/a (n.) ____________
de (prep.) ____________
dedicarse (v. r.) ____________
dirección (n. f.) ____________
doctor/a (n.) ____________
en (prep.) ____________
encantado/a (adj.) ____________
escritor/a (n.) ____________
escuela (n. f.) ____________
este/esta (pron.) ____________
estilista (n.) ____________
flamenco (n. m.) ____________
frase (n. f.) ____________
futbolista (n.) ____________
gimnasio (n. m.) ____________
gracias (n.) ____________
hospital (n. m.) ____________
jugar (v.) ____________
mesero/a (n.) ____________
mucho gusto ____________
novio/a (n.) ____________
nuevo/a (adj.) ____________
número (n. m.) ____________
pero (conj.) ____________
policía (n.) ____________
por (prep.) ____________
preparatoria (n. f.) ____________
presentar (v.) ____________
presidente/a (n.) ____________
restaurante (n. m.) ____________
secretario/a (n.) ____________
soltero/a (adj.) ____________
taxista (n.) ____________
teléfono (n. m.) ____________
tener (v.) ____________
trabajar (v.) ____________
urgencias (n.) ____________
vivir (v.) ____________

UNIDAD 2

abuelo/a (n.) ____________
amigo/a (n.) ____________
año (n. m.) ____________
banco (n. m.) ____________
carro (n. m.) ____________
casa (n. f.) ____________
cenar (v.) ____________
chavo/a (n.) ____________
chico/a (n.) ____________
computadora (n. f.) ____________
cuadro (n. m.) ____________
cuánto/a/os/as (pron.) ____________
debajo (adv.) ____________
delante (adv.) ____________
detrás (adv.) ____________
dibujar (v.) ____________
doctor/a (n.) ____________
encima (adv.) ____________
entre (prep.) ____________
familia (n. f.) ____________
foto (n. f.) ____________
gato/a (n.) ____________
gente (n. f.) ____________
guitarra (n. f.) ____________
hacer (v.) ____________
hermano/a (n.) ____________
hijo/a (n.) ____________
hora (n. f.) ____________
horario (n. m.) ____________
hotel (n. m.) ____________
joven (n.) ____________
lentes (n. f. p.) ____________
mamá (n. f.) ____________
mapa (n. m.) ____________
más (adv.) ____________
mesa (n. f.) ____________
mi/mis (adj.) ____________
minuto (n. m.) ____________
muchacho/a (n.) ____________
mujer (n. f.) ____________
papá (n. m.) ____________
país (n. m.) ____________
paraguas (n. m.) ____________
pequeño/a (adj.) ____________
primo/a (n.) ____________
reloj (n. m.) ____________
segundo (adj.) ____________
semana (n. f.) ____________
silla (n. f.) ____________
sofá (n. m.) ____________
tarde (n. f.) ____________
televisión (n. f.) ____________
tenis (n. m. p.) ____________
tienda (n. f.) ____________
tío/a (n.) ____________
tu/tus (adj.) ____________
ventana (n. f.) ____________

UNIDAD 3

acostarse (v. r.) ____________
afeitarse (v. r.) ____________
alguno/a (pron.) ____________
almorzar (v.) ____________
asignatura (n. f.) ____________
autobús (n. m.) ____________
azafata (n. f.) ____________
baile (n. m.) ____________
ballet (n. m.) ____________
bañarse (v. r.) ____________
beber (v.) ____________
bombero (n.) ____________
bueno/a (adj.) ____________
café (n. m.) ____________
camión (n. m.) ____________
casarse (v. r.) ____________
chef (n.) ____________
cocinero/a (n.) ____________
colegio (n. m.) ____________

comida (n. f.) ____________
desayunar (v.) ____________
desde (prep.) ____________
desear (v.) ____________
después (adv.) ____________
domingo (n. m.) ____________
dormir (v.) ____________
edad (n. f.) ____________
enfermero/a (n.) ____________
entrar (v.) ____________
escuela (n. f.) ____________
fiesta (n. f.) ____________
gustar (v.) ____________
hasta (prep.) ____________
huevo (n. m.) ____________
ir (v.) ____________
jueves (n. m.) ____________
jugo (n. m.) ____________
leche (n. f.) ____________
levantarse (v.) ____________
lunes (n. m.) ____________
madrugada (n. f) ____________
mantecada (n. f.) ____________
mantequilla (n. f.) ____________
mañana (n. f.) ____________
martes (n. m.) ____________
menos (adv.) ____________
mermelada (n. f.) ____________
miércoles (n. m.) ____________
naranja (n. f.) ____________
pan tostado (n. m.) ____________
pronto (adv.) ____________
queso (n. m.) ____________
regresar (v.) ____________
sábado (n. m.) ____________
semana (n. f.) ____________
siempre (adv.) ____________
también (adv.) ____________
té (n. m.) ____________
temprano (adv.) ____________
terminar (v.) ____________
todo/a (adj.) ____________
tomar (v.) ____________
tomate (n. m.) ____________
tostada (n. f.) ____________
tren (n. m.) ____________
vacaciones (n. f. p.) ____________
vecino/a (n.) ____________
vendedor/a (n.) ____________
ver (v.) ____________
viernes (n. m.) ____________
volver (v.) ____________

UNIDAD 4

alberca (n. f.) ____________
agradable (adj.) ____________
antro (n. m.) ____________
arriba (adv.) ____________
bajo/a (adj.) ____________
baño (n. m.) ____________
casa (n. f.) ____________
cine (n. m.) ____________
ciudad (n. f.) ____________
cochera (n. f.) ____________
cocina (n. f.) ____________
comedor (n. m.) ____________
cuarto (n. m.) ____________
derecha (n. f.) ____________
doble (adj.) ____________
elevador (n. m.) ____________
espejo (n. m.) ____________
estacionar (v.) ____________
fin de semana (n. m.) ____________
gabinete (n. m.) ____________
grande (adj.) ____________
habitación (n. f.) ____________
hay (v. haber) ____________
izquierda (n. f.) ____________
jardín (n. m.) ____________
lámpara (n. f.) ____________
lavabo (n. m.) ____________
llave (n. f.) ____________
microondas (n. m.) ____________
patio (n. m.) ____________
piso (n. m.) ____________
plano (n. m.) ____________
planta (n. f.) ____________
recámara (n. f.) ____________
refrigerador (n. m.) ____________
sala (n. f.) ____________
sillón (n. m.) ____________
simpático/a (adj.) ____________
supermercado (n. m.) ____________
tarjeta de crédito (n. f.) ____________
tina de baño (n. f.) ____________

UNIDAD 5

agua (n. f.) ____________
aguacate (n. m.) ____________
andar (v.) ____________
animal (n. m.) ____________
arroz (n. m.) ____________
azúcar (n.) ____________
bicicleta (n. f) ____________
caminar (v.) ____________
carne (n. f.) ____________
carta (n. f.) ____________
cerdo (n. m.) ____________
cerveza (n. f.) ____________
chile (n. m.) ____________
chuleta (n. f.) ____________
cine (n. m.) ____________
comedia (n. f.) ____________
cordero (n. m.) ____________
deporte (n. m.) ____________
discoteca (n. f.) ____________
ejotes (n.) ____________
ensalada (n. f.) ____________
flan (n. m.) ____________
fruta (n. f.) ____________
futbol (n. m.) ____________
gazpacho (n. m.) ____________
hielo (n. m.) ____________
jamón (n. m.) ____________
limón (n. m.) ____________
merluza (n. f.) ____________
mole (n. m.) ____________
música (n. f.) ____________
nadar (v.) ____________
partido (n.m) ____________
papa (n. f.) ____________
plátano (n. m.) ____________
plato (n. m.) ____________
playa (n. f.) ____________
película (n. f.) ____________
pescado (n. m.) ____________
pollo (n. m.) ____________
postre (n. m.) ____________
prender (v.) ____________
receta (n. f.) ____________
sopa (n. f.) ____________
tacos (n. m. p.) ____________
ternera (n. f.) ____________
tortilla (n. f.) ____________
tostada (n. f) ____________
viajar (v.) ____________
vino (n. m.) ____________

UNIDAD 6

antes (adv.) ____________
apagar (v.) ____________
aquí (adv.) ____________
boleto (n. m.) ____________
cambiar (v.) ____________
céntrico (adj.) ____________
cerca (adv.) ____________
colonia (n. f.) ____________
comunicado (adj.) ____________
dar la vuelta (v.) ____________
dato (n. m.) ____________
derecho/a (adj.) ____________
encender (v.) ____________
enfrente (adv.) ____________
enseguida (adv.) ____________
estación (n. f.) ____________
extraña (adj.) ____________
frío (adj.) ____________
informe (n. m.) ____________
lejos (adv.) ____________
lento (adj.) ____________
línea (n. f.) ____________
mal (adv.) ____________
malo (adj.) ____________
metro (n. m.) ____________
necesitar (v.) ____________
nota (n. f.) ____________
parada (n. f.) ____________
perdonar (v.) ____________
plaza (n. f.) ____________
poder (v.) ____________
preparar (v.) ____________
prestar (v.) ____________
rápido/a (adj.) ____________
rentar (v.) ____________
reunión (n. f.) ____________
ruido (n. m.) ____________
ruidoso/a (adj.) ____________
sale ____________
seguir (v.) ____________

sencillo/a (adj.) ____________
sentarse (v. r.) ____________
tarea (n. f.) ____________
taxi (n. m.) ____________
tomar (v.) ____________
tranquilo/a (adj.) ____________

UNIDAD 7

agradable (adj.) ____________
alegre (adj) ____________
amable (adj.) ____________
amarillo/a (adj.) ____________
azul (adj.) ____________
barba (n. f.) ____________
bigote (n. m.) ____________
blanco/a (adj.) ____________
cabeza (n. f.) ____________
callado/a (adj.) ____________
calvo/a (adj.) ____________
camastro (n. m.) ____________
claro/a (adj.) ____________
conmigo ____________
corto/a (adj.) ____________
de acuerdo ____________
dejar (v.) ____________
delgado/a (adj.) ____________
desagradable (adj.) ____________
dígame (v.) ____________
educado/a (adj.) ____________
generoso/a (adj.) ____________
gordo/a (adj.) ____________
grande (de edad) (adj.) ____________
grosero/a (adj.) ____________
largo/a (adj.) ____________
lavarse (v. r.) ____________
lo siento ____________
mejor (adj.) ____________
momento (n. m.) ____________
moreno/a (adj.) ____________
negro (pelo negro) (adj.) ____________
ojo (n. m.) ____________
oscuro/a (adj.) ____________
peinarse (v. r.) ____________
pelo (n. m.) ____________
pelota (n. f.) ____________
perfecto ____________
periódico (n. m.) ____________
piel (n. f.) ____________
platicador/a (adj.) ____________
puerta (n. f.) ____________
quedar (v.) ____________
recado (n. m.) ____________
rojo/a (adj.) ____________
rubio/a (adj.) ____________
secarse (v. r.) ____________
señor/a (n.) ____________
sol (n. m.) ____________
sombrero (n. m.) ____________
sombrilla (n. m.) ____________
toalla (n. f.) ____________
traer (v.) ____________
traje de baño (n. m.) ____________
último/a (adj.) ____________

vamos ____________
verde (adj.) ____________

UNIDAD 8

acabar (v.) ____________
aire (n. m.) ____________
así es ____________
atender (v.) ____________
ayer (adv.) ____________
calor (n. m.) ____________
cansado/a (adj.) ____________
clima (n. m.) ____________
concierto (n. m.) ____________
correos (n.) ____________
cumpleaños (n. m) ____________
diferente (adj.) ____________
encontrar(se) (v.) ____________
enfermo/a (adj.) ____________
farmacia (n. f.) ____________
final (n. m.) ____________
girar (v.) ____________
iglesia (n. f.) ____________
invierno (n. m.) ____________
llegar (v.) ____________
llover (v.) ____________
nevar (v.) ____________
nublado (adj.) ____________
otoño (n. m.) ____________
primavera (n. f.) ____________
terminar (v.) ____________
tiempo (n. m.) ____________
verano (n. m.) ____________
visitar (v.) ____________

UNIDAD 9

aburrido/a (adj.) ____________
ajustado/a (adj.) ____________
ancho/a (adj.) ____________
anillo (n. m.) ____________
antiguo/a (n. m.) ____________
apretado/a (adj.) ____________
aretes (n. m. p.) ____________
ayudar (v.) ____________
barato/a (adj.) ____________
bellísimo/a (adj.) ____________
bolsa (n. f.) ____________
café (de color) (adj.) ____________
camisa (n. f.) ____________
caro/a (adj.) ____________
chamarra (n. f.) ____________
cliente/a (n.) ____________
collar (n. m.) ____________
con descuento ____________
conocer (v.) ____________
contaminado/a (adj.) ____________
corbata (n. f.) ____________
costar (v.) ____________
divertido/a (adj.) ____________
efectivo (adj.) ____________
estrecho/a (adj.) ____________
estresante (adj.) ____________
falda (n. f.) ____________
habitante (n. m.) ____________

limpio/a (adj.) ____________
llevar (v.) ____________
mayor (adj.) ____________
medias (n. f. pl.) ____________
mejor (adj.) ____________
menor (adj.) ____________
moderno/a (adj.) ____________
montaña (n. f.) ____________
morado/a (adj.) ____________
negro/a (adj.) ____________
pantalones (n. m. pl.) ____________
pantalones de mezclilla (n. pl.) ____________
peor (adj.) ____________
playera (n. f.) ____________
rico/a (adj.) ____________
ropa (n .f.) ____________
rosa (adj.) ____________
seguro/a (adj.) ____________
sucio/a (adj.) ____________
tienda (n. f.) ____________
zapato (n. m.) ____________

UNIDAD 10

aconsejar (v.) ____________
ahorrar (v.) ____________
aspirina (n. f.) ____________
autobús (n. m.) ____________
brazo (n. m.) ____________
cabeza (n. f.) ____________
campo (n. m) ____________
cara (n. f.) ____________
cuello (n. m.) ____________
de repente ____________
dedo (n. m.) ____________
dentista (n.) ____________
descansar (v.) ____________
doler (v.) ____________
entrenar (v.) ____________
espalda (n. f.) ____________
estómago (n. m) ____________
feliz (adj.) ____________
fiebre (n. f.) ____________
garganta (n. f.) ____________
gripa (n. f.) ____________
hombro (n. m) ____________
jugador (n. m.) ____________
mano (n. f.) ____________
mejorar (v.) ____________
miel (n. f.) ____________
muela (n. f.) ____________
oído (n. m.) ____________
oreja (n. f.) ____________
pecho (n. m.) ____________
pie (n. m.) ____________
pierna (n. f.) ____________
plan (n. m.) ____________
rodilla (n. f.) ____________
social (adj.) ____________
tianguis (n .m.) ____________
vida (n. f.) ____________
vuelta (n. f.) ____________

Soluciones

UNIDAD 1

A Mucho gusto

1 1 d; **2** b; **3** c; **4** e; **5** a; **6** f

2 1 A ¿De dónde eres? **2** A ¿cómo estás? **3** A ¿Eres española? **4** A ¿De dónde eres? **5** A ¿Cómo te llamas?

3 ¿Cómo se llama usted? / ¿De dónde eres? / ¿Cómo está usted?

4 **1** A Hola, ¿cómo te llamas? / B ¿Eres francesa? / A No, soy nigeriana. ¿Y tú? **2** PABLO: María, mira, esta es Susanne. / SUSANNE: Bien, gracias. / MARÍA: ¿De dónde eres? / SUSANNE: Soy francesa, pero ahora vivo en Madrid. **3** SR. LÓPEZ: Buenos días, Susana. / SUSANA: Mire, le presento a la nueva directora, Julia Linares. / SR. LÓPEZ: Mucho gusto de conocerla. / JULIA: Gracias, igualmente.

5 **País:** Perú; Alemania; Irlanda. / **Nacionalidad-masculino:** portugués; marroquí; peruano; bielorruso; mexicano. / **Nacionalidad-femenino:** brasileña; canadiense; alemana; polaca; irlandesa; mexicana.

6 **1** Sánchez; **2** Rodríguez; **3** Zorrilla; **4** Martínez; **5** Huerta; **6** Bogotá; **7** Valencia; **8** Varsovia; **9** Túnez; **10** Ancara.

B ¿A qué te dedicas?

1

E	S	T	I	L	I	S	T	A	B
R	T	Y	Ñ	P	O	U	J	K	Ñ
M	Z	C	A	R	T	E	R	O	L
A	M	E	T	A	X	I	S	T	A
E	C	R	A	B	O	G	A	D	A
S	V	W	P	D	O	S	M	O	A
T	R	U	R	I	M	A	C	L	C
R	E	P	T	V	E	B	W	M	T
O	Y	P	O	U	S	L	U	Q	R
P	O	U	T	R	E	M	W	D	I
D	O	C	T	O	R	A	N	R	Z
A	R	V	X	L	O	P	G	F	D

2 **1** Él habla por teléfono todos los días. **2** Rosa tiene tres hijos. **3** Ignacio habla inglés y francés. **4** Nosotros comemos en casa los domingos. **5** ¿Usted habla ruso? **6** ¿Ustedes viven en México? **7** Ellos viven en París. **8** Layla estudia en la universidad. **9** Yo no trabajo ni estudio. **10** ¿Usted trabaja aquí?

3 **Ser:** soy, eres, es, somos, sois, son. **Tener:** tengo, tienes, tiene, tenemos, tenéis, tienen.

4 **1** Elena tiene dos hijos. **2** Roberto es de Buenos Aires. **3** ¿De dónde son Jorge y Claudia? **4** A ¿Son ustedes estadounidenses? B No, somos ingleses. **5** Yo tengo un novio español. **6** Mi amiga Gisela es brasileña. **7** A ¿Tienen novio? B Ella sí, pero yo no tengo. **8** A ¿Tú eres peruana? B No, soy boliviana. **9** A Julia es mi hermana, es maestra. B Yo también soy maestra. **10** Mi hija tiene una casa en Cancún. **11** A Somos argentinos. Y ustedes, ¿de dónde son? B Somos chilenos. **12** A ¿Tienes hijos? B No, no tengo hijos.

5 **Posibles respuestas:** Luis y yo estudiamos Derecho. / Renata es traductora. / Yo trabajo en un restaurante. / Ángel y Rosa tienen dos hijos.

C ¿Cuál es tu número de celular?

1 **a** 4. **b** 6. **c** 1. **d** 2. **e** 5. **f** 3.

2 **a** nueve, nueve, ocho, ocho, cuatro, cero, cuatro, seis, tres, siete. **b** nueve, cinco, uno, cinco, seis, siete, cero, ocho, cero. **c** nueve, siete, tres, siete, cero, dos, cinco, siete, ocho, siete. **d** ocho, cuatro, cuatro, cuatro, tres, ocho, cero, uno, uno, uno. **e** ocho, uno, uno, uno, cero, ocho, seis, siete, cinco, tres.

3 once, doce, trece, catorce, quince, dieciséis, diecisiete, dieciocho, diecinueve, veinte.

4 **1** Manuel. González Romero. Español. Economista. Madrid. 916543201. **2** Isabel. Jiménez Díaz. Argentina. Profesora. Madrid. 656789823. isabel.j@yahoo.com.

5 **Actividad libre.**

6 **1** Se llama José Martínez López. Es contador. Vive en Bogotá y es colombiano. **2** Se llama Noelia Montoro Ruiz. Es pianista. Vive en La Habana y es cubana.

7 **A** (1) me llamo; (2) soy; (3) Vivo; (4) tengo; (5) se llama; (6) es; (7) trabaja; (8) estudia; (9) es; (10) vive; (11) es.

B (12) me llamo; (13) soy; (14) Soy; (15) vivo; (16) Trabajo; (17) Soy; (18) viven.

C (19) es; (20) Tiene; (21) es; (22) trabaja; (23) Habla; (24) es.

UNIDAD 2

A ¿Eres casado?

1 **1** f; **2** a; **3** e; **4** b; **5** c; **6** d; **7** h; **8** g; **9** i; **10** j.

2 **Laura:** (1) se llama; (2) es; (3) tiene; (4) es; (5) es; (6) es; (7) tiene; (8) tengo; (9) Se llaman; (10) Son. **Pablo:** (1) Tengo; (2) es; (3) tiene; (4) es; (5) tiene; (6) tienen; (7) se llama; (8) es; (9) se llama; (10) es.

3 **Mercedes:** abuela; **Miguel:** esposo; **Jorge:** yerno; **Jorge:** tío; **Marisa:** mamá; **Marisa:** esposa; **José Luis:** abuelo; **Miguel y Marisa:** papás; **José Luis y Mercedes:** abuelos; **Celia:** sobrina.

4 **1** Rosa y María son colombianas. **2** Mis papás son profesores. **3** Nosotros tenemos unos gatos. **4** Ellos son casados. **5** Estos hoteles son caros. **6** ¿Tus compañeros son mexicanos? **7** Estos chavos son estudiantes. **8** ¿Tus plumas son nuevas? **9** Las ventanas están abiertas. **10** Estas son las amigas de mis hermanas.

B ¿Dónde están mis lentes?

1

C	O	M	P	U	T	A	D	O	R	A
E	W	T	A	S	G	P	I	S	E	S
L	H	V	S	Q	W	S	C	L	L	Q
U	T	S	O	F	A	P	C	E	O	G
L	O	I	W	Q	G	T	I	N	J	Y
A	M	L	V	Z	B	Q	O	T	F	C
R	A	L	T	V	S	A	N	E	G	A
C	P	A	R	A	G	U	A	S	S	R
W	A	I	Z	Q	O	I	R	W	Q	R
R	W	E	C	S	Y	L	I	B	R	O
Z	V	P	A	P	V	B	O	P	V	T

2 1 al lado de; **2** encima de; **3** entre; **4** debajo de; **5** encima de; **6** delante; **7** detrás; **8** en; **9** encima de; **10** al lado de.

3 1 Este es mi hermano. **2** Estos son mis papás. **3** ¿Esta es tu mamá? **4** Estos son sus tíos. **5** Estos son tus libros. **6** Estas son mis hermanas. **7** Estos son sus abuelos. **8** ¿Este es su teléfono? **9** Este es mi celular. **10** ¿Este es su carro?

C ¿Qué hora es?

1 1 la una y media; **2** veinte para las nueve; **3** las nueve diez; **4** las doce en punto; **5** las diez y cuarto; **6** las tres veinticinco; **7** diez para las seis; **8** cuarto para las once.

2 **a** veinticinco; **b** ochenta y siete; **c** noventa y cuatro; **d** ciento tres; **e** ciento quince. **f** doscientos treinta; **g** trescientos veintiuno; **h** cuatrocientos cuarenta y seis; **i** quinientos treinta y cinco; **j** mil doscientos doce; **k** mil novecientos treinta y seis; **l** mil novecientos noventa y ocho; **ll** dos mil quinientos cincuenta.

3 **Desayuno:** seis y media, siete. **Comida:** una, dos. **Cena:** ocho. **Clases:** ocho. **Bancos:** nueve, cuatro. **Tiendas:** siete y media, diez.

4 **Actividad libre.**

5 1 F; **2** F; **3** V; **4** F; **5** V.

6 1 Mi hermana es muy simpática. **2** ¿Tú vives con tus papás? **3** ¿Dónde viven tus papás? **4** Mi hermano mayor es doctor. **5** Mi esposo trabaja en una empresa alemana. **6** Mi abuelo vive con mis papás. **7** ¿Tus hijos estudian en la universidad?

7 **Lima:** 23848. **Santiago:** 9D. **Buenos Aires:** 15:20. **España:** 7F. **Roma:** 027.

8 1 Mis papás son italianos. **2** ¿Dónde están mis lápices? **3** Enrique tiene dos relojes. **4** El diccionario está encima de la mesa. **5** Mi hermano estudia Medicina. **6** Es la una y cuarto. **7** Este sofá es muy cómodo. **8** En mi país la gente cena a las diez.

9 1 Esta; **2** Mi; **3** tu; **4** estos, tus; **5** sus; **6** Estas; **7** su; **8** Este; **9** esta, mis.

UNIDAD 3

A Rosa se levanta a las siete

1 1 María se baña en la mañana. **2** Jorge se levanta muy tarde. **3** ¿Tú te acuestas antes de las 12? **4** Mi novio no se afeita todos los días. **5** Clarita se peina sola. **6** Yo me acuesto antes que mi esposa. **7** Mis papás se levantan temprano. **8** Peter se sienta en la última fila.

2 1 a. **2** desde, de, hasta, de. **3** de, a. **4** a, en, a. **5** A. **6** de, a. **7** en, al. **8** de. **9** en, en. **10** en, **11** a, desde.

3 1 c. **2** a. **3** f. **4** b. **5** e. **6** d.

4 **Acostarse** me acuesto, te acuestas, se acuesta, nos acostamos, os acostáis, se acuestan. **Volver:** vuelvo, vuelves, vuelve, volvemos, volvéis, vuelven. **Ir:** voy, vas, va, vamos, vais, van.

5

C	E	M	P	E	Z	A	M	O	S
I	W	R	V	O	Y	Ñ	E	M	A
E	C	I	E	R	R	A	M	H	L
R	V	E	N	G	O	B	P	X	G
R	M	Q	I	Z	M	Ñ	I	K	O
O	U	Z	M	S	A	L	E	N	C
Z	W	R	O	M	B	O	Z	Q	L
V	B	R	S	T	U	M	A	X	L

6 1 A vienes, B Vengo, voy, cierra. **2** A Vamos, B nos acostamos. **3** A empieza, B me acuesto. **4** A volvemos, B vamos. **5** te levantas.

B ¿Estudias o trabajas?

1 1 LUNES, **2** MARTES, **3** MIÉRCOLES, **4** JUEVES, **5** VIERNES, **6** SÁBADO, **7** DOMINGO.

2 1 f, **2** a, **3** c, **4** e, **5** g, **6** b, **7** d.

3 1 c, **2** e, **3** d, **4** f, **5** g, **6** b, **7** a.

4 1 aeropuerto. **2** trabaja en un supermercado. **3** son enfermeras y trabajan en un hospital. **4** es secretaria y trabaja en una oficina. **5** son meseros y trabajan en un restaurante.

5 1 se levanta. **2** se baña. **3** desayuna. **4** Lleva a la escuela. **5** Trabaja. **6** Recoge. **7** Va a nadar. **8** Cena. **9** Lee.

6 de, soy. Trabajo. muy, porque, cantantes, semanas, y, fines, salgo, el, cine.

C ¿Qué desayunas?

1 **A** B Café con leche y pan tostado. B Jugo de naranja y pan tostado con mantequilla y mermelada. **B** Sándwich de queso y un café con leche. **C** Té con leche, una mantecada y un jugo de naranja.

2 1 h.; **2** a, f.; **3** c; **4** d; **5** b, g; **6** c, e.

3 **Respuesta libre.**

4 1 guitarra; **2** paraguayo; **3** regalo; **4** goma; **5** Uruguay; **6** colegio; **7** guerra; **8** domingo; **9** pagar; **10** Noruega.

S

UNIDAD 4

A ¿Dónde vives?

1 **1** jardín, **2** cochera, **3** sala, **4** cuarto de baño, **5** recámara, **6** cocina, **7** comedor.

2 **1** En el primero izquierda. **2** En el cuarto derecha. **3** En el tercero C. **4** En el segundo izquierda. **5** En el décimo derecha. **6** En el primero derecha.

3 **1** baño, cocina. **2** recámaras. **3** estacionamiento. **4** jardín. **5** sala.

B Interiores

1 **Sala**: sillones, equipo de música, mesa, espejo. **Cocina:** gabinetes, lavavajillas, mesa, microondas. **Cuarto de baño:** lavabo, espejo, tina.

2 **1** el. **2** La. **3** Los. **4** el. **5** las. **6** El, la. **7** El. **8** los, el. **9** las, el. **10** La, las, el.

3 **1** una, **2** una, **3** un, **4** unos, **5** un, **6** unos, **7** una, **8** una, **9** un, **10** un, **11** un, **12** un, una, **13** unas, una.

4 **1** El, los; **2** un; **3** El, la; **4** Los; **5** la; **6** las; **7** un; **8** una; **9** el, una.

5 **1** Cerca de mi casa hay dos restaurantes. **2** El Museo Picasso está en Barcelona. **3** Saltillo está cerca de Monterrey. **4** Hay una estación de tren junto a mi casa. **5** Encima del espejo está el lavabo. **6** La computadora está en la habitación de mi hermano. **7** ¿Dónde hay un banco cerca de aquí? **8** Andrés está en el cine con los niños.

6 **1** está. **2** Hay. **3** están. **4** hay. **5** está. **6** Hay. **7** tienen. **8** está. **9** Tiene. **10** está.

7 **1** F: La casa de Carmen está en el campo. **2** V. **3** V. **4** F: La sala tiene chimenea. **5** V. **6** F: La casa tiene cochera. **7** F: El jardín es muy grande. **8** V. **9** F: En la casa hay alberca.

8 (1) grande, (2) Está, (3) en, (4) quinto, (5) hay, (6) recámaras, (7) cocina, (8) la, (9) porque, (10) televisión, (11) librero.

C Visita a Cuernavaca

1 **1** e; **2** b; **3** d; **4** c; **5** f; **6** a; **7** g.

2 Posibles respuestas: **1** ¿Puede decirme si hay habitaciones libres para el próximo fin de semana? **2** ¿Qué precio tiene? **3** ¿El uso de la alberca está incluido en el precio? **4** ¿El IVA está incluido en el precio? **5** ¿Se puede pagar con tarjeta de crédito?

3 **1** En Cuernavaca. **2** Que es muy bonito. **3** Restaurante, alberca, canchas de tenis... **4** Tepoztlán.

UNIDAD 5

A Comer fuera de casa

1 **Amalia:** **1** ejotes, **2** arroz, **3** huevos, **4** fruta. **Juan:** **1** pescado, **2** carne, **3** pollo asado, **4** queso.

2 **1** merluza, **2** flan, **3** ejotes, **4** espárragos, **5** milanesa de res.

3 **1** De postre, fruta de temporada para los dos. **2** De entrada yo quiero sopa de fideos. **3** De plato fuerte quiero merluza. **4** Y yo ensalada. **5** Pues yo pollo asado. **6** Para beber, agua, por favor.

Jorge: De entrada yo quiero sopa de fideos. **Ana:** Y yo ensalada. **Jorge:** De plato fuerte quiero merluza. **Ana:** Pues yo pollo asado. **Jorge:** Para beber, agua, por favor. **Ana:** De postre, fruta de temporada para los dos.

B ¿Te gusta el cine?

1 **1** A Carmen le gusta la música clásica. **2** A Pablo le gusta navegar por internet. **3** A los dos les gusta cuidar plantas. **4** A Carmen le gusta tomar fotos. **5** A Pablo le gusta ir al cine. **6** A Carmen le gusta leer. **7** A Pablo le gusta escuchar rock. **8** A Carmen le gusta esquiar. **9** A Pablo le gusta andar en bicicleta. **10** A Carmen le gusta estar con animales. **11** A Pablo le gusta ver la televisión.

2 **Actividad libre.**

3 **1** ¿A tus amigos les gusta la computación? **2** ¿A ti y a tu compañero les gusta el ciclismo? **3** ¿Te gustan los animales? **4** ¿A tu amigo le gusta ver la televisión? **5** ¿Te gusta el cine de terror? **6** ¿Te gusta el mole?

4 **1** Me gusta / No me gusta el jugo de naranja. **2** Me gustan / No me gustan los plátanos. **3** Me gustan / No me gustan las verduras. **4** Me gusta / No me gusta la leche. **5** Me gustan / No me gustan los cacahuates. **6** Me gustan / No me gustan las papas. **7** Me gusta / No me gusta el café. **8** Me gusta / No me gusta el té.

5 **Actividad libre.**

C Receta del Caribe

1 hablar, hable; trabaja, trabaje; come, coma; abre, abra; bebe, beba.

2 **1** Lava, **2** Corta, **3** Añade, **4** Mezcla, **5** Sirve.

3 **1** Prepara, **2** Compra, **3** Elabora, **4** Usa, **5** Añade, **6** Recoge.

4 **Entrada:** sopa de fideos, ensalada mixta, sopa de verduras, ejotes con jamón. **Plato fuerte:** merluza a la plancha, milanesa de res, pollo asado, chuletas de cerdo. **Postre:** helado, fruta, flan. **Bebidas:** aguas frescas, cerveza, agua mineral, vino tinto.

5 **1** Aceite de oliva, pan y vino **2** Desde hace más de cinco mil años. **3** Porque disminuye el colesterol. **4** Los pescados azules, las legumbres y las frutas. **5** En Grecia y en España.

UNIDAD 6

A ¿Cómo se llega a Garibaldi?

1 **1** llega, toma, cambia, es. **2** llega, Toma, baja. **3** llega, toma, baja, cambia, Baja.

2 **1** de, a, de. **2** de. **3** al. **4** De, a. **5** de, al, en. **6** a, en. **7** a. **8** de, a. **9** hasta, de. **10** De, a.

3 **1** V, **2** F, **3** V.

S

B Cierra la ventana, por favor

1 1 g; **2** a, **3** f, **4** h, **5** d, **6** b, **7** c, **8** i, **9** j, **10** e.

2 1 ¿Puedes poner la televisión? **2** ¿Puedes hablar más despacio? **3** ¿Puedes venir aquí? **4** ¿Puedes hacer los ejercicios? **5** ¿Puedes cerrar la puerta? **6** ¿Puedes pedir la cuenta? **7** ¿Puedes prender la luz? **8** ¿Puedes recoger la mesa? **9** ¿Puedes dar vuelta a la derecha? **10** ¿Puedes seguir todo derecho?

3 empiezo, empieza; prendo, prende; pido, pide; guarda.

4 **1** Cierra el libro. **2** Empieza a trabajar. **3** Prende la computadora. **4** Christian, siéntate ahí. **5** Siga por aquí. **6** Pide dinero a tus papás. **7** Acuéstate pronto. **8** Levántate ya, son las diez. **9** Dame un vaso de agua. **10** Préstame tu carro. **11** Muéstreme su pasaporte.

5 **1** Guarda la ropa limpia en el closet. **2** Pon la ropa sucia en la lavadora. **3** Haz la cama. **4** Coloca los libros en los estantes. **5** Pon los CD en su lugar.

C Mi colonia es tranquila

1 1 a; **2** c; **3** b; **4** d.

2 (1) es, (2) es, (3) está, (4) Está, (5) es, (6) es, (7) es, (8) está.

3 **1** corto, **2** lento, **3** bajo, **4** pequeño, **5** difícil, **6** tranquilo, **7** caro, **8** feo, **9** estrecho, **10** oscuro, **11** gordo.

4 **1** es, **2** está, **4** es (rubio), **5** es, **6** está (al lado), **7** están, **9** están, **10** Está, **11** está, **12** está, **13** está, está, **14** está, **15** es.

5 **a** avión-aeropuerto, **b** metro-estación, **c** barco-puerto, **d** taxi-parada.

6 **Actividad libre.**

7 **a** 3 (tango); **b** 4 (ranchera); **c** 2 (flamenco); **d** 1 (salsa).

8 (1) cultura, (2) ritmos, (3) salsa, (4) baila, (5) popular, (6) canciones, (7) cantantes.

9 1 F. **2** F. **3** V. **4** F.

UNIDAD 7

A ¿Dónde nos vemos?

1 **1** María: ¿Por qué no vamos a tomar algo después de trabajar?
Ricardo: Lo siento, hoy no puedo, tengo que ir de compras con mi hermano. ¿Te parece bien mañana?
María: ¿A qué hora te parece bien?
Ricardo: ¿A las seis?
María: No, mejor a las seis y media.
Ricardo: De acuerdo. ¡Hasta mañana!
2 Daniel: ¿Vamos al cine esta noche?
Carmen: No puedo, lo siento. Voy a cenar con unos amigos.
Daniel: ¿Y si nos tomamos un café antes?
Carmen: Bueno, de acuerdo. ¿Vamos al Café Central?
Daniel: Perfecto. Nos vemos ahí a las cinco.

2 **Actividad libre.**

3 1 V; **2** F; **3** F; **4** V; **5** V; **6** F.

4 1 ¿De parte de quién? **2** Ahora contesta. **3** No está en este momento.

5 1 f; **2** e; **3** a; **4** b; **5** c; **6** d.

6 1 ¿Está Pilar? **2** ¿A qué hora puedo hablarle? **3** ¿Quieres ir al cine mañana? **4** ¿Nos vemos a las seis? **5** ¿A qué hora quedamos de vernos? **6** ¿Dónde quedamos de vernos?

7 1 V; **2** V; **3** F; **4** F; **5** V; **6** V.

B ¿Qué estás haciendo?

1 1 está pintando; **2** están jugando; **3** está mirando; **4** está descansando; **5** están viendo; **6** está saliendo.

2 1 como; **2** Está haciendo; **3** lees; **4** hago; **5** hablo; **6** tienes; **7** está durmiendo; **8** Está trabajando; **9** Está estudiando.

3 (1) vive, (2) está pasando, (3) están visitando, (4) están bañándose, (5) tiene, (6) gusta, (7) están viendo, (8) cenan.

4 **1** Me estoy preparando para un examen. **2** ¿Qué estás haciendo ahora? **3** Están comiendo unos tacos **4** Estamos haciendo la cena. **5** Mi esposo está trabajando. **6** Esta semana está lloviendo mucho. **7** Mis amigos están viendo una película. **8** Claudia y yo estamos trabajando en un nuevo proyecto. **9** Las niñas están bañándose en el cuarto de baño grande. **10** ¿Qué están haciendo los niños en su habitación?

5 **1** María se está lavando la cara. **2** Luis se está afeitando. **3** Mi hermano se está bañando. **4** Me estoy peinando. **5** Susana y Rosa se están pintando los labios. **6** Yo me está bañando. **7** Mi hijo se está peinando. **8** Se está cepillando los dientes. **9** Mi mamá se está secando el pelo en el cuarto de baño. **10** Mis hermanos se están vistiendo para ir al concierto.

C ¿Cómo es?

1 1 F. **2** F. **3** F. **4** V. **5** V. **6** F. **7** F.

2 **Velázquez:** pelo largo, barba, pelo negro, bigote, mayor, alto.
Infanta Margarita: pelo largo, pelo rubio, joven.
Meninas: pelo largo, pelo negro, jóvenes.

3 **1** generoso, **2** callado, **3** desagradable, **4** alegre, **5** grosero.

4 **Actividad libre.**

UNIDAD 8

A Por favor, ¿para ir a la catedral?

1 1 e. **2** a. **3** c. **4** f. **5** d. **6** b.

2 **1 B** primera a la izquierda. **2 B** la segunda a la derecha. **3 B** la tercera a la izquierda y después la primera a la derecha.

3 Posibles respuestas: **1 A** ¿Puede decirme cómo se llega al parque? **B** Dé vuelta la primera a la derecha y después la segunda a la izquierda. **2 A** ¿Puede decirme cómo se llega al teatro? **B** Sí, la primera calle a la izquierda y después la primera a la derecha. **3 A** ¿Puede decirme cómo se llega al restaurante? **B** Sí, todo derecho y después la tercera a la derecha.

4 1 en; **2** hasta, de; **3** a; **4** de; **5** en, a; **6** En, de. **7** al, de, de; **8** a; **9** por, de, hasta, al; **10** por, a.

5 1 c, **2** d, **3** a, **4** e, **5** b.

B ¿Qué hizo Rosa ayer?

1 fue / comer, comí / escuché, escuchó / leer, leyó / empecé, empezó / estar, estuvo / jugar, jugó / salí, salió / vivir, vivió / nací, nació / trabajar, trabajé.

2 1 c (trabajo / empecé); **2** e (va / fue); **3** f (ve / escuchó); **4** b (van / jugaron); **5** d (llueve / nevó); **6** a (vamos / estuvimos).

3 (1) fuiste; (2) Fui; (3) comieron; (4) pedimos; (5) pasaron; (6) pasamos; (7) reímos; (8) Fue.

4 1 ¿A quién llamó por teléfono el jueves? A Tomás. **2** ¿Qué día tomó el camión? El viernes. **3** ¿A qué hora salió el camión? A las 11:30. **4** ¿De quién fue el sábado el cumpleaños? De María. **5** ¿A qué hora quedaron de verse? A las 5. **6** ¿Con quién fue el domingo al cine? Con Tomás. **7** ¿Cuándo vio la calificación del examen? El lunes. **8** ¿Adónde fue el martes? Al gimnasio.

C ¿Cómo está el clima hoy?

1 (1) estuve, (2) tomé, (3) vuelo, (4) río, (5) Después, (6) Más tarde, (7) salieron, (8) Finalmente, (9) tomé, (10) despedí.

2 1 Siempre deseé conocer la selva. **2** Al día siguiente salimos para Iquitos. **3** En Iquitos vimos el río Amazonas. **4** En el Amazonas se pescan pirañas. **5** En la selva nadamos en el Amazonas. **6** En el pueblo de la selva conocí a un grupo de niños. **7** Me llevé un recuerdo auténtico del Amazonas. **8** Me tomé fotos con los niños.

3 1 Ayer en México hizo calor y estuvo nublado. Hoy llueve. **2** Ayer en Argentina hizo frío. Hoy hace aire. **3** Ayer en Brasil estuvo nublado y llovió. Hoy hace frío y aire.

4 1 Unos 118 millones de habitantes. **2** 5,100 pesos. **3** Iberia y Aeroméxico. **4** Octubre, noviembre, diciembre, enero, febrero, marzo. **5** El Museo Nacional de Antropología está en Ciudad de México y las pirámides mayas están en Chiapas y en Yucatán. **6** Tienes que llevarte traje de baño para bañarte en las playas de Cancún.

UNIDAD 9

A ¿Cuánto cuestan estos zapatos?

1 1 (1) cuánto, (2) cuestan, (3) llevo, (4) con tarjeta. **2** (1) cuesta, (2) Cuesta, (3) probármela, (4) queda, (5) gusta, (6) llevo. **3** (1) cuesta, (2) gusta, (3) ve, (4) Cuánto.

3 1 ¿Tú lo traes? **2** ¿Tú las ves? **3** ¿Tú los compras? **4** ¿Tú la conoces? **5** ¿Tú lo lees? **6** ¿Tú la usas? **7** ¿Tú lo utilizas?

4 1 me; **2** la; **3** los; **4** lo; **5** lo; **6** los; **7** te; **8** Nos, los; **9** las.

B Mi novio trae corbata

1

R	W	S	U	E	T	E	R	P	O
R	P	P	L	A	Y	E	R	A	Z
E	C	V	B	E	R	T	D	N	M
A	S	R	A	M	O	S	Z	T	A
S	O	P	B	F	A	L	D	A	N
I	T	V	M	S	W	C	X	L	X
M	A	X	A	B	R	I	G	O	M
A	P	X	W	E	T	R	Y	N	U
C	A	L	C	E	T	I	N	E	S
B	Z	B	R	E	T	G	H	S	M

2 1 cartera; **2** carpeta negra; **3** grises; **4** rojos, modernos; **5** pelota amarilla; **6** azules; **7** rosa; **8** verdes; **9** bufanda naranja.

3 1 caro; **2** moderno; **3** largo; **4** incómodo; **5** limpio; **6** estrecho; **7** claro; **8** pequeño.

4 1 gasta, **2** compras, **3** cómoda, **4** de mezclilla, **5** zapatos, **6** elegante, **7** bonitos, **8** favorito.

C Buenos Aires es más grande que Toledo

1 1 Aquellos pantalones de mezclilla son más baratos que estos. **2** Yo soy menor que Juanjo. **3** El carro de Miguel es mejor que el de Ramón. **4** La silla es más incómoda que el sillón. **5** Trae el abrigo más corto que la falda. **6** Nosotras tenemos más libros que Raquel. **7** Tu carro es más moderno que el mío.

2 1 Este, corto; **2** Esa, pequeña; **3** Esos, nuevos; **4** Aquellas, cansadas; **5** esta, roja; **6** este; **7** Esas, caras, aquellas, baratas. **8** Esos, largos, aquellos, cortos; **9** Estos; **10** Esa, bonita, barata, cara, fea.

3 (1) mejor; (2) más; (3) menos; (4) más; (5) tan; (6) mayor.

4 **Actividad libre.**

5 (1) centro, (2) asentamiento, (3) conquista, (4) diseñó y fundó, (5) convento, (6) acueducto, (7) Patrimonio de la Humanidad, (8) barrocos, (9) destacado, (10) inversión.

UNIDAD 10

A La salud

1 1 rodilla, **2** dedo, **3** mano, **4** brazo, **5** hombro, **6** cara, **7** ojo, **8** oreja, **9** pelo, **10** cuello, **11** pecho, **12** pierna, **13** pie.

2 1 dedo, **2** oreja, **3** cara, **4** pie, **5** ojo, **6** rodilla.

3 1 orejas, **2** bigote, **3** brazos, **4** dientes, **5** ojos, **6** manos, **7** dedos.

4 **Sonia:** ¿Qué te sucede, Alfonso? ¿Te sientes bien? **Alfonso:** No, no muy bien. Tengo fiebre. **Sonia:** ¿Estás tomando alguna medicina? **Alfonso:** No, de momento no. **Sonia**: ¿Por qué no te tomas una aspirina y descansas? **Alfonso:** Sí, es lo

S

mejor, porque mañana tengo mucho trabajo. **Sonia:** Seguro que mañana te sientes mejor.

5 1 le duele, **2** les duele, **3** me duele, **4** le duelen, **5** te duele, **6** nos duelen.

B Antes salíamos con los amigos

1 1 d. trabajaba; **2** f. íbamos; **3** a. venía; **4** c. compraba; **5** e. me gustaba; **6** b. hacías.

2 1 vivíamos; **2** tenía, iba; **3** trabajaba; **4** tocaba; **5** eran, tocaban; **6** iba; **7** éramos, escalábamos; **8** tenía, leía; **9** existían.

3 (1) Tenía; (2) vivíamos, (3) era, (4) había, (5) teníamos, (6) iba, (7) era, (8) atendía, (9) vivíamos, (10) tomábamos.

4 1 Tenía 90 años. **2** Vivían más tranquilos. **3** No tenían ni televisión ni radio. **4** En Querétaro. **5** Era peluquero. **6** Comían muchos alimentos naturales, leche recién ordeñada y papas recogidas del campo.

C Voy a trabajar en un hotel

1 1 c; **2** b; **3** e; **4** a; **5** f; **6** d.

2 1 Juan va a lavar el carro. **2** Yo voy a hablar por teléfono con mis amigos. **3** Ana va a cenar con Pedro. **4** María y Alberto van a pintar su casa. **5** Tomás y yo vamos a reparar nuestras bicicletas. **6** ¿Vas a ir a la alberca? **7** ¿Van a venir a comer? **8** ¿Tu hermano va a correr el maratón de Ciudad de México? **9** Mis amigos no van a ver el partido en casa. Lo van a ver en un bar. **10** ¿Vas a remodelar la cocina?

3 (1) va a venir; (2) vamos a ver; (3) vamos a jugar; (4) voy a poder; (5) voy a lavar.

4 1 g; **2** c; **3** b; **4** a; **5** d; **6** e; **7** h; **8** j; **9** i; **10** f.

5 1 David va a tomar fotos a los leones. **2** Pedro va a volar sobre el Gran Cañón. **3** Alberto y Pablo van a pasear por la plaza Roja. **4** Yo voy a visitar las pirámides. **5** Tú vas a escuchar flamenco. **6** Tu novia y tú van a nadar en las playas de Copacabana. **7** Nosotros vamos a conocer las islas griegas. **8** Mis papás van a admirar la Gioconda. **9** Pablo y María van a conocer el Coliseo. **10** Tu amigo Pedro va a navegar por el Támesis.

6 1 F; **2** F; **3** V; **4** F; **5** V; **6** V.

ANEXOS

- En parejas
- Verbos
- Transcripciones

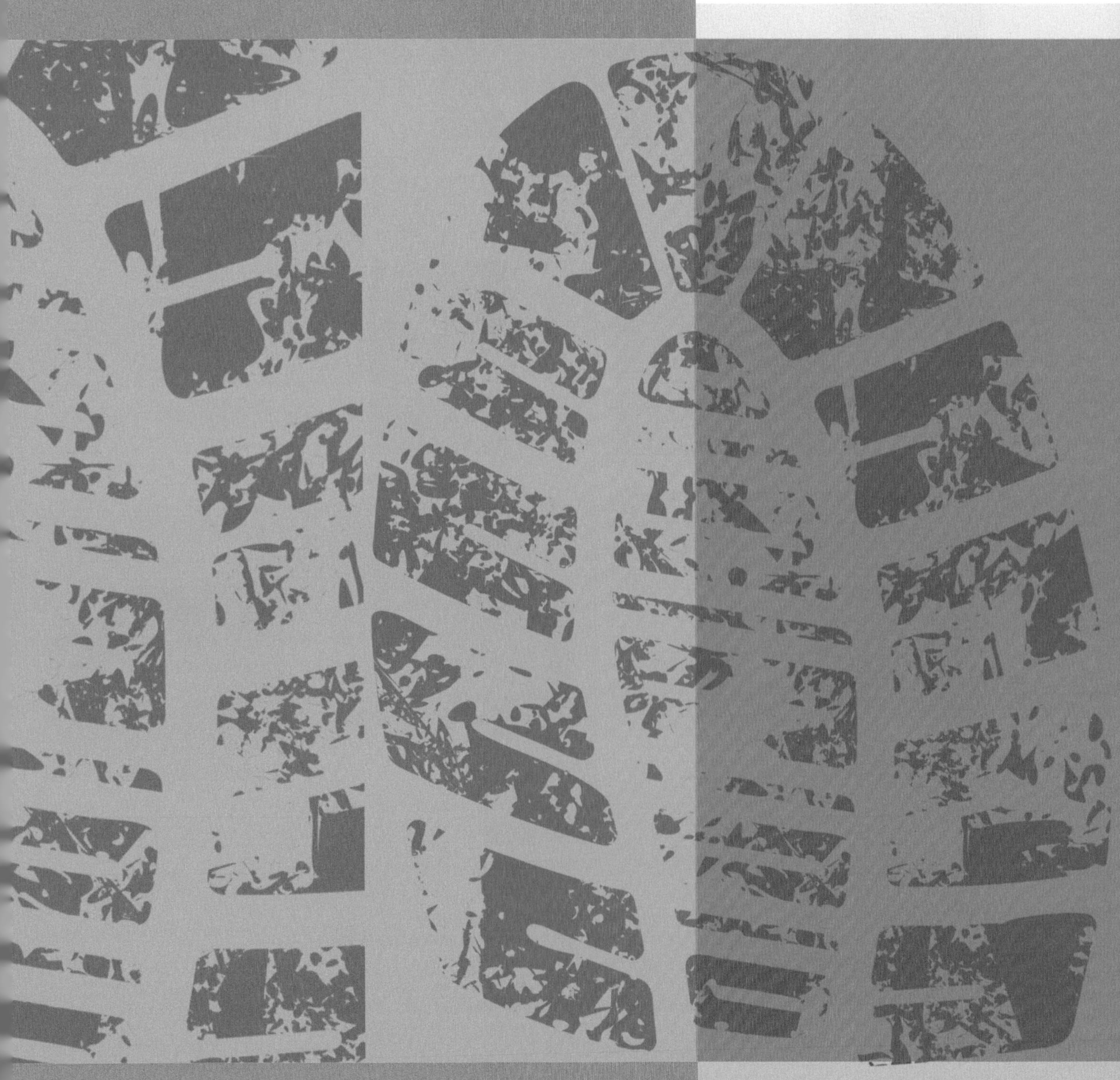

Unidad 1

Hablar

Alumno B (viene de página 19)

5 Responde a A la información sobre los números 1, 3, 5 y 7.

El número 1 se llama Isabel Allende. Es chilena. Es escritora.

1

Isabel Allende
chilena
escritora

2

______
______
______

3

Messi
argentino
futbolista

4

______
______
______

5

Carolina Herrera
venezolana
diseñadora

6

______
______
______

7

Shakira
colombiana
cantante

8

______
______
______

6 ¿Conoces a estos personajes famosos? Pregunta a A la información sobre los números 2, 4, 6 y 8.

¿Cómo se llama el número 2? ¿De dónde es? ¿A qué se dedica?

Unidad 2

Hablar

Alumno B (viene de página 29)

7 Responde a A dónde están sus objetos.

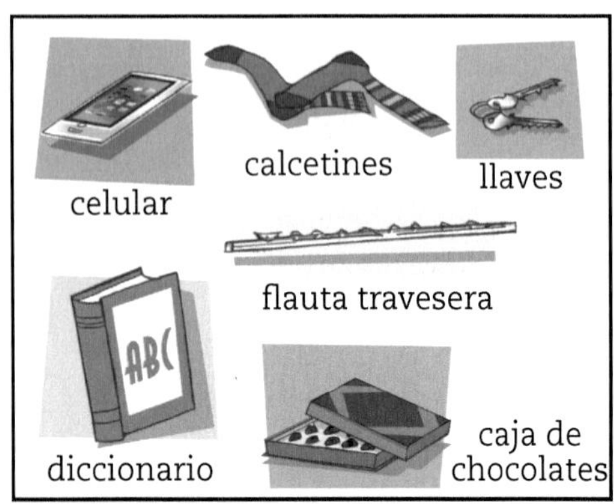

Los lentes están encima de la silla.

8 Pregunta a A dónde están los objetos del recuadro.

¿Dónde está el celular?

Unidad 3

Hablar

Alumno B (viene de página 39)

7 Responde a las preguntas de A.

NOMBRE:	Antonio García
EDAD:	42 años
TRABAJO:	Chef
PAÍS	Colombia
CIUDAD:	Bogotá
LUGAR DE TRABAJO:	Restaurante
TRANSPORTE:	Metro
FAMILIA:	Casado. Tiene dos hijos.

8 Pregunta a A y completa la siguiente ficha.

Unidad 4

Hablar

Alumno B (viene de página 49)

8 Responde a las preguntas de A.

9 Pregunta a A la información que falta en el anuncio del Hotel Miramar.

1 ¿En qué piso están: *la cafetería, la sauna y el gimnasio, el sala de conferencias?*
2 Pregunta el precio de la habitación doble: *¿Cuánto cuesta…?*
3 Pregunta el horario de la cena: *¿A qué hora se puede cenar?*

Unidad 5

Hablar

Alumno B (viene de página 59)

4 Responde a A las preguntas sobre tus gustos.

Sí, mucho. / Sí, bastante. / No, no mucho. / No, nada.

5 Pregunta a A sobre sus gustos.

¿Te gusta viajar?
¿Te gustan los perros?

	MUCHO	BASTANTE	NO MUCHO	NADA
viajar				
los perros				
las motos				
navegar por internet				
jugar futbol				
caminar				
hablar				
los niños				
leer				

Unidad 8

Hablar

Alumno B (viene de página 89)

9 Tú y tu compañero se encuentran en la esquina de la calle Argentina con la calle Ecuador. Escucha a A y dile cómo se va a los lugares que te pregunta.

10 Tú y tu compañero se encuentran en la esquina de la calle Argentina con la calle Ecuador. Pregunta a A cómo se va a los siguientes lugares:

- la panadería
- el banco
- la cafetería
- el cine
- la farmacia

- *¿Puedes decirme cómo llego a la panadería?*
- *Ve por la calle Argentina y toma la primera a la derecha, la calle Mayor. Sigue derecho y, después de cruzar la calle Colombia, a la derecha, junto al bar José, está la panadería.*

Unidad 10

Hablar

Alumno B (viene de página 109)

6 Prepara preguntas para entrevistar a A, que se sacó la lotería. Puedes añadir otras preguntas.

a Con quién / celebrar
b Qué / comprar
c Adónde / ir de vacaciones
d Con quién / ir
e Qué / hacer al regreso del viaje

7 Imagina que te vas a estudiar a un país extranjero. Prepara las respuestas para la entrevista que te hará A.

a ¿A qué país vas a ir?
b ¿Qué vas a estudiar?
c ¿Dónde te vas a quedar?
d ¿Con quién vas a vivir?
e ¿En qué vas a trabajar?

Verbos

VERBOS REGULARES

Presente	Pretérito	Imperfecto	Imperativo	Gerundio
		TRABAJAR		
trabaj**o**	trabaj**é**	trabaj**aba**		trabaj**ando**
trabaj**as**	trabaj**aste**	trabaj**abas**	trabaj**a** (tú)	
trabaj**a**	trabaj**ó**	trabaj**aba**	trabaj**e** (Ud.)	
trabaj**amos**	trabaj**amos**	trabaj**ábamos**		
trabaj**áis**	trabaj**asteis**	trabaj**abais**	trabaj**ad** (vosotros)	
trabaj**an**	trabaj**aron**	trabaj**aban**	trabaj**en** (Uds.)	
		BEBER		
beb**o**	beb**í**	beb**ía**		beb**iendo**
beb**es**	beb**iste**	beb**ías**	beb**e** (tú)	
beb**e**	beb**ió**	beb**ía**	beb**a** (Ud.)	
beb**emos**	beb**imos**	beb**íamos**		
beb**éis**	beb**isteis**	beb**íais**	beb**ed** (vosotros)	
beb**en**	beb**ieron**	beb**ían**	beb**an** (Uds.)	
		ESCRIBIR		
escrib**o**	escrib**í**	escrib**ía**		escrib**iendo**
escrib**es**	escrib**iste**	escrib**ías**	escrib**e** (tú)	
escrib**e**	escrib**ió**	escrib**ía**	escrib**a** (Ud.)	
escrib**imos**	escrib**imos**	escrib**íamos**		
escrib**ís**	escrib**isteis**	escrib**íais**	escrib**id** (vosotros)	
escrib**en**	escrib**ieron**	escrib**ían**	escrib**an** (Uds.)	

VERBOS IRREGULARES

Presente	Pretérito	Imperfecto	Imperativo	Gerundio
		CERRAR		
cierro	cerré	cerraba		cerrando
cierras	cerraste	cerrabas	cierra (tú)	
cierra	cerró	cerraba	cierre (Ud.)	
cerramos	cerramos	cerrábamos		
cerráis	cerrasteis	cerrabais	cerrad (vosotros)	
cierran	cerraron	cerraban	cierren (Uds.)	
		DAR		
doy	di	daba		dando
das	diste	dabas	da (tú)	
da	dio	daba	dé (Ud.)	
damos	dimos	dábamos		
dais	disteis	dabais	dad (vosotros)	
dan	dieron	daban	den (Uds.)	

Presente	Pretérito	Imperfecto	Imperativo	Gerundio
		DECIR		
digo	dije	decía		diciendo
dices	dijiste	decías	di (tú)	
dice	dijo	decía	diga (Ud.)	
decimos	dijimos	decíamos		
decís	dijisteis	decíais	decid (vosotros)	
dicen	dijeron	decían	digan (Uds.)	
		ESTAR		
estoy	estuve	estaba		estando
estás	estuviste	estabas	está (tú)	
está	estuvo	estaba	esté (Ud.)	
estamos	estuvimos	estábamos		
estáis	estuvisteis	estabais	estad (vosotros)	
están	estuvieron	estaban	estén (Uds.)	
		HACER		
hago	hice	hacía		haciendo
haces	hiciste	hacías	haz (tú)	
hace	hizo	hacía	haga (Ud.)	
hacemos	hicimos	hacíamos		
hacéis	hicisteis	hacíais	haced (vosotros)	
hacen	hicieron	hacían	hagan (Uds.)	
		IR		
voy	fui	iba		yendo
vas	fuiste	ibas	ve (tú)	
va	fue	iba	vaya (Ud.)	
vamos	fuimos	íbamos		
vais	fuisteis	ibais	id (vosotros)	
van	fueron	iban	vayan (Uds.)	
		OÍR		
oigo	oí	oía		oyendo
oyes	oíste	oías	oye (tú)	
oye	oyó	oía	oiga (Ud.)	
oímos	oímos	oíamos		
oís	oísteis	oíais	oíd (vosotros)	
oyen	oyeron	oían	oigan (Uds.)	
		PEDIR		
pido	pedí	pedía		pidiendo
pides	pediste	pedías	pide (tú)	
pide	pidió	pedía	pida (Ud.)	
pedimos	pedimos	pedíamos		
pedís	pedisteis	pedíais	pedid (vosotros)	
piden	pidieron	pedían	pidan (Uds.)	

Presente	Pretérito	Imperfecto	Imperativo	Gerundio
		PODER		
puedo	pude	podía		pudiendo
puedes	pudiste	podías	puede (tú)	
puede	pudo	podía	pueda (Ud.)	
podemos	pudimos	podíamos		
podéis	pudisteis	podíais	poded (vosotros)	
pueden	pudieron	podían	puedan (Uds.)	
		PONER		
pongo	puse	ponía		poniendo
pones	pusiste	ponías	pon (tú)	
pone	puso	ponía	ponga (Ud.)	
ponemos	pusimos	poníamos		
ponéis	pusisteis	poníais	poned (vosotros)	
ponen	pusieron	ponían	pongan (Uds.)	
		QUERER		
quiero	quise	quería		queriendo
quieres	quisiste	querías	quiere (tú)	
quiere	quiso	quería	quiera (Ud.)	
queremos	quisimos	queríamos		
queréis	quisisteis	queríais	quered (vosotros)	
quieren	quisieron	querían	quieran (Uds.)	
		SABER		
sé	supe	sabía		sabiendo
sabes	supiste	sabías	sabe (tú)	
sabe	supo	sabía	sepa (Ud.)	
sabemos	supimos	sabíamos		
sabéis	supisteis	sabíais	sabed (vosotros)	
saben	supieron	sabían	sepan (Uds.)	
		SALIR		
salgo	salí	salía		saliendo
sales	saliste	salías	sal (tú)	
sale	salió	salía	salga (Ud.)	
salimos	salimos	salíamos		
salís	salisteis	salíais	salid (vosotros)	
salen	salieron	salían	salgan	
		SEGUIR		
sigo	seguí	seguía		siguiendo
sigues	seguiste	seguías	sigue (tú)	
sigue	siguió	seguía	siga (Ud.)	
seguimos	seguimos	seguíamos		
seguís	seguisteis	seguíais	seguid (vosotros)	
siguen	siguieron	seguían	sigan (Uds.)	

Presente	Pretérito	Imperfecto	Imperativo	Gerundio
		SER		
soy	fui	era		siendo
eres	fuiste	eras	sé (tú)	
es	fue	era	sea (Ud.)	
somos	fuimos	éramos		
sois	fuisteis	erais	sed (vosotros)	
son	fueron	eran	sean (Uds.)	
		TENER		
tengo	tuve	tenía		teniendo
tienes	tuviste	tenías	ten (tú)	
tiene	tuvo	tenía	tenga (Ud.)	
tenemos	tuvimos	teníamos		
tenéis	tuvisteis	teníais	tened (vosotros)	
tienen	tuvieron	tenían	tengan (Uds.)	
		VENIR		
vengo	vine	venía		viniendo
vienes	viniste	venías	ven (tú)	
viene	vino	venía	venga (Ud.)	
venimos	vinimos	veníamos		
venís	vinisteis	veníais	venid (vosotros)	
vienen	vinieron	venían	vengan (Uds.)	
		VER		
veo	vi	veía		viendo
ves	viste	veías	ve (tú)	
ve	vio	veía	vea (Ud.)	
vemos	vimos	veíamos		
veis	visteis	veíais	ved (vosotros)	
ven	vieron	veían	vean (Uds.)	
		VOLVER		
vuelvo	volví	volvía		volviendo
vuelves	volviste	volvías	vuelve (tú)	
vuelve	volvió	volvía	vuelva (Ud.)	
volvemos	volvimos	volvíamos		
volvéis	volvisteis	volvíais	volved (vosotros)	
vuelven	volvieron	volvían	vuelvan (Uds.)	

LIBRO DEL ALUMNO

Antes de empezar

1 

Maestra: ¡Hola! Me llamo Maribel y soy la maestra de español. Vamos a presentarnos. A ver, empieza tú, ¿cómo te llamas?

Estudiante 1: Me llamo Marcelo.

Maestra: ¿De dónde eres, Marcelo?

Estudiante 1: Soy brasileño, de Porto Alegre.

Estudiante 2: Yo me llamo Isabelle y soy francesa.

4 

Las vocales: a - e - i - o - u.

Las consonantes: be - ce - de - efe - ge - hache - jota - ka - ele - eme - ene - eñe - pe - cu - erre - ese - te - uve - uve doble - equis - i griega - zeta.

Los conjuntos de letras: che - doble ele.

5 

ca: casa - **que:** queso - **qui:** quiero - **co:** color - **cu:** cuatro.

ga: gato - **gue:** guerra - **gui:** guitarra - **go:** agosto - **gu:** agua.

za: zapato - **ce:** cerrado - **ci:** cine - **zo:** zoológico - **zu:** azul.

ja: jamón - **je / ge:** jefe / genio - **ji / gi:** jirafa / gitano - **jo:** jota - **ju:** julio.

7 

1 erre-o-eme-e-erre-o; 2 de-i-a-zeta; 3 ge-o-ene-zeta-a-ele-uve-o; 4 erre-i-be-e-erre-a; 5 ge-i-eme-e-ene-e-zeta; 6 pe-a-de-i-ene

10 

alemán - alemana - japonés - maestro - estudiante - maestra - brasileño - hospital - estudiar - libro - lección - compañero - madre

12 

fiesta - hotel - cine - hospital - restaurante - flamenco - tango - bar - chocolate - café - salsa - playa - mariachi - guitarra - siesta

UNIDAD 1 - Saludos

2 

En clase

Isabelle: ¡Hola, Marcelo!, ¿qué tal?

Marcelo: Bien, ¿y tú?

Isabelle: Muy bien. Mira, esta es Ulrike, una nueva compañera, es alemana.

Marcelo: ¡Hola! ¡Encantado! ¿Eres de Berlín?

Ulrike: Sí, pero ahora vivo en Madrid.

En un hotel

Recepcionista: Su nombre, por favor.

Fernando: Yo me llamo Fernando Álvarez y ella es Carmen Hernández.

Recepcionista: ¿De dónde son ustedes?

Fernando: Somos argentinos, de Buenos Aires.

Recepcionista: Ah, Buenos Aires... Aquí están sus tarjetas, bienvenidos a Zacatecas.

Fernando: Gracias.

En una oficina

Díaz: ¡Buenos días!, señor Álvarez, ¿cómo está?

Álvarez: Muy bien, gracias. Mire, le presento a Marta Rodríguez, la nueva directora.

Díaz: Encantado de conocerla, yo me llamo Gerardo Díaz, y soy el responsable de la administración.

Rodríguez: Mucho gusto, Gerardo.

4 

En una cafetería

Luis: ¡Hola, Eva!, ¿qué tal?

Eva: Bien, ¿y tú?

Luis: Muy bien. Mira, este es Roberto, un nuevo compañero.

Eva: ¡Hola! ¡Encantada! ¿De dónde eres?

Roberto: Soy de aquí, de Monterrey.

7 

1 China: chino / china; 2 Irán: iraní / iraní; 3 Reino Unido: británico / británica; 4 Turquía: turco / turca; 5 Sudáfrica: sudafricano / sudafricana; 6 Colombia: colombiano / colombiana; 7 Brasil: brasileño / brasileña; 8 Francia: francés / francesa; 9 Polonia: polaco / polaca; 10 Suecia: sueco / sueca; 11 Alemania: alemán / alemana; 12 Canadá: canadiense / canadiense

9 

1 **Secretaria:** Hola, su nombre, por favor.
Claudia: Sí, me llamo Claudia Pereyra.
Secretaria: ¿Cómo se escribe su apellido?
Claudia: Pe-e-erre-e-i griega-erre-a.
Secretaria: ¿De dónde es usted, señora Pereyra?
Claudia: Soy argentina.
Secretaria: Muy bien, esta es su tarjeta.
Claudia: Gracias.

2 **Secretaria:** Hola, ¿me dice su nombre?
Francisco: Sí, me llamo Francisco Rodríguez.
Secretaria: ¿Puede repetir, por favor?
Francisco: Fran-cis-co Ro-drí-guez.
Secretaria: ¿De dónde es usted?
Francisco: Soy español, de Toledo.
Secretaria: Aquí tiene su tarjeta.
Francisco: Muchas gracias.

3 **Secretaria:** Buenos días, ¿me dice su nombre?
Elizabeth: Sí, claro, me llamo Elizabeth Henríquez.
Secretaria: ¿Puede deletrearlo, por favor?
Elizabeth: Sí, e-ele-i-zeta-a-be-e-te-hache es mi nombre y hache-e-ene-erre-i-cu-u-e-zeta mi apellido.
Secretaria: ¿Y de dónde es usted?
Elizabeth: Soy venezolana.
Secretaria: Bien, gracias, aquí tiene su tarjeta.
Elizabeth: Gracias a usted.

4 **Secretaria:** Buenos días, señor.
Manuel: Buenos días, me llamo Manuel Jiménez.
Secretaria: ¿Jiménez con ge o con jota?
Manuel: Con jota.
Secretaria: Aquí está. ¿De dónde es usted?
Manuel: Soy mexicano.
Secretaria: Muy bien, aquí tiene su tarjeta.
Manuel: Muchas gracias.

4 

Me llamo Manuel García. Soy doctor. Soy chiapaneco, pero vivo en Ciudad de México. Trabajo en un hospital. Mi esposa se llama Amelia, es maestra y trabaja en una preparatoria. Ella es oaxaqueña. Tenemos dos hijos, Sergio y Elena; los dos son estudiantes. Sergio estudia en la universidad, y Elena, en la preparatoria.

1 

1 ¿De dónde eres?
2 ¿De dónde son ustedes?
3 ¿Cómo te llamas?
4 ¿Quién es él?
5 ¿Dónde vives?
6 ¿Dónde trabaja usted?
7 ¿Dónde viven ustedes?
8 ¿Cómo se llama el esposo de Ana?

2

cero - uno - dos - tres - cuatro - cinco - seis - siete - ocho - nueve - diez

4 14

1 ■ María, ¿cuál es tu número de teléfono?
● El cinco cinco cuatro seis ocho cinco siete seis nueve ocho.
■ ¿Puedes repetir?
● Cinco-cinco-cuatro-seis-ocho-cinco-siete-seis-nueve-ocho.
■ Gracias.

2 ■ Jorge, ¿me das tu teléfono?
● Sí, es el cinco cinco tres cinco nueve siete seis ocho nueve siete.
■ Gracias.

3 ■ Marina, ¿cuál es tu número de teléfono?
● Mi celular es el cinco cinco uno cero ocho cuatro nueve tres siete dos.
■ ¿Y el de tu casa?
● Sí, es el cinco cinco siete nueve ocho cero seis cuatro tres dos.
■ Ok, gracias.

4 ■ Operadora, dígame.
● ¿Puede decirme el teléfono del Aeropuerto de la Ciudad de México?
■ Sí, anote, es el cinco cinco uno dos cinco cuatro siete ocho seis cinco.
● ¿Me puede repetir?
■ Sí, cinco-cinco-uno-dos-cinco-cuatro-siete-ocho-seis-cinco.
● Gracias.

5 ■ Operadora, dígame.
● ¿Puede decirme el teléfono de la Cruz Roja?
■ Sí, anote, es el cinco cinco siete seis nueve ocho siete ocho nueve ocho.
● ¿Puede repetir, por favor?
■ Sí, cinco-cinco-siete-seis-nueve-ocho-siete-ocho-nueve-ocho.

6 ■ Operadora, dígame.
● Buenos días, ¿puede decirme el teléfono de Radio-taxi?
■ Anote, por favor. El número solicitado es: cinco cinco dos cuatro ocho siete tres seis siete seis. El número solicitado es: cinco-cinco-dos-cuatro-ocho-siete-tres-seis-siete-seis.

7 

once - doce - trece - catorce - quince - dieciséis - diecisiete - dieciocho - diecinueve - veinte

9 

quince-uno-cuatro-veinte-ocho-siete-tres-once - cinco - seis - catorce - nueve - dieciocho - diecinueve - dos - trece - dieciséis

10 17

En un gimnasio

Felipe: ¡Buenas tardes!
Rosa: ¡Hola!, ¿qué se te ofrece?
Felipe: Quiero inscribirme en el gimnasio.
Rosa: Tienes que darme tus datos. A ver, ¿cómo te llamas?
Felipe: Felipe Martínez.
Rosa: ¿Y el segundo apellido?
Felipe: Franco.
Rosa: ¿Dónde vives?
Felipe: En la calle Reforma, número ochenta y siete, tercer piso, departamento trescientos cinco.
Rosa: ¿Teléfono?
Felipe: Cinco-cinco-ocho-seis-cero-cinco-seis-cero-nueve-siete.
Rosa: ¿Profesión?
Felipe: Maestro.
Rosa: Bueno, ya está; el precio es...

4 

- Hola, yo me llamo Francisco. Vivo en Getafe, un pueblo de Madrid. Estudio en la universidad de mi pueblo. Mi número de móvil es seis-cero-ocho dos-nueve-uno cero-siete-seis.
- Hola, me llamo Sofía y soy música. Toco la guitarra. Soy mexicana, pero vivo en Barcelona desde hace cinco años. Mi número de celular es seis-cero-nueve tres-cuatro dos-seis siete-uno.
- Yo soy Elizabeth. Soy de un pueblo, pero vivo en Caracas porque soy informática y trabajo en la universidad. Mi número de celular es seis-ocho-cero dos-tres-uno siete-seis-cinco.
- Yo soy Manuel, soy mexicano. Vivo en Málaga porque trabajo en una escuela de música, soy profesor de niños de ocho años. Mi celular es el seis-cero-seis dos-uno-cero tres-dos-nueve.

3 

1 Martínez; **2** Romero; **3** Marín; **4** Serrano; **5** López; **6** Moreno; **7** Jiménez; **8** Pérez; **9** Díaz; **10** Martín; **11** Vargas; **12** García; **13** Díez

UNIDAD 2 - Familias

2 

- Hola, soy Jorge. Soy casado y esta es mi familia. Mi esposa se llama Rosa y tenemos dos hijos: Isabel, de doce años, y David, de diez. Vivimos en Querétaro, una ciudad a dos horas de la Ciudad de México. Soy maestro de computación.
- Yo soy Luis. No tengo hermanos, no tengo novia, soy soltero y vivo en Mérida con mis papás y mi abuela. Mi papá se llama Manuel y tiene cincuenta y ocho años. Mi mamá se llama Rocío y tiene cincuenta y seis años. Mi abuela tiene setenta y nueve años y se llama Carmen. Soy estudiante de Medicina.

2 

1 las tres y media; **2** cuarto para las dos; **3** las diez y cuarto; **4** la una en punto; **5** las doce cinco; **6** veinte para las ocho; **7** las doce diez; **8** las cinco y media; **9** cuarto para la una

7 

veintiuno - veintidós - veintitrés - veinticuatro - treinta - treinta y uno - cuarenta - cincuenta - cincuenta y dos - sesenta - setenta - ochenta - noventa - cien - ciento tres - ciento once - doscientos / doscientas - trescientos / trescientas - cuatrocientos / cuatrocientas - quinientos / quinientas - seiscientos / seiscientas - mil - dos mil - cinco mil

8 

a dos; **b** veinticinco; **c** cincuenta; **d** treinta y siete; **e** trescientos veintitrés; **f** ciento treinta y cinco; **g** ochocientos cincuenta; **h** mil quinientos ochenta y nueve; **i** mil novecientos noventa y ocho; **j** mil novecientos ochenta y cinco

9 

1 ■ Hola, Clara, ¿cuántos años tienes?
● Doce.

2 ■ ¿Cuánto cuestan las naranjas?
● Treinta pesos.

3 ■ ¿Cuánto cuesta el paquete de café?
● Cincuenta pesos.

4 ■ ¿En qué año nació usted?
● En mil novecientos setenta y siete.

5 ■ Por favor, ¿cuántos kilómetros hay entre Monterrey y Guadalajara?
● Setecientos ochenta y siete.

6 ■ Por favor, ¿cuánto es por el café y la cerveza?
● Sesenta pesos.

7 ■ Disculpe, ¿qué hora es?
● Son las nueve.

8 ■ ¿Cuántas páginas tiene el libro?
● Quinientas cuarenta páginas.

9 ■ ¿Cuántos días tiene el mes de marzo?
● Treinta y un días.

10 ■ ¿Dónde vives?
● En la calle Morelos número sesenta y seis.

1 y 2 25

teléfono - lápiz - ventana - hotel - profesor - hermano - familia - música

3 

profesora - español - café - gramática - mesa - vivir - hablar - médico - autobús - Pilar - alemán - brasileña - familia - libro - examen

6 27

1 Dos de los actores españoles más famosos en el mundo son Penélope Cruz y su marido, Javier Bardem. Mónica, la hermana de Penélope, y Pilar y Carlos, la madre y el hermano de Javier, también son actores.
2 La familia Alcántara celebra la primera comunión de su hija María. Junto a la niña están sus padres, Antonio y Merche, sus hermanos, Carlitos y Toni, y su abuela, Herminia.
3 Carolina Herrera, diseñadora de moda, es reconocida internacionalmente. Con su segundo esposo, Reinaldo, tiene dos hijas. La más pequeña, Adriana, trabaja con ella diseñando vestidos.

5 28

Salidas:

- Transportes ADO anuncia su salida de las quince treinta y cinco, con destino a Michoacán, por el andén número tres.
- Transportes Del Norte anuncia su salida de las catorce treinta, con destino a la Ciudad de México. El autobús saldrá dentro de quince minutos por el andén número seis.
- Transportes ETN anuncia su salida con destino a Guadalajara, a las diez en punto, por el andén dos.

Llegadas:

- Transportes ETN anuncia la llegada del autobús procedente de Guadalajara, a las veinte horas, por el andén número once.
- Transportes Flecha Roja anuncia la llegada del autobús procedente de Querétaro, por el andén número ocho, a las dieciséis cuarenta y cinco.
- El autobús procedente de Colima, de la línea Transportes Del Norte, hará su entrada en el andén número cuatro, a las diecisiete horas.

UNIDAD 3 - El trabajo

4 

■ Y tú, Juan, ¿a qué hora te levantas?
● Bueno, yo me levanto temprano, a las seis, más o menos, me baño rápidamente y tomo café.
■ Y tu esposa, ¿a qué hora se levanta?
● Pues a las siete. Ella también se acuesta más tarde, como a las doce de la noche.
■ ¿Y tus hijos?
● Ellos cenan, ven un poco la tele y se acuestan temprano, a las diez.
■ ¿Y a qué hora se levantan?
● A las siete, porque entran a la escuela a las ocho.
■ ¿Y los fines de semana también se levantan todos temprano?
● ¡Ah, no!, claro que no, los domingos nos levantamos más tarde, a las nueve, porque, claro, también nos acostamos más tarde.

2 

- Lucía es técnica de sonido y trabaja en una emisora de radio, la Cadena Día. Tiene veintinueve años y no es casada. Vive en Querétaro, y habla inglés y francés perfectamente. Todos los días trabaja de ocho a cinco, menos los sábados y domingos. Los días laborables se levanta a las seis y sale de casa a las siete y media. Va al trabajo en camión. Los sábados en la noche sale con sus amigos a cenar y a bailar, por eso se acuesta muy tarde, a las tres o cuatro de la mañana.
- Carlos es bombero. Trabaja en el municipio de Xochimilco. Vive lejos del trabajo, por eso toma el metro todos los días. Tiene treinta y cuatro años, es casado y no tiene hijos. Trabaja en turnos de veinticuatro horas, un día sí y otro no. Si trabaja el sábado o el domingo, después tiene dos días libres. Siempre se levanta muy temprano, a las seis o a las siete de la mañana, por eso normalmente no sale en las noches. Cena a las ocho, después ve la tele y a las diez y media se acuesta.

3 31

1 ■ Philip, ¿qué se desayuna en Alemania?
● Hay muchas cosas. Algunos toman pan con mantequilla y salami y un huevo. Otros toman muesli con yogur. Y té, mucha gente toma té. Algunos toman café, claro.
2 ■ Claudia, ¿qué se desayuna en Argentina?
● Bueno, generalmente tomamos tostadas con dulce de leche o medialunas. Y para beber, mate, té o café con leche.
3 ■ Elizabeth, ¿qué se desayuna en Venezuela?
● La gente toma café con leche y arepas rellenas de queso o carne mechada, o también empanadas de harina de maíz.
4 ■ Manuel, ¿qué desayuna la gente en México?
● En México desayunamos fuerte. El platillo central suele ser huevos con frijoles y tortillas, y para beber, jugo de frutas.

6 32

Mesera: Buenos días, ¿qué desean?
Madre: Yo quiero un desayuno ranchero, ¿y tú, hijo?
Hijo: Yo solo quiero un jugo.
Madre: Come algo más: un pan dulce o un pan tostado.
Hijo: No, mamá, solo quiero un jugo de naranja.
Madre: Bueno, pues un desayuno ranchero y un jugo de naranja.
Mesera: Muy bien.

1 33

gato - agua - gota - guerra - guion

3 

1 guapo; 2 cigarrillos; 3 guitarra; 4 gastar; 5 pagar; 6 guerra; 7 Guatemala; 8 goma

4 35

■ Adriana, tú eres argentina, ¿no?
● Sí, claro.
■ ¿Y de qué ciudad?
● De Buenos Aires.
■ Cuéntame un poco los horarios habituales... Por ejemplo, ¿a qué hora se levantan?
● Nos levantamos muy temprano, a las cinco y media o las seis, porque el trabajo está lejos... y, bueno, normalmente empezamos a trabajar a las ocho.
■ ¿Y hasta qué hora trabajan?
● Hasta las seis... sí, en las oficinas hasta las seis de la tarde. Paramos una hora para almorzar, entre las doce y las dos: comemos algo rápido y, ya, volvemos al trabajo.
■ ¿Y en las tiendas?
● Bueno, el horario de las tiendas es distinto: abren también sobre las ocho de la mañana y cierran a las ocho o las nueve de la noche, y no cierran al mediodía, ¿eh?, no es como en España. Ah, y los bancos también tienen otro horario: abren a las diez y cierran a las tres, y por la tarde ya no abren.
■ Y una cosa, Adriana: cuando la gente sale del trabajo, ¿va directamente a su casa?
● Sí, sí, eso es lo normal, vamos a casa. Te-

nemos otra hora más para volver, claro. Cenamos entre las ocho y las nueve y media; y no nos acostamos tarde, sobre las once más o menos.
■ Oye, ¿y los niños?, ¿qué horario tienen en la escuela?
● Estudian solo o por la mañana o por la tarde: creo que es de ocho a doce en el turno de la mañana y de una a cinco los que estudian por la tarde.

6 

- Susana se levanta normalmente a las siete, se baña, se viste, desayuna algo rápido y sale de casa a las ocho. Su trabajo empieza a las nueve. Primero va al súper y después prepara la comida para unas treinta personas.
- Emilio se levanta tarde porque no trabaja en la mañana. Desayuna café con leche y dos panes tostados mientras lee el periódico. Come temprano porque sale de casa a las tres. Va a la universidad en metro. Sus clases empiezan a las cuatro y terminan a las ocho de la noche.
- Jaime se levanta muy temprano porque prepara el desayuno de sus hijos y los lleva a la escuela. Después va en carro a su trabajo, que está a las afueras de la ciudad. Trabaja en una gran tienda departamental atendiendo a los clientes. Su horario es de ocho de la mañana a seis de la tarde. Cuando sale del trabajo, recoge a los niños y los lleva a casa.

UNIDAD 4 - La casa

2 

Rosa y Miguel tienen una tienda de ropa en el centro de la Ciudad de México. Tienen dos hijos y viven en las afueras de la ciudad en una casa de dos plantas.
En la planta baja hay un recibidor, una cocina con un pequeño comedor, una sala grande y un medio baño.
En la planta de arriba hay tres recámaras y un cuarto de baño. La casa tiene también un jardín pequeño.

4

■ ¿Cuántas plantas tiene tu casa?
● Dos. Es una vivienda unifamiliar.
■ ¿Dónde está el cuarto de baño?
● En la planta de arriba. Y en la planta baja hay un medio baño.
■ ¿Tiene comedor?
● Sí, uno pequeño, al lado de la cocina.
■ ¿Cuántas recámaras tiene?
● Tres, están todas en la planta de arriba.
■ ¿Tienen cochera?
● No, nos estacionamos en la calle.

5 

■ Manuel, ¿cómo es tu departamento?
● Mi departamento es muy pequeño, porque vivo solo. Tiene una recámara, una sala-comedor pequeña, una cocina y un cuarto de baño, que está al lado de la recámara.
■ ¿Nada más?
● Bueno, tengo una terraza grande y ahí tengo muchas plantas.

8 

primero-primera / segundo-segunda / tercero-tercera / cuarto-cuarta / quinto-quinta / sexto-sexta / séptimo-séptima / octavo-octava / noveno-novena / décimo-décima

10 

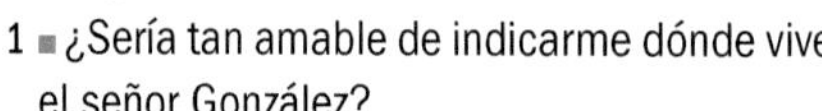

1 ■ ¿Sería tan amable de indicarme dónde vive el señor González?
● En el cuarto a la derecha.
■ Muchas gracias.
2 ■ ¿Me podría decir dónde vive doña Manuela Rodríguez?
● En el segundo a la izquierda.
■ Gracias.
3 ■ ¿En qué piso vive la señorita Herrero?
● En el tercero A.
4 ■ ¿Me podría enviar este paquete a mi domicilio, en la avenida del Mediterráneo, cinco, sexto B?
● Por supuesto, señor Acedo.
5 ■ ¿El señor de la Fuente, por favor?
● Es el inquilino del penthouse.
■ Muchas gracias.
6 ■ ¿Vive aquí la señorita Laura Barroso?
● Sí, es la hija de los vecinos del quinto E.

6 

■ Inverpiso, ¿dígame?
● Buenos días. Llamo para informarme sobre las residencias anunciadas en el periódico de ayer.
■ Con mucho gusto. Mire, la primera está en la calle Alonso Cano. Tiene ciento treinta y ocho metros cuadrados. Hay cuatro recámaras en la planta de arriba y dos baños, calefacción individual y elevador.
La segunda es una casa de tres plantas en Vasconcelos. Tiene trescientos once metros cuadrados, con jardín y alberca. Hay una sala-comedor y un baño en la planta baja, y cinco recámaras y otros dos cuartos de baño en la planta superior. La cochera es para dos carros.
La tercera residencia está en un fraccionamiento en la Rioja. Tiene trescientos metros cuadrados construidos en dos plantas. Tiene una amplia sala y cuatro recámaras. Hay un cuarto de baño en cada planta. Los materiales son de primera calidad. Hay alberca comunitaria.

2 

Recepcionista: Quinta Margarita, ¿dígame?
Carlos: Buenas tardes. ¿Puede decirme si hay habitaciones libres para el próximo fin de semana?
Recepcionista: Sí. ¿Qué desea, una habitación individual o doble?
Carlos: Una doble, por favor. ¿Qué precio tiene?
Recepcionista: Mil quinientos pesos por noche más IVA.
Carlos: De acuerdo. ¿Puede hacerme una reservación, por favor?
Recepcionista: ¿Cuántas noches?
Carlos: Viernes y sábado, si es posible.
Recepcionista: No hay problema.
Carlos: ¿Hay alberca?
Recepcionista: Sí, señor, hay una.
Carlos: ¿Admiten tarjetas de crédito?
Recepcionista: Sí, por supuesto.

4 

Recepcionista: ¿Me dice su nombre y apellidos, por favor?
Carlos: Carlos López Ruiz.
Recepcionista: ¿Dirección?
Carlos: Calle Morelos, número ciento sesenta y seis, en Guanajuato.
Recepcionista: ¿Número de teléfono, por favor?
Carlos: Cuatro siete tres siete tres tres uno seis dos uno.
Recepcionista: Entonces, una habitación doble para las noches del viernes y sábado, ¿no es así?
Carlos: Sí, correcto, muchas gracias. Hasta el viernes.
Recepcionista: ¡Hasta el viernes! Buenas tardes.

5 

Los patios

Los patios son lugares comunes para encontrarse, para jugar, para platicar, para descansar. Hay muchos tipos de patios: el patio de la escuela, donde los niños pasan el recreo; el patio andaluz, en el sur de España, lleno de macetas con flores, que en verano protege del calor y es un lugar de descanso y de conversación.

En las ciudades hay patios interiores, donde la gente tiende la ropa y habla con los vecinos de enfrente.

En Hispanoamérica muchas casas coloniales conservan bellos patios llenos de plantas tropicales que ayudan a pasar las horas más calurosas del día.

En la ciudad andaluza de Córdoba, el segundo fin de semana de mayo se celebra el Festival de los Patios. Los vecinos abren sus casas, y vecinos y turistas pueden visitar sus hermosos patios.

1 

queso - cuarto - cuanto - quinto - casa - comedor

7 

Entrevistador: Patricia, ¿dónde pasas tus vacaciones?

Patricia: Tengo una casa en Isla Mujeres, en el Caribe. Es una cabaña de dos plantas, con un jardín muy bonito, y está cerca de la playa. Siempre paso unos días allí con mi familia y algunos amigos.

Entrevistador: ¿Con quién vas este año?

Patricia: Este año voy con mi esposo, nuestro amigo Juan y su esposa. La casa no es muy grande. Tiene solo dos recámaras, pero es muy cómoda, con dos cuartos de baño, una cocina pequeña y una sala preciosa con vista al mar. También tiene una terraza para tomar el sol.

Entrevistador: ¿Comen en casa?

Patricia: No, normalmente comemos en algún restaurante cerca de la playa. Por la noche hacemos la cena en casa y cenamos en el jardín.

Entrevistador: Bueno, pues les deseamos unas buenas vacaciones.

UNIDAD 5 - Comer

2 

Mesero: Buenos días, señores, ¿qué quieren comer?

Juan: De entrada nos da un guacamole para mí y una ensalada para la señora.

Mesero: ¿Y de plato fuerte?

Teresa: ¿La carne es de ternera?

Mesero: Sí, señora. Está muy buena.

Teresa: Entonces, me trae una carne asada. ¿Y tú, Juan?

Juan: Yo prefiero unos chiles rellenos.

Mesero: ¿Y para beber?

Juan: La limonada de la casa y una botella de agua, por favor.

Mesero: Muy bien, muchas gracias.

(...)

Mesero: Y de postre, ¿qué desean?

Juan: Para mí, un flan.

Teresa: Pues, yo quiero arroz con leche.

Mesero: Enseguida se los traigo, muchas gracias.

7 

Hoy comemos fuera

En Latinoamérica, comer es algo que nos gusta compartir con amigos, familiares, compañeros de trabajo o estudio. Para la mayoría de los latinos es más importante la compañía que el tipo de restaurante.

Al escoger un restaurante preocupa la higiene, la calidad de los alimentos, pero no siempre la dieta equilibrada. En países con un clima agradable, de largos días con luz, el comer o cenar fuera de casa es un hábito extendido.

Es durante los días festivos cuando más se visitan bares y restaurantes.

3 

Mi esposo y yo siempre tenemos problemas para decidir qué hacer durante el fin de semana. A mí me gusta ir al cine los viernes y, el sábado por la mañana, ir de compras. Por el contrario, a mi esposo le gusta pasar el fin de semana en el campo: caminar, hacer ejercicio... El domingo por la tarde, lo que más le gusta es ver un partido de futbol por la tele, mientras yo navego por internet. Durante la semana lo tenemos más fácil: a los dos nos gusta leer y oír música en nuestro tiempo libre.

4 

Queridos amigos y amigas, hoy vamos a hacer un delicioso refresco de plátano. Bueno, ¿están preparados? Aquí van los ingredientes: en primer lugar vamos a necesitar tres plátanos y un vaso de leche. Como el refresco será solo para cuatro personas, vamos a utilizar únicamente un cuarto de taza de azúcar y un cuarto de taza de jugo de limón y, por último, media cucharadita de vainilla y ocho cubitos de hielo. Y ahora, para su elaboración, sigue las siguientes instrucciones:

- Primero, pela los plátanos y córtalos en rodajas.
- A continuación, mezcla los plátanos, la leche, el azúcar, el jugo de limón y la vainilla en una licuadora.
- Añade los cubitos de hielo y mézclalos con los otros ingredientes.
- Reparte la mezcla en cuatro vasos.
- Finalmente, invita a tus amigos.

9 

¿Productos de América?

Bienvenidos a nuestro programa. Hoy hablamos del origen de algunos productos. Atención a las siguientes informaciones:

1 Casi todas las piñas de los supermercados son de Hawái, pero los cultivadores originales son los indios de Cuba y Puerto Rico.

2 Es cierto que hay una variedad de cacahuate (también llamado en América "maní") que procede de Georgia, pero sus cultivadores originales son los indios de Bolivia y Perú.

3 Los italianos preparan una deliciosa salsa de tomate, pero los cultivadores originarios del tomate son los indios de México.

4 Ecuador es el mayor productor de plátanos del mundo, pero los plátanos son de origen africano.

5 Brasil es el mayor productor de café del mundo, pero el café también es de origen africano.

6 Las papas son muy populares en Irlanda, pero proceden originalmente de Perú y Ecuador.

1 

Isabel-vivir-vino-bueno-Ávila-viajar-botella-abuelo - hablar - muy bien - beber

2 54

1 ¿Dónde vive Isabel?
2 Cuba es una isla preciosa.
3 Vicente es abogado y trabaja en Puebla.
4 Las bebidas están en el refri.
5 Este vino es muy bueno.
6 Valeriano viaja mucho en avión.
7 Beatriz es de Venezuela.
8 Esta bicicleta es muy barata.
9 En Taxco no hay bastantes ambulancias.
10 La abuela de Bibiana está muy bien.

4 

1 Yo vivo en Barcelona.
2 Este licuado tiene vainilla.
3 Mesero, un vaso de agua, por favor.
4 A Isabel le gusta viajar y bailar tangos.
5 Beber agua es muy bueno.
6 ¿Este verano vas de vacaciones?
7 La botella está vacía.
8 El banco abre a las nueve.

5 

1 bala; **2** poca; **3** barra; **4** beso; **5** vino; **6** pera; **7** vaca; **8** pisa; **9** pata; **10** pez

2 

Buenos días, hoy hablamos de comida, española y también de otros países hispanos. Hay platos españoles e hispanoamericanos conocidos en todo el mundo. De México, el guacamole, que se hace con aguacate; de Perú es muy famoso el ceviche, pescado con limón, un plato que también se come en Ecuador y en otros países sudamericanos; las exquisitas arepas de Colombia y Venezuela, que se comen con jamón, con queso y otros muchos ingredientes; y cómo no, la famosa carne asada típica de Argentina, una de las mejores carnes del mundo. En Costa Rica un platillo tradicional es el gallo pinto, combinación de arroz y frijoles. La feijoada es considerada el platillo nacional de Brasil. Es un guiso de carne de puerco con frijoles negros que se suele acompañar con arroz y salchichas. En España hay un platillo que tiene fama internacional, la paella, platillo típico de la costa mediterránea, y, en especial, de Valencia. En un sartén se cocina el arroz junto con una variedad de ingredientes. Por último, en Uruguay es muy popular un sándwich de carne llamado chivito que generalmente es aderezado con mayonesa y se acompaña con papas fritas, ensalada rusa o cualquier otra guarnición.

UNIDAD 6 - **La colonia**

3 

Sergio: Disculpe, queremos dos boletos de metro, por favor.
Taquillero: ¿Sencillos o quiere una tarjeta recargable?
Sergio: Sencillos. ¿Cuánto es?
Taquillero: Diez pesos.
Sergio: Aquí tiene. Disculpe, ¿puede decirme cómo se llega de Terminal Aérea a Garibaldi?
Taquillero: Pues desde aquí es muy fácil: tome usted la línea cinco hacia Politécnico. En la primera estación cambie a la línea verde hacia Buenavista y la séptima estación es Garibaldi.
Sergio: Muchas gracias. ¿Puede darme un plano del metro?
Taquillero: Sí, claro.

1 (59)

1 ■ Carlos, siéntate en tu lugar, por favor.
● Voy.
2 ■ Venga a mi oficina, quiero hablar con usted.
● Ahora mismo.
3 ■ Pon la televisión, empieza el partido de futbol.
● Sale.
4 ■ Cierra la ventana, por favor, tengo frío.
● Sí, claro.
5 ■ Tome la primera a la derecha y después siga derecho.
● Muchas gracias.
6 ■ Da vuelta a la derecha, esa es la calle.
● Ah, sí, tienes razón.
7 ■ Haz las tareas antes de cenar.
● Sí, mamá.
8 ■ Por favor, siéntese. Ahora lo atiende el doctor.
● Bien, gracias.
9 ■ ¿Dígame?
● ¿Está el señor López?
10 ■ Alejandro, contesta al teléfono, por favor.
● Claro.

4 

Jefe: Señor Hernández, ¿puede venir a mi oficina, por favor?
Sr. Hernández: Sí, claro.
(...)
Sr. Hernández: ¿Se puede?
Jefe: Sí, sí, pase y cierre la puerta, por favor... Siéntese. Tengo una reunión en el banco el próximo lunes y necesito la información de su departamento.
Sr. Hernández: No hay problema, está todo preparado.
Jefe: Bien, haga el informe antes del lunes y ponga todos los datos de este año.

1 

rey-arroz-perro-reloj-rojo-arriba-caro-pero-diario - soltera - para

2 (62)

1 Roma; **2** Inglaterra; **3** Perú; **4** cartero; **5** compañero; **6** rosa; **7** pizarrón; **8** terraza; **9** caro; **10** ruido

3 

Pilar: ¿Sí?
Andrés: ¡Hola, Pilar! Soy Andrés.
Pilar: ¡Hola, Andrés! ¡Cuánto tiempo sin hablar contigo!
Andrés: ¿Qué tal te va por Cozumel?
Pilar: ¡Estoy muy contenta! Es una ciudad muy hermosa.
Andrés: ¿No te aburres en una ciudad tan pequeña?
Pilar: No, hay muchas cosas interesantes para conocer y, además, está el mar, hay reservas ecológicas, cenotes y playas. Y me encantan sus calles antiguas y su catedral.
Andrés: ¿Cómo te mueves por la ciudad?
Pilar: Vamos de un lado a otro en autobús o en taxi, porque normalmente hace calor.
Andrés: ¿Conoces a mucha gente ya? ¿Tienes amigos?
Pilar: Comparto departamento con dos compañeras de clase y tenemos un grupo de amigos de la universidad.
Andrés: ¿Y qué haces los fines de semana?
Pilar: Depende... Algunos sábados buceamos para hacer ejercicio, otros días conocemos pueblos o vamos a la playa... Es todo muy bonito. Bueno, ¿y cuándo vienes a Cozumel para pasar unos días en mi casa?
Andrés: Ahora tengo mucho trabajo en la oficina, pero el mes próximo puedo pedir unos días y tomar un vuelo para estar contigo y conocer tu nueva casa. ¿Qué te parece?
Pilar: ¡Fantástico! ¡Nos vemos el mes que viene!

UNIDAD 7 - **Salir con los amigos**

2 

Madre: ¿Sí, dígame?
Pedro: ¿Está Antonio?
Madre: Sí, ¿de parte de quién?
Pedro: Soy Pedro.
Madre: Enseguida contesta.
(...)
Antonio: ¿Pedro?
Pedro: ¡Hola, Antonio! ¿Qué haces?
Antonio: Nada, estoy viendo la tele.
Pedro: ¿Vamos al cine esta tarde?
Antonio: Ok, sale, ¿y qué película está?

Pedro: Podemos ver la última película de Alejandro González Iñárritu, ¿no?
Antonio: ¡Perfecto! ¿A qué hora y dónde nos vemos?
Pedro: ¿A las siete en la entrada del cine?
Antonio: No, mejor a las ocho. ¿De acuerdo?
Pedro: Sale. ¡Hasta luego!

5 

Alicia: ¿Sí?
Mónica: ¿Está Alicia?
Alicia: Sí, soy yo.
Mónica: ¡Hola! Soy Mónica.
Alicia: ¡Hola! ¿Qué onda?
Mónica: Voy a salir de compras esta tarde. ¿Vienes conmigo?
Alicia: Lo siento, hoy no puedo, tengo mucho trabajo. Mejor mañana.
Mónica: Bueno, sale. ¿A qué hora? ¿Te parece bien a las seis?
Alicia: Sí, de acuerdo.
Mónica: Hasta mañana.

Ángel: ¿Bueno?
Rosa: Hola, Ángel, soy Rosa.
Ángel: Hola, ¿qué tal?
Rosa: Muy bien. Te llamo porque Luis y yo vamos a ir el sábado a Puebla, ¿por qué no vienes?
Ángel: ¿El sábado? No puedo, lo siento, es el cumpleaños de mi mamá y voy a comer en su casa. Pero podemos vernos después. ¿Por qué no vienen a casa a cenar?
Rosa: ¿A cenar el sábado? Sale, le digo a Luis y, si podemos, luego te llamo. ¿Te parece bien?
Ángel: Perfecto. Espero tu llamada.
Rosa: Hasta luego.
Ángel: Hasta luego.

9 

■ Inmobiliaria Miramar. Buenos días.
● Buenos días. ¿Puedo hablar con el señor Álvarez?
■ No está en este momento. ¿Quiere dejarle un recado?
● Sí, por favor, dígale que la señora García va mañana a las once y media para hablar con él.
■ Muy bien, le dejo una nota.
● Muchas gracias. Adiós.
■ Adiós.

4 67

1 ■ Rosa, ¿qué estás haciendo?
● ¿Ahora mismo? Estoy peinándome porque voy a salir.
2 ■ ¡Luis, al teléfono!
● ¡No puedo, estoy bañándome!
3 ■ Niños, ¿qué hacen?
● ¡Nada, mamá, nos estamos lavando las manos!
4 ■ ¡Qué ruido hacen los vecinos!
● Sí, están levantándose ahora porque salen de viaje.
5 ■ ¡Hola! ¿Está Roberto?
● Sí, pero está afeitándose, llama más tarde.
6 ■ ¿Y Clara? ¿Dónde está?
● En el baño, está bañándose.
7 ■ Joana, ¿qué haces?
● Me estoy pintando para salir.
8 Pero hija, ¿todavía te estás vistiendo? Vas a llegar tarde a la escuela.
9 ■ ¿Está libre el baño?
● No, Jordi se está bañando.
10 ■ ¿Qué haces, Laura?
● Me estoy pintando para salir, enseguida acabo.

1 

¡Sale! - ¡Hasta luego! - ¡Qué bien! - ¡Para nada! - ¡Qué bonita! - ¡Es horrible! - ¡Perfecto! - ¡Ok!

2 

1 Claudia Schiffer es bastante fea, ¿verdad?
2 ¿Vamos al cine?
3 Mira la bolsa que me compré.
4 Tengo un departamento nuevo.
5 Bueno, me voy, ¡hasta luego!
6 Hay carne asada para comer.
7 Mira la tele, cuántas noticias malas.
8 Nos vemos a las cinco.

3 70

1 ■ Claudia Schiffer es bastante fea, ¿verdad?
● ¡Para nada!
2 ■ ¿Vamos al cine?
● ¡Sale!
3 ■ Mira la bolsa que me compré.
● ¡Qué bonita!
4 ■ Tengo un departamento nuevo.
● ¡Qué bien!
5 ■ Bueno, me voy, ¡hasta luego!
● ¡Hasta luego!
6 ■ Hay carne asada para comer.
● ¡Perfecto!
7 ■ Mira la tele, cuántas noticias malas.
● ¡Es horrible!
8 ■ Nos vemos a las cinco.
● ¡Ok!

2 71

1 Tiene el pelo largo y rubio. Tiene los ojos verdes. ¡No tiene bigote!
2 Tiene los ojos oscuros. Tiene el pelo corto y la barba negra.

3 72

1 Es moreno y tiene los ojos oscuros. Es alto y trae bigote. Tiene el pelo corto y liso.
2 Es delgada y baja. Tiene el pelo largo y rubio y los ojos azules. No trae lentes.
3 Es alta y delgada. Tiene el pelo negro, corto y liso y los ojos oscuros.
4 Es bajo y gordo. Tiene los ojos claros y es calvo. Es grande y lleva bigote y barba. Sí usa lentes.

12 73

Mónica es mi mejor amiga. Ella tiene veinte años como yo, es inteligente, guapa y muy talentosa. Las dos estudiamos música en el Conservatorio Nacional. Tocamos en una orquesta, pero Mónica toca el violín y yo la flauta. El compositor preferido de Mónica es Mozart y el mío Beethoven, y aunque compartimos la misma pasión por la música, somos muy diferentes físicamente. Mónica es alta, tiene pelo largo y negro y ojos muy grandes. Yo no soy alta, tengo el pelo corto y rubio y los ojos pequeños.

3 74

■ Estamos en la Macroplaza y vamos a entrevistar a algunas personas para saber qué hacen los fines de semana. ¡Hola! Buenas tardes, ¿eres de Monterrey?
● Sí, claro.
■ ¿Puedes contarnos qué haces normalmente los fines de semana?
● Pues los viernes salgo con mis amigas. Normalmente comemos unos aperitivos en algún bar o alguna terraza y luego vamos al antro.
■ ¿Y los sábados?
● Pues los sábados, a veces voy al cine por la tarde con mis amigas.
■ ¿Y por la noche también sales con tus amigas?
● Sí, comemos unos aperitivos y luego vamos al antro...
■ ¿Otra vez?
● Sí, nos gusta mucho bailar. Normalmente me acuesto muy tarde y el domingo duermo casi todo el día.
■ Muchas gracias.

■ ¡Hola! Buenas tardes, ¿es de Monterrey?
● Sí, claro.
■ ¿Puede contarnos qué hace normalmente los fines de semana?
● Pues los viernes por la noche siempre voy al cine con mi novia. Los sábados juego futbol por la mañana y por la noche, normalmente, vamos al teatro o a un concierto.
■ ¿Y los domingos?
● Pues normalmente vamos al Parque Fundidora por la mañana, después tomamos un aperitivo y luego nos vamos a algún restaurante a comer... A mi novia también le gusta ir a los museos de Monterrey y muchos domingos vamos a ver exposiciones: al Museo MARCO o al MUNE...

UNIDAD 8 - De vacaciones

3 

Luis: Buenos días, disculpe, ¿puede decirme cómo se llega a la plaza de Armas?
Recepcionista: Sí, ¡claro! Es muy sencillo. Al salir del hotel dé vuelta a la derecha y siga todo derecho hasta el final de la calle. Entonces dé vuelta a la izquierda. Siga derecho y tome la tercera calle a la derecha, la avenida del Sol, y al final de la avenida, a la derecha, se encuentra la plaza de Armas.
Luis: Entonces, salgo a la derecha, doy vuelta a la izquierda y en la avenida del Sol doy vuelta a la derecha. La plaza está al final de la calle, a la derecha, ¿verdad?
Recepcionista: Así es, señor. En quince minutos puede estar allí.
Luis: Muchas gracias. ¡Hasta luego!

5 

1 Desde el hotel
■ Disculpe, ¿puede decirme dónde está la farmacia más cercana?
● Tome la calle Santo Domingo, dé vuelta la primera a la derecha y, después, la primera a la izquierda.

2 Desde la iglesia de San Francisco
■ Por favor, ¿puede decirme cómo se llega a la iglesia de Santa Teresa?
● Dé vuelta a la izquierda, después tome la segunda calle a la derecha, la calle Nueva Alta, y al final de la calle, a la izquierda, está la iglesia de Santa Teresa.

6 

Ayer, como todos los días, me levanté a las siete de la mañana y me preparé para ir a trabajar. Al llegar al hospital, atendí a los enfermos de la consulta y visité a los pacientes de las habitaciones. A las cinco de la tarde, acabé de trabajar y pasé por el supermercado a comprar algo para la cena. A las seis de la tarde llegué por fin a casa, muy cansada, como todos los días. Pero ayer fue diferente: mi marido me invitó a un concierto y después cenamos en mi restaurante favorito.

8 

Soledad: ¡Oh, qué semana tan terrible! Por fin de vuelta a casa.
Federico: ¿Dónde estuviste?
Soledad: El lunes fui a Caracas para visitar a un cliente, y el martes volamos, mi jefe y yo, a Madrid, para firmar un contrato. Estuvimos dos días de conversaciones y, al fin, lo logramos. El jueves nos fuimos a Río de Janeiro para cerrar unos asuntos pendientes y hoy por fin vuelvo a casa. Y a ti, ¿cómo te fue?
Federico: Hasta el martes estuve acá, en Buenos Aires, preparando cosas para irme al día siguiente a Lima, donde estuve trabajando dos días y aproveché para conocer esa linda ciudad. Hoy fui al aeropuerto a primera hora y terminé mi semana de trabajo. ¿Qué te parece si cenamos juntos?
Soledad: Me parece muy buena idea.

1 

1 Usó lentes.
2 Comió mucho.
3 ¿Abro la puerta?
4 ¿Hablo más alto?
5 Entro a las ocho.
6 Trabajo en la mañana.
7 Estudió Geografía.

6 

En Taxco, durante los meses de invierno (diciembre, enero y febrero) hace mucho frío, pero nunca nieva. Durante la primavera (marzo, abril y mayo), suben las temperaturas y empieza a hacer buen clima. En verano (junio, julio y agosto), hace mucho calor: todos los días hace mucho sol y las temperaturas son muy altas. En otoño (septiembre, octubre y noviembre), los días son más cortos, el cielo está nublado y a veces llueve y hace aire.

8 

Estas son las condiciones del clima para el día de hoy en algunas zonas de Sudamérica. Tenemos clima inestable en Brasil, con fuertes lluvias y bajas temperaturas, sobre todo en el interior, donde tenemos ocho grados centígrados en estos momentos. En la zona del Caribe, por el contrario, hace muy buen clima, con mucho sol y una temperatura de veintidós grados centígrados. Clima inestable en la República Mexicana, con fuerte aire y cielo nublado. La temperatura en la capital es de quince grados centígrados. Próximo reporte del clima en una hora.

2 

Hay tantas cosas que ver en España que es difícil seleccionar las más interesantes. Si empezamos por el noroeste, podemos visitar Galicia y allí pararnos a ver Santiago de Compostela y su catedral. Siguiendo por la costa cantábrica, el viajero descubre paisajes inolvidables de praderas suaves y pequeñas playas entre acantilados. Desde el País Vasco nos dirigimos a Cataluña, que mira al Mediterráneo. La ciudad catalana más importante es Barcelona, puerto de mar y punto de partida y llegada de barcos de todo el mundo. Podemos seguir nuestro viaje por la costa mediterránea para disfrutar de las ciudades y playas que llegan hasta Almería y Málaga, en Andalucía. También la comunidad andaluza merece una atención especial por los restos de cultura árabe que se pueden ver en Córdoba, Sevilla y Granada, especialmente. Desde Córdoba podemos ir a Madrid, atravesando la Mancha, la tierra de Don Quijote, el héroe de Cervantes. Aquí acaba nuestro viaje por esta vez, pero aún nos quedan por ver muchos otros paisajes y ciudades.

8 

Hoy estamos en Barcelona, junto al mar Mediterráneo. Es la segunda ciudad más poblada de España. Barcelona fue la sede de la Exposición Universal de 1929 y de los Juegos Olímpicos de 1992. Muchos personajes importantes nacieron en esta ciudad:
- Montserrat Caballé, una de las grandes cantantes de la ópera, nació en Barcelona en 1933. En 1987 conoció al líder del grupo de rock Queen, Freddie Mercury. Con él grabó la canción «Barcelona», el himno oficial de las Olimpiadas de 1992.

- Joan Miró, pintor y escultor catalán mundialmente conocido, nació en Barcelona a finales del siglo XIX. En el Museo Joan Miró de Barcelona están las mejores obras de este artista. Murió en Palma de Mallorca en 1983.
- Joan Manuel Serrat, músico y poeta español, nació en Barcelona en 1943. Es un artista muy querido y admirado en toda España e Hispanoamérica. Entre sus canciones podemos encontrar poemas de grandes poetas como Machado, Lorca, Miguel Hernández o Pablo Neruda.
- Arancha Sánchez Vicario, tenista profesional, nació en Barcelona en 1971. Se convirtió en la número uno del mundo, después de ganar el torneo de tenis de Roland Garros por segunda vez.

5 

SARA: El pasado mes de mayo, después de un año de mucho trabajo, tuve quince días de vacaciones. Fui en tren a Galicia y me alojé en un hotel maravilloso. Pasé unos días estupendos yo sola, sin salir prácticamente de la playa.
LUCÍA: Mi sitio favorito para pasar las vacaciones es la Isla de Capri. Hace veinte años que fui por primera vez. Este verano llegué a la isla en barco, como siempre, para pasar mi mes de vacaciones con un grupo de amigos. Capri no es la misma de hace veinte años, pero sigue siendo única.
CARLOS: Tengo muy buen recuerdo de las últimas vacaciones que pasé con mi familia en Atacama, al norte de Chile; está a unos cuatro mil metros de altura. Alquilamos un coche para recorrer toda la zona, uno de los desiertos más secos del mundo, con unas salinas impresionantes. Fueron unas vacaciones memorables.

UNIDAD 9 - Compras

3 

Celia: Mira estos zapatos, Álvaro, son muy bonitos.
Álvaro: No están mal, pero a mí me gustan más aquellos café.
Celia: Disculpe, ¿cuánto cuestan estos zapatos negros?
Dependiente: Quinientos pesos.
Celia: ¿Y aquellos café?
Dependiente: Novecientos pesos.
Celia: ¿Novecientos pesos? Gracias, tengo que pensarlo.
Álvaro: Celia, ¿qué te parece esta camisa para mí?
Celia: Bien, ¿cuánto cuesta?
Álvaro: Solo seiscientos pesos. Voy a probármela.
Celia: Sale.
(...)
Celia: A ver... pues no te queda bien, ¿eh?
Álvaro: No, a mí tampoco me gusta.
Celia: Toma, pruébate esta chamarra, es muy bonita.
Álvaro: A ver... Pues sí, parece que me queda bien, ¿no?
Celia: Muy bien, es tu talla.
Álvaro: ¿Cuánto cuesta?
Celia: Mil quinientos pesos, es un poco cara.
Álvaro: Bueno, pero me gusta mucho, me la llevo.

Celia: Mira, ¿qué te parece este gorro? ¿Cómo me queda?
Álvaro: Bien, muy bien.
Celia: Pues me lo llevo, solo cuesta doscientos pesos.
(...)
Dependiente: Una chamarra y un gorro de lana... Muy bien, son mil setecientos pesos. ¿Pagan en efectivo o con tarjeta?
Álvaro: En efectivo.

3 

- Mi amiga Bárbara es estudiante y le gusta mucho la ropa informal. Hoy trae unos pantalones verdes, una playera roja y un collar que combina con los aretes.
- Javier es el novio de Bárbara y también es estudiante. Hoy trae unos pantalones de mezclilla, una camisa de puntos y unos tenis café.
- Ignacio es ingeniero, trabaja en una gran empresa de sistemas computacionales. Le gusta vestir bien. Para la reunión de hoy se puso una camisa azul, muy elegante, y una corbata blanca. También trae un traje oscuro.
- Marta trabaja de diseñadora en una tienda departamental y casi siempre usa ropa elegante. Hoy trae un vestido verde y unos zapatos blancos.
- Charlie es el primo de Bárbara y es fotógrafo. Hoy trae unos pantalones rojos, una camisa blanca y unos tenis amarillos.

1 

jamón - jugar - rojo - julio - joven - gimnasia - jefe - jirafa - geranio - genio - gato - goma - agua - guerra - guitarra - guapo - águila - Guadalajara - gota

2 

gusto - hago - jabón - pagar - hijo

5 

Luis: Voy a hacer mi maleta para el viaje, a ver... ¿qué llevo? Mira, estos zapatos están bien, ¿no?
Carla: No, para ir a la montaña, las botas son mejores que los zapatos.
Luis: Tienes razón. ¿Llevo los pantalones de mezclilla?
Carla: No, para el frío son mejores los pantalones de pana.
Luis: Bueno, llevo los dos y listo.
Carla: ¿Por qué llevas la maleta azul?
Luis: Pues porque es mejor que la gris, tiene ruedas.
Carla: Yo prefiero la gris, le caben más cosas. Toma el paraguas, guárdalo.
Luis: ¿El rojo? No, este es peor que el negro.
Carla: Lo siento, el negro ya está en mi maleta.

1 

MARÍA: A mí me encanta la ciudad en la que vivo. Es grande, tiene más de tres millones de habitantes y mucha oferta cultural y de actividades de tiempo libre. Puedes ir al cine, al teatro, hay varias salas de conciertos, museos y también grandes parques donde relajarte o practicar deportes. Es verdad que es una ciudad ruidosa porque hay mucho tráfico. Otro problema es la contaminación, porque la gente utiliza poco el transporte público (el metro o el camión...), pero a mí me encanta mi ciudad.
JORDI: Yo vivo en una ciudad pequeña, no llega al medio millón de habitantes y la verdad es que me gusta mucho vivir aquí. No hay una gran oferta cultural, pero tenemos mucha más tranquilidad que en una ciudad grande. Nuestros hijos viven más en contacto con la naturaleza porque hay muchos parques y tenemos la playa muy cerca. Probablemente en el futuro, si nuestros hijos van a la universidad, cambiaremos de ciudad, pero de momento no, este es el mejor lugar para vivir.

UNIDAD 10 - **Salud y enfermedad**

2 

rodilla - pierna - pecho - hombro - brazo - mano - cuello - dedo - cara - oreja - espalda - pie

3 

1 A Pedro le duele la cabeza.
2 A Daniel le duelen las muelas.
3 A Carmen le duelen los oídos.
4 A Julia le duele la espalda.
5 A Victoria le duele el estómago.
6 Ana tiene fiebre.
7 A Ricardo le duele la garganta.

4 

A **Sara:** ¡Hola, Ángel!, ¿cómo estás?
Ángel: No muy bien.
Sara: ¿Qué te pasa?
Ángel: Tengo una gripa muy fuerte.
Sara: ¿Y qué tomas cuando estás así?
Ángel: De momento, nada.
Sara: ¿Por qué no te tomas una aspirina con un vaso de limonada caliente con miel y te acuestas?
Ángel: Sí, creo que es lo mejor.

B **Raúl:** ¡No te ves bien! ¿Qué te pasa?
Luisa: Me duele muchísimo el estómago.
Raúl: ¿Por qué no vas al doctor?
Luisa: Sí, voy a ir mañana.
Raúl: Mira, tómate un té y acuéstate sin cenar.
Luisa: Sí, creo que es lo mejor.

8 

Paciente 1

■ Buenos días, ¿qué le ocurre?
● No me siento muy bien. Creo que tengo la gripa.
■ Tome una aspirina cada ocho horas y beba mucho jugo de naranja.

Paciente 2

■ Buenas tardes, ¿qué problema tiene?
● Me duele la garganta cuando hablo.
■ A ver... No está muy mal, pero tome limonada caliente con miel y no hable mucho.

Paciente 3

■ Buenos días, ¿qué le pasa?
● Mire, doctor, me duele mucho el estómago desde hace días.
■ Vaya, pues no tome café, ni fume. Coma frutas y ensaladas. Y tome estas pastillas.

2 

Elena y Emilio ya son papás. Su vida cambió cuando, de repente, se encontraron con... dos bebés en los brazos.

Elena: Antes de ser papás teníamos una vida social muy activa: viajábamos, íbamos al cine, salíamos con amigos, teníamos mucho tiempo libre. Emilio jugaba *hockey*, yo estudiaba alemán...

Emilio: Ahora todo es distinto. Dedicamos todo nuestro tiempo a Álvaro y Adrián, que son maravillosos.

8 

Martina tiene noventa y dos años. Cuando era niña, no iba a la escuela. Vivía con su mamá y sus cuatro hermanos en un pueblo pequeño del sur de México. A los ocho años, ya trabajaba en el campo con su familia: empezaba a las seis de la mañana y terminaba a las seis de la tarde. No sabía leer, ni escribir, pero tenía muchas ilusiones y planes para el futuro. A los diecinueve años se casó y tuvo su primer hijo. Los fines de semana iba con su esposo a vender las verduras de su huerta en los tianguis de los pueblos vecinos. Solo los domingos por la tarde descansaban y se reunían con sus vecinos en la plaza del pueblo.

1 

alemán - café - teléfono - cantante - árbol - canción - examen - estudiar - computadora - ventana - periódico - celular - pintura - música

2 

1 Andrés me habló por teléfono para saludarme.
2 Bárbara trabaja en una empresa de informática en México.
3 Yo estudié decoración en Milán.
4 Antes Raúl vivía cerca de aquí, pero ahora está viviendo en Chiapas.
5 Aquí hace más calor que ahí.
6 Ella es más guapa que él.
7 Los teléfonos celulares son muy cómodos.
8 Esta casa es más céntrica que tu departamento.

5 

■ Hoy vamos a hablar con la alpinista Elisa Urrutia. Está en México después de escalar el monte Everest. Elisa, ¿qué planes tienes para la próxima temporada?
● No voy a escalar el año próximo. La temporada pasada terminé agotada y tengo que tomar un descanso. El próximo semestre voy a hacer una campaña escolar en Chihuahua. Quiero ir a las escuelas y hablar con los chavos y chavas sobre este deporte.
■ ¿Cuánto tiempo vas a dedicar a esta actividad?
● Voy a dedicarme unos tres meses. Después quiero abrir un centro de alpinismo y organizar excursiones por la montaña.
■ ¿Y vas a ser una de las instructoras?
● Bueno, ese es mi objetivo. También quiero estar un poco más en casa. El año pasado me casé y creo que es el momento de pensar en organizar mi familia. Ahora estoy esperando mi primer hijo. Va a nacer el próximo otoño y estoy muy ilusionada.
■ ¡Enhorabuena, Elisa! ¡Te deseamos mucho éxito para todos tus planes!

5 (100)

Mánager: Este disco suena muy bien, es mejor que el otro.
Escorpión 1: Sí, estoy de acuerdo.
Mánager: Va a estar en las tiendas en la próxima semana y creo, amigos míos, que va a tener un gran futuro.
Escorpión 2: ¿Y cuándo nos vamos de gira?
Mánager: En diciembre vamos a dar unos conciertos por todo México y, si todo va bien, nos vamos a Sudamérica.
Escorpión 1: ¿Y vamos a salir en televisión?
Mánager: Claro, y también tengo preparada nuestra propia página web.
Escorpión 1: ¿Cuándo vamos a ir a Guanajuato?
Mánager: En septiembre, antes de empezar la gira. ¿A que no saben quién va a cantar con ustedes?
Escorpión 2: Ni idea.
Mánager: Jennifer Lopez.
Escorpión 2: ¡Vaya sorpresa!

CUADERNO DE EJERCICIOS

UNIDAD 1 - **Saludos**

4 101

1 A ¿Su nombre, por favor?
B Manuel González Romero.
A Muy bien. ¿De dónde es usted, señor González?
B Soy español, de Valencia.
A ¿Vive en Valencia?
B No, ahora vivo y trabajo en Madrid.
A ¿A qué se dedica usted?
B Soy economista.
A Muy bien. ¿Y cuál es su número de teléfono?
B Es el nueve uno seis cinco cuatro tres dos cero uno.
A Muchas gracias.

2 A Isabel, ¿cuál es tu apellido?
B Jiménez Díaz.
A ¿Jiménez con ge o con jota?
B Con jota.
A ¿Y en qué trabajas?
B Soy profesora de alemán.
A ¿Eres española?
B No, soy argentina, pero ahora vivo acá en Madrid.
A Muy bien, ¿me dices tu número de teléfono?
B Sí, es el seis cinco seis siete ocho nueve ocho dos tres.
A ¿Y tu correo electrónico?
B Isabel punto jota arroba yahoo punto com.
A Gracias.

UNIDAD 2 - **Familias**

3 

En mi país la gente desayuna a las seis y media o siete, muy temprano. Luego, en el trabajo o en la escuela almuerzan una torta y comen en casa a la una o las dos. La cena normalmente es a las ocho de la noche.
Los niños empiezan las clases a las ocho de la mañana y terminan a las doce y media. Luego, por la tarde, hay otros turnos, desde las doce y media hasta las cinco.
En cuanto a los bancos, normalmente abren desde las nueve hasta las cuatro de la tarde. Algunos bancos abren también los sábados por la mañana.
Las tiendas de comida están abiertas desde las siete y media de la mañana hasta las diez de la noche y algunas abren las veinticuatro horas.

7 

Salidas:
- El vuelo número dos tres ocho cuatro ocho con destino a Lima tiene la salida prevista a las siete cincuenta y cinco.
- Los pasajeros del vuelo con destino a Santiago número cero sesenta y cuatro con salida a las doce cero cinco deben dirigirse a la puerta de embarque nueve de.
- Los pasajeros del vuelo uno dos ocho nueve con destino a Buenos Aires y salida a las quince veinte salen de la puerta de embarque cinco be.
- El vuelo cinco siete seis con destino a España sale con una demora de quince minutos y, por tanto, la salida es a las dieciocho treinta y cinco. Pasajeros, diríjanse a la puerta de embarque siete efe.
- El vuelo cero dos siete con destino a Roma tiene su salida a las veintitrés diez.

UNIDAD 3 - **El trabajo**

1 104

A **Mesero:** Buenos días, ¿qué toman?
Señor: Yo quiero un café con leche y un pan tostado.
Señora: ¿Tiene jugo de naranja natural?
Mesero: Sí, claro.
Señora: Yo un jugo de naranja y un pan tostado con mantequilla y mermelada.

B **Mesero:** Buenos días, ¿qué desea?
Señor: Quiero dos huevos fritos con tocino.
Mesero: Lo siento, no tenemos. ¿Quiere un sándwich?
Señor: Sí, por favor, un sándwich de queso y un café con leche.

C **Mesero:** Buenos días, ¿qué desea?
Señora: Buenos días, quiero un té con leche, una mantecada y un jugo de naranja.
Mesero: Muy bien, ahora mismo.

UNIDAD 4 - **La casa**

7 

Mi casa de campo es muy bonita. Tiene tres recámaras con vistas al jardín. La más grande tiene un pequeño cuarto de baño. Tiene otro cuarto de baño grande al final del pasillo. La sala es muy amplia, con dos grandes ventanas y una chimenea para hacer fuego en invierno. Junto a la sala está el comedor y una cocina pequeña donde cocinamos mi marido y yo. Hay una cochera a la entrada. La casa tiene un jardín muy grande, con muchos árboles y flores. Tenemos una alberca para nadar en verano. Nos gusta mucho ir a nuestra casa en vacaciones.

UNIDAD 5 - **Comer**

5 106

La dieta mediterránea

¿En qué se basa esta cultura gastronómica?
Se basa, principalmente, en el aceite de oliva, el pan y el vino. Con estos productos básicos se alimentan los pueblos mediterráneos desde hace más de cinco mil años.
Los países mediterráneos consumen como grasa principal el aceite de oliva, que favorece la disminución del colesterol. También consumen gran cantidad de pescados azules, legumbres y frutas, y menos carne.
Las primeras investigaciones sobre esta dieta se centran en Grecia y en España, donde se estudian las características de su cocina, sus ingredientes, técnicas de cocción, etcétera, y se llega a la conclusión de que la dieta de estos países es la ideal para mantener una buena salud.

UNIDAD 6 - **La colonia**

3 107

■ Dígame.
● ¿Marta? Soy Beatriz.
■ ¡Hola! ¿Ya estás en México?
● Sí, estamos en el Gran Hotel, en el Zócalo.
■ Perfecto, ¿comemos juntas? Mi trabajo está cerca del hotel, si quieres puedes venir caminando, tardas unos veinte minutos.
● No, no, dime mejor cómo voy en metro, tengo un plano en la mano.
■ Mira, estoy en Isabel la Católica, en la línea uno, solo hay dos estaciones desde el Zócalo, ¿lo ves?
● Pues no.
■ Es muy fácil, toma la línea dos hacia Tasqueña y en la siguiente estación, Pino Suárez,

cambia a la línea uno en dirección a Observatorio, es solo una estación más, y estás en Isabel la Católica.

7 108

1 *Música de salsa*, 2 *flamenco*, 3 *tango*, 4 *ranchera*.

UNIDAD 7 - Salir con los amigos

1 109

1 **María:** ¿Por qué no vamos a tomar algo después de trabajar?
Ricardo: Lo siento, hoy no puedo, tengo que ir de compras con mi hermano. ¿Te parece bien mañana?
María: ¿A qué hora te parece bien?
Ricardo: ¿A las seis?
María: No, mejor a las seis y media.
Ricardo: De acuerdo. ¡Hasta mañana!

2 **Daniel:** ¿Vamos al cine esta noche?
Carmen: No puedo, lo siento. Voy a cenar con unos amigos.
Daniel: ¿Y si nos tomamos un café antes?
Carmen: Bueno, de acuerdo. ¿Vamos al Café Central?
Daniel: Perfecto. Nos vemos ahí a las cinco.

3 110

Entrevistador: Radio Centro FM. Esta noche en nuestra sección de "Espectáculos" vamos a hablar con Carolina y Pedro, una joven pareja que nos va a comentar sus preferencias cuando sale de noche los fines de semana. ¿Adónde van normalmente?
Pedro: Yo prefiero ir a un concierto. Me gusta mucho ir a conciertos de rock, pero Carolina ya está un poco harta. A ella le gusta más ir al teatro. Después, nos gusta mucho ir a tomar un aperitivo y volver a casa caminando.
Entrevistador: ¿Y tú, Carolina, qué dices?
Carolina: Me gusta mucho ir al teatro. También me gustan los conciertos de música clásica, excepto la ópera; es demasiado larga. A Pedro le gusta ir a todo tipo de espectáculos musicales, aunque son muy caros. Pero lo que más nos gusta hacer a los dos juntos es ir al cine.

UNIDAD 8 - De vacaciones

1 111

Desde niña, siempre deseé conocer la selva. Este verano estuve en Perú, un país maravilloso.
Al día siguiente de mi llegada a Lima, tomé un vuelo a Iquitos, bellísima ciudad tropical, como sacada de una película: los mototaxis, los mercados de fruta, las casas... y el río Amazonas.
Después entramos en la selva, dispuestos a pescar pirañas, nadar en el Amazonas, comer plátano frito...
Más tarde, nos detuvimos en un pueblo en medio de la selva. En unos segundos un montón de niños salieron de sus casas y me rodearon con sus rostros sonrientes.
Finalmente, me tomé unas fotos con ellos y me despedí muy contenta de llevarme un recuerdo auténtico del Amazonas.

UNIDAD 9 - Compras

2 112

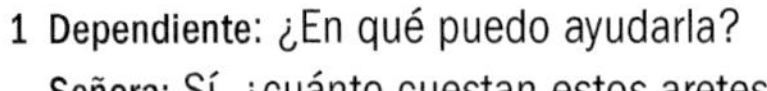

1 **Dependiente:** ¿En qué puedo ayudarla?
Señora: Sí, ¿cuánto cuestan estos aretes?
Dependiente: Seiscientos pesos.
Señora: ¿Y esos de ahí, los azules?
Dependiente: Esos tienen descuento, cuestan quinientos pesos.
Señora: Me los llevo.
Dependiente: ¿Va a pagar en efectivo o con tarjeta?

2 **Señora:** Buenos días. ¿Cuánto cuesta la falda roja del aparador?
Dependienta: Cuesta mil pesos.
Señora: ¿Puedo probármela?
Dependienta: Sí, claro, los probadores están al final del pasillo.
(...)
Dependienta: ¿Qué tal le queda?
Señora: Pues no me gusta mucho, lo siento, no me la llevo.

3 **Señora:** Mira esa playera verde, solo cuesta doscientos pesos.
Chava: Me gusta más esta, ¿por qué no te la pruebas?
Señora: Sale... A ver... ¿Cómo se me ve?
Chava: Superbien.
Señora: ¿Cuánto cuesta?
Chava: No te preocupes, yo te la regalo.

UNIDAD 10 - Salud y enfermedad

5 113

Sonia: ¿Qué te sucede, Alfonso? ¿Te sientes bien?
Alfonso: No, no muy bien. Tengo fiebre.
Sonia: ¿Estás tomando alguna medicina?
Alfonso: No, de momento no.
Sonia: ¿Por qué no te tomas una aspirina y descansas?
Alfonso: Sí, es lo mejor porque mañana tengo mucho trabajo.
Sonia: Seguro que mañana te sientes mejor.

Primera edición, 2018
Segunda edición, 2023

Produce: SGEL Libros S.L.
Avda. Valdelaparra, 29
28108 Alcobendas (Madrid)

Coordinación editorial: Jaime Corpas
Edición: Yolanda Prieto y Mise García
Corrección: Cristina González, Belén Cabal y Susana López
Diseño de cubierta e interior: Verónica Sosa
Fotografías de cubierta: Shutterstock
Maquetación: Leticia Delgado

Ilustraciones: **Pablo Torrecilla**, excepto: **Maravillas Delgado** (pág. 24 marcadores de lugar; pág. 56; pág. 82; pág. 112 marcadores del lugar; pág. 127; pág. 139; pág. 140; pág. 143; pág. 144; pág. 150; pág. 151; pág. 155; pág. 156; pág. 158), **Shutterstock** (pág. 27; pág. 37; pág. 58 Restaurante La Estancia y Vida Natural; pág. 93; pág. 109 imágenes de fondo de página web de ejercicio 3 e imagen de ejercicio 5; pág. 118 imágenes de las estaciones del año) y **Thinkstock** (pág. 58 Restaurante peruano La llama y Restaurante la Alpujarra; pág. 94 colores).

Cartografía: SGEL Libros S.L. (página 88)

Fotografías: CORDON PRESS: **Unidad 1:** pág. 11; pág. 19, fotos 1, 4 y 8. **Unidad 2:** pág. 29 foto 3; pág. 148. DREAMSTIME: pág. 18; pág. 76 ejercicio 3 foto D. HÉCTOR DE PAZ: pág. 12; pág. 133; pág. 36 fotos desayunos A-H; pág. 43; pág. 44 fotos cocina y baño. LATINSTOCK: pág. 44 foto salón. THINKSTOCK: pág. 13 foto 3; pág. 25 ejercicio 6; pág. 37 carta Cafetería Teide; pág. 47; pág. 55 foto Olga; pág. 57; pág. 59 mapas; pág. 78; pág. 86 fotos a, b, d y e; pág. 87 foto superior; pág. 88; pág. 98; pág. 102 fotos de Ana, Victoria y Carmen de ejercicio 3; pág. 105; pág. 106 fotos 1, 2, 4 y 6; pág. 108. THOMAS HOERMANN: pág. 6; pág. 12 fotos A y B; pág. 17; 37 ejercicio 5; pág. 91; pág. 103. SHUTTERSTOCK: Resto de fotografías, de las cuales, solo para uso de contenido editorial: pág. 9 foto B (Cenk Ertekin / Shutterstock.com), foto D (criben / Shutterstock.com), foto J (Kobby Dagan / Shutterstock.com) y foto N (Igor Bulgarin / Shutterstock.com); pág. 19 foto 2 (Featureflash / Shutterstock.com), foto 3 (Maxisport / Shutterstock.com), foto 5 (Joe Seer / Shutterstock.com), foto 6 (Tinswltown / Shutterstock.com) y foto 7 (Helga Esteb / Shutterstock.com); pág. 29 foto 1 (Featureflash / Shutterstock.com); pág. 53 (Tupungato / Shutterstock.com); pág. 61 (Diego Grandi / Shutterstock.com); pág. 63 (Andres Virviescas / Shutterstock.com); pág. 66 (Anton Ivanov / Shutterstock.com); pág. 67 foto autobús (Tupungato / Shutterstock.com) , foto superior (pozstos / Shutterstock.com) y foto inferior derecha (Kakimra/ Shutterstock.com); pág. 68 (Jordan Adkins / Shutterstock.com); pág. 76 ejercicio 4, Salma Hayek (Featureflash / Shutterstock.com) y Antonio Banderas (Featureflash / Shutterstock.com); pág. 8 (posztos / Shutterstock.com); pág. 87 foto inferior (Naaman Abreu / Shutterstock.com); pág. 99 (PSHAW-PHOTO / Shutterstock.com); pág. 131 foto a (krechet / Shutterstock.com), foto c /Migel / Shutterstock.com), foto f (Igor Bulgarin / Shutterstock.com); pág. 145 foto de Juan Luis Guerra (Miguel Campos / Shutterstock.com).

Para cumplir con la función educativa del libro se han empleado algunas imágenes procedentes de internet.

Audio: El Cielo Recording Studio, Crab Ediciones Musicales y Nordqvist Productions España SL

ISBN: 978-84-9778-994-3

Depósito legal: M-2662-2018
Printed in Spain – Impreso en España
Impresión: Gómez Aparicio Grupo Gráfico